Forms of the Left in Postcolonial South Asia

Critical Perspectives in South Asian History

Series Editors

Critical Perspectives in South Asian History publishes critically innovative scholarship on South Asian history from the ancient world to the present day. It focuses on three broad scholarly developments; a growing engagement with public history in South Asia, a conceptual shift that assigns agency to South Asia as the *generator* of research rather than the *object* of it and a concerted effort to study histories of neglected regions, peoples, methods and sources.

Forthcoming

Workplace relations in Colonial Bengal: The Jute Industry and Indian Labour 1870s-1930s, by Anna Sailer

Towards a People's History of Pakistan: (In)audible Voices, Forgotten Pasts, Edited by Kamran Asdar Ali and Asad Ali

The YMCA in Late Colonial India: Modernization, Philanthropy and American Soft Power in South Asia, by Harald Fischer-Tiné

The Emergence of Brand-Name Capitalism in Late Colonial India: Advertising and the Making of Middle-Class Conjugality, by Douglas E. Haynes

Political Imaginaries in Twentieth-Century India, by Mrinalini Sinha and Manu Goswami

Forms of the Left in Postcolonial South Asia

Aesthetics, Networks and Connected Histories

Edited by
Sanjukta Sunderason and Lotte Hoek

BLOOMSBURY
NEW DELHI • LONDON • OXFORD • NEW YORK • SYDNEY

BLOOMSBURY INDIA
Bloomsbury Publishing India Pvt. Ltd
Second Floor, LSC Building No. 4, DDA Complex, Pocket C–6&7,
Vasant Kunj, New Delhi 110070

BLOOMSBURY, BLOOMSBURY ACADEMIC INDIA and the Diana logo are trademarks of
Bloomsbury Publishing Plc

First published in India 2022
First published in Great Britain 2022

Cover design by Jade Barnett
Cover image © Paul Oram

This edition published with permission from Bloomsbury Publishing Plc,
50 Bedford Square, London, WC1B3DP, UK

British Library Cataloguing-in-Publication Data
A catalogue record for this book is available from the British Library.

Library of Congress Cataloging-in-Publication Data
A catalog record for this book is available from the Library of Congress

ISBN: 978-93-54352-05-8

For sale in the Indian subcontinent only

Series: Critical Perspectives in South Asian History
Typeset by Deanta Global Publishing Services, Chennai, India

Digitally printed and bound in India by Replika Press Pvt. Ltd.

Contents

Illustrations

Contributors

Kamran Asdar Ali is Professor of Anthropology at the University of Texas, Austin. He is the author of many books including *Planning the Family in Egypt: New Bodies, New Selves* (2002) and *Comparing Cities: Middle East and South Asia* (2009). His most recent book is *Communism in Pakistan: Politics and Class Activism 1947-1972* (2015). In the past few years his research has been on ethnicity, class politics, sexuality and popular culture in Pakistan.

Iftikhar Dadi is Professor and Chair of the Department of History of Art and Director of the South Asia Program at Cornell University. Publications include *Modernism and the Art of Muslim South Asia* (2010), the edited volume *Anwar Jalal Shemza* (2015), the co-edited catalogue *Lines of Control* (2012) and the co-edited reader *Unpacking Europe* (2001). Dadi serves on the editorial advisory boards of *Archives of Asian Art* and *BioScope: South Asian Screen Studies*. As an artist he collaborates with Elizabeth Dadi. Their practice investigates identity and borders, and the capacities of urban informality across South Asia and the global South.

Manishita Dass is Reader in Film & Global Media at Royal Holloway, University of London. Her research focuses on intersections of film and political cultures in South Asia. She is the author of *Outside the Lettered City: Cinema, Modernity, and the Public Sphere in Late Colonial India* (2016) & *The Cloud-Capped Star* (2020). She is currently working on a book about the impact of left radicalism on the film cultures of Bombay and Calcutta in the 1940s-50s.

Lotte Hoek is Senior Lecturer in Social Anthropology at the University of Edinburgh. She is a media anthropologist whose research focuses on the social and political life of the moving image in South Asia. She is the author of *Cut-Pieces: Celluloid Obscenity and Popular Cinema in Bangladesh* (2014; winner of the Bernard S. Cohn book prize) and co-editor of *BioScope: South Asian Screen Studies*. She is currently working on a book about the art film as a ground for political action in Bangladesh.

Harshana Rambukwella is Director at the Postgraduate Institute of English, Open University of Sri Lanka and affiliated to the School of English, University of Hong Kong. His research interests are in postcolonial literatures, and the intersections between literary history and nationalist discourse in Sri Lanka. His work has appeared in journals such as the *Journal of Commonwealth Literature, Journal of Asian Studies* and *boundary 2*. He is the author of *Politics and Poetics of Authenticity: A Cultural Genealogy of Sinhala Nationalism* (2018).

Maia Ramnath is a writer, artist, organizer and independent scholar. She has taught history at New York University, Penn State University and Fordham University. She is the author of *The Haj to Utopia: How the Ghadar Movement Charted Global Radicalism and Attempted to Overthrow the British Empire* (2011), *Decolonizing Anarchism: An Anti-Authoritarian History of Indian Liberation Struggle* (2012) and *Art for Life: Conversations with the South Asian Progressive Writers Movement on Literature, Left Politics and Internationalism, from Anti-fascism to Afro-Asian Solidarity* (2020).

Sanjukta Sunderason is Senior Lecturer (UD1) at the Department of History of Art, University of Amsterdam. She is a historian of twentieth-century modern art, left-wing aesthetics and intellectual histories of decolonization. She is the author of *Partisan Aesthetics: Modern Art and India's Long Decolonization* (2020). She is currently working on two book projects – on connected histories of post-partition visual art across India, West and East Pakistan during the 1950s to 1960s, and on the transregional aesthetics of freedom during twentieth-century decolonization.

Layli Uddin is Lecturer in the School of Politics and International Relations at Queen Mary, University of London. Her research interests focus on religion, labour and social movements in modern South Asia, and Third World internationalism. She has published on microhistory, riots and spatial politics. Her most recent article is 'Enemy Agents at Work' (2021). She is currently working on a book about subaltern politics in the making and unmaking of Pakistan, *c*. 1930s-1971

Introduction

Forms of the left in postcolonial South Asia

Lotte Hoek and Sanjukta Sunderason

In October 2016, the film *Jago Hua Savera* (Day Shall Dawn, 1959, Ajay Kardar, dir.) was to be screened at a film festival in Mumbai. Recently restored and flush with Cannes success, the film was slowly making its way through specialist screenings and audiences. Hailed as a 'lost classic' and neorealist triumph in specialist film circles, the film had been a cross-regional project with contributions of artists from across West Pakistan, India and East Pakistan (now Bangladesh), many of whom were linked to a progressive, left or communist cultural politics. The film had been controversial and badly received when released in Pakistan in 1959. Now, in 2016, while celebrated in international circuits, it incurred wrath and censorial attitudes in India. In the context of the simmering military conflict between India and Pakistan, and rising authoritarianism and exclusionary nationalism, partisan nationalist groups put pressure on the film festival to drop the film.[1]

Forms of the Left in Postcolonial South Asia asks how we might return to and recuperate such (dis)connected histories of left-wing aesthetics that persisted across South Asia's partitioned and decolonizing geographies. We pursue in this volume cultural forms of the postcolonial left that continued – via displaced, transforming and resilient forms – *beyond* the high noon of what has been retrospectively called the 'Marxist Cultural Movement'[2] of the late-colonial 1940s and the partitions in South Asia (of India in 1947, with the birth of Pakistan; and of Pakistan in 1971, with the birth of Bangladesh). Such cultural forms have slipped historiographies that fetishize national stories or dominant figures and have indeed been overshadowed by the struggles and failures of the political

1 Tanuk Thakur, 'Under Pressure, Mumbai Film Festival Drops Classic Pakistani Film', *The Wire*, 17 October 2016, https://thewire.in/diplomacy/classic-pakistani-film-jago-hua-savera-dropped-mumbai-film-festival.

2 Sudhi Pradhan (ed.), *Marxist Cultural Movement in India: Chronicles and Documents* (Vol. 1, Calcutta: Pustak Bipani, 1979; Vols. 2 and 3, Calcutta: Nabanna, 1982).

left. Our contemporary moment of authoritarian and right-wing resurgence obfuscates such forms, and more importantly, the long-standing trans-border collaborations and conversations organized by and around aesthetic forms across postcolonial South Asia.

Forms of the Left is an effort at mapping these histories via aesthetic forms of the left. This book emerges from conversations among a group of scholars who have collected stories, resonances and possibilities around the field of left-wing aesthetics across postcolonial South Asia. This field transcends South Asia's post-1947 borders and exceeds the postcolonial trajectories of the political left too. It takes shape as constellations of people, forms, networks, traces and questions around the postcolonial left as a subcontinental and transnational formation. Such constellations are at once rooted in national and locational trajectories of the new nation states born out of decolonization and partitions (1947, 1971), and are resonant of affinities, friendships and conversations across nation-state divides. They require, as we propose in this volume, new frames and questions: *Does the political left in South Asia have a recognizable aesthetic form? How have the region's climactic twentieth-century experiences – of anti-colonial and anti-imperial struggles, of famines and genocides, of partitions and displacements – recast the cultural imaginations of the political left? And how do we today write about the entanglements of the twentieth-century transnational left in dialogue with the experiences of decolonization and postcolonial modernities?*

Forms of the Left in Postcolonial South Asia has distinct methodological goals: first, of activating hitherto unexplored connected histories of the left across the new political frontiers of postcolonial, post-partition South Asia – India, Ceylon/Sri Lanka, Pakistan and Bangladesh; and second, of foregrounding therein the question of aesthetic form. Placing the question of form squarely within the particularities of the left's changing political circumstances in individual and connected contexts in the region, we intertwine here two sets of queries. The first asks how left-wing art manifested (in) cultural and social formations in the region: How were left-wing cultural forms and affiliations re-imagined post and despite mid-twentieth century displacements triggered by decolonization (see Chapters 1, 2, 5 and Afterword by Sunderason, Uddin, Rambukwella and Ali, respectively, in this volume)? In the second set, we ask how the aesthetic forms of left-wing art across postcolonial South Asia have been imagined to be politically efficacious: What modes and treatments, for instance, have been considered appropriate or appropriable to the cause and how has the efficacy of art been theorized (see Chapters 3, 4, 6 and 7 by Dadi, Ramnath, Hoek and Dass, respectively, in this volume)? By pursuing forms and connected histories simultaneously, we foreground aesthetic form as a political trope in understanding cultures of the left in postcolonial South Asia. These concerns are also intended to reframe 21st-century concerns with political aesthetics within a distinctly postcolonial and decolonial framework.

Given the left's alignments and textures of cultural action within the shifting political contours and dispensations of the region, the question of form is significant. We investigate art, film, literature, poetry and cultural discourse in postcolonial South Asia produced by artists and cultural and political activists committed to the left in various forms – through their art, and through social and ideological affiliations. Studies of aesthetic politics in South Asia, which frame and inspire our endeavours, tend to focus either on popular forms and their consolidation of political subjectivities and ideologies, or on the intertwining of art and the nation in the pursuit of modernism in colonial and postcolonial South Asia.[3] In this volume we focus instead on questions of left-wing political commitment *as* artistic and aesthetic values across productions of fine arts, *belles lettres* and cinema. We trace the particular trajectories that the left's cultural movement took during decolonization *after* its high point of radical anti-imperial cultural resistance in late-colonial South Asia in the 1940s. Dissipating both socially and ideologically after independence and partition in 1947, and along the complex transformation of Communist Parties in India and Pakistan and the left more broadly in Ceylon/Sri Lanka, the forms of the left in postcolonial South Asia took on new fluid and dynamic guises. Sharing the ethics of committed art, artist-activists formerly aligned with the Communist Party re-articulated left political-aesthetic tropes of national-popular art under new and contentious political circumstances post-1947. This produced a dense repertoire of affectively loaded forms that are recognizable and shared across South Asia in a distinct sensory regime. This repertoire is positioned adjacent to, and intersects with, the domain of popular and public culture that has been theorized for its political efficacy. Investigating the figure of the political artist, Afro-Asian literary exchanges, art film-makers, cultural collaborations, aesthetic debates and citational aesthetics, we are looking here at aesthetic forms and art-making that display great intentionality. We ask thereby how such works can

3 See, among others, Tapati Guha-Thakurta, *The Making of a New 'Indian' Art: Artists, Aesthetics, and Nationalism in Bengal, c. 1850–1920* (Cambridge: Cambridge University Press, 1992); Sumathi Ramaswamy, *Beyond Appearances? Visual Practices and Ideologies in Modern Art* (New Delhi; Thousand Oaks, CA: Sage, 2003); Christopher Pinney, *Photos of the Gods: The Printed Image and Political Struggle in India* (London: Reaktion, 2004); Srirupa Roy, *Beyond Belief: India and the Politics of Postcolonial Nationalism* (Durham, NC: Duke University Press, 2007); Kajri Jain, *Gods in the Bazaar: The Economies of Indian Calendar Art* (Durham, NC: Duke University Press, 2010).

divulge the means and the modes by which committed artists have contributed to the sensory regimes in which particular moral and political impulses were given concrete and replicable form.

The efficacy of the artistic, particularly visual, form has been a key site of debate for scholars of public culture in South Asia. The very premise of the idea of public culture as developed by Appadurai and Breckenridge was as 'an arena where other types, forms and domains of culture are encountering, interrogating and contesting each other in new and unexpected ways'.[4] Within this arena, visual and material artefacts, from religious prints and photographs to films and theatre performances, encounter and shape one another in rhythms and modes that are both of the times and formative of them. The central premise for this body of scholarship has been that the material artefacts within this arena have the capacity to exceed existing discursive fields through its figural forms.[5] Their concrete manifestations are not fully subdued by surrounding narratives about the times and places in which they exist and this provides these visual and material forms the potential to be socially and politically efficacious.[6] Much of the scholarship in the field of visual and public culture studies has been focused on popular culture, not least under the wider influence of the historians of the subaltern school. Their discussions around what lay beyond the discursive formations brought into being by colonialism, yet shaped by the global history of capital, and how to recuperate this from within an archive set up on colonial premises, fundamentally asks about the objects and subjects outwith these discursive strictures.[7] The subsequent debates about public culture inherit some of the concerns and premises of subaltern studies but explore them within the field of cultural practices, particular aural and visual forms and popular artefacts. These material forms, from music cassettes through to calendar art, are understood to not be fully incorporated into hegemonic discursive forms.[8] It is their aesthetic form that interrupts their easy equation with established narratives

4 Arjun Appadurai and Carol Breckenridge, 'Why Public Culture', *Public Culture* 1, no. 1 (1988), 6.

5 William Mazzarella, *Shovelling Smoke: Advertising and Globalization in Contemporary India* (Delhi: Oxford University Press, 2004), 43; Christopher Pinney, 'Things Happen: Or, from which Moment Does that Object Come?' in Daniel Miller, ed., *Materiality*, 256–72 (Durham, NC and London: Duke University Press, 2005).

6 See Ramaswamy, *Beyond Appearances?*; Christopher Pinney and Rachel Dwyer, *Pleasure and the Nation: The History, Politics, and Consumption of Public Culture in India* (Delhi: Oxford University Press, 2001); Pinney, *Photos of the Gods*; Jain, *Gods in the Bazaar*; Kajri Jain, *Gods in the Time of Democracy* (Durham, NC: Duke University Press, 2021).

7 Partha Chatterjee, *A Brief History of Subaltern Studies, In Empire and Nation: Selected Essays by Partha Chatterjee*, with Nivedita Menon (New York: Columbia University Press, 2010 [1998]), 289–301; O'Hanlon, Rosalind, 'Recovery of the Subject: Subaltern Studies and Histories of Resistance in Colonial South Asia', *Modern Asian Studies* 22, no. 1 (1988), 189–224.

8 Jain, *Gods in the Bazaar*, 14.

and histories, speaking to other constituencies, in different vocabularies and across new temporalities. Recent work within political history has extended this methodological approach to explore the lasting presence of revolutionary, anti-imperial and anarchic political potentialities, notably around the iconography associated with Indian revolutionary Bhagat Singh.[9] In this volume, we extend these discussions around the efficacy and lasting political potentiality of cultural forms from their focus on popular culture to inform an approach to art objects and practices that seek to understand their political efficacy within the context of left progressive politics. We argue that it is important to study the aesthetic and formal modes by which a left progressive political agenda was given shape in fine arts, art cinema and *belles lettres* during the post-independence years, not only because it illuminates transitions in political thought and shifting alliances between comrades, activists, fellow-travellers and the disenchanted but also because these aesthetic tropes travel through public and popular culture in a lasting way.

In this Introduction, we lay out the historical and conceptual domain on which we stage the question of the forms of the left in postcolonial South Asia. The Introduction is split into three segments, each thinking through the left as form *and* as history. The first – 'Histories in formation' – asks if histories of the postcolonial left in South Asia can be read and configured via the question of aesthetic forms and cultural formations. We lay out the dispersal and transformation of the 'left' as a wide political and social formation across the region in the years leading up to and after partition in 1947. We track the changing fates of the Communist Party in the different countries in the region, and within the unique parameters of the left in Sri Lanka, with new alliances made across borders – both across South Asia and across Afro-Asian solidarity networks. We also trace the conjunctural moments that offer potential connected frames and questions for intertwining histories of the postcolonial left across South Asia and in dialogue with global dynamics – whether under the political rationalities of the Cold War, of Third World solidarities or the repercussions of the global 1960s and Maoist internationalisms active strongly in the subcontinent. The second segment – 'Form' – posits aesthetic form as a means of tracing shared commitments and communities of practice in the particularly dispersed historical and political field of the left in postcolonial South Asia. Informed by long-standing discussions in South Asia about the

[9] Kama Maclean, *A Revolutionary History of Interwar India: Violence, Image, Voice and Text* (London: Hurst, 2015); Chris Moffat, *India's Revolutionary Heritage: Politics and the Promise of Bhagat Singh* (Cambridge: Cambridge University Press, 2019).

nature of realist and socially progressive artistic forms, we draw on current scholarly ideas about form and materiality to suggest that close reading and engagements with form provide an entry point to these fields of intensity that are both consciously crafted by artists as well as resistant to the dominant discursive domains they find themselves in today. The third segment – 'Contemporary articulations' – opens up the questions of left-wing aesthetics and potentialities via current artistic engagements and theoretical/epistemological questions. We consider here what sort of, and whose, histories and forms are being revalued in the contemporary context of both resurgent Maoism in rural South Asia and middle-class and elite reappropriations of these forms in contemporary art markets and NGO programmes.

Forms of the Left in Postcolonial South Asia brings together a cross-disciplinary and trans-border group of authors who bring approaches from history, art history, anthropology, film studies and literary studies to bear on the material. A few caveats are due at this stage. First, as we draw from hitherto un-addressed conversations between trans-border cultural archives in South Asia, such archives are often as informal and scattered as they are unique and untapped, and therefore in many cases hard to source (via copyright clearances) for reproduction as illustrations. We hope our readers will sense the rich texture of such archives through their detailed analyses within our chapters. Second, our selection here has been driven by resonant traces and connected forms, and we have not followed a representational rationality of covering every country in South Asia. While our archives and questions are drawn from India, Pakistan, Bangladesh, Sri Lanka and their transregional dynamics across forums of Afro-Asian solidarities, we are aware of some critical omissions – for instance, of leftist theatre and literature from Nepal, or across post-partition Punjab, or Kerala, among others. Our proposition is that conversations in this volume are taken not as indexical markers of plural histories in South Asia but as dynamic signposts for new and potential subcontinental historiographies of culture and decolonization, attuned to particular, as well as expansive and connected, histories. We hope that the organic unity of our chapters here will be self-evident.

Histories in formation

Can we configure forms of the left across postcolonial South Asia via its (connected) histories? The twentieth century offers some possibilities where the left's transnational histories can be seen to be shaped by shared questions of aesthetic form as well as manifest in particular formations – social, cultural as much as political. Here we trace some of the modalities of such (potential) formations that shape trans-border, subcontinental configurations of the left and its transnational resonances. This is aimed at providing a historical context to the artistic practices discussed in this volume. It also foregrounds the nature of relations between political formations and artistic practices as dispersed and dynamic, rather than monolithic or consistent.

A critical modality in the histories of the left in South Asia is its dispersed political spectrum, its forums spread out amidst Communist and Socialist Parties and amidst pro-communist elements scattered across centrist parties. This dispersion was contained via collaborative politics and sustained also by internal contradictions and splits that echoed regional, national and transnational shifts.[10] This dispersed modality of the South Asian left in the twentieth century exceeded party political structures and developed across extra-party forums, friendships and associations, where being on the left happens (often) from the positionality of being *outside* the party or active political left – as 'fellow-travellers' and via informal affective affiliations.[11] Across late-colonial and postcolonial South Asia this dispersed, collaborative modality was evident in the formations of the left. In British India in the 1930s for instance, the Communist Party of India (CPI; banned between 1934 and 1941) worked in incipient forms ranging from the forums of socialist politics and peasant fronts like the Congress Socialist Party and the All India Kisan Sabha (All India Peasant Congress), through growing radicalization of political prisoners, as well as via growing socio-intellectual affinities towards Marxist thought. In Ceylon likewise, the Lanka Sama Samaja Party (LSSP) was formed in 1935 out of growing discontent around the lack of national front in support of the working class, felt strongly during the Depression years in the early 1930s, and emerged to give direction to both nationalist politics and working-class politics.[12] Foundational to the formation of the LSSP were Ceylonese students returning from British and American universities with their exposure to international communist politics and Indian communism. As the Communist International itself developed the

[10] Kamran Asdar Ali, *Surkh Salam: Communist Politics and Class Activism in Pakistan 1947-1972* (Karachi: Oxford University Press, 2015); Vijay Prasad, *No Free Left: The Futures of Indian Communism* (New Delhi: LeftWord Books, 2015); Ali Raza, *Revolutionary Pasts: Communist Internationalism in Colonial India* (Cambridge: Cambridge University Press, 2020).

[11] David Caute, *The Fellow-Travellers: A Postscript to the Enlightenment* (London: Weidenfeld and Nicolson, 1973); Leela Gandhi, *Affective Communities: Anticolonial Thought, Fin-de-Siècle Radicalism, and the Politics of Friendship* (Durham, NC: Duke University Press, 2006).

[12] Kumari Jayawardena, 'Origins of the Left Movement in Sri Lanka', *Social Scientist* 2, no. 6/7 (January–February, 1974), 3–28.

transnational Popular Front politics with its programme of anti-fascist resistance in its Seventh Congress in 1935, there were late-colonial variations. In British India for instance, the 'United Front' of anti-imperialist politics was inaugurated in 1936, with the Indian National Congress under its president Jawaharlal Nehru becoming a forum for growing socialist affiliations and underground communist mobilization, even if ambiguous and irregular.[13] This (idiomatic) collaboration between nationalist and left-wing politics found echoes in a growing shared and ambiguous vocabulary of the 'people', 'popularization' and 'popular' politics/art/artist – where Gandhian populism interacted with a revolutionary popular imaginary steered by the underground left. Even when this United Front political collaboration petered out in 1941 with communist support for the imperial war effort in the defence of the Soviet Union, the sociocultural cohabitation of left-wing affinities with mainstream nationalist anti-colonial politics persisted.[14] This was felt most actively in the field of a growing cultural movement of the left that grew in dialogue with new imaginaries of political resistance – in the late 1930s through formations of forums like the All India Progressive Writers' Association and the All India Kisan Sabha, and in the early 1940s with the Indian People's Theatre Association.[15]

To comprehend the left's textured social histories, as well as its aesthetic possibilities, we therefore conceptualize the political as adjacent to, but not overdetermined by, party politics – the political read hence as both (cultural) practice and (political) theory.[16] Echoing Raymond Williams, we read the left via sociocultural formations that were 'simultaneously artistic forms and social locations'.[17] Such formations thus carried, what Michael Dennings has called

[13] For instance, at the Seventh World Congress of the Communist International in 1935, it was declared that 'the Indian communists must set aside their internal sectarianism that has thwarted their participation in anti-imperialist national politics dominated by the Indian National Congress and organizations affiliated with it, boosting Gandhi's control of the popular movement; in the new United Front, the Indian communists must consolidate all the anti-imperialist forces of the country', 'both within and without the National Congress' and broaden and lead 'the struggle of the masses against the imperialist oppressors'. Wang Ming, Report delivered at the Seventh World Congress of the Communist International, 7 August 1935, 30. See also, Subodh Roy (ed.), *Communism in India, Unpublished Documents 1935-45* (Calcutta: Ganashakti Printers, 1976); Gene Overstreet and Marshall Windmiller, *Communist Party of India, Miscellaneous Pamphlets* (Berkeley and Los Angeles: University of California Press, 1959).

[14] Roy, *Communism in India, Unpublished Documents 1935-45*; D. N. Gupta, *Communism and Nationalism in Colonial India, 1939-1945* (New Delhi: Sage Publications, 2008).

[15] On histories of the Progressive Writers' Association, the Indian People's Theatre Association and the left's cultural movement in late-colonial India see, Priyamvada Gopal, *Literary Radicalism in India: Gender, Nation, and the Transition to Independence* (London: Routledge, 2005); Sumangala Damodaran, *The Radical Impulse: Music in the Tradition of the Indian People's Theatre Association* (New Delhi: Tulika Books, 2017).

[16] Chantal Mouffe, *On the Political* (New York: Routledge, 2005).

[17] Raymond Williams, 'When Was Modernism?' in *Politics of Modernism*, 34–5.

in his study of the early-twentieth-century Popular Front in the United States, two ideas of 'politics' active within the front's notions of the politics of art: first, a 'cultural politics', that is, the politics of the allegiances and affiliations that forms the cultural field, and second, 'aesthetic ideologies', that is, the politics of form. While allegiances and affiliations represented the 'social consciousness' of the cultural front, Denning argued, the works produced by the artists and intellectuals on the left embodied a 'political unconscious'. The idea of the cultural front itself, he noted, was 'an attempt to theorize the relation of culture to politics'.[18] We extend this insight to anthropological conceptions of the political that explore the 'huge scope for different ways in which to construe the idea of the "people" as well as the idea of "representation" which supposedly binds them to the government'.[19] We also carry this dynamic to nuancing how art and politics entangled particularly during conjunctural periods across the long decolonization in South Asia, where the 'political' itself is a dispersed complex of aesthetic and ideological participation, rather than concrete party political affirmations. Modalities of the left *as form* emerge here more as a field of 'partisan aesthetics' rather than 'political art'.[20]

A second modality in reading transnational formations of the left's histories in South Asia – with or despite active patronage from the Communist Parties – would be its uniquely conjunctural character. Such conjunctures were marked by the colonial theatre of the Second World War, with famine, displacement, communal riots and partition itself at the arrival of independence, as well as the longue durée footprints of such ruptures – in structural shifts, transformational forms, memories and hauntings. This temporal modality of the South Asian left is marked by decolonization itself – its locational trails and transnational dynamics – entangled with global wars, genocides, solidarities and ideological polarizations of the Cold War. Under the accelerated time of decolonization, the left's politics gained historical momentum and radical cultural echoes as artists, performers, writers, academics and society at large strove to visualize and act upon social ruptures. Conjunctures, in Gramscian terms, are grounds upon which multiple 'forces of opposition' – political, social or aesthetic – organize, giving the time itself a particular radical charge.[21] Conjunctures connect scales of

[18] Michael Denning, *The Cultural Front: The Laboring of American Culture in the Twentieth Century* (London: Verso, 1997), xix.

[19] Jonathan Spencer, 'Postcolonialism and the Political Imagination', *Journal of the Royal Anthropological Institute* 3, no. 1 (1997), 12.

[20] Sanjukta Sunderason, *Partisan Aesthetics: Modern Art and India's Long Decolonization* (Stanford: Stanford University Press, 2020).

[21] Gramsci, *Selections from Prison Notebooks*, 178.

the regional, the national and the transnational, as the wartime decolonial decade of the 1940s amply shows. Conjunctures also cite and echo recent histories with newer, contemporary events, agendas and imagination, creating, as Stuart Hall has noted, circular possibilities of historical citations within artistic production.[22]

In British India as the wartime Bengal famine broke out along the eastern frontiers of war, with an advancing Japanese army, burning of crops by the Allied forces to quell Japanese advance and rampant black-market profiteering,[23] the CPI negotiated a political contradiction: its support for the war effort in defence of the Soviet Union (following German attack in 1941) legalized it in British India, yet the support itself marginalized its politics in the late colony steeped in the Gandhian Quit India movement. While in Ceylon, the LSSP refused the Moscow Line, affirming the national rather than foreign commitment of the Ceylonese left, the CPI in India had to re-imagine its resistance. The famine – notorious as man-made and killing and displacing more than three million across Bengal[24] – became an alternative political field for the left via activist reportage and relief work alongside anti-imperialist and anti-fascist rhetoric. Under the Party Secretary P. C. Joshi, a 'cultural front' was created where artists, performers and political activists collaborated to author an active socialist cultural critique of imperialism, one that bolstered the CPI's 'policy and work in the War of Liberation'.[25] Such a front – framed as a left-wing cultural movement – connected social struggle with political emancipation on the one hand, and on the other, a regional crisis with multiple scales of war-fronts and post-war mobilizations of decolonization across Asia. The cultural front resonated with what C. Vaughan James has described as the tendency of socialist culture not only 'to enlist the poet as philosopher, the writer as tribune and the artist as teacher in the translation of the socialist dream into reality', but also to explore 'the *almost unknown interstices* between artistic genres by uniting poet, painter, sculptor, singer, actor, dancer and director in one common socio-aesthetic system'.[26]

22 See Stuart Hall and Doreen Massey in conversation, 'Interpreting the Crisis', *Soundings: A Journal of Politics and Culture* 44 (Spring 2010), 57–8.

23 See Paul Greenough, *Prosperity and Misery in Modern Bengal: The Bengal Famine of 1943-44* (New York: Oxford University Press, 1977); Janam Mukherjee, *Hungry Bengal: War, Famine, and the End of Empire* (London: Hurst, 2015).

24 Sample Survey of the After-effects of the Bengal famine of 1943, Indian Statistical Institute, Calcutta, 1946, and the unpublished mortality data gathered by the ISI under the statistician Professor Prasanta Mahalanobis. Cited by Greenough, *Prosperity and Misery in Modern Bengal*, 305–9.

25 P. C. Joshi, *The New Situation and our Tasks, Resolution of the Central Committee of the Communist Party of India*, passed at its meeting in December 1945 (Bombay: New Age Printing Press for the Communist Party of India, 1945).

26 C. Vaughan James, *Soviet Socialist Realism: Origins and Theory* (New York: Macmillan, 1973), xii, (emphasis ours).

A third and connected modality here would be the foundationally multi-scalar nature of the left, reaching across histories and geographies of war, Comintern politics and decolonial movements, as well as in national, locational/regional and transregional dialogues with ongoing changes in the literary and artistic fields.[27] It reflected a complex 'relationality of ideas and political affiliations' that was shaped by 'the changing nature and the varying inflections of the leftist movement in India',[28] as Ali Raza argues in his excavation of the impassioned engagements of leftists with utopian ideas in colonial India. In the context of geopolitical transformations and challenges, the ongoing critique of classicism and romanticism that developed across the left's cultural movement in the subcontinent echoed the global calls for art rooted in the 'people', in dynamic aesthetics of realism – whether via social realism or with active *socialist* realist addresses.[29] The idea of 'progressive' culture upheld by the left during these years in the late colony reflected these multi-scalar transregional dynamics, as its subcontinental networks spanned from Chittagong and Dhaka in the east to Lahore and Karachi in the west, from Kashmir in the north and Colombo the south, while remaining conversant with global values and vocabularies of modernism and socialism. Across South Asian decolonizing contexts, the idea and rhetoric of progressive art drew in writers and artists rooted in the exigencies of colonial contexts as well as the modernist universalism of artistic form. By the end of the 1940s, formations of progressive art in the subcontinent would also register the global tensions between political and cultural imaginaries of the left, particularly as artists formerly associated with left-wing anti-fascist cultural resistance now began distancing themselves from the increasingly more stringent ideological regimentation around Stalinist 'Socialist Realism' that came to dominate in international socialist aesthetics steered by the Soviet Union.[30]

The multi-scalar, transregional modalities in the histories of the subcontinental left in South Asia were at once subcontinental and global. The

[27] On the transnational histories of the Comintern and the postcolonial left, see Shobhan Lal Dutta Gupta, *Comintern and the Colonial Question: The Decolonization Controversy* (Calcutta: Centre for Studies in Social Sciences, 1976); Oleska Drachewych and Ian Mckay, eds., *Left Transnationalism: The Communist International and the National, Colonial, and Racial Questions* (Montreal; Kingston; London; Chicago: McGill-Queen's University Press, 2019); see also, Jacopo Galimberti, Noemi de Haro García and Victoria H. F. Scott (eds), *Art, Global Maoism and the Chinese Cultural Revolution* (Manchester: Manchester University Press, 2019).

[28] Raza, *Revolutionary Pasts*, 10–11.

[29] For the critical debates around realism and the popular, see Theodor W. Adorno, Walter Benjamin, Ernst Bloch, Bertold Brecht, György Lukács and Fredric Jameson, *Aesthetics and Politics* (London: Verso, 2007 [1938]); also, Geeta Kapur, 'Realism and Modernism: A Polemic for Present-Day Art', *Social Scientist* 8 [Marxism and Aesthetics], no. 5/6 (December 1979–January 1980).

[30] On collectives and politics of progressive art, see Yashodhara Dalmia, *The Making of Modern Indian Art: The Progressives* (New Delhi: Oxford University Press, 2001); Sunderason, *Partisan Aesthetics.*

critical juncture of 1947–8 – our starting point in this volume – marks multiple ruptures, shaping the unique modality of the postcolonial left in South Asia that we are focusing on. In South Asia these ruptures were shaped significantly by the bloody Partition of 1947 in the wake of a communal genocide. Globally, it reflected the shifts within the international left, the Stalinist turn in the shadow of the Cold War manifesting in the split within the CPI – both ideologically and politically, with the party split between new leadership and the newly formed independent nation states of India and Pakistan. The left vacillated on the creation of Pakistan, half supporting the cause of Pakistan and half expecting the Partition to be temporary. These vacillations were visible through the mid-1940s, and by the time of the Second Congress of the CPI in Calcutta in 1948, the party was not only forced to reorganize its divided Indian and Pakistani fronts but also negotiate a shift within the party ranks. The second party congress saw a series of shifts in policy, both displacing the General Secretary P. C. Joshi and his collaborative politics, and bringing in a political hardline under B. T. Ranadive, who declared freedom in 1947 itself to be 'false'. At this second congress, it became clear to delegates from Pakistan (125 of whom attended from East Pakistan) that the party had to split to account for the new political realities of former British India, but that the East Bengal part of the new CPP should remain under the guidance of the West Bengal CPI.[31] The trajectories of the post-1947 left thus fall along and across the new lines drawn by both partition of the subcontinent and divisions within the party. Such histories were also spread across the newly redrawn frontiers – territorial and ideological – shaping under the shadow of the deepening Cold War ideological fronts. This makes histories of the postcolonial left in South Asia organically transnational and transregional, with cross-border connections and echoes in the South Asian region, even as the frameworks of the postcolonial nation state tend to make such connected histories tertiary.

The exit of P. C. Joshi at the turn of a more radical partisan shift within the party under the new leadership of Ranadive dissolved the collaborative cultural front of the 1940s, and marked a period of eclipse for the left's cultural movement. Over the 1950s the cultural momentum of the 1940s dissipated substantially – not only through the retreat of political patronage and cultural vision but also through the assimilation of a segment of the left's cultural interlocutors *into* the

[31] Moni Singh, 'Establishing the Communist Party of Pakistan', in *The Bangladesh Studies Reader: History, Culture, Politics*, eds, Meghna Guhathakurta and Willem van Schendel (Durham, NC: Duke University Press, 2013), 171.

cultural apparatus of the postcolonial state – particularly in India.[32] In Pakistan, the dissipated communist left could not sustain patronage of a progressive culture,[33] particularly under repressive policies of the new postcolonial nation state, not least with regard to the continued insurgencies among peasants, workers and tribal groups in East Pakistan that had been so effectively allied by left-committed artists in the earlier 1940s.[34] In India, the prime minister's international support for socialist culture saw an ironic repression of the communist left within the country. The party was banned in 1949, with most of its activists having to go underground. In Ceylon, John Kotelawala in the early 1950s displayed a similar two-pronged policy in the late 1940s and early 1950s. Staunchly anti-communist, he would brand the communists as 'unpatriotic' and sustain a fundamentally anti-communist politics at home, while being 'superficially pro-Communist in international affairs'.[35]

In this volume we focus on the cultural left in postcolonial South Asia across the boundaries and temporalities of the nation state. The parallel processes of dispersion and repression created a new historical formation for the cultural left – one that was transformational due to multipolar 'postcolonial displacements' – moving from the ideological cohesion under a communist culture to more diffracted forms of marginal critical socialist iconography and socially conscious artistic forms more assimilated within the mainstream modernist imaginary of the post-colonies. This dissipation and dialogue, we argue, constitutes a new critical modality of the postcolonial left in South Asia, one that requires more trans-border collaborative research and attention to the question of form and aesthetics *beyond* political party lines. Critical to this modality is the very question of freedom – and its layered meanings between immediate experiences of political independence and the longer horizons of the imaginations of liberation.[36] Sensibilities of freedom as a utopic horizon were deeply embedded in the ways in which the left interacted with the narrative of arrival and progress propounded by the postcolonial nation states, as the logic of resistance in the post-colony morphed from an anti-colonial one to one where

[32] Sunderason, *Partisan Aesthetics*, Chapter 4. See also, Dilip Menon, 'Lost Visions? Imagining a Left Culture in the 1950s', in *Land Labour and Rights – Ten Daniel Thorner Memorial Lectures*, ed. Alice Thorner (New Delhi: Tulika, 2001).

[33] See Saadia Toor, *The State of Islam: Culture and Cold War Politics in Pakistan* (London: Pluto Press, 2011); Kamran Asdar Ali, *Surkh Salam: Communist Politics and Class Activism in Pakistan 1947-1972* (Karachi: Oxford University Press, 2015).

[34] Ahmed Kamal, *State Against the Nation: The Decline of the Muslim League in Pre-independence Bangladesh, 1947-54* (Dhaka: The University Press Limited, 2009), 110–15.

[35] Ivor Jennings, 'Politics in Ceylon Since 1952', *Pacific Affairs* 27, no. 4 (December 1954), 345–52.

[36] Reinhart Koselleck, *Futures Past: On the Semantics of Historical Time*, trans. Keith Tribe (New York: Columbia University Press, 1985).

the enemy was not everywhere clear. Here the paternalistic nation state, and the promises made for its independence, seemed to temper and condition what the progressive would mean. For artists on the left, imagining and struggling towards a future often ran counter to the narratives of progress and modernity that the new nation states upheld. It heightened tensions between (postcolonial) nationalism and the utopic frontiers of socialist internationalism, where the limits of political freedom were being questioned in continuing struggles for social freedom. The left-wing artistic visions of freedom were, however, not simply of critique; such radical imaginations of futures were of hope and utopic time. This formed the cornerstone of the progressive discourse that the left had carried over from the 1940s, and which captured new potentialities in postcolonial times. Each of the chapters in this volume bespeaks these tensions around ideas of freedom.

A citational and affective economy of the left's postcolonial internationalism was visible throughout the 1950s to 1970s, alongside the will to assimilate national particularities within a transnational vocabulary – whether it be one of Third World cultural solidarities or people's resistance echoing Maoist rhetorics of people's war from China. A significant front for a transnational postcolonial left was Afro-Asian cultural solidarity. It went back as far as collectives for anti-fascist cultural resistance and Asian Youth conferences of the 1940s, and supported further by the cultural internationalism of the Afro-Asian fronts during the decolonizing decades of the 1950s – at the Bandung Conference (1955), and thereafter in conferences of the Afro-Asian People's Solidarity Association and the Afro-Asian writers.[37] For figures of the progressive cultural movement of the subcontinental left – Mulk Raj Anand in India, or Faiz Ahmad Faiz in Pakistan – navigating the spaces of international left-wing forums was at the same time a mode of negotiating nationalism and internationalism, making the sensibilities of the postcolonial left a dialogue between national identity and international affiliations.[38] Whether in Mulk Raj's assimilation in a Nehruvian modernity or Faiz's exile from a repressive regime in Pakistan alongside his patronage of postcolonial Pakistani modernism, being on the left in postcolonial South Asia suggests intertwinement of multiple histories – of both alienation

[37] Carolien Stolte and Su Lin Lewis (eds), 'Other Bandungs: Afro-Asian Internationalisms in the Early Cold War', *Journal of World History* 30, no. 1–2 (June 2019).

[38] See Annapurna Garimela, ed., *Mulk Raj Anand: Shaping the Indian Modern* (Mumbai: Marg Publications, 2005); Aamir Mufti, 'Towards a Lyric History of India', *Boundary 2* 31, no. 2 (2004), 245–74 and *Enlightenment in the Colony: The Jewish Question and the Crisis of Postcolonial Culture* (Princeton, NJ: Princeton University Press, 2007); Mohsin Zulfiqar and Fabbeh Husein, *Elusive Dawn: Faiz Ahmed Faiz: A People's Poet, A Centenary Publication* (Bradford: Kala Sangam, 2011).

and assimilation.[39] This suggests also the plural and diverse modalities in the histories of the postcolonial left in South Asia. In East Pakistan – the eastern wing of post-1947 Pakistan that became Bangladesh after the War of Liberation in 1971 – the left carried a series of intertwinements – across international, regional and national agenda's, and with dialogues between peasant, tribal and working-class politics that were allied to student movements and tied to linguistic sovereignty that took on a distinct cultural guise.[40] The left's entanglement with cultural identity was active in Ceylon/Sri Lanka too, where the language question and tensions between national culture and the politics of Sinhala and Tamil cultural imagination were echoed within left-wing discourses.

The 1960s and 1970s – critical decades in decolonization and global left-wing politics – found their unique echoes in South Asia. International tensions between the Soviet and the Chinese lines, and revolutionary edge of Maoist ideologies fascinated not only the West but also the political imaginaries of popular, particularly student, politics across the Third World.[41] In India, the CPI split multiple times during this period, the first in 1965 triggered by the Indo-China war that produced the new China-oriented CPI-M from the old Soviet-oriented CPI; and second in 1968, with the formation of the far-left, Maoist faction CPI-ML breaking away from the CPI-M. The divisions were based on both ideological lines and those of radicalism, the CPI-ML occupying the extreme left position within the new spectrum. The split also occurred around the movement of sharecroppers in Naxalbari in North Bengal, from where a new radical peasants' movement was to develop in the late-1960s. The Naxalbari movement was a trigger to re-kindle unfinished land struggles of the 1940s, and with that a new wave of peasant revolution agenda, which has been famously called the Naxalite movement. The Naxalite insurgency was hailed by China as the initiation of a Maoist resistance that would soon spread across the country. 'Spring Thunder Breaks over India', read the Chinese radio broadcasts in July 1968.[42] This was a return to the peasantry as the vanguard of revolutionary

[39] See also Lotte Hoek and Sanjukta Sunderason, 'Journeying through Modernism: Travels and Transits of East Pakistani Artists in Post-Imperial London', *British Art Studies* 13, https://doi.org/10.17658/issn.2058-5462/issue-13/hoek-sunderason.

[40] Layli Uddin, '"Enemy Agents at Work": A microhistory of the 1954 Adamjee and Karnaphuli riots in East Pakistan', *Modern Asian Studies*, online first, https://doi.org/10.1017/S0026749X19000416; Van Schendel, *A History of Bangladesh*.

[41] Sanjay Seth, 'Indian Maoism: The Significance of Naxalbari', in Arif Dirlik, Paul Healy and Nick Knight (eds), *Critical Perspectives on Mao Zedong's Thought* (Atlantic Highlands, NJ: Humanities Press, 1997); see also, Galimberti et al., *Art, Global Maoism and the Chinese Cultural Revolution*.

[42] 'Spring Thunder Breaks over India', *People's Daily*, 5 July 1967, reprinted in Seth, 'Indian Maoism: The Significance of Naxalbari', 291. See also, Sumanta Bannerjee, *India's Simmering Revolution: The Naxalite Uprising* (London: Zed Books, 1984).

resistance – an echo of the Telengana and Tebhaga peasant movements of the late 1940s, as Charu Mazumdar, the fiery Naxalite leader, announced, 'We must build our party basically among the peasant masses.'[43] By 1970, the movement had spread to urban Calcutta, and took the form of an explosive iconoclastic movement where urban-middle-class students attacked institutions, cultural icons and bourgeois establishments in an extreme bid for social revolution. Its foment can be found in the narratives and montage of Mrinal Sen's film *Calcutta 1971* (1972). As the establishment cracked down on the rebels through the early 1970s, the Naxalite movement became an explosion from within the contradictions of the postcolonial left – with party cadres turning on each other, new ideological splits and the extreme polarization of the parliamentary left and the far-left 'Maoist' activists.

The popular left-wing upsurge of the late 1960s and early 1970s was shared across South Asia in varying forms. At the start of the 1970s, histories of the far/left, of insurgency and resistance, made political and cultural geographies of South Asia coalesce. Across the border in East Pakistan, students and urban professionals joined the peasant, tribal and worker movements that had been active and actively repressed since the early 1950s, into a movement reaching a crescendo in the late 1960s. Here too, modes of resistance and insurrection were in conversation with foment in India and China while cultural representations drew parallels with Vietnam.[44] February 1969 saw a surge in resistance with the distinct socialist agenda of Maulana Bhashani – the peasant and labour leader of the National Awami Party. The Eleven-Point programme released by the student alliance of Dhaka University in January 1969 against the military dictatorship of General Ayub Khan had incorporated 'subaltern concerns', and Maulana Bhashani called for an alliance of students, workers and peasants around the rallying cry of economic and political change.[45] A revolutionary mobilization and ongoing resistance ensured a violent military repression that led to the popular insurrection and guerrilla warfare that eventually led to the

[43] Charu Mazumdar, 'Undertake the work of Building a Revolutionary Party', *Liberation*, October 1968, accessed on Charu Mazumdar-Collected Writings, http://cpiml.org/library/charu-mazumdar-collected-writings/formation-of-all-india-coordination-committee-of-communist-revolutionaries/undertake-the-work-of-building-a-revolutionary-party/. Accessed on 22 February 2019.

[44] Fahmida Akhter, 'Zahir Raihan's *Stop Genocide* (1971): A Dialectical Cinematic Message to the World', in *South Asian Filmscapes: Transregional Encounters*, eds. Elora Halim Chowdhury and Esha Niyogi De (Seattle: University of Washington Press, 2020), 233–49.

[45] See Peter Custers, 'Maulana Bhashani and the Transition to Secular Politics in East Bengal', *The Indian Economic and Social History Review* 47, no. 2 (2010), 231–59. See also, Layli Uddin, *In The Land of Eternal Eid: Maulana Bhashani and the Political Mobilisation of Peasants and Lower-Class Urban Workers in East Pakistan, c. 1930s-1971* (PhD diss., Royal Holloway, University of London, 2016).

independence of eastern Bengal as Bangladesh.[46] In Ceylon, soon to be renamed Sri Lanka, 1970 was a year of popular insurgency with militant students staging multiple attacks against the institutions of government and pushing for a more radical agenda on the left. Like the Naxalbari movement happening at the same time in India, such insurgents were inspired by Maoist ideologies of people's war, and displayed a nihilistic politics that was at the same time, generational. The April 1971 insurrection happened despite a sharply leftward turn in the elections of 1970, and due to disgruntled 'Homegrown socialist, egalitarian and populist revolutionary movements', who as an observer noted, '[. . .] will trouble regimes that are unable to solve basic social and economic problems', and will be 'poly-centric rather than mono-centric movements': 'The spectre of communism haunts Asia but it is very different from the spectre that haunted Europe earlier this century.'[47]

Histories of the subcontinental left beyond the 1980s echo more strongly our proposed call for reading ideology via imagination and dissonance rather than affirmation. The historical modalities of the cultural left in postcolonial South Asia, as we have tried to show here, were mobile and multi-nodal, consisting of partisans and fellow-travellers, with informal affiliations that were shaped but not overdetermined by the ideological and political certainties of nation states and party lines, nor the oceanic affect of revolutions and despairs of repression. Across such historical moments of the South Asian left are personal, aesthetic, national and transnational entanglements, intersections and (border) crossings. The interaction between the political and the cultural fields was steered by individuals – with different, shifting or contradictory political subjectivities. The personal trajectories of artists and cultural forms exceed the frontiers set by political borders and party lines. Our focus on the postcolonial period also foregrounds a new sociocultural matrix – marked by migration, displacement, trans-border conversations as much as inabilities to contain and converse – that shaped questions of aesthetic form.

The chapters in this volume activate these decolonial histories of the left in South Asia via form, seeing form both as a site for working through the nature of political commitments in the complex historical modalities of the left and as a trace of the networks and affiliations that produced them. We propose that

[46] Willem van Schendel, *A History of Bangladesh* (Cambridge: Cambridge University Press, 2009); Talukder Maniruzzaman, *The Bangladesh Revolution and Its Aftermath* (Dhaka: University Press Ltd, 1980).

[47] S. Arasaratnam, 'The Ceylon Insurrection of April 1971: Some Causes and Consequences', *Pacific Affairs* 45, no. 3 (Autumn 1972), 356–71, 368.

forms of the cultural left can capture what Partha Chatterjee has called the 'the fragmentary, the local, and the subjugated',[48] and thereby the 'heterogeneous time' of postcolonial modernity[49] rather than the 'homogeneous empty time' the national identities are idealized on.[50] Such forms – of disenchantment, solidarities and counter-hegemonic imaginations, as much as hauntings – as the chapters here show, can resist the drives for 'shallow homogenization', and open up for 'other, potentially richer definitions of the "nation" and the future political community'.[51]

Form

The social and political transformations and mobilizations of the left across South Asia found expression in aesthetic forms and cultural practices. These emerged in response to the central questions animating left-committed artistic practice about how to give concrete shape to, and insight into, the experiences of the people, and galvanize commitments to a transformative future. Today these forms provide a parallel register or archive through which to grasp and interpret the changing political fortunes, alliances and contestations of the postcolonial left in South Asia. In this volume, we present close readings of the aesthetic forms, artworks, texts and events to provide insight into the ways in which conceptual discussions and political passions intertwined and were given material shape. In exploring the discussions around those forms, we also gain an understanding of how those materials and their formal contingencies were considered to express and transmit those debates and passions to viewers, activists, critics and audiences elsewhere. We show how form worked to connect fields of artistic practice, centred debates and reflections, and allowed individual works or artists to be recognizably part of a broader field of political commitments, building lasting connections among artists and activists across the region.

48 Partha Chatterjee, *The Nation and Its Fragments* (Princeton, NJ: Princeton University Press, 1993), xi.

49 Partha Chatterjee, 'The Nation in Heterogeneous Time', *Indian Economic and Social History Review* 38, no. 4 (2001), 399–418.

50 Benedict Anderson, *Imagined Communities: Reflections on the Origin and Spread of Nationalism* (London: Verso, 2006).

51 Gyan Pandey, 'In Defense of the Fragment: Writing about Hindu-Muslim Riots in India Today', *Representations*, no. 37, *Special Issue: Imperial Fantasies and Postcolonial Histories* (Winter 1992), 29.

Form is a mode of representation that gives material shape to ideas.[52] Michel Foucault has distinguished resemblance and similitude as different modalities of representation.[53] Resemblance has a model to which it is faithful; it 'serves representation, which rules over it'.[54] Similitude propels series of articulations that are set apart through small differences; 'similitude serves repetition which ranges across it.'[55] The objects, phrases and images under discussion in this volume share characteristics but are not faithful copies limited by resemblance. They are connected through similitude and shift alongside the fracturing, splitting and realigning historical and social formations of the cultural left in postcolonial South Asia. They are therefore also distinct from more conventional or generic public cultural forms. In this volume we follow Lauren Berlant's idea of form as an extended repetition. Berlant distinguishes 'between *form* as an extended repetition that conscripts attention and *genre* as scene of elaborated and conventional expectation'.[56] While figure and genre point to historical and determinate norms and expectations,[57] and work along the lines of Foucault's resemblance, form captures the attention through its repetition with difference and is marked by similitude. Where genre 'is always about modalities of practice that circulate norms',[58] form is marked by similitude, which 'reveals what recognisable objects, familiar silhouettes, hide, prevent from being seen, render invisible'.[59] Form can reveal what genre conceals.

We understand form as an extended and modifying repetition of concrete material articulations of concepts and matter that draw our attention due to their break with convention, their repetition of something familiar incorporating the unexpected. The artists, critics, poets, film-makers and writers under discussion in this volume work to develop forms appropriate to their political

[52] The humanities have recently witnessed a return to formal analysis as a conceptual starting point and methodology, resulting in a reclamation of form, and practices of close reading, as sites for critical scholarship, that are proximate to some of our approaches in this volume. See Ellen Rooney, 'Form and Contentment', *MLQ: Modern Language Quarterly* 61, no. 1 (2000), 17–40; Eugenie Brinkema, *The Forms of the Affects* (Durham, NC: Duke University Press, 2014); Anna Kornbluh, *The Order of Forms: Realism, Formalism, and Social Space* (Chicago: The University of Chicago Press, 2019); Anahid Nersessian, *The Calamity Form: on Poetry and Social Life* (Chicago: The University of Chicago Press, 2020).

[53] Michel Foucault, *This Is Not a Pipe*, trans. James Harkness (Berkeley: University of California Press, 1983), 34.

[54] Ibid., 44.

[55] Ibid.

[56] Christa Robbins and Kris Cohen, 'Beyond Formaldehyde, An Interview with Lauren Berlant', *Open Set*, 2015, http://www.open-set.com/cnrobbins/o-s-form-issue/an-interview-of-form-with-lauren-berlant/ (emphasis ours).

[57] Fredric Jameson, *Marxism and Form: Twentieth Century Dialectical Theories of Literature* (Princeton, NJ: Princeton University Press, 1971).

[58] Robbins and Cohen, 'Beyond Formaldehyde'.

[59] Foucault, *This Is Not a Pipe*, 46.

and ethical commitments, in which art must be freed from convention to allow the articulation and exposure of repression and inequality, to make visible the repressed, such as in Chittaprosad's *Children* linocut series that exposed the 'underbelly of Nehruvian Indian' (see chapter 2 by Sunderason) and remained largely unseen and rejected by the party. Such forms both expose the world and reframe our understanding of it. Anahid Nersessian suggests that both poetic form and the historical moment 'effect changes in how we, as embodied beings, experience the material world, and it also makes those changes harder to grasp'.[60] In an earlier iteration, she discusses 'calamity form' as 'a poetic technique that [. . .] allows even evanescent changes in the world to become apprehensible as well as apprehensive – objects of experience and sources of anxiety'.[61] We take from this the capacity of form to be both generative of embodied ways of knowing the world and unsettling our familiarity with that world.

Making apprehensible, and even apprehensive, the evanescent changes in the world, and shaping the experience of living in cataclysmic times, were a central part of the call to arms of artists in the anti-imperialist struggle in late-colonial India. As articulated in the 1943 IPTA manifesto: 'In recent years, the depth, and sweep of the titanic events of contemporary history . . . have compelled many sensitive writers and artists to realize in varying degrees that art and literature can have a future only if they become the authentic expressions and inspirations of the people's struggles for freedom and culture'.[62] Art was to be an inspiration to those who were swept up in these events and the unfolding political struggle for freedom and change.

The question of form was central to the debate about the ways in which art and artists formed a part of these larger political mobilizations. The IPTA manifesto rejected the idea that 'art was to be an ornament' and railed against the 'soulless formalism' of nineteenth-century art in India, which 'since long had ceased to be of any great significance in the lives of the people'.[63] As Ramnath details in her contribution to this volume (see chapter 4), like IPTA, the Progressive Writers Association and the Afro-Asian writers were committed to the idea that through their art, they could 'change reality by portraying reality'. Realism was the form for an 'objective

60 Nersessian, *Calamity Form*, 4.

61 Anahid Nersessian, 'Two Gardens: An Experiment in Calamity Form', *MLQ: Modern Language Quarterly* 74, no. 3 (2013), 311.

62 In Ashish Rajadhyaksha and Amrit Gangar (eds), *Ritwik Ghatak – Argument and Stories* (Bombay: Screen Unit/Research Centre for Cinema Studies, 1987), 29.

63 Rajadhyaksha and Gangar, *Ritwik Ghatak*, 27.

representation of reality [that] was expected to reveal existing contradictions in social relations and pave the way for revolutionary change'.[64] Formalism was in many ways considered its impotent and complacent other, indicating an unnecessary play on motifs and ornamentations in art that neither expressed nor galvanized the struggles of the people. It was dismissed as 'art for art's sake', as a number of contributions to this volume demonstrate (see Chapters 3, 4, 6, 7 by Dadi, Ramnath, Hoek and Dass, respectively).

But the question of form nonetheless continued to haunt those artists who were to portray and make meaningful the contradictions that were the true nature of society and the source of its inequalities and injustices. Realism was embraced as an artistic operation, as described by Lukács, in which 'every major realist fashions the material given in his own experience, and in so doing makes use of techniques of abstraction, among others. But his goal is to penetrate the laws governing objective reality and to uncover the deeper, hidden, mediated, not immediately perceptible network of relationships that go to make up society.'[65] The question of realism was about form as illuminating, not about genre as reassuring familiarity. Left-committed artists debated the nature of this form in which material could be fashioned to express the objective reality of the people and their struggles within the context of newly decolonizing South Asian societies and states and make it newly perceptible to galvanize action. This concern continued to animate film-makers, writers and artists after the violent denouement of colonial occupation and its inheritances in the postcolonial nation states of South Asia, as they strived for 'art for life's sake'.

Folklore had presented itself before 1947 as one means of abstracting and evocatively capturing the reality of colonial society and presenting anti-colonial perspectives.[66] As expressed by Utpal Dutt, the playwright, director and actor: 'folklore tradition has already captured the struggle of its own time as well as ours in a complex manner; its apparent naivete [*sic*] is an artistic device concealing an intense moment of suffering in the life of the masses.'[67] Folklore provided a mode of presenting immanent content in an abstracted, artistic, form, that was capable of articulating the 'struggle of our time'. The problem, as Dutt saw it, was

[64] Bhaskar Sarkar, *Mourning the Nation: Indian Cinema in the Wake of Partition* (Durham, NC: Duke University Press, 2009), 70.

[65] György Lukács, 'Realism in the Balance', in Adorno et al., *Aesthetics and Politics* (London: Verso, 2007 [1938]), 38.

[66] Partha Mitter, *The Triumph of Modernism: India's Artists and Avant-Garde 1922-1947* (London: Reaktion Books, 2007), 113–22; Partha Mitter, *Indian Art* (Oxford: Oxford University Press, 2001), 191–2.

[67] Utpal Dutt, *Utpal Dutt on Cinema* (Kolkata: Seagull Books, 2009), 166.

that folkloric forms were taken up by artists, particularly in the theatre that Dutt was engaged with most centrally, in a detrimental, formalist manner.

> By knocking out precisely that content and using only the score is to replace a vision with a slogan, to misuse folklore, to descend to formalism. Form and content are thoroughly integrated in folklore; to separate them is to kill it. The score by itself is so simplistic and repetitive, even crude, that it is positively boring. And that is precisely what has been thought worth preserving in the IPTA tradition.[68]

The 'slogan' is a form cleared of content, functioning through resemblance and conforming to expectations. In Dutt's view, resonating with discussions in left-oriented circles, folklore loses its capacity for articulating in singularly strong aesthetic gestures the crises of the times when it is reduced to generic repetitions, when it becomes 'soulless' formalism.

Left-oriented artists in the early decades after independence in South Asia sought such artistic devices by which complex content could be presented in an efficacious manner, avoiding the 'slogan'. This was not only an aesthetic and artistic problem but also a political problem that set a number of artists onto a path of conflict with Communist Parties in South Asia. Given extensive repression of political organizing, the cultural domain was crucial for political mobilization and consciousness-raising. In a lengthy treatise written for the CPI in West Bengal in 1954, director, actor and writer Ritwik Ghatak laid out his vision for this cultural front. The concern with form in his call to the party to reform its relationship to the arts is worth quoting in full:

> We must proceed by admitting that in relation to Bourgeois culture we are indeed in a very bad state. We have to take all that is good in that culture, which it contains in profusion. Then we have to reshape that culture to achieve our goals, and to harness it to our purpose. [. . .]. Our comrades should creatively work among these artists in order to learn their 'melody and speech' and method of their 'utterances'; that is, to learn *their form, their mode of handling philosophical content*. This form is of decisive importance today. To understand this form means learning the trade, in its variety of uses and approaches. It means studying the past with scrupulous care.[69]

To craft efficacious modes of presenting content required deep engagements with existing forms and reworking them, as Ghatak's oeuvre, and particularly his

[68] Ibid.

[69] Ritwik Ghatak, *On the Cultural Front*, a thesis submitted by Ritwik Ghatak to the Communist Party of India in 1954 (Calcutta: Ritwik Memorial Trust, 2000), 16, emphasis in original.

Titash Ekti Nodir Naam (1973), illustrates. As Dutt would repeat subsequently, Ghatak concludes that '"Slogans" will never do here; slow, methodical, tenacious work is what is necessary'.[70] This call for a more thorough engagement with the form of bourgeois culture, and to repurpose it to serve different political ends, was not well taken by the political leadership and Ghatak's membership of the Communist Party was revoked.[71]

Ghatak and Dutt's emphasis on the use of aesthetic forms such as ('bourgeois') melodrama, folklore and mythology, or psychological tropes, as means to access and express the struggles and contradictions facing society, placed them askance of both party and canonized forms of aesthetic realism. In subsequent years, Ghatak's 'troubled relationship with realism, the privileged mode of leftist aesthetics in his time, made him seek a critical use of traditional motifs, symbolic extensions, and narrative interruptions'.[72] Writing in 1966 about his film *Subarnarekha* (1965), Ghatak notes that 'there is no trace of London in Brecht's Threepenny Opera . . . [because] at a mechanical level Brecht felt no need to know what London looked like, what coherent form it should take on, and so on, and it did not take away one bit from what he wanted to put forward'.[73] Realism, then, was far distanced from verisimilitude. As Neepa Majumdar has suggested, socially engaged 'realism' emerges in the cinema from theatrical traditions and can account for aspects of cinematic form that appear distant from realist modes.

> As a style of theater, IPTA's 'realist' social impulse did not preclude it from using a combination of song and folk performance styles, even while representing the horrors of the Bengal famine. Earlier in the century, a similar reliance on popular folk and theater styles arguably was also responsible in part for the much-vilified formal features of the Hindi sound film . . .[74]

These theatrical forms feed into the articulation of realism in cinema, producing a distinctive set of characteristics and formal conventions that are shared across very different films and other cultural practices. Realism, then, should not be equated with verisimilitude and in the final balance, painters, film-makers and authors struggled to mould a form that would capture the reality of a social context, make it legible and galvanizing to its audiences and imbue the aesthetic

70 Ibid., 17.
71 Ghatak, *On the Cultural Front*, preface.
72 Moinak Biswas, 'Two Articles by Ritwik Ghatak', *Cinema Journal* 54, no. 3 (2015), 13.
73 Ritwik Ghatak, 'On *Subarnarekha*', trans. Moinak Biswas, *Cinema Journal* 54, no. 3 (2015), 19.
74 Neepa Majumdar, 'Importing Neorealism, Exporting Cinema: Indian Cinema and Film Festivals in the 1950s', in *Global Neorealism: The Transnational History of a Film Style*, eds. Saverio Giovacchini and Robert Sklar (Jackson: The University Press of Mississippi, 2012), 182.

object with an urgency for social change, while simultaneously activating forms that were received from a range of artistic traditions in the colonial period. In this sense, left-committed realist aesthetic practices were driven by form over verisimilitude, despite the fear of the slogan and the deadening effects of formalism, and could travel from fine art contexts to music, from revolutionary street theatre to popular cinema.

As different forms were plumbed for their capacity to capture 'philosophical content', artists would also revisit crucial episodes and forms repeatedly, or trial different forms to express this content, following artistic trajectories often at odds with the political directions of dispersing and repressed left political parties. In 1946 Somnath Hore extensively sketched episodes from the Tebagha movement as a Communist Party activist (2009). In the early 1950s and within a fundamentally changed political landscape, he reworked his sketches into woodcuts.

> Hore persisted with a dogged determination in his penetration of a reality which he defines in terms of man's inhumanity to man, power riding roughshod over people, leaving them destitute and broken, with no fresh mobilization in sight. To penetrate that reality, Hore set up for himself the barriers of material which he had to break into (like wood at first, and then paper pulp . . .) . . . or mould, as with bronze . . .[75]

Here the question of material, experience and reality come together as the experience of Tebagha is revisited across political and artistic borders, and new form is once again given to that engagement. Such borrowing also occurred across the bodies of artists' works, as tropes and narratives moved between media, including in the above-mentioned *Jago Hua Savera*, for which Faiz Ahmed Faiz adapted a novel by Manik Bandopadhyay with a cast of artists drawing on the IPTA tradition. Individual artists, film-makers and writers reached for and recuperated forms which had been produced as part of the struggle, and these were recast and newly contextualized in the decolonial era. Artists brought varied embodied histories of artistic movements and cultural practice to this reworking. Sketches and woodcuts, modes of group theatre, folk motifs, styles of cinematic neorealism or particular poetic imagery continue to be re-appropriated, echoed and reframed in the works of artists whose practices intersect in ideological, social and political fields.

75 Samik Bandhyapadhya, 'Introduction', in Somnath Hore, *Tebagha: An Artist's Diary and Sketchbook*, trans. Somnath Zutshi (Kolkata: Seagull Books, 2009), 12.

The forms of the left also can be found recurring in works and sites distant from their lives within committed left-wing circles. The aesthetic forms that left-committed artists crafted to connote conscience, commitment, ethics, revolution or struggle weren't only intended for use within a community of 'believers' or 'card carrying' members of the proliferating Communist Parties, particularly as the alliances shifted and split. Both purposefully and otherwise, there was plentiful aesthetic spillage into the mainstream, in part due to left-wing artists taking up commissioned work, in part due to the ways in which left-committed artists had attempted to re-signify existing forms and emblems, and in part due to the ways in which motifs and forms that had become codified as 'committed' or serious were taken up elsewhere. In her discussion of song sequences of Bombay cinema in the 1950s set on urban streets, Manishita Dass shows how the registers by which the metropolis is presented visually, viscerally and aurally, through dance, sets, music and mise-en-scene in the 1950s cinema, drew significantly on 'the IPTA aesthetic and vision at work not only in the explicit theatricality of this sequence . . . but also in the way in which it connects performance with shared experiences of deprivation and social injustice on the one hand and with the creation of collective affect and a shared worldview on the other'.[76] Through the incorporation of artists, poets, directors and writers with IPTA experience into the Bombay film industry, IPTA's aesthetic forms and understanding of art's political role were incorporated into mainstream film. Not in any straightforward ideological set of precepts or convictions about the boundaries of realism but as aesthetic convictions and conventions that moved alongside artists and their aesthetic practices and experiences. Certain aesthetic registers, then, would become more broadly used and find expression in other cultural practices, from the architecture of war memorials, in 'art' films, to student murals and so on. In this way, the forms of the left can be understood to leak into other domains detached from their particular political context but continuing to carry its trace through form.

Forms of the left, then, acquire mobility and emerge in unexpected places to harness new collectivities and commitments, not least because of the mobile modality of left political alliances themselves. Forms of the left are not monolithic, nor self-evidently singular in their ideological potential. They are contagious, breaching domains and political valences. But they are nonetheless recognizably part of a field of artistic practices and connections, histories of

[76] Manishita Dass, 'Cinetopia: Leftist Street Theatre and the Musical Production of the Metropolis in 1950s Bombay Cinema', *positions* 25, no. 1 (2017), 116.

activism and mobilization, party political lines, funding streams and part of networks of artists, writers, critics and thinkers. They are *forms*, rather than genres or slogans, operating along the lines of similitude, in which the familiar is reworked in experimental and new ways to give concrete shape to the convictions of the artists and writers we engage in this volume. As such, a formalist approach cannot be dismissed as 'mere' attention to ornament or entertainment. With the artists and their works discussed in this volume, we must, as Sonya Posmentier articulates it powerfully, 'ask instead what a historically attentive formalism would look like. That is, how can we attend to poetic form without turning our backs on the real world or, on the other hand, falling prey to anthropomorphism and abstraction.'[77] If we understand form as thoughtful repetition and similitude across aesthetic fields, a poiesis wrought by artistic experiment that allows us to apprehend the world, this is also what we aspire to in our attention to form and formalist analysis.

In our encounter with these forms of the left, we also find an opportunity to experience the conjunctural times that these works made sensible and to return to us the complexity and unease of the moment from which they emerged. It is easy to overwrite the aesthetic forms that we explore here with a singular story of 'the left' in the twentieth century. Instead, our attention to form allows the materiality and poetry of the aesthetic object to interrupt our familiar teleological understandings of times past.[78] As Christopher Pinney has argued, 'The visual [can be] shown to be a zone in which new narratives are established that may be quite disjunct from the familiar stories of a nonvisual history.'[79] He highlights the recursivity of the image as particularly conducive to the visual inhabiting its own time, while its material form, in excess of the discursive narratives placed around it, allows it to push beyond meaning to intensities felt and experienced. Close reading and engagements with form provide an entry point to these fields of intensity that are both consciously crafted by artists and resistant to the dominant discursive domains they find themselves in today.

The chapters in this volume detail both the ways in which artists purposefully embraced certain forms for their world-renewing potential as well as mapping our own experiences of being confronted and challenged by these forms and the use and understanding of form that grounded them. We work through the building disorientation that befalls the fictional crew in Mrinal Sen's layered

[77] Sonya Posmentier, *Cultivation and Catastrophe: The Lyric Ecology of Modern Black Literature* (Baltimore: Johns Hopkins University Press, 2017), 212.

[78] Pinney, 'Things Happen.'

[79] Ibid., 265.

narrative in *Akhaler Sandhaney* (Dass, Chapter 7); the political contradictions and artistic challenges of the cross-regional production of *Jago Hua Savera* (Dadi, Chapter 3); Chittaprosad's despair with his own work (Sunderason, Chapter 1); and the Afro-Asian writers' reshaping of existing poetic form (Ramnath, Chapter 4). Each of these artists bend form to their intention and utopian aspiration while confronting us with the dense particularities of their images, poems, prints and structures. As a counterpoint that underscores the political efficacy of form, Chapter 2 shows Maulana Bhashani, the charismatic peasant leader who fundamentally shaped the popular uprising and revolution in Bangladesh, producing a political *mela* with a consciously crafted infrastructural form that was both construed from, and referenced, forms of the left. We also map the ways in which form was explicitly theorized by critics, artists and writers aligned to the left, to interpret and inform artistic practice, such as by novelists and playwrights in Sri Lanka in the context of the changing fortunes of the left (Rambukwella, Chapter 5) and film-maker Alamgir Kabir's impassioned commitment to aesthetic education in the years preceding the revolution, genocide and war in Bangladesh (Hoek, Chapter 6). In his afterword to the volume (chapter 8), Kamran Asdar Ali pursues the legacies of violence and trauma in poetic registers across South Asia. He suggests that the formal choices in the poetry of key protagonists and participants of the cultural movements we map in this volume reflect how the trauma of recurring violence in India, Pakistan, Bangladesh and Sri Lanka has demanded movements across linguistic, poetic and artistic idioms to capture the exclusions, alienations and separations that have repeatedly engulfed the region. In this way, Ali underscores the high stakes for those whose formal experiments and cultural commitments we map in this volume. The violence of the postcolonial experience, including the apocalyptic violence of Partition, the genocide in Bangladesh and the civil war in Sri Lanka, alongside the repression, censorship, arrests and attacks that befell cultural activists, to the ideological conflicts and fraught sectarianism within left circles, and the profound melancholies and alienations of the postcolonial experience in a fractured South Asia, form the backdrop against which Ali reflects on the ways in which poetry, language and film could provide a means of healing, addressing and repairing these wounds. The forms of the left detailed in the chapters in this volume were all crafted to express the conjunctural challenges and opportunities in new ways, to articulate the hopes and fears that accompanied them in unexpected and transformative ways. Today, they continue to invite us into their modes of engaging the world, to inhabit their distributed temporality. Their material forms sensitize us to the political and ethical commitments that were borne of the times in which they were conceived and that fuelled these aesthetic experiments.

Contemporary articulations

Forms of the left in the twenty-first century necessitate questions that are foundationally different from the twentieth century. Yet some of the critical energies as well as configurations of the left from the last century recur in our contemporary moment. With the fall of the Soviet Union the question of a communist left as a political force has dissipated substantially, in the Euro-American World as with vast swathes of the former Soviet Sphere in Eastern Europe and Central Asia. Globally, this closure of the Cold War encouraged myopic fantasies of the 'end of history'[80] – which while being limited by its Eurocentrism, were also blind to the dialectical energy of ideology (of the left) as history *and* as form. The early twenty-first century has only complicated this dialectic: we see a retreat of the institutional political left globally – Communist Parties and even centre–left political formations have either disappeared or have failed to find electoral majorities to the point of becoming irrelevant. A growing surge of right-wing populism has grown to occupy the centre and create an expanded political and public space for the far-right. Yet, the left is resurgent. And in this simultaneity of retreat and resurgence, we argue, there are possibilities for rethinking the question of the left as a plurality of *forms* – that persist from the past and emerge through the dialectical energies of the present. Seen as *forms* – of aesthetics and affiliations – the left is both inheritance/memory/legacy as much as strategy/intervention/affiliation. While the scope of this volume is the postcolonial twentieth century in South Asia, we see it as part of a wider contemporary reanimation of the left – its memories and momentum, its utopic thrust and perhaps also its blind spots. In opening up an academic and trans-border conversation around the subcontinental left, we provide insight into some of the contemporary cultural imaginaries of the left, to explore the aesthetic registers that are being deployed, as well as the wider historiographical questions that emerge therefrom.

To comprehend the forms of the left two decades into this century, we find aesthetics and cultural forms – rather than formal party politics – to be useful analytical tools that are deployed to animate informal/sub-national/locational/

[80] Francis Fukuyama, 'The End of History?' *The National Interest* 16 (1989), 3–18.

counter-hegemonic sites that are imaginational or dispersed, and that seek to concretize new configurations of organization. New modes of mediation are central to this new articulation of the dispersed left. The new platforms of the twenty-first century, from social media to the art biennial, allow a production and circulation of forms of the left that are linked to the political struggles of this time.

In places, the mobility of the forms of the left happens in unpredictable and newly fertile ways. In his discussion of the 'curious' 'hypervisibility of communist and radical left propaganda forms' in 21st-century mobilizations in support of statehood for Telengana separate from Andhra Pradesh, SV Srinivas notes the prominence of 'Maoist propaganda of earlier decades and cultural activists',[81] despite the absence of Maoist groups in the agitation for Telengana statehood since 2006.[82] In his detailed discussion of the trajectories of Maoist cultural forms in Andhra Pradesh, Srinivas notes how earlier forms move across media and genres and become dispersed across different screens in the contemporary moment. 'Yesterday's propaganda has been detached from the politics that spawned it and has become dispersed media content, and also acquired a political significance which has little to do with Maoism.'[83] The citationality of these forms is what allows its longevity and yoking to new political causes. 'Naxalite propaganda is invoked and quoted [in cinema, in music performances, in publicity materials] but the end product need not be directly related either to Naxalism or even to propaganda',[84] but could nonetheless be highly politically efficacious as part of the struggle for statehood, which was achieved in 2014.

The circulation of media artefacts across platforms also contributes to active and germane solidarities being forged between multiple social, political and intellectual movements. In South Asia these are active most strongly amidst assertions of Dalit politics and counter-hegemonic resistance[85] and its trans political solidarities with anti-communal protests, environmental movements or struggles for free speech. Globally we see the left returning most vividly in new anti-fascist alliances and movements and anti-capitalist, anti-racist and pro-democratic collectives. Transnational vocabularies resonate – *Black Lives*

[81] SV Srinivas, 'Maoism to Mass Culture: Notes on Telangana's Cultural Turn', *BioScope: South Asian Screen Studies* 6, no. 2 (2015), 187.

[82] Ibid., 188.

[83] Ibid.

[84] Ibid., 200.

[85] See for instance, Gary Michael Tartakov, *Dalit Art and Visual Imagery* (New Delhi: Oxford University Press, 2012); Laura R. Brueck, *Writing Resistance: The Rhetorical Imagination of Hindi Dalit Literature* (New York: Columbia University Press, 2014); Judith Misrahi-Barak, K. Satyanarayana and Nicole Thiara (eds), *Dalit Text: Aesthetics and Politics Re-imagined* (New Delhi: Routledge, 2020).

Matter resurfaces in (global) South Asia as *Dalit Lives Matter*; Hong Kong's calls for sovereignty are picked up by Kashmir's calls for *azaadi* (freedom), just as the Palestinian *intifada* has resonated in Kashmir over decades. In the past decade uprisings across the Middle East have echoed with protests in Dhaka against the political power of war criminals, captured, for instance, by political paintings and satirical cartoons by the artists Shishir Bhattacharjee, and documented by well-recognized photographers such as Shahidul Islam. Protests against environmental degradation and exploitation across the region have long-standing roots in left activist movements that themselves have produced extensive artistic output, including prominently in Amar Kanwar's *Sovereign Forest* (2012) and recently in Munem Wasif's *Seeds shall set us free* (2016–17). Across universities, museums or pedagogical concerns we find new conversations around decoloniality and indigenous politics that seek to both return to questions of (neo) imperialism and open up decolonization as an ongoing epistemic concern: the left resides across these initiatives of re-animating the questions of equality, representation, justice. Across such sites, the left seems to take shape as an *essentially* amorphous affiliation – perhaps not unlike the Popular Front period of the Communist International in the 1930s when anti-fascist solidarities had to allow fluid affiliational modalities in the transnational left, with as many fellow-travellers as active members of the political left. Then, too, culture itself had formed a modality of imagining revolutionary movements and epistemes – whether as anti-fascism or as anti-colonial and anti-imperial politics.

Today, such informal/non-official alliances of the left are surfacing once more. Such resurgences are active in artworks, curation and memory-work itself. Exhibitions, conferences and publications in the past decade have boosted this resurgence, even if as analytical frames. Whether in exhibitions like *Postwar: Art between the Pacific and the Atlantic, 1945-1965* at the Haus der Kunst in Berlin in 2016,[86] or conferences like *Axis of Solidarity* held at the Tate Modern in 2018, or in curatorial projects across documenta and biennales and art summits in Dhaka, Dubai, Guangzhou, Kochi or Venice – the left appears as history, archive, and analytical tropes as artists/curators/academics seek to bring back and reconfigure histories of anti-colonial movements, Third World solidarities and indigenous resistance from the global South.

At one level, these conversations around the 21st-century left move beyond received binaries between "West" and "East", though the Euro-American

[86] Enwezor Okukui, Katy Siegel and Ulrich Wilmes, *Postwar: Art between the Pacific and the Atlantic, 1945-1965* (Munich: Haus der Kunst, 2017).

left's tepid conceptualization, at best, of questions of race, decolonization and postcolonial modernities is in itself a critical lapse in generating global political resonance of an ideology that is an internationalist one. At another level, these new conversations point towards a potentiality of bringing back the left as a foundational transnational trope in reconceptualizing the twentieth-century decolonization – and in the process, invite scholarship and activism to rethink our positionalities.

This volume joins these current initiatives by addressing the present and its potentialities by returning to the dynamic and resonant histories of the twentieth-century left, in a region of the world that carries some of the most destructive legacies of decolonization. South Asia – with its histories of anti-colonial struggles, partitions, transnational solidarities, and tried and tortured histories of the left – provides us with possibilities of rethinking the left *as form* – whether as past forms or recurring forms or forms of possibilities. Contemporaneity sits at the heart of this historical conversation. It remains engaged time and again with the question of temporality and repetition – as mobilizing around an event, or via art's social commitment, or across historical and political ruptures (within the Communist Parties, for instance), or as citational modalities of generational memories, nostalgia and activist evocations. In pursuing this entanglement of forms of the left and historical time, it is worthwhile to make malleable ideological rigidities that tend to overwrite conversations around the (cultural or political) left as well as its contradictory histories. This malleability is not a gesture towards deradicalization but rather an invitation to rethink the left as an entangled historical, political as well as aesthetic episteme.

1

A melancholic archive

Chittaprosad and socialist art in postcolonial India*

Sanjukta Sunderason

A melancholic archive

In this chapter, and in the spirit of the questions we are pursuing in this volume, I am focusing on the postcolonial trajectory of the communist artist Chittaprosad. I will work with drawings, paintings, prints, draft sketches, book illustrations, correspondence and miscellaneous writings that the artist produced between 1948 – the year of his dissociation from the Communist Party of India (CPI), of which he was a dedicated member and artist-cadre since the early 1940s – and 1978 – the year of his demise.

In the early 1940s, Chittaprosad had shot to prominence as what can be called an 'artist-cadre' – a politically committed artist and a working member of CPI. In a lengthy piece titled 'Chhabi-r Sankat' (roughly translatable to 'crisis/dilemma of the image'), written in 1943 for *Arani* – one of the left's cultural organs – Chittaprosad had called for turning art into an 'agitator and organizer'.[1] Within the documentary conventions of journalistic drawings, his famine sketches – trailing death, displacement and grassroots relief-work across famine-ravaged districts of undivided Bengal (from Chittagong in the east to Midnapore in the west)[2] – had introduced a new expressionistic realism in Indian art, a drift he both

* Parts of this chapter have appeared in my book, *Partisan Aesthetics: Modern Art and India's Long Decolonization* (Chapter 4: 'All the more real for not being preached: Forms and Futures of Socialist Art in Nehruvian India').

1 Chittaprosad, 'Chhabi-r Sankat', *Arani*, October 1943.

2 The famine is known to have killed and displaced more than three million. Chittaprosad's visual diary – *Hungry Bengal, A Tour through Midnapore District, by Chittaprosad, in November 1943* (Mumbai: New Age Printing Press, 1944) – remains one of the most iconic documentations of the famine. The British government is said to have burnt 5,000 copies after its publication in 1944, as recalled by Gouri Bhattacharya, the artist's sister in a collection of reminiscences on the artist and

pioneered and shared with some of his peers. Through the 1940s, he organized and composed for ballets of the Indian People's Theatre Association – a front organization set up during the famine years of 1943–4. During these heydays of the left's cultural movement, idealized retrospectively as the 'Marxist Cultural Movement',[3] Chittaprosad also became the first and complex protagonist of socialist realism in Indian art, a visualizer of the communist rhetoric of culture as *front*, art as *weapon*, artists as *cultural workers* and touring collectives of performers as *cultural squads*.[4]

As India became independent, Chittaprosad quit the CPI in 1948, when the party's general secretary and his mentor, patron and confidant, P. C. Joshi, was expelled at the party's Second Congress in Calcutta in 1948, on charges of 'bourgeois reformism'. His post-1948 works were made almost entirely in withdrawal, with next to no patronage, as the artist lived in isolation in his ground-floor room in the working-class neighbourhood of Andheri in Bombay/Mumbai. None of these works were exhibited in India in the 1950s to 1970s, outside perhaps the occasional exhibition in Calcutta among the artist's limited circle of friends and admirers (as we see in his letters). They never entered art critical conversations or published profiles on postcolonial Indian artists either, beyond a few stray pieces. Many works from the period are in fact lost and damaged in mishandling and property disputes since his death, as the artist's sister notes in her memoirs of him in 2002, in a volume I will begin with here.[5]

A critical minority of the material I will discuss here – the artist's letters, memoirs of his friends/comrades and sister, and his own (unfinished/undated) essays – were published in 2002 in Calcutta in a volume titled *Kshudarto Bangla*, a reprint from an earlier little magazine edition from *Jogasutra*. A lion's share of my material, however, comes from the decades long excavation on the artist undertaken by the private art gallery circuits steered by the Delhi Art Gallery (DAG) since the 1990s and Osian's in Bombay/Mumbai: the culmination of this was the monumental retrospective on the artist in 2011, with accompanying

his authored short articles, *Kshudartho Bangla* (Hungry Bengal). See Benoy Ghosh, ed. *Kshudartho Bangla* (Kolkata: Kathabarta, 2002).

3 The expression was popularized with the publication of three volumes of collected papers from the period by one of the activists of IPTA, Sudhi Pradhan. See Sudhi Pradhan, *Marxist Cultural Movement in India: Chronicles and Documents* (Vol. 1, Calcutta: Pustak Bipani, 1979; Vols 2 and 3, Calcutta: Nabanna, 1982, 1983).

4 These vocabularies and sensibilities are spread across reports and editorials in CPI organs, and manifestoes of the Progressive Writers' Association and the IPTA.

5 Gouri Bhattacharya, 'Nihsangha Paribrajak', reproduced in Ghosh, ed., *Kshudarto Bangla*, 41.

publications of catalogues/essays/sketchbooks/letters.[6] The DAG's substantial retrospective on the artist displayed an entire paraphernalia of objects (sketchbooks, leaflets, catalogues, photographs, book illustrations, tools, pens, puppets, fragments from the artist's book collection, among others) alongside the art works: the more familiar 1940s' works on famine and popular protests that he had published in the CPI organs *People's War* and *People's Age* (and their regional editions); but more importantly, a host of never-displayed material from the 1950s to early 1970s. The objects and works that the artist held on to dearly during his lifetime – now exhibited for the first time in this scale – made Chittaprosad an active name as reporters and critics hailed the artist of "hunger and resistance". Yet such celebrations ironically revealed also, the *unconscious* of such belated retrievals – the artist's own unique *withdrawal* that he had held on to till his death.

Chittaprosad's works have since circulated in auctions, exhibitions, biennales and indeed increasing scholarship that have been made viable due to the visibility of the works (my own trajectory in writing on the political in Indian art has been a product of that visibility). Chittaprosad is celebrated now as the artist of hunger and humanism, a hallmark in contemporary (transnational) curations on art, decolonization and Third World solidarity movements of the twentieth century. Yet this miscellaneous archive of his works/letters resonates beyond the artist's recent art world salvage of the 2000s. The salvage/visibility itself, as I will argue here, is laden with a shadow history of absence.

Growing up in India in the 1980s to 1990s and across my university life in the 2000s, I encountered or chanced upon Chittaprosad's iconography in random sites and flashes: amidst peeling political graffiti on Calcutta street walls (before their sanitization over the 2000s); pastiches of (far)left student activist posters, graffiti and wall-writing in university campuses; most memorably, on walls in India's tribal hinterland caught during train journeys (travelling across India's Maoist 'Red Corridor' in the Bastar region, for instance); or indeed, in the sudden find amidst bristling counters of little magazines in Calcutta's annual book fairs. For the longest period, it can be safely argued, Chittaprosad's art thrived in serendipitous encounters, almost *in absence*, rather than in (its current) dynamic visibility. What produced his absence in postcolonial India, particularly after his immense popularity in the 1940s? And what works – artworks or thought-works – did this absence produce? Along the same grain, what questions can

[6] Mallik, Sanjoy. *Chittaprosad.* Vols 1 and 2 (New Delhi: Delhi Art Gallery, 2011); *A Sketchbook of 30 Portraits by Chittaprosad* (New Delhi: Delhi Art Gallery, 2011); *Yours Chitta: Translated Excerpts from Select Letters of Chittaprosad* (New Delhi: Delhi Art Gallery, 2011).

such absence pose – for art history/historiography of twentieth-century India, and for a transnational understanding of socialist art itself?

Elsewhere, I have pursued some of these questions to understand the peculiar (after)lives of socialist art in postcolonial India, particularly after its high noon in the 1940s under a Marxist cultural movement.[7] In this chapter, I want to dwell more specifically on the question of absence, by remaining as close as possible to Chittaprosad's letters, writings and artworks. My purpose is to listen in (amidst his letters), to trace (from the marginalia of his drafts and sketches) and to see *in his terms* (and hence, via the artist's deeply personal vantage points) how socialist art was imagined and experienced by an artist both committed to and torn from the legacies of the left.

Chittaprosad's letters here date mainly from the early 1950s until the early 1970s. They were written to his former comrades, his family (his mother and sister), friends – old and new – in the United States, Denmark and the then Czechoslovakia. Given his own withdrawal from the cultural circuits of postcolonial India, such letters carry unique entry-points into the terrain of associations, and thoughts that he sustained; they also very significantly help us trace the different projects he engaged himself in, or failed to pursue, or even rejected. The letters are steeped in his wishes, plans, frustrations and euphoria; most persistently, they reveal his loneliness and disillusionment, that are, I argue, at once deeply personal and ideological. They are also, in Stuart Hall's words, a 'living archive' that is made alive by the heterogeneity and multiplicity of discourses – '[...] not only of practice but of criticism, history and theory, of personal story, anecdote and biography [. . .]'.[8]

Chittaprosad's correspondence and the artworks/drafts from the 1950s to the 1970s also present, as I propose here, a *melancholic archive* of the cultural left – a field of personal reflections and negotiations from the CPI's cultural activists that negotiated both the dreams of a socialist culture and the disappearing or at best limited political patronage. They reveal a dialectical affiliation that captures both intimacy to and longing for the lost realms of solidarity, as well as a rejection of the politics of the present – what Walter Benjamin had called the regression of left-wing melancholy.[9] Yet, along Enzo Traverso's arguments, while the 'memory of the left is a huge, prismatic continent made of conquests

7 Sunderason, *Partisan Aesthetics*.
8 Stuart Hall, 'Constituting an Archive', *Third Text* 15, no. 54 (2001), 89–92.
9 Walter Benjamin, 'Left-Wing Melancholy', in *The Weimer Republic Sourcebook*, ed. A. Kaes, M. Jay and E. Dimendberg (Berkeley: University of California Press, 1994).

and defeats', melancholia is a 'feeling, a state of the soul and a field of emotions'.[10] Pursuing the analytical thread of left-wing melancholia, Traverso argues, suggests therefore 'going beyond ideas and concepts' and into 'imagination, not doctrine'.[11] This realm of the personal and the imaginational – of hopes and frustrations – is also a uniquely individual entry-point into a structural question, an artistic negotiation of a political transition, even failure.

What remains of Chittaprosad's belated archive, I will argue, is a (potential) discursive field that constitutes the individual histories of a collective aesthetic of the left's cultural movement, and thus carries deeply subjective vantage points that can refract monolithic, celebrational narratives – whether of national culture, or ideological cultures. They help us conceptualize both the aesthetic *and* individual forms that political histories of the left took during the 1950s to 1970s – decades steeped in postcolonial state-building as much as of the ideological horizons shaped by Afro-Asian decolonization and the Cold War. They might even offer a (continued or potential) agency for a cultural left in its dialectic with the political left.

Dialectical affiliations: Art and the party

The relation of the left with India's post-independence government under Jawaharlal Nehru was complex. After the Second Congress of the CPI held in Calcutta in February 1948, the party had adopted a political hardline that echoed a rejection of the idea of independence itself: 'Yeh azadi jhooti hai'/'This freedom is false', the incoming party secretary, B. T. Ranadive is known to have said. While the CPI under P. C. Joshi had pledged support for the national leadership under Nehru, the new party line in 1948 took an anti-Nehru line, in support of the Telengana movement (for regional sovereignty in the princely state of Hyderabad), and remained at war with the Indian state until the movement was officially withdrawn in 1951. By 1949, the CPI was banned in Bengal and its activists jailed, as the new nation state remained ever cautious about communist action.[12] For the cultural movement itself, the impact was disastrous; political opposition to the nation state disbanded the cohabitation of liberal and communist cultural workers within a wider rhetoric of social

10 Enzo Traverso, *Left-Wing Melancholia: Marxism, History, and Memory* (New York: Columbia University Press, 2016), xiii.

11 Ibid., xv.

12 Benjamin Zachariah, *Nehru* (London: Routledge, 2004), 184.

responsiveness of art – what Joshi had crafted in the 1940s; at an international level the formation of the Cominform and consolidation of the political line of Andrei Zhdanov made ideological control over cultural expression more active. Apathy towards the cultural movement saw many artistes leave the party during the late 1940s and early 1950s; some were expelled for critiques, and those who remained struggled with disillusionment.

Ranadive drove the party into a blind lane, writes the poet Subhash Mukhopadhayay, in his recollections of Chittaprosad published in *Kshudarto Bangla* (2002); those who could escape, removed themselves completely, and some others became sensitive, and then there were those who while retreating completely still struggled with hope and disillusionment, Chitta being the latter. Mukhopadhyay calls this Chitta's 'abhiman' – untranslatable in English, but coming very close to dejection/disappointment, a melancholic withdrawal from (or complaint against) the object of desire itself, not a renunciation of a cause.[13] His separation was neither simple nor complete, as his letters show, resonating with disappointment with the party and the stifled potential of the cultural movement, while he remained in conscious isolation, half-expecting the party to acknowledge his art. While his commitment to art's social address was perennial, there were degrees of tension that he negotiated with the legacy of the left itself. Despite an active and permanent rift from the party, an artist like Chittaprosad, writes his former comrade and lifelong communist activist Hirendranath Mukhopadhyay, was a socialist at heart: 'what Marx had called "The party in the grand historical sense of the term"'.[14]

Chittaprosad's dissociation from the party appears across his letters as a curious dialectic. His letters to his friends – Murari Gupta, the poet Subhash Mukhopadhyay and his wife, Gita Bandopadhyay, the writer and activist of the international defence for children movement – bristle with the artist's dialectical affiliation with the communist cause, at once rejecting association with the party and working diligently for its forums. He writes to Gita Bandopadhyay, for instance, about his linocuts for the International Conference for the Defence of Children, with which Bandopadhyay was closely involved: 'I have already sent 22 illustrations to Tara (Yagnik) in Berlin. . . . Before leaving Berlin Tara has handed over the illustrations to Madame Simone. They are going to be published in a women's bulletin apparently [. . .].'[15] Yet when the couple invite him to

[13] Subhash Mukhopadhyay, 'Reminiscences on Chittaprosad', in Ghosh, ed., *Kshudarto Bangla*, 24.

[14] Hirendranath Mukhopadhyay, 'Chittaprosad Smaran-e', in Ghosh, ed., *Kshudarto Bangla*, 21.

[15] Chittaprosad's letter to Gita Mukhopadhyay (nee Gita Bandopadhyay), 15 October 1951. Reproduced in Ghosh, ed., *Kshudarto Bangla*, 25.

decorate the conference for the defence of children in Calcutta with his works, he refuses, writing that that his involvement with an event would immediately give it a 'partisan' character; it is much better, he writes, if they invite veteran artists like Jamini Roy, or Ramendranath Chakraborty, or Ramkinkar Baij: 'If you begin the work with artists outside the party, then I can get involved as a general worker.'[16] 'The main issue', he notes, 'is that until the party gives leadership, it will be difficult to find people who will think and work hard in organizing. And without that, even if a couple of people sacrifice themselves in the process, nothing can be built.'[17]

Writing in 1952, we see him drawing for party journals like *Unity*, getting weekly commissions from *Crossroads* (the journal of the communist activist and entrepreneur Romesh Thapar), and taking photographs for IPTA conference exhibitions – for which he is often not paid, or his works used unacknowledged.[18] During the same period, in 1952–3, he writes to Murari Gupta about the new sketches of famine victims he was doing in the hunger-ravaged districts of Maharashtra. He had returned from a famine-ravaged district of Mangi with 70 sketches and more than 650 photos, hoping that the party would exhibit his works. He was met instead with a dithering party response, which to him revealed more than financial backtracking on exhibition costs. 'The route to an artist's link with his country, in this land and these times', he notes lamenting the failure of Mangi famine drawings to draw patronage, 'is so unfathomably far that it fails my sight, energy and intellect.'[19] 'And even if it were possible', he writes referring to the exhibition the party had promised him, 'I doubt whether it would serve its purpose because it amounts to challenging Nehru. Had there been a support from the Kisan Sabha it could have been successful.'[20] What seemed revolutionary art in the 1940s appeared to him untenable to the party in independent India. The Mangi sketches remained invisible in his lifetime. His letters to his former comrades and friends resonate with a sense of disappointment with the party and the stifled potential of the cultural movement. Even the annual conference of the IPTA, where he hoped to show his works, had become, he notes, 'merely a dance-of-the-ghosts', 'people's theatre minus the people'.[21]

16 Chittaprosad's letter to Gita Mukhopadhyay, 9 February 1952. Reproduced in Ghosh, ed., *Kshudarto Bangla*, 26.

17 Chittaprosad's letter to Gita Mukhopadhyay, 9 February 1952. Reproduced in Ghosh, ed., *Kshudarto Bangla*, 27.

18 Letter to Somnath Hore, 31 October 1952, reprinted in Ghosh, ed., *Kshudarto Bangla*, 183.

19 Letter to Murari Gupta, 26 June 1953, in Mallik, ed., *Yours Chitta*, 14.

20 Ibid., 11.

21 Chittaprosad's letter to Murari Gupta, 21 May 1953, in Mallik, ed., *Yours Chitta*, 9.

His frustrations with his own initiated works ring through the letters; to Murari Gupta he writes in 1953:

> My experience in trying to materialise the children's album of linocuts only increases my fear and worries about the party and this country at large. Not because they could not comprehend my worth, but because they have forgotten to put good work, relevant and necessary work, to good cause. This can only be called unsophisticated savagery; and that is frightening. Had my efforts alone been sufficient I wouldn't have despaired, for I know despair is an illness.[22]

Elsewhere, in the same letter, he writes:

> my heart and life lies in the country's revolutionary struggles. I am dying because nobody seems to have any need of me. Nuts and bolts come to life only if the whole machine remains active and if the nuts and bolts are accorded their proper spaces [. . .] And having joined the party I have learnt one thing, that it is impossible to realise what is to be given and how it is to be given unless one knows whom to give [to] and why.[23]

We also see in the letters that he is invited off and on by the world of left-wing theatre and film practitioners in Bombay, many of who had IPTA lineages. For instance, for a week-long celebration around the 'Paul Robeson birth anniversary', he makes a 'mural-like oil, 7 feet high and 12 feet long': 'I visited on the inaugural day of the meeting – wasn't looking too bad in the Jehangir Hall.'[24] It is likely that his former comrades Balraj Sahani and K. M. Abbas would have invited him to work on the Robeson anniversary. Yet, in his own writings he admits his difficulties with market-driven commercial art commissions. In a brief unfinished essay, he writes that he has been told by 'friendly agents' that artists like him have consciously destroyed their own potential by being 'too artistic' and 'uncompromising temperamental'; that a little bit of adjustment to suit the 'client' would benefit both him and the cause of modern art.[25] Yet his rejection of the 'culture-barons of this nation' remains strong, even as he copes with the reality of having next to no income.[26]

In a letter to Chittaprosad in 1967, the Marxist poet and Chittaprosad's former comrade-in-arms, Jyotirindranath Moitra writes: 'Bhule jao byarthota-r nesha – obokshoy tomar shaje na' – roughly translated as 'Abandon your addiction

22 Letter to Murari Gupta, 26 June 1953, in Mallik, ed., *Yours Chitta*, 14.
23 Ibid., 14–15.
24 Letter to Murari Gupta, 25 April 1958, in Mallik, ed., *Yours Chitta*, 23.
25 Chittaprosad, 'Chitrakar bonam bigyapan-er dalal', reproduced in Ghosh, ed., *Kshudarto Bangla*, 57.
26 Letter to Murari Gupta, 27 June 1959, in Mallik, ed., *Yours Chitta*, 48. See also, Prabhash Sen, 'Chittaprosad, Kichhu Smirticharan', in Ghosh, ed., *Kshudarto Bangla*, 31.

to failure – disintegration is unbecoming of you.'[27] Failure, however, is in itself a form of affirmation; failure carries a tension between 'non-fulfilment and expectation', and is therefore, a complex form with 'connotation, symbolic charges and cultural roles, which are often diverse and contradictory'.[28] Chittaprosad's failures echo contradictions that drove the transformation of socialist art in the post-colony. Desire and despair were as much a part of the dialectical aesthetics of the postcolonial left as were the new artistic negotiations between socialist commitment and modernist experimentation.

Chittaprosad's dialectical affiliations echo similar voices from the cultural left in the 1950s. Striking, for instance, is the auteur Ritwik Ghatak, who in 1952 was expelled from the CPI upon submitting to the party his programmatic text – *On the Cultural Front: A Thesis Submitted to the Communist Party of India* – where he laid out a foundational critique of the left's cultural patronage, and raised the call for a cultural agenda rooted in formal rigour and participation in collective art-making as much as in political address. 'Reshape the past, hammer the present and forge the future',[29] Ghatak writes in the thesis; the 'problem of culture', he notes, is a problem of organization, not ideology, and hence rooted 'at the levels of the Party, the Platform, and Art'.[30] The 'use' of 'Culture' to the party is mechanistic, Ghatak notes, either as a 'money-making machine' or as 'mobilizer in meetings and conferences to keep the crowd (and not the masses) engaged with whatever the artists can offer'.[31] His appeal, on the contrary, was for participation in the pursuit of form: 'Our comrades must creatively work among these artistes in order to learn their "melody and speech" and "method of their utterances"; that is, to learn *their form, their mode of handling philosophic content*.'[32]

In his thesis Ghatak addressed the slippage of left-wing artistes into nostalgia; the habitation of the past for Ghatak is not one of nostalgia (an echo thus of the Benjaminian critique of left-wing melancholy), but an unrelenting commitment to the dialectic of the past and future: 'We are not seeking a "golden period," but a proper place in the body of the Party, and our share in Party rights and responsibilities.'[33] This denial of cultural nostalgia or revolutionary promise is

27 Jyotirindranath Maitra-s letter to Chittaprosad, 8 May 1967, reproduced in Ghosh, ed., *Kshudarto Bangla*, 180.
28 Susana S Martins, 'Failure as Art and Art History as Failure', *Third Text*, online, 2 (August 2015), accessed 18 May 2016.
29 Ghatak, *On the Cultural Front*, 13.
30 Ibid., 15.
31 Ibid., 14.
32 Ibid., 16.
33 Ibid., 15.

striking: 'Drop the idea that Revolution is round the corner. It is not. Forget about that former previous "elation", former "enthusiasm", and that romantic feeling of Revolutionary "zeal" – in a word, all that guided us up to at least 1950.'[34] Form, he insists, 'is of decisive importance today':

> 'To understand this form means learning the trade, in its variety of uses and approaches. It means studying the past with scrupulous care, and learning the experiments and achievements of the past'; it means learning the whole process; from the inception of 'theme-content', through stages of development, to the final product.[35]

This aesthetic labour, he argues, cannot be hasty, or steeped in sloganeering: 'slow, methodical, tenacious work is what is necessary'.[36]

Ghatak had joined the IPTA in 1948 and remained active through the party's underground years since 1949. This document was his reflection, manifesto, programme statement on art, party and the people. It triggered at first no response, and finally a rustication from the party. Ghatak's material, he admits, is directed mainly towards what he calls 'collective' arts – theatre, opera, ballet – and not 'individual' arts like poetry, painting, crafts; yet, the crisis – of both patronage and imagination – that he raises, can be seen to entangle – even if in slightly divergent ways – with Chittaprosad's own thoughts from the same period. In both, we trace a frustration that is both individual and collective, as much organizational as formal. In Chittaprosad, this formal unrest would result in a host of experimental works that he did in isolation, morphing at each turn as if in response to a lack of party interest, reaching out for wider horizons of transnational solidarities and ending up in deeply personal story-worlds of children's illustrations that can be seen to carry the (transformation of) socialist affiliation he himself negotiated via desire and dissociation.

Chittaprosad's withdrawal – from the party and the art spheres of postcolonial India – was symptomatic, both of his own personality and of the prerogatives of such spheres. He is indeed the split subject of the afterlives of the left-wing cultural movement, half caught in the visual ethics of committed visual reportage from his famine years with the Joshite CPI, and a growing sensibility of the futility of the cultural agenda of the party under Nehruvian India. Chittaprosad's anxiety reveals the culpabilities of both the CPI and independent India, producing in him an ironic eye, rare in the national-modern aesthetic of Nehruvian India.

[34] Ibid., 65.
[35] Ibid., 16.
[36] Ibid., 17.

Through the mid-1950s, Chittaprosad produced linocuts that etched and drew this irony.

'Bhejal itihash-er desh-e': In the shadows of Nehruvian India

Chittaprosad's cartoons all through 1947 visualized a nation in transition, fraught by an arrival of political independence the cost of partition, genocide and displacement. Decolonization appears in his works as a complex battlefield – of people and state, class and capital. Workers, peasants, Hindus and Muslims tower over territories hacked apart, as they fend off duelling politicians and unholy ententes of capitalists, princes and bureaucrats. Elsewhere, a Khadi-clad politician wields the axe of the Public Safety Bill over protestors agitating for food, clothing and housing, while British and Indian capitalists perched on a steam-roller crush their bodies. In another work, a monumental barricade of Indians, Turks, Arabs, Vietnamese and Chinese fighters towers over scorched lands, thwarting stealthy Anglo-American forces with the triumphant flag of 'Quit Asia'. These cartoons were some of the earliest expressions of people's struggles that continued under the shadow of political independence. Across 1947, such cartoons revealed movements that marked the complex questions and scopes of freedom at the hour of independence. For instance, a cartoon made in April 1947 at the hour of the All India States Peoples' Conference held in Gwalior in April 1947 foregrounds the right of the people of Kashmir to seek their own relation with the Indian Constitution, and against the dominance of the Hindu ruler Hari Singh. Made under the shadow of Sheikh Abdullah's imprisonment during the conference, Chittaprosad's sketch here is resonant of a people's movement that was both integral to the arrival of Indian independence and yet at threat of being subsumed under a new hegemonic narrative of the nation state.[37] Resonance of this can be seen till date in the burning question of freedom/*azaadi* in contemporary Kashmir. Other cartoons feature, for instance, stances that the left took over partition – support for the cause of sovereignty of the 'Muslim people' and a fight for the provision of popular mandate for a future Pakistan parliament – vis-à-vis 'princely interests' and those of the 'upper classes'.[38]

Chittaprosad's dissociation from the party is a critical turning point, not necessarily in the work the artist was doing, but indeed for the forums in which

[37] *People's Age*, 13 April 1947, 12.
[38] *People's Age*, 3 August 1947, 3.

such work would appear – a crisis of (political) patronage thus, rather than the impulse of creating (politically) committed art. The late 1940s or the early 1950s reveal a curious period in Chittaprosad's postcolonial trajectory, where he can be seen to continue the impulses of documentational art from the margins, drawing from sites of hunger and labour, from the shadows as it were, of postcolonial freedom. In the early 1950s, he did a series of linocuts around suburban Bombay, capturing rural hinterlands and working-class neighbourhoods. Somnath Hore – a fellow communist artist – recalls meeting him in the residences of Prabhash Sen and illustrator Khaled Chowdhury in the early 1950s, when he would still visit Calcutta – something that would reduce increasingly; he recalls Chittaprosad's ongoing works with the subaltern peoples around Bombay: fisherfolk, vegetable vendors, labourers, urban youth.[39]

Chittaprosad's letters carry traces of some of the works he did during this period, and the forums in which they got circulated. In his letter to Gita Bandopadhyay, for instance, he complains about the quality of reproduction of his work on the coverage of *Parichoy*, edited by her husband, Subhash Mukhopadhyay: the image looks grim, he writes, unfit for reproduction in red and too big for the cover page.[40] Reproduced here (Figure 1.1), this *Parichoy* cover page shows one of the most iconic sketches of Chitta that he is today known for – a vagrant boy snatching morsels of food from the garbage bin, fighting off crows – an echo both of famine years, but alive not only in the India of the 1950s but indeed of 2021. From these letters, we also see that Chittaprosad illustrated Subhash Mukhopadhyay's early collection of essays: *Amar Bangla* and *Jokhon Jekhane*. These drawings illustrated Mukhopadhyay's journalistic writing, and upheld labour in integral ways to foreground national and capitalist extraction, a striking illustration from *Amar Bangla* for instance, showing tribal women pushing a cart for extracting coal from the mines.

In series of linocuts that he did without any patronage, Chittaprosad made labour his core theme – for refracting a unilinear narrative of the promises of Nehruvian modernity, by drawing from the underbelly of the national-modern project itself. Labour morphs into rural displacement, quotidian struggles of migrant daily wage-earners in the city, working-class solidarities forged in labour and leisure, as well as urban destitution. Here suburbia's industrial landscapes capture a grinding social disintegration that feeds urban poverty.

[39] Somnath Hore, 'Chittaprosad' (written in 20 August 1991), reproduced in Ghosh, ed., *Kshudarto Bangla*, 37–8.

[40] Chittaprosad's letter to Gita Mukhopadhyay, 9 February 1952. Reproduced in Ghosh, ed., *Kshudarto Bangla*, 28.

Figure 1.1 Chittaprosad, cover page in *Parichoy* 1358/1951. Image source: http://sanhati.com/porichoy/.

In the early 1950s, Chittaprosad did illustrations for Bimal Roy's film on rural displacement *Do Bigha Zameen* (1953), where rural marginalization and displacement are shown to generate urban pauperization – another recurring trope in Chittaprosad's works from the 1940s. The prints reveal, for instance, the journey of a rural peasant who loses his land and bearings, and is displaced to the city, where he struggles to secure livelihood, for himself and family. During these years Chittaprosad also made a series on urban labour and semi-urban construction sites (Figure 1.2) that foregrounded the corporeality of labouring bodies rather than the meta-structure of the factory itself, which had been a critical marker of Nehruvian socialist celebrations of industrialization.[41] Linocuts were particularly suited for this nocturnal, dark landscape to emerge, or for bringing out the expressionistic rupture of displacement itself, for instance in his new works on draught and flood victims that he did in 1953 from his travels in rural Maharashtra. These works too seem to disturb, almost consciously, a very

[41] Works from this series were published in the international literary journal, *The Literary Review*, Summer 1961.

Figure 1.2 Chittaprosad, Untitled linocut, early 1950s. The image was also published in *The Literary Review*, Summer 1961. © DAG, New Delhi.

similar idiom of the rural used in the current Nehruvian socialist imagery, where celebration of rural plenitude was a way of marking the hegemonic imagination of postcolonial promise.[42] Labour captures the artist's identifications of, and with, precarious living – street children on the edge of lunacy, child labourers in bidi (tobacco) factories in grim drudgery as mice nibble at their morsels, child newspaper vendors in frozen monotony of daily toil, a child boot-polisher sleeping by the wayside. Crows, mice, roosters and rushing vehicles inhabit these

[42] For a discussion of this genre of imagery, see Srirupa Roy, *Beyond Belief: India and the Politics of Postcolonial Nationalism* (Durham, NC: Duke University Press, 2007) and Sandria B. Freitag, 'Consumption and Identity: Imagining "Everyday Life" Through Popular Visual Culture', *Tasveer Ghar: A Digital Archive of South Asian Popular Visual Culture*, 2010, accessed 20 April 2016.

linocuts, thrusting into the living spaces of destitutes. These works displace also the allegorical traces of the nation in art.

In 1952, Chittaprosad put together these linocuts on tissue paper in an album that, as he writes to Gita Bandopadhyay, were sent to Vienna for the International Conference for the Defence of Children.[43] The works remained marginal to the postcolonial artistic imagination in India, and entered visibility of sorts only in the 1970s, when the album was published in 1969 as *Angels without Fairy Tales* under the Danish UNICEF Committee. His efforts to popularize linocuts as a cheap production system to reach people continued, despite his frustration with patronage. He sought the potential of linocuts to reach the people, seeking to develop this genre of graphic art with 'legends of the country on a national scale, even on a global scale', which he writes, 'is impossible with paintings that are part of an exhibition-patron circuit or the journal dependent black-and-whites'. 'But linocuts too require assistance', he writes, 'from mass organisations, progressive printing presses, implying mainly that there is no art-consciousness in a party – all my efforts will be a futile waste of energy like the *Children* series.'[44]

Chittaprosad's absorption in drawing the underbelly of Nehruvian India is reflective of a wider critique he had of postcolonial freedom. His linocuts of displacement and child labour echo this foundational melancholia. This is reflected, most starkly, in a couplet from a poem he can be seen writing to Sunil Janah – noted for his photography for the CPI, of the Bengal famine of 1943 and popular movements and by the 1950s, a photographer too of Nehruvian development projects. Nestled amidst this long poem is a sliver of what the artist felt about postcolonial India:

> [. . .]
> *Bhejal itihash-er deshe*
> *Bhejal kainda bhejal hneshe*
> *Bhejal deshprem-e bheshe*
> *Dilli giya hoilam na nabab*
> *Bharat shadhin hoilo tobu moilo na shabhab*
>
> [author translation]
> In a nation of tainted histories
> With tainted tears and tainted smiles

[43] Chittaprosad's letter to Gita Mukhopadhyay, 9 February 1952. Reproduced in Ghosh, ed., *Kshudarto Bangla*, 27.

[44] Letter to Murari Gupta, 26 June 1953, in Mallik, ed., *Yours Chitta*, 15.

And adrift in tainted patriotism
I could not become an emperor in Delhi,
India is free but not of its afflictions.[45]

The idea of tainted (also translated as fake, contaminated, or polluted) histories reveals a deep historical melancholia that marks artistes like Chittaprosad; in postcolonial film-making, this is reflected most starkly in Ritwik Ghatak's films on partition too. In Chittaprosad, this melancholia around freedom is rooted in his own encounters with hunger, displacement, apathy and political failures; it blends also with his deep-seated doubts about a market-driven art world, and an insistence too, on withdrawal.

Chittaprosad's marginal living in India was matched by his visibility across a defined transnational circuit of socialist art. This visibility, however, was rooted in his own non-movement. He never left India; his plans for visiting Europe were thwarted, at times by himself.[46] Yet his works on transnational commissions reveal a unique trajectory of socialist internationalism in the 1950s to 1960s – one that formed, often through ideological affiliations and friendships rather than active exchange and travel – the hallmarks of artistic internationalism that marked the Cold War years.

Home and the world: Internationalism and stasis

Chittaprosad's letters reveal a tension between his desire to remain in Bombay and that of leaving – to Calcutta, or across India or to Europe. Time and again, his letters show this undulation of the home and the world. This also marks, one can argue, the curious internationalism he – and like him many other artistes who developed a locational internationalism without the global circuits of travel/exchange – sustained during the critical post–Second World War decades.

Since 1949 Chittaprosad had participated in the world peace movement, and in 1951–2 he made a series of linocuts on the living conditions of children in India. Chittaprosad's involvement with the world peace movement since 1949 is key in understanding a new series on peace that he begins in 1952. This is, in many ways, a return to the utopic trope, which dominated his works of popular resistance and collective culture from the post-1945 period. The idiom of socialist realism is strongest here, matched also by his dedication to the Soviet Union. There are

45 Chittaprosad's poem-letter to Sunil Janah, 23 September 1959, reproduced in Ghosh, ed., *Kshudarto Bangla*, 86.
46 Sen, 'Chittaprosad, Kichhu Smirticharan', reproduced in Ghosh, ed., *Kshudarto Bangla*, 33–4.

anti-imperialist fronts and anti-war solidarities here that demand peace, wield the flag 'Hands off Asia', kicking away Uncle Sam – the signifier of post-war American capital and financial aid – while the British pound sterling gnaws at his feet. Post-war US capital spreads over tilled lands as vermin and worms, and a chuckling Uncle Sam crowned with daggers, dangles the atom bomb, while his pet vultures guard over pyres burning truth, freedom or progress, and fresh supplies of crime, terror, spies, filth and lies abound. Some of these, made for the World Peace Council, suggest the artist's continuing affiliation to a socialist internationalism and the global left against a waning party enthusiasm at home. India's prime minister, Jawaharlal Nehru, is a staple in many of these cartoons that mock the moral assumptions of Nehruvian non-alignment, showing him repeatedly as a dithering statesman in the crafts of the Cold War. In an undated cartoon, probably from 1950, Nehru rises over the globe with a garland held in open arms to welcome a battered Uncle Sam, who hides a dagger behind a beaming sack of dollars, while being kicked out by a Vietnamese peasant. Unlike the more widely circulated cartoons of Shankar, whose protagonist, the 'Common Man', shadowed Nehru's trails and policies with satirical bafflement,[47] Chittaprosad's Nehru is the eager victim of US imperialism, a pawn in post-war neo-colonialism. Nehru's recurrence in Chittaprosad's cartoons and letters are cues to the anxieties of socialist art in postcolonial India.

Anti-imperialism gains defined socialist-realist aura in Chittaprosad's posters for the World Peace Council. Indeed against the backdrop of a waning party enthusiasm for cultural activism, these posters gave Chittaprosad a purpose to sustain a socialist cause, and are indeed pointers towards his political subjectivity that remained deeply ideological, bordering on the dogmatic at various points. His support for Stalinist USSR, for instance, even in the early 1950s is noteworthy, as he writes to his friend and comrade Somnath Hore with great pride, of his prints being published in *Ogonyok*, one of Soviet Union's oldest illustrated weekly magazines.[48] Under the shadow of the Cold War, these posters for the World Peace Council made between 1949 and 1955 were invoking the visual rhetoric of anti-fascist cultural resistance of the Popular Front period.[49] When the exhibition of socialist realist art from the USSR came to Bombay in 1952, Viktor Klimashin,

[47] Ritu Gairola Khanduri, *Caricturing Culture*: Cartoons and History in the Modern World (Cambridge: Cambridge University Press, 2015).

[48] Chittaprosad, Letter to Somnath Hore, 31 October 1952, reprinted in Ghosh, ed., *Kshudarto Bangla*, 181–2.

[49] The WPC, though apparently non-aligned, was itself was Soviet dominated. See Günter Wernicke, 'The Unity of Peace and Socialism? The World Peace Council on a Cold War Tightrope Between the Peace Struggle and Intrasystemic Communist Conflicts', *Peace and Change* 26 (2001), 332–51.

Soviet watercolourist and the chief artist for *Ogonyok* visited Chittaprosad (photographs of this visit appear in the collection of the DAG) and collected Chittaprosad's pastels and gouache works of peasant women singing during the Bezwada conference of the Kisan Sabha of 1944.[50] Klimashin's own poster-exhibit – 'Stalin gently looking down from a poster (poster in poster), smiling friendly to the poor Indian families' was made specifically for this show to resonate the Soviet promise: 'We stand for peace and champion the cause of peace. Stalin.'[51]

In the mid-1950s, Chittaprosad was also corresponding with a wider network of transnational socialist movement, for instance, the *Daily Worker*, as his mention of Barbara Niven (an artist who worked for many years for the *Daily Worker*, becoming the head of its 'Fighting Fund') shows. In 1955, Sidney Finkelstein noted the monumentality of Chittaprosad's linocuts, writing in the New York *Daily Worker*.[52] His works were also published in *Aufbau* (Vol. 8, No. 2, p. 637, 642, 1952), a review on which appeared in the French Marxist journal *La Pensée*, where Chittaprosad is wrongly attributed to being a socialist artist from Iran. His name appears alongside Polish-born French artist Louis Mittelberg.[53] *Aufbau* was a New York periodical of the Jewish diaspora. It is likely that Harold Leventhal would have been instrumental in printing his works. Leventhal – who appears across Chittaprosad's letters – was one of the members of the Allied army who had frequented the studio of Jamini Roy and the left-wing circuits in wartime Calcutta and Bombay.[54] Reaching India in 1944 he is known to have headed straight to the CPI office in Bombay, and procured a copy of '*People's Front*' (should be *People's War*).[55] He would later go on to form the American Friends of India (AFI). Leventhal was also the promoter for left-wing music, steering the careers of artistes like Pete Seeger, Arlo Guthrie, Phil Ochs and so on. His love for Indian art aside, his correspondence with Chittaprosad can resonate a wider world of socialist aesthetic that sustained through friendships and solidarities. These new friendships and Chittaprosad's works for the WPA in the early 1950s fostered his visibilities in the socialist world. In one of the linocuts he made during this period, the artist shows himself with works of Nâzım Hikmet

[50] Letter to Somnath Hore, 31 October 1952, reprinted in Ghosh, ed., *Kshudarto Bangla*, 181–2.

[51] See Tanja Zimmerman, 'Yugoslav Partisan Poetry: Songs for the Leader', in *Partisans in Yugloslavia, Literature, Film and Visual Culture*, eds. Miranda Jakisa and Nikica Gilic (Verlag: Bielefeld, 2015), 50.

[52] Sidney Finkelstein, 'Chittaprosad', *Daily Worker*, 16 November 1965.

[53] *La Pensée: revue du rationalisme moderne, arts, sciences, philosophie*, 50–5 (September-October 1953), 141.

[54] Michael Kleff, 'Speaker of the (Carnegie) Hall: An Interview with Harold Leventhal', https://www.woodyguthrie.org/harold.htm#kleff; accessed 4 May 2020.

[55] https://www.independent.co.uk/news/obituaries/harold-leventhal-317765.html; accessed 4 May 2020.

and Pablo Neruda, a staging of his own ideological and affective affiliations with the transnational left-wing cultural movement during the Cold War.

By the late 1950s, Chittaprosad was also developing close ties with the then Czechoslovakia, a connection he would continue to nurture through friends like Frantisek Salaba, the Indologist Dr. Miloslav Krasa, or the film-maker Pavel Hobl.[56] The first international exhibition of his works was organized in the communist bloc at Prague in 1954, mainly at the initiative of Krasa. Pavel Hobl would later make a documentary on his life, *Konfesse*/Confession, which received a special award at the World Peace Council in the 1970s. Chittaprosad's friend in Denmark, Erik Stinus, continued to exhibit/publish/sell his works in the Scandinavian world. His archive is full of letters/postcards/photographs/ poems (that Chittaprosad himself translated) from Stinus; a July 1968 letter to his mother, for instance, notes: 'Erik had published some of my pictures along with snippets [of his poems]'.[57]

In the 1960s, we see Chittaprosad writing in his letters that he was receiving money from Europe: '[. . .] I too will receive some money from Europe in a couple of months' time – the works have been sold – the payment is being delayed because it is a foreign transaction'.[58] In the letter to his mother in September 1965, he writes that the National Art gallery of Czechoslovakia has acquired his paintings worth over 1,500 rupees, he signed a contract too, but got no further response from them.[59] By the early 1970s, he writes to his sister Gouri Bhattacharya, that more and more foreigners were buying his works in the early 1970s: 'Staying in Kolkata I would lose all contact with these foreigners', he writes, '[. . .] These foreign friends of mine visit Bombay – hardly ever Kolkata [. . .] If your *dadamoshai* has to survive by painting, he must continue to live in Bombay [. . .]'.[60] He also notes that a new exhibition of his works was to be organized in Bombay 'with the administration and support of his Czechoslovak friends'. His new 'Indian friend' Subrata (Subrata Banerjee, the early associate

[56] Arany Banerjee, 'Chittaprosad and Czechoslovakia', an essay from Orbit Press Agency, reproduced in Malik, *Chittaprosad 2*, 159–61. For extended discussion of Chittaprosad's transnational networks, particularly in Czecoslovakia, see Simone Wille, 'A Transnational Socialist Solidarity: Chittaprosad's Prague Connection', *Stedelijk Studies 9, Modernism in Migration. Relocating Artists, Objects, and Ideas, 1910-1970*, Gregor Langfeld and Tessel M. Bauduin (eds.), Fall 2019; See also, Sanjukta Sunderason and Jaroslav Strnad in conversation with Simone Wille, in Simone Wille, 'Chittaprosad's Linocut Prints at the National Gallery in Prague: Understanding Indo-Czech Cultural Relations in the Postwar Era', *Bulletin of the National Gallery in Prague*, 2020.

[57] Letter to Mother, 29 July 1968, in Mallik, ed., *Yours Chitta*, 104. Also letter of 27 December 1968, in Mallik, ed., *Yours Chitta*, 110.

[58] Letter to Mother, 10 March 1965, in Mallik, ed., *Yours Chitta*, 75.

[59] Letter to Mother, 14 September 1965, in Mallik, ed., *Yours Chitta*, 83.

[60] Letter to Sister, 1 July 1968, in Mallik, ed., *Yours Chitta*, 139.

editor of the *Illustrated Weekly of India*), he writes, was 'uppermost in convincing the Indo-Czech friendship committee'.[61]

Chittaprosad laments time and again that he cannot get a passport – neither from Bombay – not from other cities: 'In fact travelling abroad is not in my destiny – no matter how much it ought to be.'[62] Yet apparently, when all arrangements had been made for him to visit Czechoslovakia, writes Prabhash Sen in his memoirs on the artist, he refused. Chitta, he writes, got to know the Czech ambassador to India, artists and critics from the country visited him, collected his drawings and linocuts, exhibited them in Czechoslovakia. But his trip itself did not happen; he declined to go at the last minute stating that he is disillusioned with the form global communist movement had taken by the 1960s, particularly in countries that have a communist government. Sen notes that Chittaprosad stated that he has left the Communist Party not out of disillusionment with Marxism, but in rejection of the particular form Communist Parties and in particular ruling communist governments have taken. To him Czechoslovakia was no exception; he felt there he would face the repression other artists were facing from the government. This would make him sacrifice his independence or his honesty. As a guest he would not be able to critique the government that invited him, hence it was best to not go. Sen further states that this decision did not alter despite repeated invitations.[63]

Chittaprosad's association with home itself is curious – torn between his love for the land and his deep suspicion of postcolonial modernity in India, his transnational horizons and a foundational desire to walk across the rural hinterlands of India. His absorption in his own rented Ruby Cottage room permeates his letters: 'Should you come now you will simply be surprised', he writes to Murari Gupta, '[. . .] The puppet stage glows exactly beneath the R. I. N. painting; my "children" staring out wide-eyed at all, whichever direction you may choose to cast your eyes on.'[64] In another letter, and indeed in many, his loneliness reverberates:

> Now it's exactly one o'clock at night. Took a bath but still no sign of sleep, a wind is blowing, I can hear murmur in the coconut-palm leaves, the curtain on the window is tense like a sail, I am feeling good, and feeling extremely lonely [. . .].[65]

[61] Ibid., 139.

[62] Chittaprosad's letter to Gita Mukhopadhyay (nee Gita Bandopadhyay), 15 October 1951. Reproduced in *Kshudarto Bangla*, 25.

[63] Sen, 'Chitaprosad, Kichhu Smirticharan', in Ghosh, ed., *Kshudarto Bangla*, 33–4.

[64] Letter to Murari Gupta, 31 July 1957, in Mallik, ed., *Yours Chitta*, 21.

[65] Letter to Murari Gupta, 30 May 1959, in Mallik, ed., *Yours Chitta*, 41.

He seems to be both tied to this haunt, yet yearning to leave: 'No, not Kolkata', he writes to Gupta, 'The forests, mountains, unknown cities and villages, uninhabited terrain, tell me, how do I explain it.' Yet obstacles hinder him, he writes: 'each day they twine around in tighter spirals.'[66] In 20 November 1960, he writes about a plan for touring Bengal on foot, to illustrate the history of Bengal in pictures:

> I had begun work based on it from Dinesh Sen's *History of Bengal,* that sound be something like 25 years ago – an infantile attempt. Now source materials are galore in Bengali – the prominent among which is Ashok Mitra's *Census Report of Bengal.* But I do not at all wish to visualize an academic history-in-pictures. I will tour Bengal on foot as far as possible – for two years. The tour programme will be prepared from textual references in advance. Then I will bring back photographs of historic Bengal from my tour in cities-villages-open terrain – a glimpse of the past as seen through my contemporary vision – and then I will write and paint my book based on how my modern mind feels and responds. I have given this a thought – such a book is essential not only in Bengal – every region of India needs a history of new India from a new vision. And that is only possible from regional artists and writers. It isn't essential to make use of pictures as the saddle-horse of history. At least I don't intend to do that – pictures won't merely be a supplement to the text. Had my famine sketches not been supported by reportage, even then the pictures would have spoken for themselves. What is essential is that the life-rhythm of the pictures maintains a connection with the *flux of history,* and that is precisely why I must tour Bengal on foot.[67]

Chittaprosad never left Bombay, until before his death when he had to be brought to Calcutta for failing health. His accumulated world of books, art, ongoing work – despite his active withdrawal – seem to carry a restless weight, one that he himself could not share. Writing to his mother, this becomes stark:

> And this single room contains the accumulated wealth of the past twenty years, the yield of my toil, the wealth of my pain. So many books, so many paintings, puppets, gifts from abroad, expensive brush and paint. Further, utensils and clothes as well. And – at night there's the menace of the tree-rodents here, they had broken into my suitcase and nibbled to bits my expensive warm clothes and suit.[68]

[66] Ibid., 39.
[67] Letter to Murari Gupta, 20 November 1960, in Mallik, ed., *Yours Chitta*, 31.
[68] Letter to Mother, 10 March 1965, in Mallik, ed., *Yours Chitta*, 75.

His nostalgia for Cox's Bazar remains; writing to his mother in December 1967:

> Cox's Bazar was true heaven – such splendid hills and forests – so many flowering plants – the huge areas full of the *champa* and the *nagkeshar.* The countless varieties of divine orchids and ferns. And there's no comparison between the Bay of Bengal and the Arabian Sea. I have not seen shells and cowries here till date [. . .].[69]

Home also provides to him a new domain for re/creating new story-worlds, where his own lineages in socialist art, his melancholic withdrawal away from postcolonial art worlds, as well as his socialist internationalism come together. Since the late 1950s, Chittaprosad rediscovered himself as a narrator and illustrator of folk tales, retold and illustrated by himself, and as a maker of puppet theatre.

Socialist story-worlds

Writing to Murari Gupta on 31 July 1957, Chittaprosad mentions his Czech friend Salaba gifting him money for a puppet project, 100 Rupees each month for a period of six months. Salaba also gifted him a puppet stage. Chittaprosad named his puppetry theatre group 'Khelaghar' – translatable as an 'abode of play'. He mentions composing shorter theatrical pieces to be staged for puppet shows. 'I have become addicted to puppets since then', he writes,

> I have already composed two plays in the meanwhile number one – *Shakuntala.* Entirely rearranged, complete in three acts, a matter of about one-and-a-quarter hours. The last act is completely mine, a little bit of Kalidasa in the initial two. Number two, a fifteen-minute sarcastic drama.[70]

Khelaghar became his obsession, threading into his daily life and his melancholic affiliations:

> [. . .] the entire noon I spend with the hammer and the saw, build the limbs of the puppets and fume at not receiving your letter. In the evening I sit down with needle thread and scissors to prepare the puppets' dresses and get furious over Tara [. . .].[71]

[69] Letter to Mother, 22 December 1967, in Mallik, ed., *Yours Chitta*, 95.
[70] Letter to Murari Gupta, 31 July 1957, in Mallik, ed., *Yours Chitta*, 19.
[71] Ibid., 21.

Somnath Hore recalls that Chittaprosad nurtured these puppets like his own children, despite tremendous financial strain.[72] He assembled his own crew for the puppetry project, and ruminated on the new possibilities of creating puppets in more vernacular idioms:

> One of the members is an engineer. He is preparing the torso of the puppets, trunks with legs, in the factory following the Czech technique, I will supply the heads. I have already produced some five such whole figures. . . . Since I am still under the spell of foreign prototypes, the puppets continue to follow a naturalistic schema. But other fresh plans are filling my imagination; intend to 'puppetise' the folk wood and terracotta toys.[73]

Writing to Murari Gupta in 1958, Chittaprosad mentions writing a play for puppet theatre about 'a drongo bird':

> This will require nearly 17 puppets, ten are ready as on today. The painting of details in the faces is also finished – only the dress remains. All the characters have turned out to be very amusing, really, extremely amusing. And the puppets are of a completely new kind too, they would even stun the Czechs. And equally simple.[74]

Khelaghar created a new story-world around him:

> Increasingly, I am observing that a new kind of life is growing up for me centred around the puppet performance. New acquaintances, young boys are gathering around me. Even the ruling authority seems interested . . . . The meek, docile puppet is commanding me to toil enormously, day in and day out.

Yet he remains anxious about this becoming too public:

> It is certainly exciting, nevertheless I do not wish to get too entangled and dissipated in an outside world. The joy in work can never be achieved unless I move away from the hustle and bustle of the world of exchange. Yet my own blood goads me on to work, and work invariably implies establishing a relationship with the market. This is an indescribable situation.[75]

He talks about his fascination for Radost, a famous puppet group from Prague; Radost was also to view Khelaghar's performance.[76]

72 Somnath Hore, 'Chittaprosad' (written in 20 August 1991), reproduced in Ghosh, ed., *Kshudarto Bangla*, 37–8.
73 Letter to Murari Gupta, 31 July 1957, in Mallik, ed., *Yours Chitta*, 21.
74 Letter to Murari Gupta, 25 April 1958, in Mallik, ed., *Yours Chitta*, 24.
75 Ibid., 24.
76 Letter to Murari Gupta, 22 September 1958, in Mallik, ed., *Yours Chitta*, 27.

Yet Khelaghar too runs into crisis. The artist writes about the lack of 'manpower' and 'effort': 'This is not a one-man's job – one needs a team, both boys and girls.'[77] As 'fresh visitors keep passing by attracted by Khelaghar', Chittaprosad writes of the difficulty with 'necessary monetary support for the expenses'.[78] In November 1958 he mentions shutting down Khelaghar.[79] In 1959, he writes to Murari Gupta, 'The truth is that without a real patron it is still impossible today to construct something really artistic with the support of these film-people. One cannot produce art with the support of speculators.'[80]

In the late 1960s, Chittaprosad can be seen illustrating children's stories, many of which were published in periodicals in Eastern Europe, for instance in Czechoslovakia, the image reproduced here being published in the Czech journal *Novy Orient* in May 1957 (Figure 1.3). Last ten to fifteen years of his life he composed poems alongside children's book illustrations, including writing scripts for puppet plays. As his own health deteriorated, he continued to work on children's illustrated books on the epics, *Ramayana* and *Mahabharata*, with calligraphic writing on one page and illustrations on the other; but this work remained incomplete; Prabhash Sen recalls seeing some of these works.[81] During these years Chittaprosad was also writing poems. Writing to his friend and fellow artist Sanjoy (he is referring to the noted commercial artist Sanjoy Sengupta here), he writes in 1966: 'You had asked for new poems – that inspired me to pen these twenty poems in the past three days [. . .].'[82] He invites his friends (refers to commercial artists Sanjoy Sengupta and Dilip Dasgupta here) to illustrate and publish the poems – similar to Sengupta's publication of Chittaprosad's comrade from the 1940s – the Marxist poet Sukanta Bhattacharya's poem collection *Ek je chhilo Raja.* Sanjoy Sen Gupta was part of the Shilpayan Artists' Society – one where one of the first retrospectives of Chittaprosad was organized after his death. By 1967, however, he is alienated from the group, as he writes in a letter to his sister, asking her to pick up the collection of his works from Sanjay Sen Gupta's house.[83] In these letters he is also writing about his illustrations for children's *Ramayana.*

In a July 1968 letter to his sister he mentions Subrata Banerji's piece on him in the *Illustrated Weekly of India.*[84] His images were published in March and April

77 Letter to Murari Gupta, 31 July 1957, in Mallik, ed., *Yours Chitta*, 9.
78 Letter to Murari Gupta, 30 November 1958, in Mallik, ed., *Yours Chitta*, 27–8.
79 Ibid., 29.
80 Letter to Murari Gupta, 30 May, 1959, in Mallik, ed., *Yours Chitta*, 41.
81 Sen, 'Chittaprosad, Kichhu Smirticharan', in Ghosh, ed., *Kshudarto Bangla,* 34.
82 Letter to Sanjoy, 11 October 1966, in Mallik, ed., *Yours Chitta*, 7.
83 Letter to Sister, 4 April 1967, in Mallik, ed., *Yours Chitta*, 138.
84 Letter to Sister, 1 July 1968, in Mallik, ed., *Yours Chitta*, 139.

Figure 1.3 Chittaprosad, Draft Illustration for *The Frogs and the Elephant*. The image was also published in the *Novy Orient*, 14 May 1957. © DAG, New Delhi.

editions of *Illustrated Weekly of India*. Banerji's brief article on Chittaprosad strikes a sharp balance between Chittaprosad's own radical lineages and his conscious absorption in (and translation into) folk idioms and puppetry – a point completely missed by Mulk Raj Anand, the Marxist writer and key figure in Nehruvian national-modern culture, who while introducing Chittaprosad in the mid-1950s to an American audience had described him rather tepidly, as a carrier of 'folk traditions' in the line of a 'village artisan';[85] Chittaprosad himself mentions in his letters time and again, the ill-treatment he received from Anand, including never being paid for his works that Anand had published.[86] The artist's absorption in fairy tales, as noted in Banerji's piece – one of the rare writings

[85] Mulk Raj Anand, 'Introducing Chittaprosad', 1955, unpaginated (accessed from the private papers of Chittaprosad, DAG). The note most likely accompanied a portfolio of the artist published in an American magazine.

[86] Letter to Mother, 26 July, 1963, in Mallik ed., *Yours Chitta*, 65–6.

on Chittaprosad – was an 'escape'. *The Kingdom of Rosogolla and Other Tales* – Chittaprosad's illustrated children's book – was 'hardly representative' of the artist's talents and lineages, wrote Banerji; he was, he noted, the artist of famine, earthy people rooted in the soil, 'the artist of the struggle'. The 'sensitive soul' of this artist 'reacted violently', he wrote, to the reality of post-independence India, one that was a far cry from his own dreams; his retirement from active political life brought him to his art as a 'refuge'. His withdrawal, Banerji writes, makes it appear 'as if he had ceased to exist', and 'he is appreciated more abroad than at home'. The artist, Banerji writes, carried 'a deep sadness in his eyes', with a 'raging passion' – a 'lonely man', and yet 'full of love'. Banerji concluded with a fragment of a poem the artist had sent him:

> *In loneliness, there is no happiness*
> *Brother.*
> *No happiness in a crowd.*
> *The happiness in friendship brother,*
> *Even in a temple is not to be found.*[87]

Staying along the grain of Banerji's own encounters with and readings of the artist, one could still ask: Is the child's world of story-telling an escape? The question of childhood in itself is an important cornerstone – not only in Chittaprosad's postcolonial career but also for the wider story-worlds of transnational socialism. Childhood appeared as a critical point of deflection in Chittaprosad's 1950s' child labour linocuts, one that refracted a Nehruvian narrative of a young nation of promise. In the late 1950s, childhood enters a domain of narration, animation and a reinvented popular itself, as Chittaprosad dedicated himself to puppetry. This was a striking moment in his career, one that was otherwise deep in withdrawal. Khelaghar also exposes him to a new world of public-ness, one that is rooted in making art, yet removed from the art circuits:

> Till date, my fate relating to my pictures has exclusively been mine alone. I mean to say that a couple of individuals, or probably ten at the most, have made me their own from near or far, but it's never the crowd; I have been able to continue in my own world of peace. Puppets are a world apart, gathering a crowd around them is their profession. Having started it, I am surely not going to give up, but it is equally certain that I am not going to allow myself to be traded away. A limit must be maintained, and that is the concern that keeps me engaged presently.[88]

[87] Subrata Banerji, 'Jottings', *Illustrated Weekly of India*, 30 June 1968, 12.
[88] Letter to Murari Gupta, 25 April 1958, in Mallik, ed., *Yours Chitta*, 24.

In his illustrations for children's books, his projects on illustrating *Ramayana* or fairy tales, the artist can be seen to enter into his own uniquely personal vocabulary of the social, one that is rooted in translating art into story-telling, imagination into pedagogy. This is its own kind of abstraction – in this case, from his own lineages in socialist expressionist art that visualized hunger, struggle and displacement. It echoes, in a very different way, his friend and former comrade Somnath Hore's 1970s' abstract white-on-white prints called the *Wounds* series, where Hore himself withdrew from realistic or expressionist portrayals of hunger and politics by creating textured pulp prints with deep gashes and burns signifying corporeal/material rupture. Chittaprosad's (further) withdrawal into fairy tales – while echoing a wider socialist culture of children's book illustrations – can also be read as a peculiar trajectory for former CPI artist-cadres like him whose postcolonial careers were marked by disjunctures from the party, and constant negotiations around how to carry on the radical socialist impulses within the wider postcolonial condition.

The *Ramayana* pictures, Chittaprosad notes in his (only) interview, given to the Czech film-maker Pavel Hobl for his documentary *Konfesse* (Confessions), was his last venture: 'The events of old myths fascinate me today. This is my last job. Transcript of the ancient Indian epic *Ramayana*.'[89] *Konfesse* was made in 1972, which reveals the rich world of story-telling and illustration Chittaprosad had created around him. As 'confessions', the artist's words in the short fifteen-minute documentary, also brought together an almost pivotal moment combining testimony and testimonial.

Confessions: Testimony and testimonial

Konfesse begins with a scattered set of catalogues that show Chittaprosad's transnational footprints and book illustrations: we see reproductions from the Czech periodical *Novy Orient*/and its English edition *New Orient*; in Danish from the 'Dansk Unicef Komite' (Danish UNICEF Committee); Den Ny verden (The New World: For International Illumination of Nordic Peasant Culture); 'Chittaprosad, Born uden aeven'; Chitta's own illustrated story-book *Kingdom of Rosogolla*; the Czech magazine Indické Bajky a Pohadky; also paper cuttings from Danish periodical '*Fredens Ärstid*'.

[89] Transcript of *Konfesse*. I am thankful to the art historian Simone Wille for providing me with the transcript.

The film begins with the camera zooming into a Bengal rural landscape and terracotta temples; village fairs; rural homes with decorated walls, thresholds; it cuts into, seamlessly, the artist's own room in Bombay – a sign are the masks (from his puppets) hanging on the walls, in what seems to be afternoon light; the artist's own story moves alongside montages of the famine, displacement and decimation of population. We hear the artist's own voice in Bengali, very briefly, as we see him sprawled on the floor, showing his drawings to Hobl (possibly); before the Czech voiceover overtakes it very soon: 'I felt the eagerness to put art and art education to the use of mankind and society first and most clearly during the war.' The music moves from classical notes to folk rhythms, to songs of the Indian People's Theatre Association – the left's front organization in the 1940s, of which Chittaprosad was a visualizer, making in fact the IPTA icon of a drummer beaconing the people to action. At moments it seems that the artist himself is singing (which is likely given he composed songs and designed attire for IPTA performances), as the documentary weaves from decimated landscapes, to displaced populations and, suddenly, a battleground. The shift seems seamless when we are alerted to the scenes actually shifting to the Liberation War and genocide in East Pakistan at its hour of becoming Bangladesh in 1971. The artist is showing Hobl drawings tied to the Liberation War in Bangladesh; while these could have been drafts for the Liberation War painting that he poses with (Figure 1.4), many of these drawings have not been shown anywhere else. They show the artist's experimentation with a figuration of evil – anthropomorphic images of battleships, humanoids, army generals as grimacing animals – striking additions to a genre of works that artists in India were doing in response to the Liberation War in Bangladesh,[90] yet ones that remained invisible, and in fact lost today.

The use of the term 'confession' itself is interesting – it echoes the idea of testimonial and testimony; the artist's own recollection appearing not only as a mode of staging his own lineage of political art but also connecting a narrative of (postcolonial) Bengal from both sides of the border. Speaking to Hobl, Chittaprosad's confessions reveal the inner lives of communist art in twentieth-century India, one where deeply individual and subjective interfaces with political art become tangible:

> The more I wanted to stay away from political life in my life and pursue only art, the more my country's life returned me again and again into the arms of politics. It is so. After all, the artist is a human being, nothing more and nothing less, which has been tied to the fate of his homeland since his birth. Whether

90 Devika Singh, 'Indian Art and the Bangladesh War', *Third Text* 31, no. 2–3 (2017), 459–76.

Figure 1.4 Chittaprosad with his painting on the Bangladesh Liberation War, *c.* 1971–2. © DAG, New Delhi.

> the artist is aware of it or not, whether he likes it or not, he becomes part of the future of his fellow citizens. (music, shooting, war, singing)[91]

'And so, in the face of death', he continues, 'I always realize again what is art and its value'. The more 'the essence of humanity is threatened', the more an artist's message 'must be stronger': 'Perhaps it seems trivial to those who have survived.' The black-and-white 'essence' of graphic art, to him, creates the unique possibility of 'quick and cheap reproduction', and is 'the most effective means of communication for both learned and unspoken'. His confessions echo both the received histories of the left he was part of and the wider worlds of radical popular art he felt the nation failed to produce:

> Every artist must sooner or later consciously or unconsciously express his moral and political standpoint. Through my work, I am committed to the tradition of moralists and political fighters. To save people is to save the art itself. Artist's activity is an active denial of death.[92]

In a way Chittaprosad's letters *are* his confessions. They often veer closely towards his own incapacity, as much as he rejects the structures of the art market and official

[91] Chittaprosad in conversation with Pavel Hobl, used in *Konfesse*. I am grateful to Simone Wille for providing me with the transcribed English script of *Konfesse*.
[92] Chittaprosad in conversation with Pavel Hobl.

patronage. 'The urban formula for a successful exhibition is entirely different', he writes in 1958, pondering over having his own exhibition, 'one needs a friend like Salaba in this case, or a Harold. But let's quit that thought. [. . .]'.[93] Writing on W. G. Archer's book *India and Modern Art*, he writes in one of his letters:

> While I was reading the book, I had this feeling that, unknowingly, I traversed through all the phases from Aban-*thakur* to Sher-Gil in my personal pictorial endeavours along the rise-and-fall of the core perspectives pertaining to the practice. I am telling you, in truth. However, such direct and clear-cut intellectual formulations have never been possible from me, and will not be possible either, that I know. One cannot view oneself without a mirror. Art critics are mirrors to the artists. Accordingly, I felt I saw my work and its entire background – distinct in certain places, not so distinct in others.[94]

Ultimately, Chittaprosad's letters carry the confessions of an artist unsure of his own legacy, as much as he is unsure of his own sustenance:

> My greatest worry today is my future [. . .] And my life-sacrificed heap of paintings and books – how and to whom will I entrust them, brother Murari? The stinging words due to loan, the prospect that I may be on the streets for the final few days, are trivial, most trivial, I am ready for it today. But will I have to hand over this small world created by me to the gutters, those worse than asses and pigs – those are my disturbing sleepless thoughts, brother Murari.[95]

Gouri Bhattacharya writes that in a legal quagmire, all of the artist's belongings were languishing in lock-up, and by thc time she got access after the case was closed, only 50 per cent of his things survived decay; only some artworks and a few thousand books remained; among these was his crushed leather bag – one that he carried with him in all his tours of rural India since 1939: 'with this bag hung over his shoulders and with a mere bottle of water, Dada (elder brother) would roam the nooks and corners, rural expanses of India. The bag contained his drawing tools, sketchbooks, notebook and packets of cigarettes.'[96]

Afterword: Memory/montage/manoeuvres

As Chittaprosad's archive went on display at the 2011 DAG retrospective, and appear time and again across transnational exhibitions, its salvage, like I noted

93 Letter to Murari Gupta, 29 December 1958, in Mallik, ed., *Yours Chitta*, 38.
94 Letter to Murari Gupta, 30 May 1959, in Mallik, ed., *Yours Chitta*, 43.
95 Letter to Murari Gupta, 26 June 1959, in Mallik, ed., *Yours Chitta*, 46.
96 Gouri Bhattacharya, 'Nihsangha Paribrajak', reproduced in Ghosh, ed., *Kshudarto Bangla*, 41.

Figures 1.5a–c Montages of Chittaprosad's images at Jawaharlal Nehru University, New Delhi, and the Kolkata People's Film Festival. Image source: Author's personal photographs.

at the start, echoes beyond the art world or narrative of Indian/global modern art. In capturing at the same time, the artist's own absence, this belated archive, as I have argued, carries melancholia that is both historical and individual. It bristles with the more granular histories of (postcolonial) freedom, where narratives of national identity are undercut by those of displacement and hunger, and legacies of the left's activist movement too are not monolithic inheritances. Yet in appearing, even if belatedly and as fragments (that were also re-distributed across a private auction market) – Chittaprosad's re/discovery at a national and now transnational scale has carried distinct resources for the very popular movements that the artist himself would have been enthused by. In contemporary times, the artist's melancholic archive – and the visuals from these works made in withdrawal – are becoming resource for montage and manoeuvres of contemporary emancipatory political cultures, and as such, are activating a potentiality that continues to make present, the politics of absence and peripherality.

Chittaprosad's images appear as flashes today (Figure 1.5) – in protest marches, university graffities, people's film festivals – also across mugs, bags, posters sold at sites where there are conscious citations of radical people's histories, for instance here at the Kolkata People's Film Festival (bottom panel). His works join – as montage – fragments from revolutionary poetry or combined with iconic political art (like with the *Guernica* as from walls of Jawaharlal Nehru University, New Delhi) or with works of his fellow artists from the 1940s (with Zainul Abedin or Ramkinkar Baij) at the reception of the Kolkata People's Film Festival in 2020) – upholding critical constellation of past histories and struggles as they resonate in our times. These are conscious manoeuvres – from students, activists and grassroots organizers – to generate through citational montages – new memory practices around people's art and its twentieth-century lineages in India – even if such memories have remained marginal in art/historiographies in the country. This popularization *via* citation, one could argue, is perhaps also the closest afterword that the artist himself would have desired for his practice and the lineages he carried, or craved.

2

Kagmari Festival, 1957

Political aesthetics and subaltern internationalism in Pakistan

Layli Uddin

In February 1957, the Awami League (AL), the ruling party in East Pakistan, held their council convention at Kagmari, a small sleepy village 50 miles north of Dhaka, the political capital of the East Wing. The Kagmari Sammelon, described as a *mela* (festival), *sanskritik sammelon* (cultural gathering) and an Afro-Asian cultural convention, had profound consequences for the politics of Pakistan and Bangladesh.[1] The event precipitated the break-up of the AL, the most popular political party in the East Wing, during the only time they held power in both the Province and Centre prior to the 1971 war. This split over issues of foreign policy marked the radical entry of international affairs and internationalism into domestic politics. There are few historical instances, if any, where domestic parties that were not explicitly communist have fractured over non-domestic issues.

This chapter presents a microhistory of the 1957 Kagmari Sammelon, offering a thick description of the event from memoirs, photos, novels, correspondence between organizers and foreign dispatches. Over the course of six days, AL delegates and visitors from the wider region debated and discussed the Cold War, Afro-Asian politics, military pacts, anti-imperialism and decolonial futures in a large rapidly constructed tent-city. Conversations on national and international politics often confined to the parliament chambers, university halls, debating

[1] Although the Kagmari Sammelon finds a mention in extant scholarship on Pakistan and Bangladesh, it is a cursory reading of the event. The more substantive work is in Bengali, see Syed Abul Maksud, *Maulana Abdul Hamid Khan Bhashani* (Dhaka: Agami Prokashoni, 2014), 172–213; Syed Abul Maksud, *Kagmari Sammelon: Maulana Bhashani Purbo Banglar Swadhikar Samrajyobadbirodhi Sangram* (Dhaka: Prothoma Prokashon, 2017); Mohsin Shoshtropani (ed.), *Kagmari Sammelon Smarakgrantha* (Tangail: Kagmari Sammelon 50 Borsho-Purti Palon Jatiyo Kamiti, 2011).

clubs and mansions of Dhaka migrated to the rural *maidan* (public space) of Kagmari, foregrounding the participation of those excluded from the formal spheres of politics. It is in these unlikely settings that the demand for radical anti-imperial friendships and solidarity with the Third World triumphed over the case for more arms spending and military pacts with the United States and other associated powers. The subaltern was not the parochial subject, nor the elite the international actor as traditionally imagined.

Scholarship on left-wing aesthetics has largely emphasized elite artistic practices associated with privileges such as access to capital, social networks and mobility. The focus is commonly on a material cultural object (book, film, or painting), or the individual artist, and their understanding of universal ideas and values.[2] A reading of Kagmari extends the analysis of left-wing aesthetics in South Asia by focusing on a subaltern cultural form – the mela, until now associated with the construction of communal or national identity and considered for its specific elements rather than as a whole.[3] The Kagmari Sammelon was a curated experience that melded popular culture, artistic practices and aesthetics, with the intention of evoking specific emotions and creating new subjectivities, beyond the local or national.

In this chapter, I show how Kagmari was a collective aesthetic production that embodied a prefigurative radical politics of a syncretic socialist internationalism. We can see this in the Sammelon's lively local rural arts: stick-fighting, fisherfolk songs, dancing girls, wrestling and colourful gates. Kagmari as a whole was a unique syncretic combination of a wide range of (largely) South Asian cultural forms: the *mela*, the *urs*, collective village labour, the Mughal camp and Congress meetings. The Sammelon had an international dimension too, drawing from the nineteenth- and twentieth-century World Fairs and Afro-Asian events, reflecting international cultures in arches named after figures

[2] Here, I am referring to scholarship on the Marxist Cultural Movement where subaltern contribution is often discussed in terms of influencing or inspiring elite authors or artists, but their role is never fully sketched out. See, Priyamvada Gopal, *Literary Radicalism in India: Gender, Nation and the Transition to Independence* (London: Routledge, 2005); Talat Ahmed, *Literature and Politics in the Age of Nationalism: The Progressive Episode in South Asia, 1932-56* (New Delhi: Routledge, 2008); Yashodara Dalmia, *The Making of Modern Indian Art: The Progressives* (New Delhi, Oxford University Press, 2001); Nandi Bhatia, *Acts of Authority/Acts of Resistance: Theatre and Politics in Colonial and Postcolonial India* (Ann Arbor: University of Michigan Press, 2004).

[3] Scholars have often focused on specific elements rather than entire form of the mela itself, see: Atreyee Gupta, *The Promise of the Modern: State, Culture and Avant-Gardism in India (c. 1930–60)* (PhD diss., University of Minnesota, 2011); Sonal Khullar, *Worldly Affiliations: Artistic Production, National Identity, and Modernism in India, 1930-1990* (Los Angeles: University of California Press, 2015); Sanjukta Sunderason, *Partisan Aesthetics: Modern Art and India's Long Decolonisation* (Stanford: Stanford University Press, 2020).

such as Shakespeare, Lincoln and Mao.[4] In a sense, Kagmari was an immersive political theatre, a 'total work of art' (*Gesamtkunstwerk*); it disrupted the borders between politics and performance, artist and audience, sacred and profane, and the past and the future. This was unsurprising since the main organizer was Maulana Abdul Hamid Khan Bhashani ('the Red Maulana'), a 'rabble-rousing' rebel politician and Sufi saint. Bhashani, since his early training in a rural *jatradol* (folk theatre troupe), and education at Deoband, was no stranger to the provocative blurring of boundaries.[5]

Kagmari showed the possibilities for re-ordering spatial and temporal configurations of power, and building left futures. Kagmari was a form of progressive prefigurative politics. Carl Boggs, the author of the term, defined it as the 'embodiment, within the on-going political practice, of those forms of social relations, decision-making, culture and human experience that are the ultimate goal'.[6] Bhashani deployed several prefigurative strategies by which people could behold, hear and experience different aspects of the desired future, and hence, disrupt the current dispensation. The collective production of Kagmari, for one, embodied the promise of a non-hierarchical and egalitarian world where everyone held value. The desired future was to be achieved, not through heroic individual enterprise but by collective effort. For Kagmari participants, the future was represented as an ongoing, experimental and creative site, drawing on the rich histories of the present, rather than the year zero of some modernist project.[7] This was reflected in the reworking of traditional cultural practices and forms, something that Craig Jeffrey describes as 'productive improvisations', a vital characteristic of prefigurative politics.[8] Kagmari's aesthetics, in line with the event's wider politics, were enacted through vernacular, subaltern forms, consciously socialist and internationalist, but locally rooted in rural and Indo-Islamic traditions. Finally, Kagmari's production of a specific 'affective atmosphere', mainly joy, was central to the prefigurative politics. Subaltern

4 The re-working or experimentation with existing aesthetic practices and forms appears to be a defining characteristic of the left in South Asia, see Iftikhar Dadi, Lotte Hoek and Sanjukta Sunderasan's chapters in this volume.

5 See, Layli Uddin, *In The Land of Eternal Eid: Maulana Bhashani and the Political Mobilisation of Peasants and Lower-Class Urban Workers in East Pakistan, c. 1930s-1971* (PhD diss., Royal Holloway, University of London, 2016).

6 Carl Boggs, 'Marxism, Prefigurative Communism, and the Problem of Workers' Control', Libcom.org, 13 Sept 2010, available online: https://libcom.org/library/marxism-prefigurative-communism-problem-workers-control-carl-boggs (accessed 10 September 2020).

7 Boris Groys, *The Total Art of Stalinism: Avant Garde, Aesthetic Dictatorship, and Beyond*, trans. Charles Rougle (Princeton: Princeton University Press, 1992), 19.

8 Craig Jeffrey and Jane Dyson, 'Geographies of the Future: Prefigurative Politics', *Progress in Human Geography* 20, no.10 (2020), 1–18.

constituencies saw how ideas of solidarity, equality and freedom emanated from the cultural forms that enriched their daily lives. Moreover, the physical feeling of collective joy and togetherness generated by the laughter, chattering and the hustle-bustle at Kagmari offered a physical embodied sense of diverse popular gatherings and the power that a demotic left future could bring to the people.

I begin with situating Kagmari in the wider politics of Pakistan during this period. Moving on, I look at the ways in which the Kagmari Sammelon created the capital in a village, examining the progressive ideas, practices and futures invoked in this upside-down world. Although Kagmari borrowed from traditional forms and practices, I argue that it produced a new aesthetic that brought together rural, religious, internationalist and socialist ideas and practices in one space. Thereafter, I examine specific cultural aesthetics and the ways that they were used for left pedagogy and organizing. To conclude, I show how a microhistory of Kagmari generates conceptual insights by critically engaging with the ideas of Lefebvre on the creative politics of collective social space and Rancière's ideas of politics as aesthetics. This chapter speaks to present conditions by emphasizing the importance of occupied space in progressive left politics. Central to this Kagmari narrative is the figure of Maulana Bhashani, introduced earlier, the primary organizer, who appears throughout the story as multiple figures: saint, politician, teacher, Mughal king and worker. I use Bhashani's various roles as a way of thinking about subaltern interventions in left aesthetics in postcolonial Pakistan.[9]

Desher Dak: We are the 95 per cent

The AL, established in East Bengal in 1949 by Maulana Bhashani on a progressive manifesto of land reform, nationalization and provincial autonomy, emerged as one the first organized opposition to the Muslim League government in the Centre and Province. In 1954, Bhashani and Suhrawardy, the two senior leaders of the AL, were instrumental to the sweeping victory of the Jukto Front coalition in the provincial elections in the East Wing. However, within months of that victory, in May 1954, the Central Government in Karachi stating that 'enemy agents' were at work ousted the Jukto Front, arrested and exiled many of its

9 I am using Gramscian concept of *the organic intellectual* to think through Maulana Bhashani's role here as someone whose political organizing and intellectual activities were directed by subaltern constituencies. For more, see Antonio Gramsci, *Prison Notebooks: Volume II*, ed. and trans. Joseph A. Buttigieg (New York: Columbia University Press, 1996).

leaders, and established Governor's Rule in East Pakistan.[10] This was followed up with a ban on the Communist Party in both wings. However, almost two years later, there was a turnaround of events. In September 1956, the AL found itself in the unlikely position of holding power in the Centre and Province, the only time that this would happen in the history of a united Pakistan. On 5 September, rocked by industrial protests, hunger marches and Bhashani threatening civil disobedience, the Centre invited the AL to form a provincial ministry. This was swiftly followed up with changes at the Centre itself, with Suhrawardy taking up the post of prime minister of Pakistan on 12 September, heading a mixed AL-Republican coalition in government. However, it was this actual prospect of power that provoked a crisis within AL over the possible futures of Pakistan, with the differences between Bhashani's and Suhrawardy's visions coming to a head at the Kagmari Sammelon.

On 9 December 1956, a helicopter carrying Suhrawardy landed on the Salimullah Hall lawns at the University of Dhaka. He had come to address a student gathering on his foreign policy position. He offered an impassioned defence of Pakistan's extant military pacts, the claim on Kashmir and enmity with India, while denouncing Soviet intrigue and the weakness of the Arab world. Suhrawardy, invoking familiar tropes of fear, suspicion and vulnerability, stressed the necessity of strong military alliances. He firmly stated: 'these hands of mine are not there to make Pakistan weak.'[11] The implication here was that to suggest anything contrary would be construed as anti-national. In many ways, there was nothing unusual about Suhrawardy's position; it echoed that of his predecessors. But Suhrawardy was also the leader of the AL, and this was a complete U-turn from the party's stated position since 1953: the demand for complete withdrawal from the bilateral and multilateral security agreements, such as the Baghdad Pact, South East Asian Treaty Organisation (SEATO) and the Mutual Defence Assistance Agreement with the United States, and a free and independent policy.[12]

The founder-president of the party, Maulana Bhashani, was all too aware of how far the party had shifted from its original position. His commitment to anti-imperialism and Third World solidarity, however, was strengthened through his encounters with international left organizations and figures abroad. During

[10] Layli Uddin, '"Enemy Agents' at Work": A Microhistory of the 1954 Adamjee and Karnaphuli Riots in East Pakistan', *Modern Asian Studies* 55, no. 2 (2021), 629–64.

[11] Shah Ahmed Reza, *Bhashani-r Kagmari Sammelon O Swayatsashoner Shongram* (Dhaka: Gonoprokashoni, 1993), 44.

[12] Oli Ahad. *Jatiyo Rajniti 1945 Theke 1975*, fifth edn (Dhaka: S. M Raisuddin, 2012).

his time in exile in Europe from 1954 to 1955, he attended the British Labour Party conference in Scarborough and World Peace Council in Stockholm.[13] In 1955, he participated in the Conference of Asian Countries on the Relaxation of International Tension in Delhi.[14] The Anglo-French intervention in Suez in 1956 further solidified his position.[15] For Bhashani, the question of foreign policy was not outside of everyday politics but intimately tied to the question of sovereignty, power and the fate of Pakistan. The people could not really be the 'masters' of Pakistan as he described them, while tied into these asymmetrical relationships of power, and being drawn into wars that were not of their making.

Conscious of an imminent showdown between him and Suhrawardy, Bhashani called for the Awami League Council Convention to be held in February 1957.[16] He also saw it as an opportunity to challenge the political complacency that he sensed among AL Party workers since coming to power. He characterized their attitude as '*montrira desh shashon koruk, amra barite bisram ney*' (Let the Ministers rule, and we'll relax at home).[17] It soon became clear that Bhashani was not intending just another run-of-the-mill political gathering. The Kagmari Sammelon would be held in a village instead of Dhaka, go on for six days and be much more than a convention. The formalized and routine matters of delegates' reports, adoption and ratification of resolutions and the election of members to various committees would feature at Kagmari, but without dominating the proceedings. Bhashani had a more ambitious plan in mind. This was going to be an event that undermined Suhrawardy's onward march in defence of the military pacts and bolstered Bhashani's demands for love and friendship between the newly decolonized Afro-Asia bloc.

In early February, Kagmari organizers put out advertisements titled '*Desher Dak*' (Call of the Nation) in various newspapers (see Figure 2.1).[18] Harun Chowdhury, an attendee at Kagmari, remarked that the publicity around the Sammelon had all the makings of a 'political jamboree of all progressive elements – the first of its kind in Pakistan. The word Kagmari was on everyone's lips in Pakistan.'[19] In other iterations of the adverts, the 'nation' was presented

13 Khondoker Mohammed Elias, *Bhashani Jakhan Europe-e*, 6th edn (Dhaka: Muktadhara, 1978).
14 Carolien Stolte, '"The People's Bandung": Local Anti-Imperialists on an Afro-Asian Stage', *Journal of World History* 30, no. 1–2(2019), 125–56.
15 Layli Uddin, *In the Land of Eternal Eid*, 181.
16 Saeed-ur Rahman (ed.), *Maulana Bhashani: Bhashan o Bibroti* (Dhaka: Jagroti Prokashani, 2000), 55.
17 Ibid.
18 Awami League O Birat Sanskritik Sammelon', *Daily Sangbad*, 1 February 1957.
19 S. H Harun Chowdhury, *The Working of Parliamentary Government in Pakistan, 1947–1958: With Particular Reference to the Central Government and Major Political Trends* (PhD diss., Durham University, 1970), available online: http://etheses.dur.ac.uk/8039/, (accessed 3 May 2013), 428.

Awami League and huge cultural festival place: Kagmari-Santosh (Tangail).

6th February – Provincial AL Workers Conference

7th and 8th Feb – Provincial Awami League Council Convention

9th, 10th and 11th – Cultural Festival

Desher Dak (Call of the nation)

1) This call is for the fulfilment of provincial autonomy for the survival of 45 million Bengalis

2) This call is for the realisation of the historic 21-points

3) This call is for unity and togetherness of all peasants, labourers, blacksmith-potters, businessmen, intellectuals and artists

4) This call is for the freedom of Asian and African countries from the clutches of imperialism

5) This call is for the establishment of 60,000 AL units in the villages of East Bengal.

Participate in this conference in groups.

Servant: Abdul Hamid Khan Bhashani

Chair – East Pakistan Awami League

P.S., From the 7th February, there will be a huge exhibition on agriculture, labour, health and education, please send a product from your various districts to help out.

Figure 2.1 Desher Dak. 'Awami League O Birat Sanskritik Sammelon', *Daily Sangbad*, 1 February, 1957. Table has been produced from the text in the newspaper article.

with information on the timings and locations of public transport organized for them, requested to bring their own blankets, mosquito nets, as well as 'rice, vegetables, pots, pans, cows-goats, whatever any one wishes to donate'.[20]

What 'nation' was being invoked and invited to participate in Kagmari? The participants were intended to be different to Suhrawardy's constituency of students and intellectuals from metropolitan Dhaka. On 13 January 1957, Bhashani's petition stated, 'the country does not belong to ministers, members and government workers', the typical attendees of political conventions. He

[20] Mohsin Shostropani, 'Kagmari Sammelon: Pariprekhita O Tatparja', in Shoshtropani ed., *Kagmari*, 35.

appealed instead to the '95% of those who were poor cultivators, labourers, blacksmith, potters, etc., and with all those whose money the country runs' to attend Kagmari.[21] These kinds of population distributions have usually been thought about in terms of communal majorities or minorities, but at Kagmari, they took on a class complexion. With his religious title removed from these petitions and advertisements, Bhashani as the '*nogonno khadem*' (insignificant servant) opened up the event to all '*dol, mot, jati o dhorom*' (party, opinion, caste or community and religion).[22] The demand for Afro-Asian emancipation, international invitations and the connection between the '*Desher Dak*' to the Bengali working-class diaspora in the UK also suggest that the understanding of 'nation' was not circumscribed to those residing within the territorial bounds of the state.[23] The AL Party political convention, usually a closed-door session, was now thrown open to all of the people that Suhrawardy and the other senior AL workers did not find necessary to include in their discussions on Pakistan's future.[24]

The upside-down village: Infrastructure, aesthetics and labour

Kagmari was a changed landscape over the period of the Sammelon. Those who organized or attended the event describe how the '*ajparagaon*' (backward village) transformed into an *ostayi rajdhani* (temporary capital).[25] This was not just a remark on the thousands of people that descended onto the small village, including the prime minister, the chief minister of East Pakistan, politicians, international guests and foreign diplomats, but a reference also to the infrastructural and aesthetic makeover that the village received. Kagmari was the material manifestation of Bhashani's occupation of two modes of power,

21 Ibid, 35.

22 Ibid.

23 Sarah Glynn in her work on the Bengali diaspora in the UK mentions a monthly newspaper *Desher Dak* ran by Tasadduk Ahmed, Bengali community activist, from 1954 to 1962. When Bhashani was in London in 1954, he stayed with Tasadduk Ahmed. It is possible that Kagmari's *Desher Dak* was either inspired by Tasadduk's paper or an appeal to the diaspora. However, the *Desher Dak* was also a commonly used phrase by anti-colonial revolutionaries. See Sarah Glynn, *Class, Ethnicity and Religion in the Bengali East End: A Political History* (Manchester: Manchester University Press, 2014), 32–56.

24 Senior Awami League officials in their conversations with Stockwell Everts, the US Vice Consul, told him them that they were not 'willing to spend time in the villages of East Pakistan to find out for himself what the peoples' views were on different issues'. See, US Consul, *Dhaka to the Department of State, Washington, 28/2/1957* (Central Decimal File 1955–9, Record Group 59, Box No. 3862, US National Archives) (hereafter *Everts Report*).

25 Maksud, *Maulana*, 173.

the modern and vernacular, which helped to visibilize and magnify his power as well as his constituencies, vis-à-vis Suhrawardy.

The expression 'all roads lead to Kagmari' was in common use over this period.[26] This was not just a simple turn of phrase or a metaphor for the attention or publicity that surrounded the Kagmari Sammelon, but an actual representation of the massive network of unmetalled roads that were constructed to enable attendees from different parts of East Pakistan to travel to Kagmari.[27] Mr Stockwell Everts, the American Vice Consul, who travelled to the conference using the congested and dusty Dhaka-Tangail road, jostling alongside the passenger cars, jeeps and buses that were transporting people to the conference on a road not yet concretized, surmised that this much traffic or police had not been seen on the roads since the Second World War.[28] The construction of these unmetalled roads stood in stark contrast to the monumental failure of the recent road-building project between Dhaka and Tangail. In 1952, an Italian road-building firm had secured a contract to put down thousands of miles of roads in East Bengal connecting Dhaka to outlying districts and towns. However, since 1954, bitter, long and fruitless wrangles between the provincial government and Italian contractors had meant that machines were turned off and laid to rust, 25 miles of built roads washed away by floods and a debt of five crore rupees (50 million) owed to the Central Government.[29] As much as the unmetalled roads narrated a story of government failure and neglect, it strengthened the perception of Bhashani as someone who could make things happen. Although not much is known about the extent of road construction, the people that built it (perhaps Bhashani's *murids* [disciples]), or of Bhashani's own role in this enterprise, he had come across as someone who could bring Dhaka closer to other parts of Pakistan, as well as connect the different most remote parts of the province to each other. Ironically, Bhashani was popularly known for his use of boats, the traditional mode of communication and movement across the riverine delta.

However, the roads that led into Kagmari were not the only physical transformation. The sights, sounds and smells normally associated with the small towns or villages in East Bengal were not to be found. Instead, what the residents and attendees encountered was a well-lit village connected to the electricity grid, constant supply of clean water, latrines which produced no strong

26 Chowdhury, *The Working of Parliamentary Government*, 428.
27 Ibid.
28 *Everts Report*.
29 'Road Building in E. Wing Stalled', *Dawn*, 1 February 1957.

and strange odours, huge furnace ovens used to cook food fit for foreign guests, and medical arrangements on standby.[30] The estate of the former Maharajah of Santosh, unused and abandoned since partition, recovered some of its earlier power and splendour in its new role as the actual site of the Sammelon. One of the three mansions was used for the accommodation of foreign guests. The Nat Mandir, 'a graceful building, open to the outside world, consisting merely of a roof supported by pillars', formerly part of a temple complex used to stage dramas, dance and musical performances, as well as accommodate large gatherings during festivals, was put to use once more as a stage for another set of performances, the Awami League Council Debates.[31]

Roads and electricity, of course, have a basic function, the circulation and exchange of capital, goods, people and ideas. The city and its productive hinterlands as spaces ordered and regulated by capital are where the main arteries of road and electricity networks are embedded. However, infrastructure does not simply have a technical function; they are objects of collective fantasies and desires. Roads and electricity are simultaneously symbols of, and experienced as, progress, modernity and freedom.[32] The city, by extension, becomes invested with similar ideas and emotions. On the other hand, villages are endowed with fixed and essentialized qualities, as deeply hierarchical, unequal and mythical spaces.

The rural village, which during the colonial era had captivated the anti-colonial nationalist imagination, lost much of its political valence in the postcolonial period.[33] The dominance of the urban over the rural was apparent in East Pakistan by the mid-1950s. In September 1956, as villagers poured out of boats and ferries onto the riverbanks of Dhaka to take part in a hunger march, the police fired shots at them.[34] The city was where people came to articulate basic socio-economic and political claims and be seen by the modern state. The changing infrastructure and aesthetics in Kagmari presented a vision of the power and possibilities contained within rural spaces and constituencies, a role otherwise denied to them. The village did not have to continue to be marked by stubborn decline and immizeration. It could be revived and reimagined, not as

30 Maksud, *Maulana*, 184.

31 *Everts Report.*

32 Brian Larkin, 'The Politics and Poetics of Infrastructure', *Annual Review of Anthropology* 42 (2013), 427–43; Naveeda Khan, 'Flaws in the Flow: Roads and their Modernity in Pakistan', *Social Text* 24, no. 4 (2006), 87–113.

33 Uddin, 'Enemy Agents at Work'.

34 'Dhakai Michiler Upar Polisher 27 Round Gulibarshan', *Daily Azad*, 5 September 1956; 'Khadyar Janya Dabi Janaite Giya Dhakar Rajpathe ghate 8 Jan Nihat O 7 Jan Ahat', *Daily Sangbad*, 5 September 1956; 'At Least 3 Killed and 4 Injured in Police Firing', *Morning News*, 5 September 1956.

some romanticized version of a village of a by-gone era, but as a place that could boldly face the future if equipped with infrastructure. What would Pakistan be like if modern facilities only encountered in towns and big cities - electricity, cars, telephones, telegrams, water filtration, sewage system, hospital, libraries and roads - could also exist in those spaces?

These transformations can be interpreted as more than just attempts at reproducing the power of the city. They can be understood as the practical or generous efforts of the hosts in ensuring the Sammelon accommodated the guests. But, perhaps, conversely, those changes were also there to mock those in power, so distant from majority realities that they could only be lured to the village through the availability of creature comforts and the veneer of modernity. Kagmari was additionally a rebuke to those in the AL, such as Suhrawardy, who thought that politics could only happen in modern spaces. Bhashani could have put together an event where urban elites confronted rural realities, but that would have most likely confirmed commonplace assumptions. By showing that peasants and other rural inhabitants were as modern, progressive and capable of political thought as their urban and elite counterparts, Kagmari displaced elite knowledge and power. The Sammelon was a manifestation of Rancière's 'principle of axiomatic equality – the equality of anyone with anyone'.[35] Moreover, creating the capital in a village simultaneously disrupted how the village *and* the city were sensed, perceived and understood. By encouraging people to come together, eat, sleep, discuss politics and have fun for six days, the Kagmari Sammelon showed how the city too could be lived differently outside capital's ordering of time and space.

The power of the rural space and inhabitants was not just presented through future-oriented visions but also through the instantiation of precolonial ideas and practices of kingship. The arrangements for Prime Minister Suhrawardy, Chief Minister Ataur Rahman Khan, other high-ranking officials and delegates received no less attention from Maulana Bhashani and the organizers. An elaborate 'tent city' was set up, which in the meticulousness of its arrangements was strikingly reminiscent of the 'immense white pavilion', that is the movable imperial camps of Akbar during royal tours and military expeditions.[36] Sinopoli in her work shows how these camps, which were the locus of Mughal political activity when the emperor was on the move, became temporary capitals.[37]

[35] Mustafa Dikeç, *Space, Politics and Aesthetics* (Edinburgh: Edinburgh University Press, 2015), 33.

[36] John F. Richards, *The Mughal Empire* (Cambridge: Cambridge University Press, 1995), 41–2.

[37] Carla M. Sinopoli, 'Monumentality and Mobility in Mughal Capitals', *Asian Perspectives* 33, no. 2(1994), 293–308.

The camp arrangements at Kagmari also reflected an attempt to mimic the organization of power and hive of activity that once was expected in the capital. The rows of tents set up for Prime Minister Suhrawardy, Chief Minister Ataur Rahman Khan and the central and provincial ministers demonstrated sensitivity to those relationships of power with each tent getting bigger and extravagant in line with the status of its occupants. Suhrawardy's tent, thus, was the most adorned.[38] Each tent was fixed with temporary phone lines, telegrams and secretaries to ensure that business continued as normal. Armed military guards, intelligence and police officers brought in to provide round-the-clock protection formed the outer ring of the tents. On the outside of the ring was the cantonment of hundreds of temporary straw-thatched huts to accommodate almost 900 councillors, arranged according to geographical division.[39] According to Zirwat Chowdhury, in imperial times the camps 'asserted the sovereign status of its chief occupants'.[40] However, at Kagmari, the emphasis was not on the power and authority of the man with the biggest tent but on the man behind it all – Maulana Bhashani. Suhrawardy sat stuck in his tent, trapped by his political position, answering calls and giving instructions, while Bhashani ran around organizing and working alongside the people. In many ways, the contrasting roles illustrated the distance that had developed between the AL and its constituencies since coming into power.

On his entry to Kagmari, Mr Everts was taken to the double-storied mansion where Maulana Bhashani, dressed like the typical Muslim villager in his '*longi, pirhan, tupi*' (sarong, shirt and cap) and barefooted, was waiting to escort him to his room. Evert's room was extravagantly decorated, chandeliers hung from the ceilings, and eighteenth- and nineteenth-century Romantic paintings of the Maharaja of Santosh and his several wives, as well as members of British Royalty adorned the walls. Everts's hope for a conversation with the Maulana never materialized. He noted in his report that after Bhashani had lain out the Persian rugs in the room, and seen to guests who had come looking for him, he had 'slipped out, in hot pursuit, no doubt of some bearer or handy man'.[41] However, he had not done so without entrusting Everts to the care of two of his most reliable men. The picture that Everts and others draw of Bhashani flitting in and out of rooms, his obsessive attention to detail, overseeing of tasks and

38 Shostropani, 'Kagmari Sammelon', 38.
39 Ibid.
40 Zirwat Chowdhury, 'An Imperial Mughal Tent and Mobile Sovereignty in Eighteenth Century Jodhpur', *Art History* 38, no. 4 (September 2015), 668–81.
41 *Everts Report.*

hospitality towards guests was not new or out of character. Being a gracious host were the signs of cultivated good and proper manners, or in other words '*adab*'. Ira Lapidus defines this as the 'correct knowledge and behaviour in the total process by which a person is educated, guided and formed into a good Muslim'.[42] In the Mughal period, training in *adab* was essential for kings, princes, courtiers, judges, scholars and Sufi saints.[43] Although Bhashani employed and revived symbols and practices of Mughal kingship and zamindari authority, it was not the figure of the benevolent zamindar that was being idealized or assumed. Bhashani had chosen to cast his authority in the role of a worker. Bhashani's physical presence rather than reflecting the charisma associated with his position as organizer and pir drew power through his actions, through his labour.[44] These imperial practices of the tent-city and *adab* were after all drawing upon a greater authority. While the king himself does not build the tent-city, his authority comes from his command over labour, and *adab* is also about a kingly labour, the work that the ruler puts in to rule.

Bhashani's own performance of labour was to show that he was part of a much larger collective that made and occupied the space of Kagmari during this period. They had built the roads, set up the lighting, pitched the tents, slaughtered the animals, cleared the site, dug ditches, baked clay pots and plates, and set up the *pandals* (canopies). The labour of the people, many who came from the poorest constituencies, was the political energy that transformed this *ajparagaon* village into a political capital. Joinuddin's account of the preparations of the conference reveals how Bhashani projected this power of labour. Days before the conference, Joinuddin, a volunteer helper, travelled with two other members of the Preparatory Committee, Khondoker Elias and Kazi Mohammed Idris, to ask Bhashani whether the cheque of two hundred thousand rupees that had been given by the Central Government should be accepted. Bhashani instructed them to reject the offer with the rather inscrutable answer that Allah was the provider; he then proceeded to offer them a tour of the festival area. Bhashani took them through dense thickets, along the way he indicated to a small building that had been constructed to operate as the Kazi Nazrul library, and once he reached the

42 Ira Lapidus, 'Knowledge, Virtue, and Action: The Classical Muslim Conception of Adab and the Nature of Religious Fulfillment in Islam', in *Moral Conduct and Authority: The Place of Adab in South Asian Islam*, ed. Barbara Daly Metcalfe (Los Angeles: University of California Press, 1984), 39.

43 Meltcafe, *Moral Conduct*.

44 There is ample scholarship on the charismatic body in theories of kingship, notable works include Ernst H. Kantorowicz, *The King's Two Bodies: A Study in Medieval Political Theology* (Princeton: Princeton University Press, 1957); A. Azfar Moin, *The Millennial Sovereign: Sacred Kingship and Sainthood in Islam* (New York: Columbia University Press, 2012); David Graeber and Marshall Sahlins, *On Kings* (Chicago: Hau Books, 2017).

actual festival area, he showed them the impressive 10 meter-long ditch dug next to the large reservoir of water, and which was to function as the stoves over the festival period.[45] The questions of finance and patronage, which engulfed the festival in controversy later on, were secondary, if not irrelevant to Bhashani's purpose.[46] The emphasis on labour augmented Bhashani's authority in several ways; he had spoken to the constituencies in a language that they understood, but, more importantly, he unveiled the radical and transformative potentialities of these collective endeavours. Labour emerged as the connective tissue between people, space and politics. After all, the prime minister of Pakistan had come to discuss the future of the nation-state with the peasants and workers.

The hybrid mela

Mr Everts, a keen observer for various reasons, described a rambunctious and lively atmosphere at Kagmari. He wrote of the crowds 'milling around the scores of shops and stalls' and the many hundreds of 'workers' who had come to 'cheer and watch the fun' besides the actual councillors.[47] Atiqur Rahman Eusufzai recalled his excited eight-year-old self, travelling with his father to Kagmari by rickshaw and foot to attend the 'huge village fair'. He was left awestruck at the sight of various shops, food stalls, colourful gates and the prominent leaders sitting on the dais.[48] Joinal Fakir, a murid (disciple) who attended the Sammelon, described it as a *birat shobdo* (loud noise) and *hoyhulla* (celebratory noise), with stalls, music and 'people coming from all directions carrying sticks and spears'.[49] The few visual traces that exist of the event corroborate the carnivalesque nature of gathering, capturing carousels, Ferris wheels and crowds in motion.[50] Kagmari Sammelon turned out to be a huge *mela* (festival). Kagmari, a fairly typical setting for melas, set in the rural interior, and home to the shrine of Pir Shah Jaman as well as the famous living saint Maulana Bhashani, was certain to draw in peasants, workers and devotees from the surrounding villages and

45 Maksud, *Maulana*, 182–3.

46 Uddin, *In The Land of Eternal Eid*, 209–17.

47 *Everts Report.*

48 Atiqur Eusufzai, 'Memoirs: As We Saw A Great Leader', in *Moulana Bhashani: Leader of the Toiling Masses*, ed. Anisuzzaman Chowdhury (New York: Maulana Bhashani Foundation, 2012), 269–322.

49 'Bhashanir khuje-dwityo porbo/Joinal Fakir', *Maulana Bhashani Archive,* 30 April 2021, available online: https://www.facebook.com/111882550723553/videos/788333825454026 (accessed 30 April 2021).

50 Pictures of Kagmari can be found on Facebook pages dedicated to Maulana Bhashani.

elsewhere, who would not have otherwise attended or been invited to a political convention in Dhaka.[51]

Historically, festivals have been imbricated in the everyday rhythms and cycles of daily life. Their occurrences tied to agricultural and religious calendars coincide with the planting and harvesting of crops, holy days and pilgrimages. But they were also exceptional events, set outside the bounds of everyday life, involving the suspension or transgression of social norms, practices and relationships.[52] Festivals offered alternative and new images and experiences of the self, community and world at large. Bakhtin argued that festivals symbolized the 'transfer from the old to the new, from death to life.'[53] In the historiography of melas in South Asia, similar form of openness can be found. Raminder Kaur in her study of Ganapati festival described this as the 'character of multivalency'; these festivals were sites of negation, contestation and negotiation, and hence extremely political.[54] Although the festivals in South Asia usually have religious and cultural underpinnings, they have often been used for the pursuit of a myriad of political agendas. Chris Bayly, William Gould and Kama Maclean have shown how the Kumbh and Magh mela in Allahabad emerged as arenas of conflict between the colonial rulers and their subjects. The pilgrim communication networks enabled the spread of nationalist messages, and mela aesthetics were used for the instantiation of a Hindu nation.[55] In the postcolonial context, the mela continues to have political significance. Thomas Blom Hansen shows how the Shiv Sena have instrumentalized the highly charged atmosphere, drama and emotions produced at the Ganapati and Shivaji Jayanti festival to legitimate their claim to represent and practice a form of plebeian politics.[56]

[51] In the Bengal District Gazetteer, the Sufi saint of Kagmari is referred to as Pir Shah Jamal and Pir Shahjaman, all that we know of him is that he lived during the reign of Emperor Shah Jahan (1592–1666), see F. A. Sachse, *Bengal District Gazetteers: Mymensingh* (Calcutta: Bengal Secretariat Book Depot, 1971).

[52] Interesting accounts of these transgressions can be seen in Robert Darnton, *The Great Cat Massacre: And Other Episodes in French Cultural History* (New York: Basic Books, 1984); Mikhail Bakhtin, *Rabelais and His World*, trans. Hélène Iswolsky (Bloomington: Indiana University Press, 1984).

[53] Bakhtin, *Rabelais*, 166.

[54] Raminder Kaur, *Performative Politics and the Cultures of Hinduism: Public Uses of Western Religion in Western India* (Delhi: Permanent Black, 2003), 27.

[55] C. A. Bayly, *Rulers, Townsmen and Bazaars: North Indian Society in the Age of British Expansion, 1770-1870* (Cambridge: Cambridge University Press, 1983); William Gould, *Hindu Nationalism and the Language of Politics in Late Colonial India* (Cambridge: Cambridge University Press, 2004); Kama Maclean, *Pilgrimage and Power: The Kumbh Mela in Allahabad, 1765-1954* (New York: Oxford University Press, 2008).

[56] Thomas Blom Hansen, 'Politics as Permanent Performance: The Production of Political Authority in the Locality', in *The Politics of Cultural Mobilization in India*, ed. John Zavos, Andrew Wyatt and Vernon Marston Hewitt (New Delhi: Oxford University Press, 2004), 19–36.

Muslim festivals such as Muharram and *urs* (death anniversary of a Sufi saint) have had similar political connotations and effects. Nile Green's work on 'barrack Islam' states how 'urs celebrations by Muslim sepoys in colonial Hyderabad', which included 'feasts, a fairground and the singing of the *tawaif* (dancers, prostitutes)' were treated with great suspicion by their British commanding officers.[57] The unruliness and indiscipline of the lower ranks at the time of Muharram and *urs* created the fear that the sepoys might once again become mutinous subjects. In 1920s and 1930s Bengal, Pir Abu Bakr of Furfura, whose spatial and spiritual reach spanned across fifty-two districts of Bengal and Assam, saw the *urs* celebrations as an opportunity to create a more politically conscious Muslim community around signs of moral and economic piety and conservatism.[58] The Kagmari Sammelon had all the characteristics of an *urs*: the feasting, crowds and the devotees who had come to witness the *karamat* (remarkable deeds) of their saint.

Kagmari Sammelon built on the traditions of religious festivals of South Asia to firmly locate the 'people' in the politics of the nation state through their physical and symbolic participation and representation at the event. However, unlike these festivals, whose polyvalent nature has meant that the political message presented itself in more nebulous and ambiguous forms, Kagmari was ostensibly political. The religious or cultural elements of the festival were arranged according to the political agenda. Political melas are not new, and Kagmari shared resemblances with various political events of the colonial period, particularly to the 1938 Haripura Congress Session. Here, Vital-Nagar, a small village, was also transformed into a 'space of/for politics', and the masses drawn in using the spectacle of the mela to witness a political showdown between leaders.[59] However, where Haripura was about the construction of a nationalist space bankrolled by the major business houses of the day, Kagmari was about the instantiation of an anti-imperial and anti-capital internationalism.[60]

But Kagmari drew on other kinds of festivals too. The late nineteenth and twentieth centuries saw a flourishing of World's Fairs, or international expositions in Europe and North America, showcasing scientific, industrial and cultural 'achievements' of different cultures, advocating putatively universal

[57] Nile Green, *Islam and the Army in Colonial India: Sepoy Religion in the Service of Empire* (Cambridge: Cambridge University Press, 2009), 118.

[58] Pradip Kumar Datta, *Carving Blocs: Communal Ideology in Early Twentieth Century* (Oxford: Oxford University Press, 1999), 88–94.

[59] Gupta, *The Promise of the Modern*, 63.

[60] Indian National Congress, *Report of the 51st Indian National Congress: Haripura (Dt. Surat. Gujarat) 1938* (Ahmedabad: Navajivan Press, 1938).

ideas of progress, science and modernity. In fact, the World's Fairs were a material manifestation of imperial desires and 'cultures of abundance'.[61] In the postcolonial era, the Afro-Asian conference and Soviet-organized events like the World Peace Council and World Festival of Youth offered counter-projects of decolonized, anti-imperial futures.[62] Kagmari was a hybrid of these forms, offering an alternative model of abundance, of progressive, flexible socialist futures based on South Asian vernacular culture, aware of international models, but confident in advancing its own path.

Subaltern politics of joy: Gates, arts and lectures

The Kagmari Sammelon, however, was not just a spectacle designed to put Suhrawardy in his place or to stupefy the senses of the workers and peasants who attended these festivities in large numbers. Bhashani argued that the AL could not 'hoodwink' the people for long, and that their *bicarkhamata* (ability to judge) and *buddhibibecana* (intelligence and thought) were not to be underestimated.[63] Kagmari was turned into a pedagogical space, which could appeal to those specific qualities of intelligence and judgement of the subaltern constituencies. Bhashani saw Kagmari as a crucial platform for cadre building. The target of 60,000 AL units set out in the adverts was to happen through recruitment and consciousness-raising of existing and potential cadres at Kagmari. Bhashani, thus, constructed a powerful and compelling case for autonomy, anti-imperialism and internationalism in ways that he could secure the hearts and minds of those at the festival. So what pedagogical strategies and resources did Bhashani employ to secure support on issues that appeared so far removed from the everyday realities of his constituencies?

Central to the task was to give people a sense of what futures built on subaltern internationalism would look like by prefiguring some of the political connections, emotions and experiences at Kagmari.[64] Subaltern

[61] Robert W. Rydell, *World of Fairs: The Century-of-Progress Expositions* (Chicago: University of Chicago Press, 1993), 35–7.

[62] Patryk Babiracki and Austin Jersild (eds), *Socialist Internationalism in the Cold War* (Cham, Switzerland: Palgrave Macmillan, 2016); Quỳnh N. Phạm and Robbie Shilliam (eds), *Meanings of Bandung: Postcolonial Orders and Decolonial Visions* (London; Rowman & Littlefield, 2016); Su Lin Lewis and Carolien Stolte, '*Other Bandungs: Afro-Asian Internationalisms in the Early Cold War*', *Journal of World History* 30, no. 1–2 (2019), 1–20.

[63] Rahman (ed.), *Maulana Bhashani*, 61.

[64] See Lotte Hoek's discussion on the relationship between aesthetic training and left pedagogy in the volume.

internationalism is understood here as the productive alliance between the globally disenfranchised.[65] The idea was that if people were to see that it was possible to inhabit the world differently, then they would want to change it. However, the world was to be experienced in an abstract way but through local, concrete and visible forms – through things that can be touched, seen, smelt and heard. These sensations were central for producing thought and energy.

Bhashani, no stranger to organizing political events with cultural components, organized Kagmari for a specific reason. The intent was not just to draw crowds but produce an atmosphere of fun and happiness. Festival laughter was seen as a generative and powerful energy for confronting the present and building new futures.[66] The significance of subaltern humour is shown by Shankar Ramaswami in his excellent work on *mazaak* (fun) among metal factory workers in Delhi; he writes: 'Mazaak affirms life . . . asserts the urge and passion to create, connect, and unify, and the desire to live, contra the drives of mere self-preservation.'[67] In contrast to traditional confrontations with power, where peasants and workers are either seen to be pleading or protesting, Bhashani used the positive laughter emanating from the festival to project new images of community. However, this politics of joy was not meant as a performance for Suhrawardy and the elite, but to orientate subaltern communities towards left futures.[68] At Kagmari, joy, laughter and happiness were integral to the experience and intellection of solidarity and internationalism.

Bhashani drew on three festival techniques and practices to persuade and educate his constituency: the use of gates, folk culture and lectures. The gates, translated from '*turon*' in Bengali, were one of the most striking sights of Kagmari Sammelon. They were memorable enough to merit a mention in Sunil Gangodpadhyay's epic partition novel '*Purbo Paschim*' (East West), where one of the main characters attending the events at Kagmari remarks on the 'beautifully made gateways'.[69] Everts, who also noticed them, was less appreciative about

65 I am building here on David Featherstone's excellent study on solidarity, see David Featherstone, *Solidarity: Hidden Histories and Geographies of Internationalism* (London: Zed Books, 2012).

66 Bhashani's interest in subaltern laughter as an important political energy can be seen throughout his career, in a way it hasn't been for other leaders of South Asia. Bhashani in 'Mao Tse-Tung-er Deshe', the only book he is said to have written, devotes the first one or two pages to thinking about the importance of laughter. See Uddin, *Eternal Eid.*

67 Shankar Ramaswami, 'Masculinity, Respect and the Tragic: Themes of Proletarian Humor in Contemporary Industrial Delhi', *International Review of Social History* 51, supplement no. 14: Coolies, Capital and Colonialism: Studies in Indian Labour History (2006), 203–27.

68 Here, I am using Sara Ahmed's work on happiness as an orientation towards an object rather than away from it. See Sara Ahmed, 'The Politics of Good Feeling', *Australian Critical Race and Whiteness Studies Association e-journal* 4, no. 1 (2008), 1–18.

69 Sunil Gangopadhyay, *East West: Purbo-Paschim*, Vol. 1, trans. Enakshi Chatterjee (New Delhi: Sahitya Akademi, 2000), 362.

them as he described the 'flimsy arches' that dotted the 4–5 mile route from Tangail to Kagmari: he counted up to 50 gates, though estimations of as many as 100 were also made.[70] The gates were most likely the work of one of the key organizers, Quamrul Hassan, a '*patua*' (folk) artist and founding member of the Dacca Art School in 1948. According to Lala Rukh Selim, Nandalal Bose's artwork for the 1938 Haripura Congress Session was one of the main influences in Quamrul Hassan's work.[71] Bose had been in charge of designing the fifty-one gates and pandals in Vithal Nagar; the gates constructed out of locally produced materials such as wood and bamboo were decorated with art panels depicting quotidian activities and features of village life.[72] Although we know little about the design and construction of the Kagmari gates, they were meant to signify something quite radically different to Haripura's representation of the village in India.

The Kagmari gates had the names of political, religious and cultural figures, mainly men, emblazoned on them, ranging from Mao, Stalin, Ataturk, Shakespeare, Prophet Muhammad to more regional and local leaders, such as Gandhi, Chittaranjan Das, Haji Shariatullah, Rabindranath Tagore.[73]Although it was Jinnah, and not the Prophet, whose name was printed on the most lavish and highest number of gates, there was no serious attempt to arrange these gates or endow ornamental or hierarchical privilege on any identifiable category. The names had different levels of familiarity and associations for the audience. For example, whereas Everts regarded the inclusion of 'Indian independence heroes' as a suspicious gesture, the eight-year-old Yusufzai conflated Ali brothers, Abul Kalam Azad, Chittaranjan Das, Bose and Gandhi, as all 'revered leaders of the subcontinent'.[74] However, it is possible that the groups who derived some, if not the most, pedagogical benefits from the gates were the workers and peasants for whom many of the names were unfamiliar.

Although, it is not possible to retrieve the stories that were told or imagined by subaltern constituencies as they walked through the gates and noticed the Prophet's name before and after rows of unfamiliar names, perhaps some speculation can be allowed.[75] It is possible that the row of arches, a structural

[70] *Everts Report.*

[71] Lala Rukh Selim, 'Art of Bangladesh: the Changing Role of Tradition, Search for Identity and Globalization', *South Asia Multidisciplinary Academic Journal* 9 (2014), 1–21.

[72] For more information on Haripura, see the following: Gupta, *The Promise of the Modern*; Khullar, *Worldly Affiliations; Indian National Congress, Report.*

[73] Uddin, *In The Land of Eternal Eid*, 195–6.

[74] *Everts Report*; Eusufzai, 'Memoirs', 298.

[75] Saidiya Hartman writes about the necessity for Speculative History when it comes to writing the histories of marginalized, see Saidiya Hartman, 'An Unnamed Girl, A Speculative History', *New*

feature in Mughal imperial architecture, paradoxically played a similar as well as a radically different function in Kagmari. Historically, they have denoted the king's rule and power and the connection between different spaces.[76] The arches at Kagmari demonstrated a similar veneration for authority, but it was not vested in a single individual, idea, past or geography but rather to multiple and variegated geographies, peoples, religions and cultures. Where the military pacts offered belonging to an exclusive club of nation-states, the gates were infused with a spirit of radical equality. The peasants and labourers were shown that they were part of a wider and richer moral and cultural universe, where lessons and examples from Mao, Lenin or even Abraham Lincoln could be drawn upon, although perhaps not given the same weight. The haphazard ordering of the gates, were, perhaps, not arbitrary as initially assumed but designed to place emphasis on the connections between those life-worlds – revolutionary cultures – rather than what divided them.

The performing arts were also used for similar pedagogical effect at the Kagmari festival. Around the beginning of the festival period, in the dead hours of the night, the camp-dwellers and villagers of Kagmari were startled out of their sleep. Bhashani, Suhrawardy and the other guests, curious to see what was going on, came out of their dwelling. The sounds coming from a mile off were the deep and powerful voice of a folk singer from the *char* (sandbank) areas of Habiganj, Parimal Dasgupta, accompanied by his troupe as they approached the festival space.

> Oh Mountbatten Sahib,
> In whose hands did you place your pleasure baton?
> You left your beautiful mansion in darkness,
> Oh Mountbattern Sahib, where did you go?[77]

This was the subversive and salacious Mountbatten *mangal kabya* (epic poem), Hemanga Biswas's farcical song of blessings for the last Viceroy of India.[78] The performance was the prelude to the ambitious and varied programme of music, dance, martial arts, films and lectures that took place on the various platforms

Yorker, 9 February 2019, available online: https://www.newyorker.com/culture/culture-desk/an-unnamed-girl-a-speculative-history (accessed 2 April 2019).

76 Ebba Koch, *Mughal Architecture: An Outline of its History and Development, 1526-1858* (Munich: Prestel, 1991).

77 'Mount Batten Saheb O (Mount Batten Saheb O) … Hemanga Biswas Song of IPTA', *YouTube*, 8 March 2012, available online: https://www.youtube.com/watch?v=PLkHwI-mw7w&ab_channel=DipankarSinha (accessed 4 August 2013). The author has translated the lyrics.

78 Mahfuzur Rahman, 'Kagmari Sammelone Koyekjon Sangit Shilpi', in Shoshtropani ed., *Kagmari*, 75–80.

erected on Kagmari's maidan. The crowds came, lured by the energetic and frenzied martial arts performances of *lathi-khela* (stick-fighting) and various forms of swordplay such *as ram-da khela* and *tarbari.* The highlight of the programme though were the various folk artists and troupes that had come from all areas of the province, even some parts of West Pakistan, to perform. This included the illustrious Sufi communist *kabigan* singer Romesh Shil and his troupe from Chittagong, *jarigan* singer Tosher Ali and his group, *bhawaiya* performer Abbas Uddin, baul of Sylhet Shah Abdul Karim and various other troupes from Sherpur, Faridpur, Rangpur, Mymensingh and Dhaka.[79] Mary Frances Dunham, in her work on *jarigan* in Bangladesh, refers to the massive audiences that attended these musical events, with many villagers travelling from afar and for several days for performances that lasted for hours and even days.[80] The popularity of these art forms was not just based purely on entertainment or the evocation of particular moods and emotions, but also on their pedagogical function, found in the form and content. The songs at Kagmari featured strong anti-colonial and anti-capitalist themes that drew upon the diverse life-worlds of the performers. Romesh Shil, a virtuoso performer in the *kabigan* genre (musical duels) from the Napit caste in Chittagong, whose compositions reflected his association with the left movement from the colonial period and onwards, turned to his audience at Kagmari and asked: 'How have our minds and bodies been freed living in Pakistan? How is a state running on foreign wealth free?' [81]

Romesh Shil's performance, and that of the others, demanded and built on the generative noise and response of the audience. In turn, the audience also became performers producing the political content. The immersive nature of these performances helped to form anti-imperial political subjectivities at Kagmari. These different art forms were also expressions of a collective form of life built around labour, caste, religion and locale. Where *lathi-khela* and swordplay was the 'literal and metaphorical flexing of peasant muscles',[82]and expressed a dignity in manual labour, the music told the stories of the different lives of Bengal. The *bhawaiya* songs, which were from Dinajpur and Cooch Bihar, were sung by the tribal communities and drew upon their lives, while the *bhatiali* and *sarigan* were sung by fisherfolk communities of East Bengal at times of leisure or during

[79] Ibid.

[80] Mary Frances Dunham, *Jarigan: Muslim Epic Songs of Bangladesh* (Dhaka: University Press, 1997).

[81] Maksud, *Kagmari,* 139, see also Syed Mohammad Shahed, *Romesh Shil Rochonabali* (Dhaka: Bangla Academy, 1993).

[82] Shahid Amin, *Event, Metaphor, Memory: Chauri Chaura, 1922-1992* (Berkeley: University of California Press, 2001), 124.

boat competitions.[83] I suggest that the performance of these songs outside their normal environment was a way to make these communities visible, and show the qualitative and quantitative difference between them and their rulers. Can those who sat in Dhaka convincingly claim to represent all of these different political communities that were there at Kagmari? However, these performances were not alone for those in power; they presented ways that different constituencies could think about and relate to each other, and forge anti-imperial and radical solidarities between them.

It was not simply male performers that graced the stages at Kagmari, Madame Azurie from the west wing also performed with her dance company. Azurie, of German-Indian descent, was the 'first great item dancer of Hindi cinema'.[84] In the 1930s and 1940s, she appeared in popular and low-budget movies as a dancing girl, performing Arabic, Turkish or other seemingly Oriental dancing forms.[85] After partition, she had migrated to Pakistan with her husband, where she had opened her dance school in 1945, enraging the 'maulvis of Rawalpindi'. She wrote, 'they were after my blood. They delivered sermons in mosques and spread as much venom against me as they could.'[86] Azurie found acceptance only among Karachi elites and the film circles in Pakistan. So, what does her performance in this village in East Bengal, at the site of a Sufi shrine, and in front of a mixed audience, comprised mostly of rural peasants and workers imply? On the one hand, Madame Azurie's performance taps into older traditions of professional dancers at Sufi shrines.[87] On the other, it speaks to this attitude of openness to difference that Bhashani and the other Kagmari organizers wanted to cultivate, where the public performance of a woman was a normalized event rather than something exceptional. After all, Azurie as a *kathakar* (classical Hindustani dancer) was only doing what the other male performers had done, telling stories and educating people through her art and labour.

The calibre of music, dance, art and film was matched by the equally impressive lectures on a broad spectrum of subjects ranging from religion, language and literature, public health and economy. This was an august gathering of renowned

[83] See Iftikhar Dadi's discussion on folk songs and instantiation of communities in this volume. See also Wakil Ahmed, *Bangla Loksangit Sari Gan* (Dhaka, Shilpakala Academy, 1998); Wakil Ahmed, *Bangla Loksangit: Bhatiali Gan* (Dhaka, Shilpakala Academy, 1997); Wakil Ahmed, *Bangla Loksangit: Bhawaiya* (Dhaka: Shilpakala Academy, 1995).

[84] S. Richard, 'Azurie', *Dances on the Footpath* (blog), 24 May 2013, available online: https://roughinhere.wordpress.com/2013/05/24/azurie/ (accessed 15 April 2014).

[85] Usha Iyer, *Dancing Girl: Choreographing Corporeal Histories in Hindi Cinema* (New York: Oxford University Press, 2020), 91–138.

[86] Feriyal Amal Aslam, *Choreographing (in) Pakistan: Indu Mitha, Dancing Occluded Histories in the 'Land of the Pure'* (PhD diss., University of California, Los Angeles, 2012).

[87] See fn. 57.

international, national and local academics, practitioners, both men and women. Dr Hasan Habashi, who had just finished his doctorate at the School of Oriental and African Studies under the supervision of Professor Bernard Lewis, and was in the cultural wing of the Egyptian Embassy, spoke about the medieval Islamic scholar Ibn Hajar al-Ashqalani.[88] Charles Adams, based at Princeton and then later at McGill's Institute of Islamic Studies, spoke about the poetry of Allama Iqbal.[89] There was a considerably large Indian delegation, which included writer and politician Humayun Kabir; theosophist Sodia Wadia; Bengali translator of Omar Khayyam's writings, Narenda Dev; and the founding member of the Muslim Sahitya Samaj, Kazi Abdul Wadud. The speakers from West Pakistan included Maulana Abdul Qadir, director of Pashto Language Academy and Zaibunnisa Hamidullah, Pakistan's first female political columnist, who spoke about the role and status of women in Pakistan. From East Pakistan itself, there were a number of celebrated authors, scientists and public health experts, including Dr Mahmud Shahidullah, Muhammad Qudrat-i-Khuda, Dr Govinda Chandra Dev and Shamsunnahar Mahmud.[90] However, apart from the title of the talks, we know little about the content, the languages in which they were delivered, whether translation facilities were available and the response of the audience to these talks. Nonetheless, we do know that these talks were open to all since they took place on the maidan.

Where music, arts and *lathi-khela* operated within the realm of popular culture and entertainment, lectures on specialist or technical topics fall within the ambit of a narrower and more exclusive field. Hence, it is worth considering what pedagogical value these talks held for peasants and workers, who were most likely to have low levels or no education. AbdouMaliq Simone's work on 'gathering' in Islamic thought and practice offers some answers here. In Surah Al-Qiyamah and Surah Al-Israh, the reader is told the Qur'an must be gathered, and the people must gather together to understand it. Knowledge acquires form and meaning through a community of learners.[91] This hermeneutic process of collective interpretation is central to the project of Islam, and Bhashani's politics of gathering up different constituencies and fragments of knowledge reflects this. Moreover, in the context of East Bengal, peasants and workers were used to

[88] Hasan Habashi, Historical studies on the 'Inba' al-Ghumr' of Ibn Hajar (PhD diss., SOAS, UK, 1955).

[89] Wael B. Hallaq and Donald P. Little (eds), *Islamic Studies Presented to Charles J. Adams* (Leiden: E.J Brill, 1991).

[90] For an extensive, but not the complete list, see Shostropani, 'Kagmari Sammelon', 61–2.

[91] AbdouMaliq Simone, 'Muslim Hoedowns, Tenuous Language and the Uncertain Lives of an Urban Majority', *International Journal of Urban and Regional Research*,43, no. 6 (2019), 1193–208.

attending lectures and assemblies in the form of *waz mahfils* and *bahas*, where fairly complex and detailed discussions on Islamic jurisprudence took place.[92] These lectures were not restricted to doctrinal matters, but covered a wide range of secular issues. Even if not immediately comprehensible, similar to learning the Qur'an, the emphasis was on listening, and that knowledge would inevitably follow. There is no reason to assume that peasants and workers did not gather in order to learn from the lectures at Kagmari, trying to draw closer to a world that seemed so far from them. Nor should it be assumed that they were passive receptacles of knowledge; these gatherings involved manifold exchanges and conversations, some between speaker and audience, and others between the members of the audience themselves.

In mid-1944, the East Pakistan Renaissance Society had arranged a three-day cultural festival in Calcutta's Islamia Hall. The festival with its rich programme of folk music, artists and writers had also attracted the attention of senior Muslim League politicians such as Suhrawardy and Nazimuddin. Neilesh Bose has described this festival as the 'epicenter of Bengali Muslim literary, intellectual and political engagement and a meeting of intergenerational energies dedicated to Bengal Muslim self-definition'.[93] However, while the 1944 festival was used to define a narrower and particularistic identity of the Bengali Muslim, Kagmari was the demand for a more open identity that could build out of nationalism.

The foreign policy *bahas*

At Kagmari, Bhashani's strongest and most explicit attempt to recruit and organize an AL cadre against the various military pacts and treaties, and support the demand for autonomy and Afro-Asian freedom was through his public address and exchanges with Suhrawardy. His speeches undermined, if not shattered, any façade of unanimity that might have existed between them both.

Kagmari was as much an adaptation of the popular rural tradition of the bahas as it was of the mela. Bahas were public religious debates between rival religious parties that took place in the villages of Bengal, their peak occurred during the period of religious revivalism in the nineteenth century. Occasions

[92] Rafiuddin Ahmed, *The Bengal Muslims, 1871-1906: A Quest for Identity* (Delhi: Oxford University Press, 1996); Max Stille, *Islamic Sermons and Public Piety in Bangladesh: The Poetics of Popular Preaching* (London: I.B. Tauris, 2020).

[93] Neilesh Bose, *Recasting the Region: Language, Culture and Islam in Colonial Bengal* (New Delhi: Oxford University Press, 2014), 209.

of much fanfare, they lasted for several days and drew in huge crowds from surrounding villages and elsewhere. According to Rafiuddin Ahmed, bahas imparted among the peasantry and village-dwelling communities a 'new pride in their "Muslimness" and knowledge of what it involved'.[94] Kagmari was a bahas on foreign policy, and inextricably linked to that was the question of what it meant to be a postcolonial subject. The Nat Mandir, the site for the meetings, was fitted with loudspeakers to reach a larger audience beyond that of the council workers and party workers. Naveeda Khan writes how the introduction of loudspeakers in 1950s Pakistan 'amplified and broadcast' conflict;[95] Bhashani wanted everyone to know that this was a public disagreement between him and the prime minister of Pakistan. Like the mela itself, Bhashani's speech was to be a co-constituted performance, relying on the interruptions of the crowd with sounds of approval and disapproval to defeat Suhrawardy. Bhashani's familiarity with rural theatrical form from a young age, his experience as a pir and long-standing relationship with subaltern constituencies meant that he knew how to perform in such settings. However, this was not the case for Suhrawardy, confronted with an audience different from his usual listeners, a factor exacerbated by his long absence from East Bengal since his entry into the Central Cabinet in 1955. Once again, Bhashani's ability to combine the different forms – bahas, political debate and folk theatre – enabled him to reprimand the AL for their indifference to subaltern life-worlds, and on a broader level, demonstrate the transformative collective power of subaltern constituencies.

Bhashani's address to the crowd was firm in its denunciation of the military pacts and in the demand for a free and independent foreign policy. His performance betrayed none of the confusion or vacillation that was reported of his closed-door performances.[96] He bellowed at the prime minister:

> Shohid, you are asking me today to support the Pak-US military pact. If you put me in front of the barrel of a gun and ask me, I will say, no! If you put me in front

[94] The activities at Kagmari in many ways mirrored Rafiuddin's descriptions of some of these nineteenth-century *bahas*, like the one that took place in Murshidabad and was captured in the religious tract, the *Saif al-Momenin*: 'The cooking was under way with great fanfare. Stacks *of golab, attar* and *sorma* had already been stored in a room. Folded betel leaves with varieties of spices were presented in a number of *dalis* with great care . . . food was cooked in many colours and there were lots of vegetables . . . countless people came and had their meal there . . . what a scene! The two villages took the guise of two bazaars of happiness. The shopkeepers were happy and so were the shoppers. Happiness filled the hearts of everyone in the two bazaars', see Ahmed, *Bengal Muslims 1871-1906*, 81.

[95] Naveeda Khan, 'The Acoustics of Muslim Striving: Loudspeaker Use in Ritual Practice in Pakistan', *Comparative Studies in Society and History* 53, no. 3 (2011), 571–94.

[96] Uddin, *In the Land of Eternal Eid*, 201–9.

> of a canon and ask, I will say no! No! If you go to my grave and ask me, from there I will shout out no, no![97]

The image must have been majestic, terrifying and even plausible, especially for the murids and others who did not think that the idea of the Maulana shouting from his grave was so impossible. Even for those who did not think of Bhashani as a pir, his roar resonated for a long while in their ears.[98] Bhashani's arguments, however, did not hinge on bellows and roars, or these majestic and striking images and phrases alone, powerful as they were. In many ways, the strength in Bhashani's address resided in his ability to make a direct and personal connection between foreign policy to the relatable and quotidian experiences and emotions of peasants and workers. The interconnectedness of struggles at the international, national and local levels were made clear, and the relationships of mutuality and cooperation that existed in the fields and factories, villages and industrial areas were elevated to an aspired status at the international level.

Bhashani argued that the pressing concern for newly independent people and states was social and economic development, the path to being fully human. As a newly independent state, all that Pakistan wanted was a peaceful life. However, the defence pacts did the very opposite; they centred war, making it an oppressive and omnipresent reality in the lives of people. As Bhashani stated, 'the people of Asia and Africa oppressed for hundreds and hundreds of years have only managed to escape the "nagpas" of imperialist powers as a result of one world war after another.'[99] The story of nagpas, the mythological snake in the Ramayana and Mahabharata that wound itself around the neck of its victim as a noose, tapped into cultural memory of colonial violence. It was a reminder of the horrors of the Second World War and the resulting Bengal famine of 1943, when physical constrictions had robbed life from the body of many a peasant and labourer. Bhashani told his audience that the postcolonial world held even greater horrors. The 'age of the atom' meant that the powerful states now possessed weapons and technologies to destroy human civilization. For new states to bind themselves to imperial powers who 'would not hesitate to create rifts and bring neighbouring countries to war' was akin to an act of suicide.[100] Bhashani's highlighting of this newer and potentially more destructive

[97] K. A. M. Sa'aduddin, 'Kagmari Sammelon: Age O Pore', in Shoshtropani ed., *Kagmari*, 15–25. For a variation of the speech, see 'Jibaner Sheshdin Parjonto Shakti Diya Shamasto Sarbaprokar Samarik Cuktir Biruddhita Kariba', *Daily Sangbad*, 7 February 1957.

[98] Sa'aduddin, 'Kagmari Sammelon', 22.

[99] Rahman (ed.), *Maulana Bhashani*, 65.

[100] Ibid., 66.

threat spoke to the worst fears of those peasants and workers, who had only just escaped death in the last war, and whose lives, since independence, had been so precariously balanced on a knife-edge.

Bhashani used the language of dignity most powerfully to underscore the danger of military pacts. He claimed that though Pakistan needed economic development, this was not to be achieved by riding on the tailcoats of, or as the '*talpi-bahak*' (porters) of imperial powers such as the United States or Britain.[101] There was no dignity, and therefore, no freedom where a nation had to barter peace for economic help. He argued that it was only through entering into relationships, networks and exchanges with nations where they were co-equals that Pakistan's dignity and freedom could be restored. *Shohardiyo* (friendship) and *shompriti* (love) with newly independent countries within the Asia and Africa bloc would weaken the power of imperialism and help Pakistan achieve that 'genuine freedom and peace'.[102] This discourse of dignity and self-respect and solidarity was not an abstract one, but one that had familiar, and particular resonance in the lives of the workers and peasants. The food crisis; the precariousness of their employment; the strikes, closures and marches pointed to their narrative of indignities and their struggle to restore that dignity. It should be stated this was not just an audience comprised of peasants or workers. The presence of rural and urban middle class and intelligentsia meant undoubtedly that there was not just the one, but also multiple readings being made of Bhashani's speech and activities at Kagmari. But in the context of an imminent famine, increased cost of living and first fall in industrial production since independence, Bhashani's caution against war and championing of freedom and dignity was likely to have had some impact on all the classes.[103]

As the public debate between Suhrawardy and Bhashani wound down, shouts of '*bisbashakti zindabad*' (long live global solidarity) could be heard from the crowd, instead of the usual '*Pakistan zindabad*' (long live Pakistan). The festival signalled a dramatic defeat for the prime minister of Pakistan, unable to convince the assembled crowd of peasants, workers and other groups of the need for a militarised future. Everts observed that Kagmari saw a weakening of Suhrawardy's position with the majority of 'rank-and-file' AL workers and

[101] Ibid.
[102] Ibid.
[103] Y. V Gankovsky and L.R Gordon-Polonskaya, *A History of Pakistan (1947-58)* (Lahore: People's Publishing House, 1962), 216.

supporters, who were convinced that Bhashani had triumphed, an outcome that Suhrawardy himself conceded.[104]

Conclusion

On 13–14 June 1957, Suhrawardy secured the victory that he failed to obtain at Kagmari. The AL convened another council meeting in Dhaka, far removed from its predecessor in almost all aspects. The meeting, held in the political capital of Dhaka with none of the fanfare, had a much narrower and clearly defined audience and agenda. Suhrawardy received an overwhelming validation, with an estimated 775 councillors voting in favour of the government's position on foreign policy, and only 46 dissenting.[105] However, Suhrawardy's consolidation over the AL prompted the gathering of some very formidable opposition forces under Bhashani's leadership. In July 1957, at the gathering of the 'All-Pakistan Democratic Worker's Convention' in Dhaka, the National Awami Party (NAP) was born, with Bhashani as the president. Ajoy Ghosh, a member of the Communist Party of India, described the formation of NAP as a 'moment of historic import for the Pakistani people'.[106] The radical futures and energies of Kagmari were sustained through the activities of NAP, which after the banning of the Communist Party, emerged as the foremost left-leaning and progressive party in Pakistan. NAP members, particularly Bhashani, would be involved in some of the most militant subaltern movements across Pakistan in the 1960s and early 1970s.

Kagmari Sammelon reframes our understanding of the history, politics and aesthetics of the left in South Asia. As a historical event, Kagmari has received inadequate attention from scholars. It acquires significance mainly for Bhashani's remark of 'salaam' (goodbye) to the Centre, seen as an indication of the prevalence of Bengali-nationalist sentiment in East Pakistan.[107] In this way, Kagmari is read as just another event in the seamless narrative of Bengali nationalism. However, Kagmari Sammelon shows, even at this high point of Bengali representation, the fault lines of Bengali nationalism, as an insufficiently hegemonic project unable to suppress other political aspirations and possible

[104] *Everts Report.*
[105] US Consul, *Dhaka to Department of State, Washington, 27/6/1957* (Central Decimal File 1955-9, Record Group 59, Box No. 3862, United States National Archives).
[106] Ajoy Ghosh, *Pakistan Portent* (New Delhi: Communist Party of India, December 1958), 13–14.
[107] Uddin, *In the Land of Eternal Eid*, 209–17.

futures. Kagmari offers a more radical narrative, the prefigurative politics of futures beyond nationalism.[108] Kagmari is the story of internationalism versus nationalism. In most studies, internationalism is the hallmark of state or elite actors, and their formal gatherings in metropolitan spaces. The focus is on the auditoriums and conference hall, the impressive addresses of the participants and the formal resolutions that are made. Kagmari contests such readings, as well as the Subaltern Studies, claim that the limits of the subaltern in progressive politics were shaped by their inability to engage or imagine worlds beyond what they were familiar with.[109] Instead, I have shown how peasants and workers connected their everyday lives to the international through the material and cultural practices of the mela. Kagmari was about the forging of a new political community that rejected muscular nationalism in favour of affective solidarities between the newly decolonized nations. The freedom and dignity of the '95 per cent' could only be realized through a class-based internationalism.

Viewing Kagmari as a collective cultural project allows us to foreground different forms of agency, practices, values and functions constitutive of art and aesthetics. We can think about Kagmari's creative transformation of the village into an artificial, temporary city celebrating a subaltern politics of progressive internationalism using Lefebvre's idea of social space. He described the tendency towards collective creative production of rural and urban landscapes as an *oeuvre*, 'closer to a work of art than a simple material product . . . a production and reproduction of human beings, rather than a production of objects'.[110] By aiming to enact spaces for human fulfillment, pleasure and sociality, rather than profit and consumption, the oeuvre generates use value rather than exchange value. For Lefebvre, the clearest and most concentrated expression of space as oeuvre, or use value, is *la fete* – the festival.[111]

We can approach Kagmari as an aesthetic event in a second way, drawing on Rancière's idea of politics as a creative process that opens up new ways of relating to the world. I suggest that Kagmari changes how people thought of the villages and peasants of East Bengal in the politics of united Pakistan; most importantly how the participants understood themselves. Politics, for Rancière,

[108] See Introduction in the volume.

[109] Ranajit Guha, 'On Some Aspects of the Historiography of Colonial India', in *Subaltern Studies I: Writing on South Asian History and Society*, ed. Ranajit Guha (Delhi: Oxford University Press, 1982), 1–9, see also Ranajit Guha, *Elementary Aspects of Peasant Insurgency in Colonial India* (Delhi: Oxford University Press, 1983).

[110] Henri Lefebvre, *Writing on Cities*, trans. and ed. Eleonore Kofman and Elizabeth Lebas (Oxford: Blackwell Publishers, 1996), 101. For more analysis on oeuvre, see Andrzeg Zieleniec,'Lefebvre's Politics of Space: Planning the Urban as Oeuvre', *Urban Planning* 3, no. 3 (2018), 5–15.

[111] Henri Lefebvre, *Critique of Everyday Life: Volume 1*, trans. John Moore (London: Verso, 1991), 250.

is a rupture of the existing order resulting from an irruptive event enacted by 'those who have no part'. Echoing Bhashani's concept of the 'have-nots', Rancière describes this group as the 'class of the uncounted that only exists in the very declaration in which they are counted as those of no account'.[112]By forcing the government to come out of the city to a rural village and bringing in peasants and workers generally excluded from formal politics, Kagmari disrupted traditional arrangements of power between spaces and populations towards greater equality. This case study of Kagmari highlights the areas where Rancière's theorization on politics can be developed. Rancière's privileging of politics as shared speech appears to overlook the problem of difference, while his focus on 'speaking beings' reduces the rich and complex cultures and ways of being political in South Asia. At Kagmari, peasants and workers participated in the language of internationalism, equality and radical citizenship in different ways that did not always involve words. Moreover, while elites usually own the modes of communication and perform political power using the spoken and written word, Kagmari highlights the communicative power of labour, an aspect ignored by Rancière. Under normal conditions, labour is commodified, anonymous and the property of capital. However, in the temporary setting of Kagmari, the voluntary, ongoing and living labour of the workers conveyed their productive power and agency, generating feelings of solidarity and pride. Rancière has been criticized for focusing on the event; Bhashani's politics took the radical energies of Kagmari forward into a sustained and organized project in the form of NAP.

Finally, Kagmari offers a different perspective to the usual story about subaltern constituencies, left politics and agency in South Asia. The willingness of peasants and workers to work creatively and accommodate the seeming contradictions between sacred and secular, tradition and modernity, and the history and future shows how subalterns were actively shaping the intellectual trajectories of the left in postcolonial South Asia. These creative accommodations generated some of the more radical images of a decolonized future. At the heart of the story of Kagmari is the centring of joy as an indispensible emotion in subaltern left politics. It was a joy that connected people to left politics but also kept them fighting for its future.

As students of left aesthetics, Kagmari deserves our attention for thinking about how more creative and alternative left politics, cultures and futures were

[112] Jacques Rancière, *Disagreement: Politics and Philosophy,* tran. Julie Rose (Minneapolis, London: University of Minnesota Press, 1999), 38. See also: Jacques Rancière, *Dissensus: Politics and Aesthetics*, ed. and trans. Steven Corcoran (London: Continuum, 2010), Dikeç, *Space, Politics and Aesthetics.*

fashioned by different constituencies. Some of the most important progressive political movements of recent years have come from occupied space: Shaheen Bagh, Tahrir Square and the Indignadoes movement. These, and other creative protests, have reworked and combined existing cultural forms for progressive ends. In the UK and beyond: Reclaim the Streets reinterpreted the free-party as a site of environmental and workers resistance; Climate Camp envisioned the festival as collective labour and co-education; and Occupy reimagined the assembly as radically democratic and rebellious. This tradition of cultural politics has a longer history and at Kagmari we see a unique South Asian example. There are criticisms of the ability of these movements to physically sustain themselves outside the limited space of their occurrence, leading to disunity and fragmentation. Yet, the events themselves do continue to have political effects; perhaps, we can say that their enduring legacy has been to change the way people see the world long after the movement is finished. In short, left futures once seen cannot be unseen. The task of the radical scholar is perhaps to help trace and gather the scatter of those visions, and ask how we can use them to vitalize and interrupt the present, to build futures anew.

3

Between neorealism and humanism

Jago Hua Savera

Iftikhar Dadi

Jago Hua Savera (A New Day Dawns) (1959, dir. A. J. Kardar) is the only prominent example of a neorealist Pakistani film from the 1950s and 1960s. Its aesthetics are comparable to the art and parallel cinema of India, rather than to feature productions from within Pakistan from that era that were primarily commercially oriented melodramas and social films.[1] This chapter posits a series of inquiries to *Jago Hua Savera* and offers a preliminary reading of the film's intellectual and social contexts.[2] Despite adhering to the formative Italian

1 This chapter has benefited from numerous suggestions and advice by Kamran Asdar Ali, Tariq Omar Ali, Shaina Anand, Manishita Dass, Lalitha Gopalan, Salima Hashmi, Lotte Hoek, Rini Bhattacharya Mehta, Aamir Mufti, Madhuja Mukherjee and Sanjukta Sunderason. Anjum Taseer kindly provided me with a DVD copy of the film.

Jago Hua Savera can nevertheless be situated on the horizon of progressive cultural politics of the mid-century. In the Urdu cinema of Pakistan, writers and directors associated with progressivism played a key role in feature films during the 1950s and even the 1960s. These individuals include many of the leading writers and directors: W. Z. Ahmed, Riaz Shahid, Khalil Qaiser, Zia Sarhadi and many more. Serious films made in Dhaka in Bengali during this period include *Asiya* (1960, dir. Fateh Lohani); for a discussion see Zakir Hossain Raju, *Bangladesh Cinema and National Identity: In Search of the Modern?* (London: Routledge, 2015), 84, 132–9. Many of Zahir Rahian's Bengali-language films from the 1960s are widely regarded as ambitious aesthetic and political ventures, most notably *Jibon Theke Neya* (Glimpses from Life) (1970), for an analysis see Fahmida Akhter, '*Jibon Thekey Neya* (*Glimpses Of Life*, 1970): The First Political Film in Pre-Liberation Bangladesh and a Cinematic Metaphor for Nationalist Concerns', *Journal of the Asiatic Society of Bangladesh* 59, no. 2 (2014), 291–303. Raihan had served as assistant director for *Jago Hua Savera*, and its lead actor Khan Ataur Rahman also plays a central role in *Jibon Theke Neya* as actor, music composer and singer. See Lotte Hoek's chapter in this volume for a discussion of the collaborative work between Raihan, Khan Ata and fellow-travellers.

2 *Jago Hua Savera*
Released in 1959
Director: A. J. Kardar (screenplay)
Based on a novel by: Manik Bandopadhayay
Story by: Faiz Ahmed Faiz (story, lyrics, dialogues)
Producer: Noman Taseer
Music: Timir Baran
Cinematography: Walter Lassally
Assistant Directors: Shanti Kumar Chatterji and Zahir Raihan

conception of neorealism and drawing from contemporary Indian productions, *Jago Hua Savera*'s realism is marked by fractures in form, narrative and address. Its formal fissures include many visible joints across its aesthetic assemblage: it deploys both colour and black-and-white film stock, includes songs in an ostensibly neorealist narrative and uses multiple linguistic registers that are not close to everyday language but are primarily an artifice. In its narrative, *Jago Hua Savera* shuttles between a humanist vision that envisioned traditional rural life as timeless and perennial and on the other hand a progressive understanding of exploitation and poverty as having become unsustainable. The film's production team was diverse, and its elements included dialogues and songs drawn from diverse backgrounds. In doing so, *Jago Hua Savera* makes a gambit or opening towards a larger alternative South Asian cinema after the Partition of 1947. Moreover, its audiences were neither fully envisioned, nor actualized, and this contributed to its failure in reception. In this chapter, I will read these fault lines as symptoms of a larger challenge, of artistic form and its adequacy to its context. Rather than analysing the film as a unified totality, a riven and divided social formation is instead visible in its ruptures, and is potentially productive for further engagement and experimentation.

Jago Hua Savera was the result of a collaboration of themes and personnel from within and beyond Pakistan. Directed by Akhtar Jung Kardar (1926–2002), brother of the established Bombay-based director Abdur Rashid Kardar (1904–89), the lyrics and dialogue were written by leading progressive Urdu poet Faiz Ahmed Faiz (1911–84).[3] Faiz had loosely adapted the overall story from the famous Bengali realist novel *Padma Nadir Majhi* (The Boatman on the River Padma) (1936) by Indian writer Manik Bandopadhyay (1908–56).[4] Zahir Raihan (1935–72), who served as an assistant director, subsequently emerged as

3 A short profile of A. J. Kardar was published as 'Introducing A. J. Kardar', *Eastern Film* 5, no. 5 (June 1963), 44.

4 The novel and its author remain unacknowledged in the film's opening credits. Overall, the story is far more ambitious and complex in its narrative scope than *Jago Hua Savera*. For example, the story has Hindu and Muslim characters, but the film does not depict a mixed community. The middleman in the story is Housain Miya who has multiple preoccupations, one of them being an attempt to reclaim a low-lying deltaic island, settling it and making it agriculturally productive. All this is absent in *Jago Hua Savera*, which has a more streamlined and unified narrative that moves forward towards a cinematic denouement. For an English translation of *Padma Nadir Majhi*, see Manik Bandyopadhyay, *Padma River Boatman*, trans. Barbara Painter and Yann (Lovelock, St. Lucia: University of Queensland Press, 1973). Bandopadhyay himself was sensitive to the need for realism in cinema: 'The common audience may not apply conscious judgment . . . but with the times their taste is changing. They want the story of real life and living humans in film . . . cinema cannot satisfy people any longer by resorting to romance, thrills, mythology and religion.' Quoted and translated in Moinak Biswas, 'In the Mirror of an Alternative Globalism: The Neorealist Encounter in India', in *Italian Neorealism and Global Cinema*, edited by Laura E. Ruberto and Kristi M. Wilson (Detroit: Wayne State University Press, 2007), 83.

a gifted and committed film-maker who made a number of important Urdu and Bengali films during the 1960s, and the documentary *Stop Genocide* in 1971.[5] Khan Ataur Rahman (1928–97), who plays the lead character Kasim, had been involved in emerging media and cultural productions in Karachi and in Europe during the 1950s. After *Jago Hua Savera* he went on to have a significant career as an actor in Zahir Raihan's films and as a director of Urdu and Bengali cinema (see Lotte Hoek's chapter in this volume for further discussion on Zahir Raihan and Khan Ata).

The team included Walter Lassally (1926–2017), a rising young German British cinematographer who later became prominent for his work on *Zorba the Greek* (1965) and won an Oscar for it; he also worked on Jamil Dehlavi's *Blood of Husain* (1980).[6] Experienced Indian film personnel also assumed key roles in the production of *Jago Hua Savera*. Shanti Kumar Chatterji, the other assistant director, had served as assistant director for Satyajit Ray's *Pather Panchali* (Song of the Little Road) (1955).[7] And Indian Bengali composer Timir Baran (1904–87) had composed the music for *Jago Hua Savera*.[8] Baran was the music composer for the iconic film *Devdas* (1935, dir. P. C. Barua) from India, as well as for the Pakistani Urdu films *Anokhi* (Singular) (1956, dir. Shah Nawaz), *Fankar* (Artist) (1956, dir. Mohammad Hassan) and later the Bengali film *Jog Biyog* (1970).[9] The lead actress of *Jago Hua Savera*, Tripti Mitra (1925–89), was also Indian. She had been involved with the Indian People's Theatre Association (IPTA), which was founded in 1943 as a leftist cultural organization and produced numerous realist plays across South Asia, many of which deployed songs, music and performance in innovative ways.[10] Mitra had acted in Khwaja Ahmad Abbas's realist film *Dharti Ke Lal* (Children of the Earth) (1946), as well as in many Indian Bengali-

[5] Raihan was disappeared and killed, probably by collaborators associated with the Pakistani Army in 1972.

[6] Walter Lassally, *Itinerant Cameraman* (London: J. Murray, 1987), 44–55, 164–8.

[7] 'Santi Chatterjee', *IMDb*, accessed 17 July 2017. http://www.imdb.com/name/nm0154155/.

[8] 'With Faiz himself contributing the lyrics, the music for the film was composed by Timir Baran, who was part of a New Theatres triumvirate that included R.C .Boral and Pankaj Mullick', noted Saibal Chatterjee in 'A Treasure Regained: A Neo-Realist Gem Shows Pakistani Cinema in a New Light', *DNA India*, 11 June 2016, https://www.dnaindia.com/analysis/column-a-treasure-regained-2222123.

[9] 'Timir Baran | Movies & Music of India', accessed 23 June 2016. https://iyerbhaskar.wordpress.com/2012/03/29/movies-music-of-india-timir-baran/.

[10] Sumangala Damodaran, *The Radical Impulse: Music in the Tradition of the Indian People's Theatre Association* (New Delhi: Tulika Books, 2017); Malini Bhattacharya, 'The Indian People's Theatre Association: A Preliminary Sketch of the Movement and the Organization, 1942–47', in *Modern Indian Theatre: A Reader*, ed. Nandi Bhatia (Delhi: Oxford University Press, 2009); Nandi Bhatia, 'Staging Resistance: The Indian People's Theatre Association', in *The Politics of Culture in the Shadow of Capital*, eds. Lisa Lowe and David Lloyd (Durham, NC: Duke University Press, 1997); Rustom Bharucha, 'The Indian People's Theatre Association (IPTA)', in *In the Name of the Secular: Contemporary Cultural Activism in India* (Delhi: Oxford University Press, 1998).

language films.[11] Participation of experienced international personnel in *Jago Hua Savera*'s production helped alleviate the glaring lack of experience by the Pakistanis involved – director A. J. Kardar had never made a film, and the production was also a first for Faiz.[12] I posit that in enlisting a broad production team, the makers of *Jago Hua Savera* sought to expand the scope of progressive cultural production beyond national limits.

This broader context suggests that while *Jago Hua Savera* might be considered a 'Pakistani' film, it cannot be understood without developments in India, with which Pakistani film-makers would have had varying access during the 1950s.[13] We can understand *Jago Hua Savera* in a wider South Asian context and as a contribution to and a manifestation towards what has been termed 'global neorealism'.[14] As I demonstrate later in this chapter, realism in South Asian cinema has multiple lineages since the 1930s across diverse cultural forms, with 'neorealism' notating a trajectory from 1952 onwards that drew from the influential Italian developments, but sought also to develop, refine, incorporate and partly repudiate popular cinematic codes and narrative tropes associated

[11] On the making of the film, see the primary documents assembled in Sudhi Pradhan, ed., 'The All India People's Theatre Association: Annual Report–1946', in *Marxist Cultural Movement in India: Chronicles and Documents* (Calcutta: Santi Pradhan, 1979), 239–40. On Tripti Mitra's work with IPTA (as Tripti Bhaduri) in the 1944 play *Jabanbandhi*, see pages 254 and 372 of *Marxist Cultural Movement in India*. Writing in *People's War* (13 February 1944), Hiren Mukherjee writes of her performance: 'No praise, however, can be adequate for Tripti Bhaduri and Anoo Das Gupta, who in their roles of peasant women could beat any professional hallow [*sic*] . . .' (372).

[12] Sayyid Mazhar Jamil, *Zikr-e-Faiz* (Karachi: Department of Culture, Government of Sindh, 2013), 501. Jamil notes that A. J. Kardar had proposed adapting the story to film. Faiz liked the idea, enthusiastically wrote the script, screenplay and dialogues, and even helped out with the direction.

[13] Indian cinema was increasingly restricted for distribution in Pakistan beginning in the mid-1950s, and completely prohibited within a decade. Protests by film-makers in Lahore against the import of Indian cinema in 1954 are termed the '*Jaal* agitation', because the lightning rod for this protest was the import of the Indian film, *Jaal* (1952) to West Pakistan. Mushtaq Gazdar observes that 'The restriction on Bombay cinema opened a new free and non-competitive market for local productions. 1956 proved to be the most fruitful year of the first decade in terms of box-office returns from indigenous cinema'. (52). See Mushtaq Gazdar, *Pakistan Cinema, 1947–1997* (Karachi: Oxford University Press, 1997), 49–53. On exchanges of film, personnel and themes between India and Pakistan, also see Salma Siddique, 'Meena Shorey: The Droll Queen of Partition', *BioScope: South Asian Screen Studies* 6, no. 1 (1 January 2015), 44–66; Salma Siddique, 'Archive Filmaria: Cinema, Curation, and Contagion', *Comparative Studies of South Asia, Africa and the Middle East* 39, no. 1 (1 May 2019), 196–211.

[14] The concept of 'global neorealism' is a recent one in cinema studies, emphatically not one where the Italian development serves as a master template and all others are secondary, but precisely the opposite – it takes each local articulation seriously in its own right, sees all of them as fully legitimate and situates them in the post–Second World War period and the onset of decolonization, when varieties of neorealism were developed in many locations. Laura E. Ruberto and Kristi M. Wilson, eds. *Italian Neorealism and Global Cinema* (Detroit: Wayne State University Press, 2007); Saverio Giovacchini and Robert Sklar, eds. *Global Neorealism: The Transnational History of a Film Style* (Jackson: University Press of Mississippi, 2011). For an overview account, see Geoffrey Nowell-Smith, 'The Second Life of Italian Neo-Realism', *Journal of the Moving Image* 12 (2014), 46–58.

with the 'studio *Social*' film.[15] *Jago Hua Savera* was awarded a gold medal at the First Moscow Film Festival in 1959 and was also Pakistan's Oscar submission.[16] For decades, it had been lost and not available either nationally or internationally, yet had acquired a mythical aura domestically. In his memoir, Walter Lassally observes that 'by the time of my second visit to Pakistan in 1976, *Day Shall Dawn* had become a sort of *Birth of a Nation* of the Pakistani Film Industry, a film which, even though they hadn't necessarily seen it, was discussed by local film buffs in reverend tones'.[17] Since its rediscovery and subsequent restoration, the film has been shown at numerous film festivals, such as the Three Continents Festival in 2007, the New York Film Festival in 2008 and the Festival de Cannes in 2016.[18] The version available now is apparently the one meant for foreign distribution. The local version included a song-and-dance sequence in colour, whose incorporation raises important questions as to how 'highbrow' leftist artistic projects understand their own social appeal in relation to the widespread allure of popular cinema in South Asia. I discuss the importance of songs in *Jago Hua Savera* and the question of its audiences in more detail later in this chapter.

Plot summary of *Jago Hua Savera*

Set in the village of Shaitnol on the banks of the Meghna River some 30 miles from Dhaka, the film focuses on the everyday life of ordinary fishermen and their families. Mian is the main character. His family consists of his crippled wife Fatima, who is in poor health and has recently delivered a baby; their children; and an adopted orphaned young man named Kasim (who accompanies Mian as a fishing partner). Mala, the visiting sister-in-law, is a young woman who falls in love with Kasim over the course of the film. Ganju is another fisherman who lives with his paralysed mother. Neither Mian nor Ganju own their own boats, and thus much of the earnings of their labour are handed over to the boat owner. They are also compelled to sell their catch to Lal Mian, a middleman of some means who is deeply involved with everyday matters of the village, at prices over

15 On the concept of the 'Studio Social', see Biswas, 'In the Mirror of an Alternative Globalism: The Neorealist Encounter in India'.

16 '1st Moscow International Film Festival', *Wikipedia*, 17 June 2017. https://en.wikipedia.org/w/index.php?title=1st_Moscow_International_Film_Festival&oldid=786104691.

17 Lassally, *Itinerant Cameraman*, 55.

18 Ali Raj, 'Pakistan's First Oscar Submission "Jago Hua Savera" Goes to Cannes', *The Express Tribune*, 1 May 2016. http://tribune.com.pk/story/1095386/pakistans-first-oscar-submission-jago-hua-savera-goes-to-cannes/.

which they have little say. In order to purchase their own boats, Mian and Ganju save part of their meagre earnings after each expedition – these are also 'banked' with the grasping but indispensable Lal Mian. Ganju has saved more but is in very poor health.

When a Pakistani government delegation comes to conduct an auction for the renewal of fishing rights, Lal Mian wins by outbidding other middlemen, and he uses this as a pretext to further squeeze the fishermen (Figures 3.1a–c).

Figures 3.1a–c Auction of fishing rights for the next year by the Pakistani government, *Jago Hua Savera*. © Anjum Taseer, courtesy of Anjum Taseer.

Towards the end of the film, when Ganju has finally saved enough, Lal Mian delivers a vessel to him, having it dramatically hauled upland to his hut. But Ganju is now far too ill and collapses in a coughing fit. Lal Mian repossesses the boat, ostensibly to resell it in order to provide for Ganju's mother. Watching this, in desperation, Mian scrounges up the savings of all members of his household to add to his savings already banked with Lal Mian. But when Lal Mian's *munshi* (accountant) tallies up all of Mian's savings, they are tantalizingly close to Lal Mian's asking price but still insufficient, and suspiciously lower than Mian's own reckoning of how much he has banked with Lal Mian. Mian and his family's hopes for achieving greater financial independence and taking ownership of the 'means of production' are frustrated for now (Figure 3.2). These emotional events constitute a denouement in the film that is otherwise characterized by subdued drama throughout.

Similar to its beginning, the film ends with a lyrical sequence of boats launching at dusk, initiating another seemingly eternal cycle of events. But the cycle's previous iteration had sharpened social contradictions and created greater consciousness in some characters, suggesting that existing hierarchies are not fated to repeat endlessly. This is most evident in the development of Kasim's character, marked by integrity, independence and growing consciousness. Kasim

Figure 3.2 Mala and Fatima watch as Mian fails to purchase Kasim's boat from Lal Mian, *Jago Hua Savera*. © Anjum Taseer, courtesy of Anjum Taseer.

accompanies Mian on the boats and is subject to the same forces of exploitation as other fishermen who do not own their own vessels. Unlike others, however, Kasim refuses to bank his savings with Lal Mian, and this quiet assertion of independence unpleasantly surprises the latter when he learns of this. Kasim is also aware of Lal Mian's pursuit of Mala and protects her from his advances. And when one of Mian's children has a broken leg that the faith healer brought in by Lal Mian is unable to heal, Kasim insists on taking the child to Dhaka for treatment in a modern hospital, accompanied by Mala. As an outsider to the family unit, Kasim is perhaps freer to breach social custom. In this interlude, the film depicts the bustling streets of Dhaka and its commercial and public spaces, suggesting that for the next generation, the small rural world of Shaitnol will no longer remain a self-enclosed one.

Remarkably, the film depicts virtually every character in the film engaged in saving money. In addition to the fishermen Ganju, Kasim and Mian, Mian's crippled wife and their young son are all preoccupied with saving even small coins, assiduously reckoning their sums, and resorting to unusual stratagems to accomplish this. This depiction probably sharply contrasts with the probable reality of rural Bengal at mid-century where debt had long figured as a central problem plaguing its rural poor – the emphasis on saving in the film perhaps charts a fantasy of responsible rural life, an imaginative trajectory towards a transformed future.[19]

[19] Thanks to Tariq Omar Ali for this observation and for the citations below that span the years 1914–52. These describe jute cultivators, but may well also characterize the general economic scenario of rural East Bengal during the early to mid-twentieth century:

> The crores of rupees paid for the raw article have had no visible effect on the manliness or contentedness of the agricultural classes or even on their material prosperity. They have no idea of saving, and in most cases their earnings from jute are frittered away on profitless extravagances long before the next crop is on the ground. By increasing their credit the inflated prices of jute have deepened rather than diminished their general indebtedness (F. A. Sachse, Settlement Officer, Mymensingh to Revenue Dept., Government of Bengal, 21 February 1914. Proceedings A, Agriculture Dept., Agriculture Branch, List 14, Bundle 28, National Archives Bangladesh).

> There is a kind of poverty, which while not amounting to insolvency, nevertheless makes for precarious and uncertain living. It is this latter class of poverty, which is the real cause of indebtedness among agriculturists in Bengal (Bengal Provincial Banking Enquiry Committee, Vol. I, 1933, 73–4).

'Poverty, illiteracy, indebtedness, love of litigation have however all combined to reduce many cultivators to the position of landless labourers. He neither can realize the importance nor can he afford to take recourse to improved methods of intensive farming for cultivating the small holding which he might yet own' ('Note by Cooperative Directorate for the Agricultural Enquiry Committee', 1952, MSS EUR F235/303, India Office Records, British Library).

Exploitation is depicted as part of daily routine and is not excessively dramatized. Even Lal Mian is involved in acts of welfare, and his accumulative motivations are not depicted as being starkly evil. His actions are deeply intermingled in the everyday life of the community: he constitutes nothing less than being 'a part' of the village's 'fate', according to the opening credits. By contrast, the state remains distant – the only event where the Pakistani government intervenes in the village is when its official, wearing a *sola topi*, arrives in a large boat flying the national flag, to auction off annual fishing rights (Figure 3.1a). There is no trace of development activities in the village – no clinic, post office, bank or school – suggesting that the state remains resolutely colonialist, an absentee landlord, interested primarily in the extraction of revenue via middlemen who are in turn deeply involved in everyday acts of exploitation and maintenance of the poor fisherfolk at a bare subsistence level.

Jago Hua Savera: Style and reception

The look or style of *Jago Hua Savera* is lyrically cinematic, deploying strong lighting contrasts and editing sequences that track the narrative, punctuated by strong graphic shots of the countryside and the water. The frame compositions are well conceived. The film was shot mostly on location, and the sense of realism of the everyday is heightened as the camera lingers on details of evidence and events.[20] The fisherfolk's desperation is portrayed with restraint. The narrative unfolds slowly but steadily – its pacing aligns with the gentle waves of water which the film's evidentiary focus highlights.

Jago Hua Savera is singular in its stark 'realist' portrayal, as film historian Mushtaq Gazdar has noted in his landmark study, *Pakistani Cinema 1947–1997*:

> *Jago Hua Savera* was the first realistic and experimental movie of Pakistan. It was the story of an East Pakistani fisherman who strives hard to build a boat, a symbol of livelihood and sustenance for his entire family. All-pervasive poverty, deprivation, ill-health and ignorance are the major obstacles he has inherited from his environment. The film is more about the lives of such people than a series of dramatic events.[21]

Gazdar equates the values of realism here with experimentalism. And part of its realist value is the 'focus on the lives' of ordinary people, rather than on

[20] According to Lassally, the interior shots were done in Dhaka in a set constructed outdoors. Lassally, *Itinerant Cameraman*, 48–9.

[21] Gazdar, *Pakistan Cinema*, 78.

'dramatic events.' These attributes set *Jago Hua Savera* against mainstream Pakistani cinema of the 1950s in which social concerns are largely subordinated to, or placed within, a melodramatic narrative. Gazdar is certainly correct in descripting *Jago Hua Savera* as offering a new set of aesthetic and moral values to cinema produced in Pakistan. The booklet accompanying the film claims that it 'marks the beginning of the avante guard [*sic*] movement in this country!'[22] But the film failed to find a receptive domestic audience, and 'was taken down from Karachi's Jubilee Cinema . . . in just three days.'[23] This is despite the domestic version being reported to have included the song in colour precisely to broaden the film's local appeal.

The political environment in Pakistan was not conducive to a film affiliated with progressive politics. The country had been allied with the United States from the early 1950s and hostile to leftist cultural and political projects. The Rawalpindi Conspiracy Case of 1951 is an important landmark, in which members of the Communist Party of Pakistan were tried for conspiring to overthrow the government. Faiz was jailed for four years between 1951 and 1955.[24] The All Pakistan Progressive Writers Association and the Communist Party of Pakistan were also banned in 1954. These events had a repressive effect on cultural expression.[25] Ayub Khan's coup in 1958 put an end to political instability between 1951 and 1958, but right after seizing power, Ayub Khan exerted greater authoritarian control over journalism, criticism and cultural policies, including his notorious takeover of Progressive Papers Limited in 1959, the publisher of *Pakistan Times*, the largest-circulation English-language daily, which Faiz had edited before his imprisonment in 1951, and *Imroze*, an important Urdu newspaper.[26] Ayub Khan was reportedly unhappy with *Jago Hua Savera* and attempted to thwart its release just three days prior to its screening.[27] The producer's son Anjum Taseer recalls:

> My father financed the entire production from his own resources, and although the project was risky, idealism and passion were two driving forces that he could not resist . . . the film was shown in February 1959, but the reception was poor.

22 *Jago Hua Savera* (booklet) nd., np.

23 Ali Raj, 'Pakistan's First Oscar Submission "Jago Hua Savera" Goes to Cannes.'

24 Hasan Zaheer, *The Times and Trial of the Rawalpindi Conspiracy, 1951: The First Coup Attempt in Pakistan* (Karachi: Oxford University Press, 1998).

25 Intezar Husain, *Chiraghon Ka Dhuan: Yadon Ke Pachas Baras* (Lahore: Sang-e-Meel Publications, 2003), 65–79.

26 Chatterjee, 'A Treasure Regained.'

27 'The India-Pakistan Masterpiece That Fell through the Cracks', *BBC News*, 5 June 2016, sec. India, https://www.bbc.com/news/world-asia-india-36417007.

> Firstly, people were not ready for neo-realism, and also, I believe the distributors were pressured to cut short the viewings.[28]

The question of *Jago Hua Savera*'s audience and its reception must be further parsed in terms beyond ideological suppression. Was the film intended to circulate locally and do the sites of circulation include Shaitnol? Dhaka? Karachi? Or was it intended also for, or perhaps even primarily for, the international film festival circuit, which had recently been very receptive to films from India, as Neepa Majumdar has noted, '1954–57 were particularly good years for India's cinematic morale'.[29] This quest for international recognition was no anomaly – as even in India, despite its more cinematically literate public and state support, Satyajit Ray observed that his work was possible only via European film festival support.[30]

Jago Hua Savera's devastating failure in the domestic market, coupled with the state's political and aesthetic conservatism of the late 1950s, meant that *Jago Hua Savera* has remained largely a singular experiment in *Pakistani* cinema.[31] But if one extends the scope of analysis across South Asia, one can situate *Jago Hua Savera* in relation to other films being produced at the time. Moreover, its collaborative production process underscores that it also can be viewed as a broader move in South Asia towards an embrace and localization of neorealism during the 1950s. *Jago Hua Savera* can be posited as attempting to create a progressive cultural form that had cross-regional address, not unlike earlier IPTA productions, as well as meetings of the All India Progressive Writers' Association (PWS) during the 1940s that Faiz was intimately familiar with and participated in. Exchange of cinema between India and Pakistan since the mid-1950s was however in the process of attenuation, with national borders that were becoming increasingly harder to traverse, and protests in Lahore in 1954 against the import of Indian cinema.[32]

[28] Nandini Ramnath, 'Made in Pakistan with Some Help from India, Lost and Found Again: The Story of "Jago Hua Savera"', Scroll.in, accessed 8 May 2018, https://scroll.in/reel/817995/made-in-pakistan-with-some-help-from-india-lost-and-found-again-the-story-of-jago-hua-savera.

[29] Neepa Majumdar, 'Importing Neorealism, Exporting Cinema: Indian Cinema and Film Festivals in the 1950s'. In *Global Neorealism: The Transnational History of a Film Style*, ed. Saverio Giovacchini and Robert Sklar (Jackson: University Press of Mississippi, 2011), 181.

[30] Satyajit Ray, 'Problem of a Bengali Film Maker', in *Our Films, Their Films*, 3rd edn (Bombay: Orient Longman, 1993), 42–3.

[31] Jamil, *Zikr-e-Faiz*, 501–3.

[32] On the '*Jaal* agitation' of 1954, which started to see Indian films being screened less in Pakistan, see note 13 above. Nevertheless, the realist social film *Aadmi* (1958) was directed by Lahore-based Luqman, who was close to celebrated Indian actor Dilip Kumar. The story was written by Ayub Sarwar, elder brother of Dilip Kumar, who wanted Dilip to star in it initially. See Gazdar, *Pakistan Cinema*, 70; Urmila Lanba, *Life and Films of Dilip Kumar, the Thespian* (New Delhi: Vision Books, 2002).

Realism in South Asian cinema before 1952

The move towards realism in the cinematic and performing arts of South Asia began from at least the late 1930s. Apart from neorealist works from the mid-1950s, mid-century Indian cinema contains a variable register of aesthetic values and concerns, across which various manifestations of realism are marshalled. Thus, the social film of the 1940s is imbued with a kind of Hollywood realism, and in many Indian productions the focus of themes and motivations relevant to society are coupled with the 'heterogeneous attractions' of the commercial Indian film.[33] To examine the embrace of realism in 1950s Indian cinema in more detail, in this chapter I draw on the work of Moinak Biswas and Neepa Majumdar.[34] Both scholars have shown that this development was not simply due to exposure to Italian neorealism, but conditions were being prepared within the trajectories of Indian cinema during the 1940s for the neorealist turn to unfold in the 1950s the way it did – long before the fateful 1952 First International Film Festival that introduced Italian neorealist cinema widely to Indian film-makers.

Founded in 1936, the Progressive Writers' Association 'sought to extend the progressive, rationalist trends in nationalist culture into a critical and socialist direction. Realism was conceived of as an ethic that could oversee this "progress"'.[35] (See Ramnath and Rambukwella's chapters in this volume for the widespread influence of the Progressive Writers' Association across South Asia.) The subsequent founding of the IPTA in 1943 was extremely consequential for theatre and cinema overall, producing a vibrant 'movement that in the next ten years or so would directly or indirectly influence almost every important artist in the country'.[36] In cinema, developments in realism that Biswas terms the 'studio *Social*' had begun in 1940 with films such as *Aurat* (Woman), directed by Mehboob Khan. Furthermore, the Bengal famine of 1943 created new artistic, photographic and theatrical depictions of its grim reality, as discussed by Sanjukta Sunderason in this volume and in her book-length study.[37] Rustom Bharucha

33 N. Majumdar, 'Importing Neorealism, Exporting Cinema', 187.
34 Biswas, 'In the Mirror of an Alternative Globalism'; N. Majumdar, 'Importing Neorealism, Exporting Cinema'.
35 Biswas, 'In the Mirror of an Alternative Globalism', 77.
36 Biswas, 'In the Mirror of an Alternative Globalism', 78. For an overview of the development of IPTA, see Nandi Bhatia, 'Staging Resistance: The Indian People's Theatre Association', and Malini Bhattacharya, 'The Indian People's Theatre Association: A Preliminary Sketch of the Movement and the Organization, 1942–47'.
37 Sanjukta Sunderason, *Partisan Aesthetics: Modern Art and India's Long Decolonization* (Palo Alto: Stanford University Press, 2020).

has stressed how audiences 'discovered for the first time' in Bijon Bhattacharya's play *Nabanna* (New Harvest), first performed in 1944, 'the extraordinary impact of realism in the dialects and street cries of the actors, the minutiae of their gestures, movements, and responses, and the stark simplicity of the set and the costumes'.[38] Notably, these influences were relayed into subsequent cinema.[39] Khwaja Ahmad Abbas's *Dharte Ke Lal* (Children of the Earth) (1946) serves as a landmark film in 'terms of its realism', notes Neepa Majumdar.[40] This was followed by another key film, the 1950 Bengali-language *Chinnamul* (The Uprooted), directed by Nemai Ghosh. Both films were supported by IPTA and embraced codes of realism, yet in many ways also remained tied to values associated with the 'studio *Social*'.[41]

Two international films also have relevance for the development of realism in South Asian cinema, and especially for understanding *Jago Hua Savera*. *La Terra Trema* (The Earth Trembles) (1948), directed by Luchino Visconti, focused on the exploited lives of a fishing village in Sicily.[42] I undertake a more extensive comparison between *La Terra Trema* and *Jago Hua Savera* later in this chapter. The other significant film is *The River* (1951), directed by Jean Renoir and shot in India. *The River* has been widely recognized for its technical and artistic quality, with its 'innovative use of technology, documentary sequences, and realist aesthetics'.[43] It forms another significant reference, more so as the young Satyajit Ray, who had not yet ventured into film-making, assisted in its production. *The River*'s emphasis on the cyclical nature of time marked by the river's flow serves to foreground the temporal dramas of the protagonists, with a 'combination of smoothness and disruption'[44] that is emphasized by its sophisticated and limpid cinematography and editing. Renoir spliced the drama of the largely European characters together with documentary ethnographic vignettes, creating a kind of realist epic in which everyday events in the characters' lives were placed adjacent

38 Rustom Bharucha, *Rehearsals of Revolution: The Political Theater of Bengal* (Honolulu: University of Hawaii Press, 1983), 49.

39 Biswas, 'In the Mirror of an Alternative Globalism', 81. Also see Manishita Dass, 'Cinetopia: Leftist Street Theatre and the Musical Production of the Metropolis in 1950s Bombay Cinema', *Positions: Asia Critique* 25, no. 1 (February 2017), 101–24.

40 N. Majumdar, 'Importing Neorealism, Exporting Cinema', 178.

41 Biswas, 'In the Mirror of an Alternative Globalism', 81.

42 It was released the same year as Vittorio De Sica's landmark neorealist film *Ladri di biciclette* (*The Bicycle Thief*, 1948).

43 Parkash Younger, 'The River: Beneath the Surface with Andre Bazin', in *A Companion to Jean Renoir*, edited by Alastair Phillips and Ginette Vincendeau (Chichester, West Sussex, UK: Wiley-Blackwell, 2013), 166.

44 Sarah Cooper, 'Henfi Agel's Cinema of Contemplation: Renoir and Philosophy' in *A Companion to Jean Renoir*, edited by Alastair Phillips and Ginette Vincendeau (Chichester, West Sussex, UK: Wiley-Blackwell, 2013), 322–3.

to the eternal cycle of life epitomized by the steady flow of the river and the performance of timeless Hindu rituals that acknowledge that birth and death are cyclical.[45] Film historian Sarah Cooper stresses that Renoir accomplishes this by 'the use of dissolves, hastening the pace of time but in a languorous manner, suggesting connections rather than cuts from one moment to the next, and thus a form of continuity across the boundaries of difference'.[46] And while *The River* has been criticized for its expatriate orientalist and rose-tinted view of India that disregards social exploitation and risks trafficking in colonialist clichés, for our purposes, what is significant is how subtly it modulates the relationship between epic time and everyday actions and decisions of human actors.[47] As I argue later, *Jago Hua Savera* also calibrates cyclical time with everyday life, but unlike *The River*, it gestures instead towards the impossibility of the cycle of seasons playing out endlessly in the social life of its protagonists.

Neorealism in Indian cinema after 1952

The most consequential context for experimental Indian cinema of the mid-1950s onwards was its encounter with Italian neorealism. The embrace of an intensified realism, more in keeping with Italian neorealist principles, accelerated after 1952 even in mainstream cinema, such that by the mid-1950s, 'one can find a continuum of films ranging from mainstream studio products such as Zia Sarhadi's *Footpath* (1953) to hybrid independent and studio films such as Bimol [Bimal] Roy's *Do Bigha Zamin* (Two Acres of Land, 1953) to state-supported independent films such as *Pather Panchali*', notes Neepa Majumdar.[48] The latter film was released in 1955, the first of the celebrated *Apu Trilogy* by Satyajit Ray, who acknowledged the decisive impact of this aesthetic after his viewing of *The Bicycle Thief* (1948): 'I knew immediately that if I ever made *Pather Panchali* –

45 Priya Jaikumar, *Where Histories Reside: India as Filmed Space* (Durham, NC: Duke University Press, 2019), 155–69.

46 Cooper, 'Henfi Agel's Cinema of Contemplation', 323–4. The highly influential post-war cinema critic André Bazin proclaimed *The River* a 'pure masterpiece' whose achievement was nothing less that the revelation of reality itself: 'In The River the screen no longer exists; there is nothing but reality. Not pictorial, not theatrical, not anti-expressionist, the screen simply disappears in favor of what it reveals.' André Bazin, 'A Pure Masterpiece: The River' in *Jean Renoir* (New York: Simon and Schuster, 1973), 118. For an assessment of Bazin's influence in the post-war era, see Rochona Majumdar, 'Art Cinema: The Indian Career of a Global Category', *Critical Inquiry* 42, no. 3 (1 March 2016), 588.

47 For a summary of these criticisms, see Younger, 'The River'.

48 N. Majumdar, 'Importing Neorealism, Exporting Cinema', 179.

and the idea had been at the back of my mind for some time – I would make it in the same way, using natural location and unknown actors.'[49]

The mid-to-late 1950s thus emerged as a key period for the embrace of Indian cinema of a restrained realism. Biswas notates the key players – Bimal Roy, Prakash Aurora, Zia Sarhadi, Amar Kumar, Raj Kapoor and Khwaja Ahmad Abbas – and its aesthetic values that embraced 'lower-middle-class poverty, unemployment, homeless children on the street, and the experience of the urban subalterns'. In terms of cinematic style, 'the change is visible in the use of location, space, and light'.[50] But if Hollywood productions and aspects of the earlier 'studio *Social*' can also be labelled as realist, the question arises: What characterizes a neorealist film in South Asia? And how do we situate films like *Pather Panchali* and *Jago Hua Savera* specifically as neorealist rather than broadly realist? (Dass's chapter in this volume also examines these questions.) For Biswas, it is the crystallizing impact of Ray's contribution in finally equating serious realism firmly with neorealism:[51]

> *Pather Panchali* established as a fully formed aesthetic what was only partially operative in earlier Indian cinema, that is, the realist textual principle. The success of this aesthetic was measured in terms of its ability to free itself of impulses characteristic of traditional Indian cinema – textual heterogeneity, lack of individuation, non-secular narrative logic, and the predominance of spectacle over narrative. After *Pather Panchali,* these same impulses were associated with popular cinema.

The problem of what constituted serious realism was thus not simply cinematic but also literary, and, indeed, the neorealist turn was premised on imaginatively adapting literary forms into film.[52]

The bifurcation of Indian cinema into serious and commercial trajectories begins at this juncture. But while serious Indian cinema is often viewed in

49 Ray, 'Introduction' in *Our Films, Their Films*, 9.

50 Biswas, 'In the Mirror of an Alternative Globalism', 85.

51 Ibid., 72–3.

52 Here I also note the analysis of realism in the Indian novel offered by Ulka Anjaria, which bears relevance for our discussion. In her analysis of realism's purported belatedness and its ambivalences in South Asia, Anjaria observes: 'Although a realist novel may seem to support colonial or nationalist hegemony, its instability allows it to elude any rigid ideology . . . a realist representation of the rural poor is not solely a means of incorporating that population into the universal fold of the nation, but can simultaneously show the *inability* of realism to capture the reality of social inequality. . . . realism is sometimes complicit with dominant ideology, sometimes resistant, but mostly neither – or somewhere in between. This ambivalence is not always aesthetically pleasing but sometimes clumsy, reading at times more like inconsistency and hesitation.' Anjaria suggests that realism in its awkward silences and contradictions offers an aesthetic and social critique that cannot be neatly folded into a national register. See Ulka Anjaria, *Realism in the Twentieth-Century Indian Novel: Colonial Difference and Literary Form* (New York: Cambridge University Press, 2012), 8.

national terms, it was shot through with diverse subnational and transnational vectors. For Neepa Majumdar, the question of nationalism in realist cinema hinges on issues of state patronage and formal and technological constraints, set against a commercial industry that did not receive analogous legal and financial recognition by the government: 'In its negotiations and compromises in grafting Italian neorealist aesthetics to an Indian studio-based realism, mainstream cinema lost the historical battle of neorealist status to state-supported filmmakers such as Ray.'[53] Biswas has argued that while realism in Indian cinema is partly associated with Nehruvian nationalism, its full scope and diversity cannot be captured via a nationalist framework.[54] This 'serious' aesthetic crucially also received legitimacy from recognition in international film festival circuits.[55] Satyajit Ray himself stressed the importance of foreign patronage in making his cinematic experiments possible.[56]

Moreover, in Indian cinema, realism was foregrounded as a facet of mainstream commercial cinema itself even after the genre division. 'The emphasis on realism and humanism was indicative of global discussions in cinema after the Second World War', stresses Rochona Majumdar.[57] As Biswas notes, 'A new popular film emerged around the same time that the new realist cinema arrived. It incorporated neorealist elements even as it launched an advanced dialogue with Hollywood – the 1950s films of Raj Kapoor and Guru Dutt are good examples.'[58] Biswas perceptively remarks that the impact of neorealism 'helped Indian cinema break away from a set of restrictions and lay the basis of modern ways of working with its own material. . . . its reality lying outdoors, . . . its people living out there, . . . its novels, poems, and pictures'.[59] And Manishita Dass observes that IPTA film-makers, upon moving to work in Bombay cinema in the 1940s and 1950s, 'in their roles as directors, actors, scriptwriters, lyricists, and composers . . . drew on the IPTA experiment to reorient Bombay cinema toward the mass subject and the mass public . . . and fashion a mass cultural critique of the postcolonial nation-state's failure to extend the rights of social citizenship to the vast majority of Indians'.[60] This is also the case for West Pakistani cinema in Urdu

[53] N. Majumdar, 'Importing Neorealism, Exporting Cinema', 190.

[54] Biswas 'In the Mirror of an Alternative Globalism', 78.

[55] As Neepa Majumdar notes in 'Importing Neorealism, Exporting Cinema', 181, 'If success abroad was the measure of pride in a national cinema, then 1954–57 were particularly good years for India's cinematic morale. At the Cannes Film Festival in each of these years, an Indian film won either an award or a special mention.'

[56] Ray, 'Problem of a Bengali Film Maker', 42.

[57] R. Majumdar, 'Art Cinema: The Indian Career of a Global Category', 588.

[58] Biswas, 'In the Mirror of an Alternative Globalism', 76.

[59] Ibid., 89.

[60] Dass, 'Cinetopia', 109.

of the 1950s and 1960s, where realist tropes and social critique in commercial cinema include films directed by W. Z. Ahmad, Luqman, Hassan Tariq, Khalil Qaiser and Riaz Shahid. Mid-century realism in South Asia thus cut across subnational (Bengali), national and transnational orbits.

In sum, it is worth stressing not simply the divergent values of 'serious' neorealist cinema from the commercially oriented social film, but also their resonances – themes drawn from literary narratives, and a shared focus on social issues. Nevertheless, the neorealist juncture of the 1950s also created a dividing framework of production and reception that placed 'serious' and 'artistic' films *against* the mainstream popular cinema, even as the latter was partially realist as early as in 1940. This emergence of post-war realist cinema must also be seen in relation to the wider context of Cold War humanism globally, which I discuss further.

Form and style in Italian neorealism

The Italian background for the emergence of neorealism during and after the 1940s is that of a nation emerging from under fascist rule, with limited equipment and resources available to film-makers after the end of the Second World War, and with continued extreme uneven development between the industrialized North and the impoverished South. For film-makers working in South Asia in a context of linguistic and social heterogeneity and unevenness, also with limited technical and financial resources, but wanting to address serious topics such as poverty and exploitation, the ideas and aesthetics associated with Italian neorealism understandably had tremendous resonance.

Many foundational theorizations of neorealism by Italian film-makers and critics remain salient to the South Asian context. Here I summarize key ideas of screenwriter and theorist Cesare Zavattini (1902–89), who among his numerous contributions also wrote the screenplay for Vittorio De Sica's hugely influential film *The Bicycle Thief* (1948).[61] In his manifesto published in English translation in 1953, Zavattini exhorts neorealism to avoid illusory narrative plots and stories in order to focus on the truth of everyday life. Since reality itself is 'hugely rich', the film-maker can create a film that will encourage people to 'reflect . . . on the real things, exactly as they are'. Zavattini marks a sharp distinction between Italian neorealism and American cinema, as in the latter, 'reality is unnaturally

[61] For a good discussion of the intellectual genealogy of neorealism, including a discussion of Bazin and Zavattini, see Torunn Haaland, *Italian Neorealist Cinema* (Edinburgh: Edinburgh University Press, 2012), chapter 2.

filtered, . . . lack of subjects for films causes a crisis, but with us such a crisis is impossible. One cannot be short of themes while there is still plenty of reality'.[62] He thus situates poverty itself as a plentiful resource for film-makers, rather than rendering technical impediments as lacking. Zavattini accordingly repudiates congealed expectations of apparatus and infrastructure that attend to film-making as a capitalist artefact.[63]

This everyday reality can be apprehended by the neorealist film-maker through 'a minute, unrelenting, and patient search', that 'must sustain the moral impulse . . . in an analytical documentary way'.[64] The materials for the film must be brought together by exercising one's 'poetic talents on location, we must leave our rooms and go, in body and mind, out to meet other people, to see and understand them'.[65] This moral imperative has a technical and aesthetic dimension, in terms of the film-maker's sensitivity and focus on seemingly minor sites, events and characters, so that 'when we have thought out a scene, we feel the need to "remain" in it, because the single scene itself can contain so many echoes and reverberations, can even contain all the situations we may need'.[66] He urges a turn away from a focus on individual heroism of characters,[67] and exhorts film-makers to be sensitive to local linguistic expressions, 'the best dialogue in films is always in dialect. Dialect is nearer to reality. In our literary and spoken language, the synthetic constructions and the words themselves are always a little false.'[68] However, this focus on authentic and local linguistic expression will become a fraught issue for Visconti's *La Terra Trema*, and also for *Jago Hua Savera*, as both films attempt to straddle fidelity to local authenticity with the problem of the film's implied audience and actual reception in metropolitan and global cine circuits.

Jago Hua Savera and *La Terra Trema*

La Terra Trema (The Earth Trembles) (1948) is an Italian neorealist film directed by Luchino Visconti. Although the film has been criticized for being didactic

[62] Cesare Zavattini, 'Some Ideas on the Cinema (Italy, 1953)', in *Film Manifestos and Global Cinema Cultures: A Critical Anthology*, ed. Scott MacKenzie (Berkeley: University of California Press, 2014), 125.

[63] 'Neorealism . . . rejects all those canons, which . . . exist only to commodify limitations. Reality breaks all the rules, which you can discover if you walk out with a camera to meet it.' Zavattini, 'Some ideas on the Cinema', 131.

[64] Zavattini, 'Some Ideas on the Cinema', 126,

[65] Ibid., 133.

[66] Ibid., 126.

[67] Ibid., 130.

[68] Ibid., 132.

and stylistically unresolved,[69] it nevertheless remains a key milestone in the development of Italian neorealism and the subject of analysis by major film critics and theorists, such as André Bazin and Gilles Deleuze. My purpose here is to foreground a comparison between *La Terra Trema* and *Jago Hua Savera*, in order to better elucidate the character of the latter. *La Terra Trema* focuses on the exploitation of fishermen in a Sicilian coastal village of Aci Trezza. Considered remote, underdeveloped and exotic to the inhabitants of cosmopolitan Rome, the film was sponsored by the Italian Communist Party and was initially intended to be a documentary on the exploitation of the fisherfolk community. Visconti instead created a lengthy poetic and cinematic epic by adapting a late-nineteenth-century novel by Giovanni Verga and using local, unprofessional actors. Bazin has observed that Visconti's camera deployed a deep depth of field both indoors and outdoors, so that all of the reality of Aci Trezza that came into the frame of the camera was always in-focus.[70] The mise-en-scene throughout the film remains resolutely situated in the inner and outdoor spaces of Aci Trezza, which produces the effect of oppression and claustrophobia in the viewer, in sympathy with the perceived worldview of the suffering villagers.[71]

One of the fascinations for Visconti in the site of Aci Trezza was that it had scarcely changed at all since Verga described it in his novel, sixty years earlier. The location has powerful mythical associations with the Homeric epics and with Ovid's *Metamorphosis* that are evoked in both the novel and in Visconti's film. In a detailed study of the site in Verga's novel and earlier photography that informed the making of *La Terra Trema*, Noa Steimatsky has noted that 'Visconti's prospects for a Marxist' series of films that might suggest 'an impending revolution' is 'disrupted already in Verga by an enclosed, cyclical, rhythmic sense of time, a mythical order of fate'.[72] Visconti departs from other neorealist films in that rather than repudiating myth, *La Terra Trema* instead embraces the epic mythical aura of the site and situates its natural setting and built form as a theatrical set for the ensuing drama enacted by the actors – who encompass the life of the village itself as a totality.[73]

[69] '*La Terra Trema* is a great bore, a colossal aesthetic blunder and a monumental confusion of styles', noted Satyajit Ray in his damning critique. See Ray, 'Some Italian Films I Have Seen', 122.

[70] André Bazin, *What Is Cinema? Volume II*, trans. Hugh Gray (Berkeley: University of California Press, 1971), 43.

[71] Paul Thomas, '"Gone Fishin"? Rossellini's "Stromboli," Visconti's "La Terra Trema"', *Film Quarterly* 62, no. 2 (Winter 2009), 22.

[72] Noa Steimatsky, *Italian Locations: Reinhabiting the Past in Postwar Cinema* (Minneapolis: University of Minnesota Press, 2008), 90.

[73] 'Visconti endows the suffering of his characters with an aura of grace and grandeur . . . [and] boldly grafts diverse visions, scales, spaces, narrative and historical orders in a resonant chorale . . . [the] cinematographic grasp of the location as an enframed chorale suggests a conception of nature

By contrast, the fishing village of Shaitnol on the banks of the Meghna River is endowed with no such archaic myth, but is instead imagined in *Jago Hua Savera* in the context of post-war humanism, which I discuss later in this chapter. Film critic Alamgir Kabir has compared the extended opening scene of *Jago Hua Savera* as being very similar to that of *La Terra Trema*.[74] Both open with an extended lyrical take several minutes long, in which humble fishing boats slowly return back to the shore at twilight. In both films, this creates a mood of immersion in the life-worlds of the locations, echoing Zavattini's call for 'cinema's original and innate capacity for showing things that we believe worth showing, as they happen day by day – in . . . their longest and truest duration'.[75] *Jago Hua Savera* maintains this mood of immersion in everyday life throughout the film, an aesthetic that was brilliantly deployed earlier by Satyajit Ray in *Pather Panchali*. In *Jago Hua Savera*, certain visual tropes are effectively repeated: the face of Ganju's paralysed mother, the emphasis on the structure, silhouette and architectonics of the boats, the preparation and eating of rice, the torn vests of the fishermen and the lyrical riverine landscape.

The picturesque rendering of the landscape in *Jago Hua Savera*, aspects of which one might also find in a documentary promoting tourism, is an aesthetic issue that neorealism faces at large. Torunn Haaland notes that for Zavattini, the neorealism film is a 'lingering in the intersection between anthropological study and a poetic discovery', premised upon 'the director's artistic autonomy and presence in the reality encountered'. This vantage provides 'subjectivity of selection and perspective', which are 'decisively . . . creative acts. This essentially is what distinguishes the [neorealist] social documents from documentaries.'[76] Bazin also stressed these ideas – for both thinkers, 'realism appears to be a question of integral representation, to be achieved through uninterrupted long takes'.[77] The experience of the viewer then becomes an immersive phenomenological encounter with the filmed event or object: 'Zavattini defines [this] as *pedinamento* or the act of shadowing . . . that reveals the multifarious aspects and dimensions of the studied object, decidedly emancipating the

as a contained, determinant, humanized stage – and a conception of reality as itself such a set.' Steimatsky, *Italian Locations*, 105, 115.

74 'Its opening sequence that portrays the homecoming of the fishermen just before sunrise after a whole night's fishing in the river has been overwhelmingly influenced by a surprisingly similar sequence from Luchino Visconti's "La Terra Trema", a masterpiece based on the plight of the Sicilian fishermen. Whether this was a conscious imitation or an accidental coincidence is not really important. The scene certainly added a lyrical quality to the severely austere mood of the story.' Alamgir Kabir, *The Cinema in Pakistan* (Dacca: Sandhani Publications, 1969), 71–2.

75 Zavattini, 'Some Ideas on the Cinema', 126–7.

76 Haaland, *Italian Neorealist Cinema*, 52.

77 Ibid., 53.

spectator from all *a priori* interpretations.'[78] The lengthy opening shots of both *La Terra Trema* and *Jago Hua Savera* can thus be understood as orienting the viewer into an immersive experiential perception of the mise-en-scene, in order to prepare for the encounter with life-worlds starkly different from those of the films' audiences. The long takes and depth of field in the films' cinematography immerse the viewer in-location, and which is animated by actors whose characters are drawn from everyday life.

Both films primarily subject everyday life to their scrutiny and conclude on an expectation of the future horizon that is freighted with the possibility of change. While exploitation is present throughout social and temporal incidences and cannot be dislodged in a single transformative event, and while the cycle of time still retains its hold, there is the suggestion of 'the unsustainable nature of these hitherto unchanging realities'[79] in *La Terra Trema*, as well as in *Jago Hua Savera*. In the latter, the film closes with Kasim being engaged to Mala, and with Mian and his family more united than ever. The family has been exposed to the healing power of modern medicine, which means that the future generation will not be afflicted by being crippled, unlike Mian's wife, who suffers daily. And they are now aware that their savings aggregated together is already close to meeting Lal Mian's asking price for a boat. The endless cycle of unremitting stasis and exploitation is thus not fated to continue forever. This sensibility is brought out subtly but powerfully in *Jago Hua Savera*.

Humanism in *Jago Hua Savera*

The difference in worldviews between the lives of the characters and the lives of film-goers is central to both films in their concern with authentic and exotic locale. While *La Terra Trema*'s site of Aci Trezza becomes resonant via Visconti's epic archaism, *Jago Hua Savera* draws on the trope of timeless continuity-in-adversity of Bengali riverine life, which was resorted to not only in Renoir's *The River* but also had a hold on West Pakistani conceptions of East Pakistan. Consider, for example, a photo essay titled 'River Life in East Pakistan' by A. B. Rajput published in the journal *Pakistan Quarterly* in 1964. In keeping with the journal's national developmentalist agenda and its celebration of diverse facets of Pakistani cultural life, the essay weaves statistical details about commerce

[78] Ibid.

[79] Lara Pucci, 'History, Myth, and the Everyday: Luchino Visconti, Renato Guttuso, and the Fishing Communities of the Italian South', *The Oxford Art Journal* 36 (2013), 434.

Figure 3.3 Opening pages of A. B. Rajput's essay, 'River Life in East Pakistan', *Pakistan Quarterly*, Summer 1964.

on East Pakistani rivers with touristic observations. All the photographs accompanying the text are picturesque (Figure 3.3). The essay characteristically concludes on a lyrical note that acknowledges hardship, but subsumes it within aesthetic pleasure of human accommodation to the cycles of the natural order:

> The rivers of East Pakistan, thus, hum with unceasing activity, day and night, with boats carrying passengers and cargo, with men and womenfolk bathing, washing, fishing and filling the air with soft melodious music of flutes and sentimental songs. The day dawns with a beautiful breeze and the rays of the sun gradually turn the silvery water into liquid gold. The entire area around is full of green glory, providing a romantic background to the golden-brown hamlets. . . . Life goes on unabated, full of adventure and supreme satisfaction in these highly romantic yet extremely precarious conditions, and this has been going on since time immemorial.[80]

[80] A. B. Rajput, 'River Life in East Pakistan', *Pakistan Quarterly* (Summer 1964), 42. Also see Layli Uddin's discussion in this volume (page 74) as to how the Kagmari Festival in 1957 enacted a transformed understanding of rural Bengal: 'The changing infrastructure and aesthetics in Kagmari presented a vision of the power and possibilities contained within rural spaces and constituencies, a role otherwise denied to them. The village did not have to continue to be marked by stubborn and inexorable decline and immiseration. It could be revived and reimagined, not as some romanticised version of a village of a by-gone era, but as a village that could boldly face the future if equipped with infrastructure.'

It bears stressing that this is not simply the specific colonialist view held by urbane West Pakistanis.[81] Zakir Hossain Raju has argued that two early Bengali-language films released from Dhaka in 1956 and 1960 portray the region as 'a rural idyll . . . depicting the riverine landscape of the delta and its beauty'.[82] And cyclical time had been arrayed earlier in *The River*. And in the post–Second World War context of the Cold War, human experience in traditional societies and its place in eternal cycles was widely disseminated by influential magazines such as *Life* whose photo essays depicted life in traditional and rural locales around the world as precisely such tropes.[83] The celebrated *The Family of Man* (1955–ongoing) exhibition curated by Edward Steichen, which travelled globally over decades, also reiterated this sense of humanist realism; its mythological presumptions Roland Barthes has incisively critiqued.[84] The prominence of this mid-century Western documentary aesthetic must be viewed in the Modernization Theory context of the Cold War – in which social transformation would be achieved primarily by modernization directed from above, rather than by leftist, collective or community mobilization from below. Unlike revolutionary or leftist depictions of workers, strikers or peasants engaged in struggle against exploitation and transformation, Western post-war mid-century humanist realism also works as a prophylactic against the more radical claims that visual and performative realism could marshal via Marxist and leftist initiatives, some of which were prevalent in Bengal of the 1940s with the activities of IPTA and the work of artists like Chittaprosad.[85] Pakistan's alliance with the United States from the very beginning meant that in the establishment of publications such as *Pakistan Quarterly*, traditional society was viewed in humanist terms as eternal and passive, with transformation to be bestowed upon it from statist, institutional and capitalist developments.

81 In her chapter in this volume on the film *Akaler Sandhaney* (In Search of Famine) (1980, dir. Mrinal Sen), Manishita Dass observes how urban leftist Indian film-makers repeatedly misconstrued and romanticized rural conditions in West Bengal even as late as in 1980.

82 Raju, *Bangladesh Cinema and National Identity*, 138. His extended discussion on the files and their aesthetics is on pages 132–8.

83 Erika Doss (ed.), *Looking at LIFE Magazine* (Washington, DC: Smithsonian Institution Press, 2001).

84 Jean Back and Viktoria Schmidt-Linsenhoff (eds), *The Family of Man 1955–2001: Humanismus und Postmoderne: Eine Revision von Edward Steichens Fotoausstellung = Humanism and Postmodernism: A Reappraisal of the Photo Exhibition by Edward Steichen* (Marburg: Jonas Verlag, 2004); Blake Stimson, 'Photographic Being and The Family of Man', in *The Pivot of the World: Photography and Its Nation* (Cambridge, MA: MIT Press, 2006); Mary Anne Staniszewski, *The Power of Display: A History of Exhibition Installations at the Museum of Modern Art* (Cambridge, MA: MIT Press, 1998), 235–59. Roland Barthes's influential critique of this exhibition is 'The Great Family of Man', in *Mythologies: The Complete Edition, in a New Translation*, trans. Richard Howard and Annette Lavers, 2nd edn (New York: Hill and Wang, 2013), 196–9.

85 Sunderason, *Partisan Aesthetics*.

How do we situate *Jago Hua Savera* against this cultural and ideational landscape? I argue that *Jago Hua Savera* is a project caught between eternal humanism and a recognition of the need for change to arise from below. A clue is provided by the rhetoric employed in the film booklet:

> East Pakistan is a land of rivers. . . . In such a land, there live many communities remote from the hubub [*sic*] of modern civilization . . . . This is a story of the people of the river: of those who spend their life, in dazzling sun and blinding rain, to hunt for fish that swarm the surrounding waters. . . . of their little human weakness and strength . . . and deep down of their undaunted, undefeatable spirit.

As is evident, these tropes of ethnographic fascination with remote people whose lives are synchronized with natural cycles are no departure from those deployed by A. B. Rajput given earlier and with Cold War humanism in general. One can, however, posit that *Jago Hua Savera* is both complicit in, and critical of, this view. In lyrically celebrating the unchanging rhythms of Bengal's riverine village life, *Jago Hua Savera* partakes in West Pakistani exoticism.[86] However, as a neorealist film, it also poetically dwells on the sensory and material character of the environment, and attempts to inhabit the life-world of the protagonists. It proffers both continuity and change – the cycle will repeat again, but the present traversing of it has introduced a consciousness of exploitation and the promise of modernity in many of its characters. This is not a strong revolutionary stance that proffers that conditions for dramatic transformation are immanent, but it's not fully a humanist one either.

The booklet's excited description of *Jago Hua Savera*'s pioneering cinematic accomplishment as a kind of conquest is therefore also in character with the tropes of exoticism (see Appendix A).[87] The unsettling militarist metaphors in it notwithstanding, it is the case where conditions for filming were difficult and the infrastructure lacking – this is confirmed by the anecdotes narrated by cinematographer Walter Lassally in his memoir.[88] However, the booklet's claim of the pioneering inexperience of the film-makers must be tempered with the proficiency and perspective the international team members brought to the project. Still, given the inexperience of the director and many of the key personnel involved, and far more significantly, the absence of critical discourse in

[86] Another example is an article taxonomizing various types of boats in Bengal. M. A. Ahmed, 'River Craft in Modern Bengal', *Pakistan Quarterly* 4, no. 2 (Summer 1954), 37–9.

[87] *Jago Hua Savera* (booklet) nd., np.

[88] Lassally, *Itinerant Cameraman*, 44–55.

Pakistan on cinema means that we must evaluate *Jago Hua Savera* as a pioneering experiment, rather than the product of a thriving environment in which such a film project would have emerged within established local precedents in critique and praxis.[89]

Songs in *Jago Hua Savera*

Songs in *Jago Hua Savera* condense many of the issues discussed earlier and merit closer examination. The opening and closing sequences of the film with lyrical long takes are attended by the incantation of the poem '*Bhor hui ghar aao majhi*' (It's dawn, return home boatman), attended by plaintive melodious notes from a single flute, evoking a sense of extended temporality and relationship of human presence within the sensory materiality of nature.[90] The film opens with a long take, an extreme wide-angle shot that divides the screen in half, with the open sky above and water below, over which the titles and credits appear. In the distance, some twenty boats with fluttering white sails are visible. Swaying gently, the camera traverses the space, immersing the viewer in the journey across the water. The song bridges the journey's crepuscular atmosphere into a stilled darkness in which stationary boats with lowered sails and the fishermen are etched by strongly directional lantern light, a realm marked by extended waiting and sudden exertion. After hauling fish, as the fish gasp for air, Kasim and Mian struggle to catch their breath, evoking themselves as precarious and vulnerable beings also (Figures 3.4a and b).

The next song '*Ab kya dekhen rah tumhari*' (Still awaiting for your return) also plays extradiegetically, this time attending the sequence when Kasim first goes to fetch Mala. He stands up alone in a boat and manoeuvres the vessel in

[89] See Lotte Hoek's chapter in this volume on how critic Alamgir Kabir positioned *Jago Hua Savera* as an influential but troubling exemplar for socially committed cinema in Bangladesh.

[90] The long take and cinematic immersion in the riverine landscape is also celebrated in the early Bengali productions from Dhaka, Bengali *Mukh o Mukhosh* (The Face and the Mask) (1956, dir. Abdul Jabbar Khan), and *Asiya* (1960, dir. Fateh Lohani). Zakir Hossain Raju observes that both films 'combin[e] images and sounds that quite ably represent East Bengal's traditional lifestyle and the beauty of rural nature. Lohani himself admits that he was accused of using long takes of the natural scenery of rural East Pakistan. . . . I argue that the . . . long sequences of natural beauty and of folk culture in rural East Bengal actually portrayed the relationship of Bengali-Muslim identity within its local setting . . . . *Asiya* also repeatedly presents long shots of boats, rivers and clouds, and medium shots of water lilies. Moreover, it combines various scenes such as a snake-play by a snake-charmer in a rural market and women singing folk songs whilst thrashing paddy. These images are only remotely connected with the narrative development of the film, but are significant constituents of the rural culture of the Bengal delta. East-Bengali folk literature also plays important role in the film. Not only are there a number of folk songs in the film, but sometimes the protagonists, the two young lovers, converse using folk riddles.' Raju, *Bangladesh Cinema and National Identity*, 137.

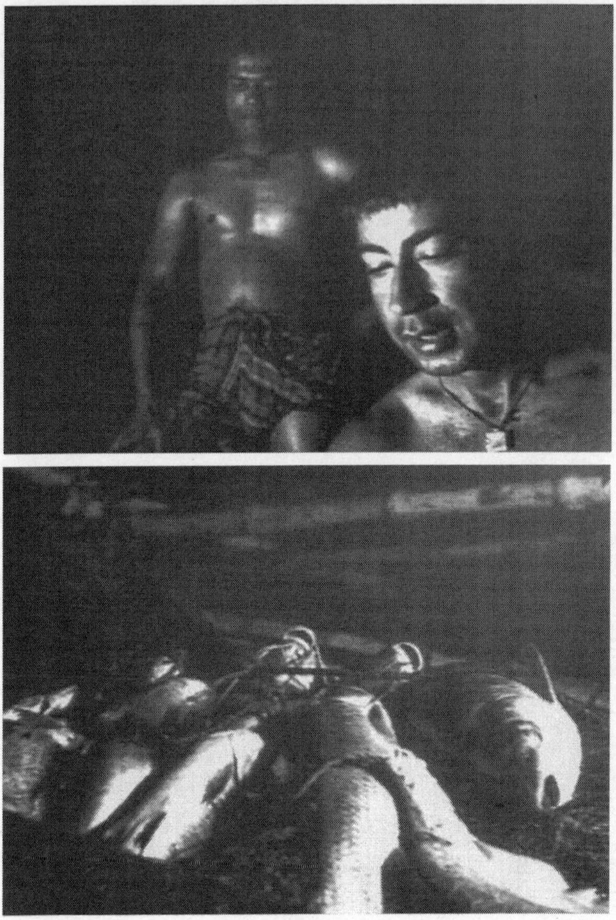

Figures 3.4a and b Kasim and Mian catch their breath after hauling their catch, as the fish gasp for air, *Jago Hua Savera*. © Anjum Taseer, courtesy of Anjum Taseer.

waterways with a bamboo staff. The sequence is a combination of long shots and medium close-ups of the upper half of Kasim's labouring body and of his legs planted on the deck of the boat (Figures 3.5a and b). Faiz's diction is simple in both poems, and draws on Bhojpuri and registers of North Indian languages with folk associations. In both songs, lyrics are set to compositions that recall folk music. Lotte Hoek and Sanjukta Sunderason have noted that these songs are modelled after *bhatiali*, a folk form sung by boatmen especially in East Bengal – these were also deployed 'in the Left's national-popular rhetoric in the 1940s'.[91]

[91] Email communication, 31 October 2016.

Figures 3.5a and b Sequence of Kasim manoeuvring the boat with the extradiegetic song '*Ab kya dekhen rah tumhari*' ('still awaiting for your return'), *Jago Hua Savera*. © Anjum Taseer, courtesy of Anjum Taseer.

In her detailed study of music in IPTA productions, Sumangala Damodaran observes: 'The use of the "folk" idiom and the need to focus on it . . . was the subject of much discussion within the IPTA tradition. . . . particularly in terms of its identification as "truly people's music".'[92] Indeed IPTA's 1946 Annual Report

[92] 'The engagement with the indigenous saw a wide variety, ranging from presenting indigenous artists or their music, to using indigenous forms and tunes with political lyrics, to interpreting, mixing and borrowing between different forms, involving substantial aesthetic transformations.' Damodaran,

accorded a special and elevated status to folk traditions in Bengal, in relation to other regions of South Asia:[93]

> [W]here classical influence is least felt, folk art has its richest traditions. Having no big temples as in the South or big royal courts like those of the Mughals and Rajput princes as in the North, before the coming of the British, where classical dance and music grew to its full stature under the patronage of princes and priests, Bengal developed its folk forms of art almost to a perfection. Today among all the provinces it is perhaps the richest in folk music, dance and drama.

Damodaran notes that when artists use folk songs, usually the songs would be presented 'as they were', in order to introduce them to urbanized audiences.[94] However, in IPTA, the fidelity of folk music motifs to their original form was also a subject of contentious debate, as Anuradha Roy points out.[95] It may be recalled that Tripti Mitra and Timir Baran had been associated with IPTA, and would have been deeply familiar with this debate.[96]

A *bhatiali* song is included in the Smithsonian collection *Folk Music of Pakistan* (1951), which was compiled with the assistance of the Pakistani government. Willem van Schendel observes that radio broadcasts in rural areas had popularized such folk songs across East Bengal.[97] A translation of a poem mentioning *bhatiali* was published in the *Pakistan Quarterly* in 1954.[98] The poet Jasimuddin published a six-page article in the *Pakistan Quarterly* in 1956, explaining various styles of folk music in East Bengal that included *bhatiali*.[99] Kardar and Faiz's exposure to *bhatiali* is thus also no mystery. But in

The Radical Impulse, 153. Also see page 119, where she notes that the singer Hemanga Biswas included *bhatiali* songs in his performances.

93 Sudhi Pradhan (ed.), 'The All India People's Theatre Association: Annual Report – 1946', 251. Also cited in Anuradha Roy, *Cultural Communism in Bengal, 1936–1952* (Delhi: Primus Books, 2014), 202.

94 Damodaran, *The Radical Impulse*, 153.

95 Roy, *Cultural Communism in Bengal*, 202–4.

96 'Timir Baran's own classical training and work/travels with Uday Shankar and the milieu of the IPTA in the 1940s and 1950s does open up a new mode of producing (and affirming) a lyrical scape, at once classical and folk.' Sanjukta Sunderason, email communication, 4 October 2017.

97 'Regional genres came to be appreciated across the region, such as the wistful love songs from the north – bhaoaya . . . and the haunting boat songs – bhatiali . . . from the east and south.' Willem van Schendel, *A History of Bangladesh* (Cambridge: Cambridge University Press, 2009), 156. Also see Zakir Hossain Raju's discussion of the first film made in Dhaka, *Mukh o Mukhosh* (The Face and the Mask) (1956, dir. Abdul Jabbar Khan), specifically the lyrics and picturization of the 'song by the boatman'. Raju, *Bangladesh Cinema and National Identity*, 137.

98 *Folk Music of Pakistan*. Folkways Records, 1951. 'Program notes by John Gonella ([4]p.) inserted in slipcase'. Songs available online for streaming at http://www.aspresolver.com/aspresolver.asp?GLMU;71822; Jasimuddin, 'The Fisherman', trans. Winfred Holmes, *Pakistan Quarterly* 4, no. 2 (1954), 40.

99 Jasimuddin, 'The Folk Songs of East Bengal', *Pakistan Quarterly* 6, no. 3 (1956), 45–50. *Bhatiali* is discussed on page 50.

Jago Hua Savera, the songs have been rendered into a North Indian linguistic register. Can we posit that the two songs are transcreations when rendered in the linguistic registers of Bhojpuri and Purbi? And if so, can this move be situated with reference to the IPTA debates regarding how closely to adhere to folk forms when deploying them in a progressive framework?

The third song was markedly different. And as noted earlier, only the local version of the film included a song-and-dance sequence in colour, with a selection of verses from Faiz's poem '*Shishon ka masiha koi nahi*' (The shattered glass has no savior), and are reproduced in the *Jago Hua Savera* booklet. Here, the diction is closer to Urdu, with more Persianized vocabulary: Is this choice of diction an implied critique of West Pakistani linguistic and economic colonialism over East Pakistan?[100] The song was reportedly performed as playback in the film by noted ghazal singer Iqbal Bano, 'whose melodious voice had a spellbinding effect on the listeners', notes Agha Nasir, former managing director of Pakistan television. Nasir's observations are valuable in providing us with a sense of the character of this lost song sequence:[101]

> The film is in black and white, but the scenes with the dancer Rakhshi are in color. They show a large hall in a magnificent mansion, where a spirited party with a dancer is carrying on [*mehfil-e raqs-o surud barpa hai*], with big landlords, industrial tycoons, high government officers, and corrupt politicians in attendance. The door to the hall is closed. Outside the mansion in semi darkness, the poor faithful servants overhear what's transpiring inside. The cameraman shot these scenes with great skill and ingenuity, such that the shift between color and black and white clearly signified the stark difference between the exploiter and the exploited.

In his memoirs, however, Lassally recalls only the difficulties in filming this sequence:[102]

> To complicate matters further, A. J. [Kardar] had inserted a short colour sequence in the film, a musical number intended to be included only in the version of the film to be released locally – in fact considered essential for obtaining a

[100] The poem was written in 1952. For the Urdu text of poem with a gloss on its context, see Agha Nasir, *Ham jitay ji masruf rahe* (Lahore: Sang-e-Meel Publications, 2008), 139–43. The poem recited by Faiz is available on YouTube: 'Shishon ka masiha koi nahin (Faiz Ahmad Faiz)', accessed 21 April 2020, https://www.youtube.com/watch?v=I_O3CbVhjCQ&t=16s.

[101] Agha Nasir, *Ham jitay ji masruf rahe*, 260–1 (translation mine). Also quoted in Jamil, *Zikr-e-Faiz*, 502–3. On the dancer Rakhshi, see Amjad Parvez, 'Rakhshi—the First Vamp/Dancer of Lollywood', *Daily Times*, 14 April 2020, https://dailytimes.com.pk/595320/rakhshi-the-first-vamp-dancer-of-lollywood/.

[102] Lassally, *Itinerant Cameraman*, 50.

> local release at all. But the shooting of this musical sequence caused us a lot of headaches, the first being the set – the only one to be built inside the stage – which represented the living room of a smart modern villa.

Nasir's remarks underscore the importance of the song, but Lassally clearly does not accord much significance to it. While in Lassally's recollection, this song was yet another 'complication', Nasir's remarks stress how the aesthetics of the song and the cinematography underscore the film's symbolic message. How to understand this sharply contrasting significance of the song? And what to make of the aesthetic disjuncture – between colour employed only for this sequence and black-and-white for the entire remaining film? The song sequence has unfortunately not surfaced so far, but we can speculate on its role based on the two remarks earlier.

In South Asian cinematic lexicon, an 'item number' is a sexualized song-and-dance sequence gratuitously inserted in a cinematic narrative in order to increase audiences, often where the female dancer has no other role in the film.[103] Indeed, in *Jago Hua Savera*, Rakhshi's screen presence is limited only to this sequence. Nevertheless, Nasir's remarks suggest that this sequence has importance beyond its 'item number' status and greatly contributes to the film's meaning in the South Asian context by distilling the sense of social disparity in a heightened and concentrated affective register. Which audiences are being activated by this song? Does inclusion of this possibly melodramatic picturization of '*Shishon ka masiha koi nahi*' only for *local* distribution cause *Jago Hua Savera* to vacillate between the neorealist and the social film genres, but remain a 'serious' film when seen abroad? We cannot definitively answer the latter question without viewing the lost song sequence, but Anna Morcom's gloss of the term 'filmi' provides a useful contrast. The term suggests 'the larger-than-life, showy, glittery, glamourous and overly dramatic film world, as opposed to the ordinary and mundane real world'.[104] Do these breaches of form, between colour and black-and-white footage, and the inclusion of a 'flimi' or commercial song-and-dance for a local audience in an otherwise austerely shot and scored film, suggest that we might understand this film's composition as a kind of pastiche, or an assemblage? This quality of artifice is also underscored by the *bhatiali* songs that are not presented here 'as they were' and as IPTA practitioners would have done,

[103] On the 'item number' see for example, Amanda Weidman, 'Voices of Meenakumari: Sound, Meaning, and Self-Fashioning in Performances of an Item Number', *South Asian Popular Culture* 10, no. 3 (2012), 307–18.

[104] Anna Morcom, *Hindi Film Songs and the Cinema* (Aldershot: Ashgate, 2007), 85.

but recast in Bhojpuri and Purbi and composed as extradiegetic aurality in an otherwise neorealist film.

Language and the limits of humanism

From the previous discussion, we can understand *Jago Hua Savera* as positioning itself between the humanist focus on the observation of difference that is primordial and eternal, and offering a critique of economic and social exploitation, or suggesting that existing conditions are unsustainable. The difficulties of this straddling are most evident on the question of linguistic aporia, across which subaltern voices are translated into dominant linguistic registers. In *La Terra Trema* Visconti had followed a peculiar strategy of deploying Sicilian as the spoken language of the film, rather than Italian. The dialogues were first developed with the actors, 'without a pre-established script, allowing the performers to form their characters and formulate the most authentic ways of expressing a given narrative situation or certain sentiments'.[105] But once finalized, the dialogues 'were endlessly rehearsed to ensure clarity', lending a sense of stilted unnaturalness to the final performance. Haaland stresses that 'no other film encapsulates the oral quality of neorealism or its exclusion of standard Italian with such rigour and with such sacrifices'. And Ray has observed that the acting is 'deliberate and stylized to the point of ballet'.[106] The voiceover in Italian interferes with the call for phenomenological immersion that the visuals hearken towards. Haaland notes that this creates a sense of 'estrangement' and disturbs the viewing experience, leading to the film's poor reception, but 'this anti-realistic effect may forge critical moments of self-awareness Visconti himself would have known in approaching the long-neglected South as a privileged Northerner'.[107]

Language in *Jago Hua Savera* is in some ways opposite to that of *La Terra Trema*. In *Jago Hua Savera*, the dialogue is spare, and meaning is conveyed primarily by cinematic composition. And rather than rigorously using a local vernacular in its dialogue, *Jago Hua Savera* deploys mostly a kind of pidgin North Indian language register understandable to Hindi and Urdu speakers. At rare moments, female characters do speak very briefly in Bengali, but they do

[105] Haaland, *Italian Neorealist Cinema*, 151.
[106] Ray, 'Some Italian Films I have Seen', 122.
[107] Haaland, *Italian Neorealist Cinema*, 151–2.

not speak much throughout the film.[108] Its eccentric character was 'a peculiar mixture' of simplified Urdu and Bengali that was 'easily understandable to neither communities',[109] and which contributed to its failure according to Alamgir Kabir.[110] Naeem Mohaiemen has termed the film an 'iconic, but ill-fated, hybrid (featuring an invented Urdu patois for East Bengal)'.[111] Rather than seeing linguistic difference itself as an issue that the film might have addressed in narrative terms, the film instead posits a kind of synthetic resolution, using a form that emphasizes cinematic and visual compositions and editing, but spare dialogue, to strive towards broader intelligibility. And the larger framing of the project itself brings up issues of how subalternaity is viewed from the vantage of gendered privilege – in this case with the additional twist in that it was enjoyed by the largely West Pakistani team of film-makers.

The film was not alone in this striving towards a shared intelligibility between Urdu and Bengali. For example, a 1959 essay in the establishment-oriented *Pakistan Quarterly* (Figure 3.6) argued on the basis of linguistic evidence that dominant regional languages of North India and West Pakistan and including Urdu and Bengali were derived from a common 'Primitive Prakrit' origin. Rather than evaluating the merits of the essay's argument, here I underscore the choice of the theme itself, which stresses a shared history that spans all the major regional languages of East and West Pakistan, and includes Urdu in its capacious ambit. Moreover, the text of the essay is placed in a symbolic graphic layout, framed by letters of the Urdu and Bangla alphabets. The left column is composed of Urdu letters linked together with calligraphic flourishes, while the right column attempts the same with the Bangla alphabet. On the top, the calligraphed English title is comparatively small in size, and placed in a dominant field of floating elements composed of the letters of the two alphabets and foliate patterns. The quest for linguistic breadth that would override the difference between Bengali and Urdu is thus enacted here through aesthetic form as well.

But by 1959, the year of *Jago Hua Savera*'s release and the publication of the article discussed earlier, this project of harmony was already freighted. The question of language differences between East and West Pakistan had emerged

[108] Sanjukta Sunderason comments: 'The question of dialect in *Jago Hua Savera* had struck me while watching the film. The minimal smattering of Bengali used in the film seems to have a sharp west Bengali accent. It could be an evident slip from the actresses from Calcutta, showing further how the local in the film was pastiche formulation.' Email communication, 4 October 2017.

[109] Kabir, *Cinema in Pakistan*, 43.

[110] Ibid., 71.

[111] Naeem Mohaiemen, 'Simulation at Wars' End: A "Documentary" in the Field of Evidence Quest', *BioScope: South Asian Screen Studies* 7, no. 1 (1 July 2016), 35.

Figure 3.6 Layout of Muhammad Shahidullah's essay, 'Common Origin of Urdu and Bengali', *Pakistan Quarterly*, Autumn 1959.

in 1948, right after the creation of Pakistan.[112] The 1952 language movement was suppressed violently; it became central to the consciousness of East Pakistanis in subsequent years, and it is commemorated by the Shaheed Minar located at the centre of Dhaka, first erected in 1952 in a makeshift guerrilla act during curfew. (In its permanent form, it is perhaps Bangladesh's most iconic monument now). And *Hamari Zaban* (Our Language), a film produced in Karachi, whose theme is reported to assert the position of Urdu against Bengali, had been released in 1955.[113] The issue of language would have been quite a central problem especially for leftist intellectuals, who had already witnessed the traumatic effects of the Partition, in which the Hindi–Urdu divide was central.

The specific linguistic character of Faiz's contribution to the lyrics and the dialogue of *Jago Hua Savera* can perhaps be understood through Aamir Mufti's detailed analysis of a poem by Faiz written in 1965, right after the war between India and Pakistan. Mufti notes that in '*Sipahi ka marsiya*' ('Soldier's Elegy') Faiz eschews the Persianate diction of 'high' Urdu, and instead 'turns to an idiom whose resonances are . . . "Hindavi"'.[114] Mufti further notes:[115]

[112] For an overview, see Willem van Schendel, *A History of Bangladesh*.

[113] 'Hamari Zaban'. *Motion Picture Archive of Pakistan*, accessed 8 August 2017. http://www.mpaop.org/mpaop/pak-film-database/chronological-of-films/1955-2/hamari-zaban/. I have been unable to find a copy of *Hamari Zaban*.

[114] Aamir Mufti, *Enlightenment in the Colony: The Jewish Question and the Crisis of Postcolonial Culture* (Princeton: Princeton University Press, 2007), 230.

[115] Mufti, *Enlightenment in the Colony*, 231.

> The poem opens up a window on the vast linguistic-literary vista – Braj, Avadhi, Bhojpuri, Dakhni, Maithli, Rajasthani, to name just a handful of the vernacular language forms that the northern region (and its southern outposts) have produced over the centuries – that has been occluded from view in the standardization of rival 'Hindi' and 'Urdu' registers . . . [in the poem] the surface of modern language is peeled off to reveal submerged sounds and meanings.

One might therefore consider the experiment in the language of *Jago Hua Savera* analogously: as an attempt to bring the intimate stranger into an affective relation with the self. Nevertheless, one notes that Bengali remains absent in the linguistic register Mufti has identified earlier, falling outside intelligibility even by this expanded North Indian linguistic register. The problem of linguistic incommunicability in *Jago Hua Savera* thus could not be addressed by dialogic incorporation towards a greater synthesis.

On the other hand, it is also the case that progressive writers were concerned to focus on issues of social exploitation that would elicit wider solidarities, rather than focusing on ethnic and linguistic divisions that was fuel to the fires of communal divisions and violence that led to and attended the 1947 Partition. Moreover, an argument can be made that during the late 1950s, a film attempting to reach a wider audience in South Asia (including eastern Bengal) might deploy the widely legible and simplified Hindi–Urdu that Bombay cinema had broadly popularized. David Lunn and Madhumita Lahiri have independently argued that 'Hindustani', an emerging spoken composite idiom, developed in the commercial films from Bombay after the arrival of the talkies in 1931.[116] Lahiri notes:

> Unfolding in the Marathi speaking region of western India, with numerous Bengali, Punjabi and Urdu speakers in the mix, Hindustani, in the sense of a mixed, accessible argot becomes the de facto and de jure language of this commercial sound cinema known as Bollywood, which I use here to refer to a consolidated filmmaking idiom, not simply any film made in Bombay (now Mumbai). The language . . . is a flexible, miscible, endlessly expanding collage, using the syntactical structure common to Hindi and Urdu, but throwing in words from other languages at will: Persian, Sanskrit, Punjabi . . .

Although commercial films' aesthetics have been endlessly disparaged by purists, yet this is an arena in which serious writers affiliated with the Progressive Writers'

[116] Madhumita Lahiri, 'An Idiom for India: Hindustani and the Limits of the Language Concept', *Interventions: International Journal of Postcolonial Studies* 18, no. 1 (2016), 60–85; David Lunn, 'The Eloquent Language: Hindustani in 1940s Indian Cinema', *BioScope: South Asian Screen Studies* 6, no. 1 (1 January 2015), 1–26.

Association consciously participated in. They had been committed to Hindustani as a language that could overcome regional and religious divides.[117] And in a largely nonliterate South Asia of the mid-twentieth century, they understood film's vast potential to address audiences far beyond the reach of other mediums. It's worth stressing that many Hindi–Urdu films had been produced in Calcutta, including several in the mid-1930s by director Abdur Rashid Kardar (none other than the brother of A. J. Kardar). Bengal was thus no stranger to the production and circulation of Hindi–Urdu cinema. Indeed, the use of an idiom that Bombay and Lahore cinemas had helped forge was also prevalent in cinema in both East and West Pakistan, and Dhaka in the 1960s emerged as an important centre for film-making in Urdu, with over fifty releases by 1971.[118] Moreover, exchange of film personnel between Lahore and Dhaka was not unusual, and Lotte Hoek has argued: 'Between 1958 and 1971, the film industry of Pakistan straddled Lahore, Karachi, and Dhaka in a cross-wing love affair between stars and audiences, producers and profit, directors and fame, which could not always be assigned exclusively to either East or West, Urdu or Bengali.'[119]

On the other hand, East Bengal's focus on Bengali-language cultural forms during the mid-twentieth century marked its departure from the multiple porous layers of cultural forms in Calcutta and West Bengal. Willem van Schendel has stressed that emerging developments in East Bengal after 1947 were forging a new national cultural trajectory that diverged from both Calcutta and Lahore, which was 'not bilingual (Bengali–English or Bengali–Urdu)', and in which expression in Bengali language was central.[120] Consequently, the absence of

[117] Madhumita Lahiri, 'An Idiom for India: Hindustani and the Limits of the Language Concept', 76–7.

[118] 'Movies from East Pakistan, Dacca', *Pakistan Film Magazine*, accessed 4 April 2021, https://pakmag.net/film/db/EastPakistanFilms.php. Bengali/Urdu double versions number 13, while another 41 are Urdu-only releases through 1971. Moreover, industry personnel would move across Dhaka, Lahore, and Karachi from the 1950s onwards, and this continued after 1971, as exemplified by the team involved in the blockbuster Lahore film *Aina* (Mirror) (1977, dir. Nazrul Islam). See Lotte Hoek, 'Mirrors of Movement: *Aina*, Afzal Chowdhury's Cinematography and the Interlinked Histories of Cinema in Pakistan and Bangladesh', *Screen* 57, no. 4 (Winter 2016), 488–95. Alamgir Kabir notes that the release of the Dhaka made Urdu film *Chanda* (1962, dir. Ehtesham) marked a shift in films made in Dhaka for a few years until about 1965, with more emphasis on Urdu-language productions. Alamgir Kabir, *Film in Bangladesh* (Dacca: Bangla Academy, 1979), 27. Also see Raju, *Bangladesh Cinema and National Identity*, 84–5.

[119] Lotte Hoek, 'Cross-Wing Filmmaking: East Pakistani Urdu Films and Their Traces in the Bangladesh Film Archive'. *BioScope: South Asian Screen Studies* 5, no. 2 (1 July 2014), 105.

[120] 'The Pakistan period was not only a time of political and economic struggle; it was also a time of crucial cultural change. After 1947 the inhabitants of the Bengal delta had a lot of rethinking to do. What did it mean to be a Bengali now that the old centre of Bengali culture, Kolkata (Calcutta), had become inaccessible . . . . What set this emerging elite apart was that they were not bilingual (Bengali–English or Bengali–Urdu) and that their frame of reference was the Bengal delta, not the entire subcontinent or all of Pakistan. Their new cultural style was . . . popular rather than aristocratic, open-minded rather than orthodox and delta-focused rather than national. Most importantly, it was expressed in the Bengali language. Dhaka and other rapidly growing towns in East Pakistan became

Bengali-language materials or explanation, in *Jago Hua Savera*'s opening credits, as substantive dialogue, as song, as subtitle or in the booklet is telling – it marks the unawareness in West Pakistani intelligentsia of the specificity of the emerging public linguistic and cultural sphere in East Pakistan.

Closing thoughts

Jago Hua Savera is best seen as an experimental project and a kind of opening gambit, rather than a product of a mature ecology of serious, experimental film-making accompanied by a robust discursive reception that would subject such ventures to critical scrutiny in Pakistan. It might have been received as a serious film in a wider South Asian context, and as we have seen, its production and its theme emphatically invites such a reception. But political and cultural currents ran in the reverse direction. Growing tensions between India and Pakistan since the 1950s led to the banning of new Indian films in Pakistan by 1962. The 1965 war between India and Pakistan put an end to all exchange of films across borders. Widespread systematic racism among West Pakistanis towards the inhabitants of East Pakistan also foreclosed genuine critical possibilities for dialogic understanding across languages, ethnicities and life-worlds. In contrast to the parallel cinema that developed in India with government support, in Pakistan, conditions of patronage and reception were not conducive to build upon the experiment in a sustained manner.[121] The project of leftist film-making in Pakistani commercial cinema continued, however, in the films of Khalil Qaiser and Riaz Shahid of the late 1950s and 1960s, some of which also examine minor and subaltern lives under exploitative circumstances.

The project of *Jago Hua Savera* also had to confront impassable aporias: its relevance for local publics and its legibility in the film festival circuit abroad; its breach of neorealist aesthetics in its songs and dialogues; and the strangeness of its linguistic register as it sought to overcome divides that were to become intractable. Moreover, as primarily the vision of West Pakistanis, *Jago Hua Savera*

centres of this cultural renewal.' Willem van Schendel, *A History of Bangladesh*, 152. Also cited in Raju, *Bangladesh Cinema and National Identity*, 116.

121 Faiz wrote lyrics for the film, *Sukh Ka Sapna* (Distant Dream) (1962, dir. Masood Pervaiz). The leftist journalist and writer Hamid Akhtar (1924–2011) contributed its dialogues. I have been unable to find a copy of this film. On Akhtar, see Kamran Asdar Ali, *Communism in Pakistan: Politics and Class Activism, 1947-1972* (London: I. B. Tauris, 2015). Faiz also contributed lyrics to the Khalil Qaiser directed films *Shaheed* (Martyr) (1962) and *Farangi* (The European) (1964); *Qaidi* (Prisoner) (1962, dir. Najam Naqvi, and *Ghoonghat* (The Veil) (1962, dir. Khurshid Anwar). On Faiz's involvement in cinema, see Jamil, *Zikr-e-Faiz*, 500–9.

was caught between a humanism that saw rural life in East Bengal as lyrical and timeless, and a progressive stance that viewed these conditions as exploitative and unsustainable. Nevertheless, I propose that it is precisely *Jago Hua Savera*'s fault lines that are most salient for today's context. The film asks important questions about the relevance of an artistic form for its historical, social and aesthetic significance. To what degree is fidelity to a genre like neorealism meaningful in South Asia where the commercial film has long reigned supreme? Who are the publics for a socially relevant cinema? How does a narrative artistic form overcome ethnicity, language and other differences in its address without losing its locational specificity? Alamgir Kabir was sharply critical of *Jago Hua Savera* precisely for its awkward language and for its exoticizing of the riverine landscape of East Bengal. Nevertheless, his comment, that *Jago Hua Savera* 'still remains the only example of efficient film-making in Pakistan', published in his book as late as in 1969, suggests that Kabir also valued the cinematic approach of *Jago Hua Savera*, as well as the questions that it raised, as being important for subsequent serious cinema to grapple with, and which is discussed by Lotte Hoek in her contribution in this volume.[122] Writing about the film six decades later, one acknowledges that *Jago Hua Savera* has played a spectral role in subsequent cultural developments, and that it holds important lessons for the future. Above all, it serves as a stark reminder of collaborative progressive paths not taken, and that still need to be revisited, if South Asia is ever to emerge from its ongoing predicament brought upon by exclusivist and hostile nationalisms.

Appendix A

Excerpts from the *Jago Hua Savera* booklet

On the 31st of December, 1957, an event, now cinema history, took place at Shaitnol, a tiny fishing village, on the banks of the river Meghna, 30 miles from Dacca, the capital of East Pakistan. In the darkness of the New Year's eve lit by kerosene and gas lamps, the first short of JAGO HUA SAVERA was taken.

On the 19th of April, 1958, three and a half months later, the unit that had assembled from half way around the world to shoot the film, disbanded. Between these three and a half months lies the story of one of the great pioneering efforts in cinema history. In 1958, East Pakistan had practically no film production

[122] Kabir, *Cinema in Pakistan*, 71.

tradition. A government sponsored film corporatirn [*sic*] had just been initiated. A makeshift laboratory and a small floor were the only apparent signs of film production in the country.

Equipment had been ordered but most of it was either still in crates or under shipment from U.K. and U.S.A. There was hardly a technician in the country with feature-film experience.

The task of setting up camp at Shaitnol was a major problem in itself. East Pakistan has few roads and the only means of communication open to the unit was slow river transport. Every single item necessary for the intricate requirements of a feature film had to be packed and taken to the location – unto fresh water supplies! Prefabricated hutments, tents and house-boats were assembled to house the unit. The whole operation was planned and tackled with the precision of a military objective. The three and a half months' time schedule allowed no room for mistakes or retakes.

A FOREWARD [*sic*] on behalf of the Producers by NAUMAN TASEER

By far the greatest problem was that of casting. Hundreds of persons were interviewed and photographed before billing almost a dozen major roles. With the exception of one artiste, every other member of the cast was appearing before the camera for the first time. Never before have so many new faces been cast in a film – never before have so many emerged as 'stars' from any one film.

The unit that set to work on JAGO HUA SAVERA was indeed strange by any normal standard. The director was carrying out his first assignment. His previous experience was nil. Trained for the merchant marine he had given up his love for the sea for his passion for filming. A young German cameraman and an equally young British sound recordist comprised the team. A well-known leading poet of Pakistan threw in his lot to write the story – his very first brush with cinema!

The entire film was shot on location in a minimum of time – 48 working days – and with the barest of equipment. A hand-held camera had to take the place of a dolly. Throughout most of the shooting a blimp was not available. The artistes, many of whom were picked from the location itself, had to record each dialogue, after the day's shooting, for dubbing later.

Seldom has a team dared so much . . . Seldom has it achieved so much . . .

It is too early, yet, to assess the impact of this film on Pakistan's film industry, but this much is certain: JAGO HUA SAVERA marks the beginning of the avante guard [*sic*] movement in this country!

4

Lotus roots

Transposing a political-aesthetic agenda from South Asia to Afro-Asia

Maia Ramnath

Introduction

The Afro-Asian Writers Association, literary wing of the Soviet-backed Afro-Asian People's Solidarity Organization, used its triennial journal *Lotus* as a vehicle for its mission of renewal and resistance in the global south, thereby playing a key role in the cultural Cold War on Third World fronts. But from another angle, *Lotus* can also be seen as the direct culmination of the aesthetic and political agenda of the South Asian Progressive Writers Association, a project based upon enlisting culture as a weapon against the forces of reaction and as a tool for progressive auto-transformation, but now expanded from a subcontinental to a transcontinental scale.

When the PWA was launched in the 1930s by Indian radical intellectuals then in London, they positioned themselves as a force for progressive change inside India (setting themselves against what they read as the symbiosis of colonial rule and capitalist exploitation with the homegrown forces of feudal, patriarchal and religious oppression), and simultaneously as the Indian branch of a global cultural front against fascism. During the 1940s they mobilized cultural activists in support of the war effort, the national liberation struggle, famine relief and communal harmony.

But for the Progressive Writers and the Communist Party(s) to which many of them belonged, the realization of formal independence for India and Pakistan in 1947 did not mark the endpoint of the struggle for true liberation. That would require socialist revolution in the subcontinent, and independence in the parts of Asia and Africa still subject to colonial and neocolonial rule. Thus their mission remained unchanged, though the domestic and geopolitical conditions had evolved into a new phase. The Cold War too was born in 1947; this was the context that framed the PWA stalwarts' affiliation with the AAWA and defined their post-war field of transnational activity, even as the organization seemed to have passed the peak of its stature and influence at home.

Some observers and historians called the convening of a 1956 Asian Writers' Conference in Delhi the PWA's 'last significant achievement'[1] before fading into a period of decline. But from an international(ist) perspective, this was not an end but a transition, and their first significant step towards launching a new phase for their work: a shift to another forum wherein they made up in international prominence what they lost in domestic clout. Not that they would necessarily have chosen that trade-off; why not both?

Several of the key founders and architects of the PWA played equally important roles in the AAWA, and left their unmistakable fingerprints upon its mission statement and its style. Most notably, these included memoirist Sajjad Zaheer and novelist Mulk Raj Anand, who had both helped draft the initial PWA manifesto and laid the groundwork for its organizational birth and sustainment in India and overseas, and the renowned poet Faiz Ahmad Faiz, one of the earliest leaders in the progressive literary movement and later nearly synonymous with its development in Pakistan. Zaheer, Anand, Faiz and Bengali poet Subhash Mukhopadhyay all served at some point on the *Lotus* editorial board (Faiz as editor-in-chief from 1978 to 1984) or the Lotus Prize literary adjudication committee. Clearly after the mid-1950s they didn't disappear but rather shifted aspects of their work increasingly abroad, in a concentric broadening of focus.[2] Therefore the best window through which to glimpse the PWA's political concerns manifesting through aesthetic imagery from that point onward may be in the pages of *Lotus*.

From PWA to AAWA

At the peak of their influence during the 1940s, the PWA had sought no less than to democratize art, changing the nature of literature to reflect the lives and interests of peasants, workers and emancipated women instead of aristocratic or bourgeois elites, and in essence to change reality by portraying reality, in all its

1 Rakhshanda Jalil, *Liking Progress, Loving Change: A Literary History of the Progressive Writers' Movement in Urdu* (Delhi: Oxford University Press, 2014), 359.

2 For an exposition of this idea see Faiz, 'The Artist's Three Circles of Being', *Lotus* 57 (1986), 9–12.

dialectic dynamism. Their oft-repeated guiding principle was 'art for life's sake, not art for art's sake'. Artists had to be engaged, not secluded; intellectuals were to work on the ground, not in the ivory tower. In a struggle of good and evil (or in other words, progress and reaction), neutrality was impossible; writers could only be partisan. 'Our faith . . . in literature as a weapon is beyond question', wrote one member taking part in a discussion reassessing the direction of the movement in 1953. 'The last two decades have further reinforced our belief that there is no literature that does not take sides and that no writer can pretend to be neutral and free from politics.' This should not, however, make them dogmatic and sectarian.[3] And while progressivism was deemed to reside primarily in content rather than in form, there were still strong recommendations for the forms most suitable to render such content effectively to its desired audiences.

For prose, in effect this came to mean socialist realism in line with the prescriptions of Andrei Zhdanov, the Soviet cultural policy chief who had so rigorously matched an aesthetic to a political party line. For poetry, it meant adding a new index of meaning for the repertory of imagery (gardens, roses, nightingales, moths and flames, dark nights and bright mornings, lonely roads, taverns, winecups) familiar in the Hindustani and Persian poetry traditions, layering a third resonance under the one that already equated the language of erotic love and longing to ecstatic union with the divine; now the same tropes signified oppression, revolution, liberation. For drama, it meant agitprop street theatre: many of the Progressive Writers were also closely associated with the Indian People's Theatre Association (IPTA), which, along with revolutionary mushairas, enabled them to reach audiences far beyond the pool of the literate and educated. Making use of traditional folk forms of music and performance, they delivered content on contemporary political and social issues such as the exploitation of the people by factory owners, foremen, moneylenders and landlords; the brutality of imperial rule and fascist aggression; communal violence and the famine that devastated Bengal through decidedly non-natural causes during the war years.

After 1947, the PWA and IPTA became more closely associated than ever with the CPI and especially with the new CPP. As the party went through a hard-left sectarian phase in both countries between 1948 and 1950, so did the associated cultural apparatus. This interlude proved very damaging to the organization, leaving it dangerously vulnerable to state repression, while alienating or

[3] *Indian Literature* #2 (1952). In Sudhi Pradhan (ed.), *Marxist Cultural Movement in India: Chronicles and Documents, vol III* (Delhi: National Book Agency, 1979).

ostracizing many artists and writers from the larger community of culture. Although they retreated from that level of ideological strictness and attempted to revive the organization in India, they never quite managed to recover the level of zeitgeist dynamism they had enjoyed prior to partition.

Meanwhile in Pakistan, they were virtually wiped out for the time being by Ayub Khan's military dictatorship. Embracing an alliance with the United States through its Cold War security pacts and CIA-backed cultural initiatives, Ayub's efforts to crush the domestic left included heavy censorship of journalists and academics, proscribing of socialist literature from libraries and bookstores, and detention of activists. Faiz and Zaheer were jailed in connection with a 1951 conspiracy case teaming communists with disgruntled army officers in a failed effort to overthrow the government. The CPP was banned in 1954, along with organizations deemed a threat to national security. This included the PWA insofar as it engaged with political and not just literary activity; their definition of literature, of course, made it inseparable from the political. Upon coming to power in 1958, Ayub destroyed any socialist literature to be found in public libraries, shut down the People's Publishing House bookshop in Lahore and took over Progressive Papers Limited and its various PWA-edited publications. According to Hafiz Malik, this loss of income and outlet for left voices was the final blow.[4] With Faiz again jailed in 1958 – after his return from an Afro-Asian writers meeting in Tashkent and Moscow, Habib Jalib took up the mantle of next-generation Progressive poet-warrior, beloved of workers and students, weaponizing his mushairas against the regime and its cooptation of writers.

Meanwhile the soul of the Progressive movement (and along with it, Progressivism's outward-looking Afro-Asian sensibility) may have found a refuge in the eastern wing, where the fact that the popular party could be portrayed as both too left-ish and too Indian-ish (in a word, too Bengali) for the Western-based rulership was a harbinger of their eventual separation. In 1957 the National Awami Party was established in Dhaka, merging left and progressive formations. In any case, whether in the west or east, the progressive cultural forces were now in a repressed and oppositional position relative to the government, in contrast to the patriotic renown they had enjoyed during the independence movement. Upon being released from jail, Faiz began a long and influential cultural career in Pakistan while Zaheer returned to India.

[4] According to Hafiz Malik, Qasmi had edited *Imroz* since 1953, and Faiz had returned to the *Pakistan Times* after his release in 1955. Malik, 'The Marxist Literary Movement in India and Pakistan', *Journal of Asian Studies* 26, no. 4 (August 1996), 660.

In the early 1950s both PWAs returned to the ideal of a united front, both domestically and internationally, this time locating themselves in an international context defined not primarily by anti-fascism as in the 1930s, but by Afro-Asian solidarity in the decolonizing world. Anti-imperialism and anti-racism provided the threads of continuity between the two political articulations. In July 1956, PWA co-founder Mulk Raj Anand along with other Progressive Writers active in the World Peace and Afro-Asian Solidarity movements formed a committee to organize an Asian Writers' Conference in Delhi.[5] The draft agenda listed topics such as the current state of literature in Afro-Asian countries, cultural exchange, writers' freedom and the writer's trade.[6] Some items reached grandly, but vaguely, beyond the strictly literary towards a 'common search for a new life in Asia', enrichment of 'her common culture . . .[,]civilization', and language. Writers from India, Burma, China, Korea, Nepal and Vietnam signed an appeal asserting that 'During the centuries of foreign domination . . . many strands of our traditional civilizations were disrupted, integral ways of life disturbed or broken, our educational systems perverted, and our whole cultures sought to be debased. . . . Now, writers of Asia should meet' to analyse these disruptions, evaluate their cultural heritages, and together seek conditions for new creation.[7] Two hundred delegates attended, from the previously mentioned countries plus Egypt, Iran, Japan, Mongolia, Syria and Pakistan, each delivering reports on their national literatures. It was agreed, controversially, that controversial issues (i.e. partisan commentary relating to the politics of the Cold War) would be kept off the agenda. The gathering then split into four working groups which would present reports on the last day, on topics that reflected some long-standing preoccupations of the PWs while previewing those of the AAWs: freedom of speech and how to balance writers' autonomy with their social responsibility; the need for greater cultural exchange; Asian cultural traditions (this working group was certain there was indeed such a thing as an Asian culture, although they struggled to articulate exactly what that was); protection of writers' interests as a trade and infrastructure for maximizing dissemination of their work to readers. In closing, the Chinese delegation suggested that a committee be formed to plan a second conference, and Uzbek poet Zulfia Khanum extended an invitation on behalf of the Soviet Writers' delegation to hold it in Tashkent.

5 Sajjad Zaheer, 'Yaden', in *Marxist Cultural Movement in India: Chronicles and Documents*, vol. I, ed. Sudhi Pradhan (Delhi: National Book Agency, 1979), 6.

6 M. V. Desai, 'The Asian Writers' Conference December 1956: New Delhi', *Books Abroad* 31, 3 (Summer 1957), 243–5.

7 Ibid., 243.

The Soviet delegation had sent formal greetings from 4,000 writers of 60 languages, claiming to represent a multinational Soviet literature with significant Central Asian elements. Among them Anatoly Sofronov (Soviet Writers' Union secretary) recalled that attending the conference left his compatriots 'full of emotion. At Delhi we considered questions concerning the consolidation of all the progressive forces of Asia. [And] We discussed the fate of the struggle for the African continent, which at that time was still closed to us.'[8] To his home organization, both strategically and idealistically, the cultural workers of the decolonizing global south were crucial Cold War partners. To Zaheer, the significance of the event was that so many Asian and Soviet writers were able to encounter one another as part of a greater 'current of liberation and renaissance . . . sweeping among the hitherto subject peoples of Asia, Africa and Latin America.'[9]

The following year, the inaugural meeting of the Afro-Asian People's Solidarity Organization (AAPSO) was held in Cairo (December 1957 to January 1958). Then in November 1958, 200 delegates from about 40 countries gathered in Tashkent, its public squares decked out in flags and the conference emblem of hands from five continents joined together, to welcome its guests. Some arrived from places of exile, others from working on Radio Moscow's various language programmes in Russia.[10] Aside from the Central Asian Soviet republics the biggest delegation was India's, with ample PWA representation among its twenty-eight members.[11] Pakistan was represented by only two writers: Faiz and Hafeez Jalandhari. As a member of the conference organizing committee, Faiz had hoped to include a large Pakistani delegation, but the government, wary of displeasing the United States, would grant only these two visas.[12] The PWA imprint on the 1958 Tashkent conference closed a circle begun in the 1930s, when the Soviet Writers' Conference had influenced the founding of the anti-fascist International Congress of Writers for the Defense of Culture, and the PWA.

The South Asian writers were particularly eager to meet their Central Asian colleagues, with whom they traced cultural ties dating back many centuries 'since the days of Kanishka', when Buddhism spread to central Asia, and from

8 Anatoli Sofronov, *Lotus* #26 (October–December 1975), 17.
9 Zaheer, 'Yaden', 7.
10 Krishnalal Shridharani, 'Association and Isolation at Tashkent', *Indian Literature* 2, no. 1 (October 1958 to March 1959), 60.
11 Zaheer, 7. These were Anand, Zaheer, Haldar, Sharma, Yashpal and others.
12 Ali Madeeh Hashmi, *Love and Revolution: Faiz Ahmed Faiz, the Authorized Biography* (New Delhi: Rupa Publications, 2016), 186.

where a millennium later the Mughals themselves had entered India. The ancestors of Amir Khusrau and Ghalib, lights of classical Urdu literature, were, like the Mughal founder Babar, from Uzbekistan. Certain words, practices, bits of architecture or music and elements of cuisine all felt uncannily familiar to the South Asians. Future *Lotus* editor-in-chief Youssef el-Sebai described the city as a paradise of gardens and fruit trees, mixing new apartment blocks in its various ethnic quarters with old houses furnished in traditional Islamic style, with rugs and low divans. Meanwhile model hospitals, schools and collective farms never failed to make a big impression on visitors, who marvelled at machines harvesting cotton while ruddy, healthy peasants made music and danced.[13] So Tashkent was special to them, representing perhaps the aspirational quintessence of Afro-Asian-ness, in that it combined its resonance of ancient cultural kinship with its modernity as well-equipped capital of a socialist republic.

Indian journalist Krishnalal Shridharani simultaneously experienced an exciting sense of camaraderie as an Asian, and 'a splendid isolation or utter loneliness' as a writer. Half the Indian delegation, he felt, were ideologues or at least 'willing to look at poetry and drama and life through ideological eyes'. Yet he thought that it was his colleagues' Indian-ness – their cultural specificity – not their communism, that brought something unique to the conference, because the communism was like everyone else's. India's message, however, was 'that a conference of writers should be a conference of writers and not of politicians or of willing or unwilling tools of politicians'.[14] In other words, the AAWA should be distinct from (while supplementary to) the AAPSO. Perhaps this was because Indian writers were tracing the origins of this gathering to the 1956 Delhi Conference, which they proudly claimed as the extension of a twenty-year-old literary movement,[15] whereas the Soviets were tracing its origins to the 1957–8 Cairo Conference, making it the extension of a one-year-old political body. In a sense *Lotus* was the child of both parents.

It was also a question of emphasis. The Indians asserted literature's link to life and politics beyond any doubt; that was their foundational principle. But they still foregrounded literature. Colonialism was the context for their concerns with freedom of expression and the growth of indigenous literatures, but this

[13] *Lotus* #23 (January–March 1975). See also Faiz's *Mah-o-Sal-e-Ashnae* (1979); Mahmuduzzafar's *Quest for Life* (1954).

[14] Shridharani, 'Association and Isolation at Tashkent', 57–8.

[15] Zaheer in 'Afro-Asian Writers Movement', *Contemporary Indian Literature*. 10, no. 3–4 (1970). remarks that Indian writers should be proud that this thing began in India, at the Asian Writers Conference in Delhi in December, 1956.

wouldn't be a writers' conference if they were to speak only of instrumentalizing literature for struggle, or how various playwrights and poets had also battled colonialism. And yet, at hearing such notions, 'whispers filled the magnificent corridors of the Navoi Theatre' where the conference was taking place '. . . to the effect that the Indian delegation was anti-anti-colonialism'. Shridharani recalled consulting with delegation spokesperson Tarashankar Bannerjee (of the original Bengal PWA), who said, 'We have fought against colonialism and we will continue to fight against colonialism. We go even further. We are opposed to any form of domination of one country by another.' However, he stressed that 'threats to freedom come in many forms and from many quarters', including, he did not say aloud, conformist peer pressure, postcolonial governments or authoritarian socialist ones, 'and so the writer should be ever vigilant to his conscience'.[16]

Might this have had something to do with the fact that India already had its independence, while not all of those present yet did? If so, it would explain India's eagerness to emphasize culture-building whereas those still under colonial rule felt the greater urgency of resistance. They were simply at different stages of the process. Shridharani, too, noted that some '[had] not yet won their independence and the maturity which is its result',[17] although his unfortunately patronizing tone suggests either short-sightedness or a short memory. The other moments of discord Shridharani identified had to do with the fact that 'We were meeting in a country whose writers even fail to see any difference between art and propaganda, between the writer and the "engineer of the soul"', a phrase referencing Zhdanov/ Stalin in 1934, 'on the ground that life is one' with art.[18] However, the issue was not really about *whether* art was connected to life, but *in what way* life was suffused with explicit politics.

Would *Lotus* indicate an answer to this conundrum? Along the delicate balance its creators walked between political instrumentality and artistic expression, the fact that it was a literary magazine is perhaps the answer. AAPSO already circulated a monthly *Afro-Asian Bulletin* edited by M. Kalimullah, the Indian member of the AAPSO Permanent Secretariat and a veteran of the PWA.[19] This was a digest of news updates, organizational and policy documents,

[16] Shridharani, 'Association and Isolation at Tashkent', 59.

[17] Ibid., 59–60.

[18] Ibid., 59.

[19] AAPSO, 66–7. Kalimullah appears as Lahore branch spokesperson in 1946 reports: See Pradhan, 330–6; he had attended PWA meetings in Bombay back in the 1940s: see Hamid Akhtar, *Rudad-e-Anjuman* (Lahore: Book Home Publishers, 2011).

reports on the doings of the various national branches and occupational sections (including Writers', Jurists', Women's and Youth wings). The *Bulletin* sometimes printed poetry, and *Lotus* printed special sections of documents from the major AAWA conferences transcribing agendas, addresses and resolutions, but *Lotus*'s function did not replicate the *Bulletin*. It pledged allegiance to the same agenda, but via the artistic and literary niche specific to cultural workers. While propagandists might insist that the list of analytical points, policy priorities and slogans determined at the latest conference needed to be repeated in every text, writers argued that since they were a part of the same larger organization, adherence to these points should go without saying; poems and stories should be unencumbered to express the emotions of Afro-Asian struggles and the experiences of Afro-Asian realities.

Back home, the Indian Writers Association for Afro-Asian Solidarity had its first meeting in Calcutta, in November 1961. Former PWA general secretary Abdul Aleem presided over the first session, opening with a recitation of Tagore's poem 'Africa', after which fraternal delegates from the USSR, Indonesia and the Arab League presented greetings. In the rhetoric generated, one might easily have taken any of the PWA statements from the previous twenty years and simply replaced the word 'India' with 'Afro-Asia', and the word 'unity' with 'solidarity':

> We the Indian writers, wholeheartedly welcome the great upsurge for solidarity, which is sweeping across Asia and Africa, and which is lending courage and sustenance to the freedom fighters in various lands. It is this great awareness of our common destiny, that has forced imperialism and colonialism to retreat and suffer defeat after defeat. It is our united struggle that is responsible, to a great extent, in staying the hand of imperialism for unleashing another world war.[20]

Eighty writers attended from throughout the country, PWA veterans prominent among them. As the Indian branch of the AAWA, the Indian Writers Association for Afro-Asian Solidarity was now virtually indistinguishable on paper from the AIPWA. Its declaration made two observations about India's position in the world freedom struggle. First, that '[t]hough India has attained freedom, the fight for social and economic justice and equality', for complete democracy and prosperity, still continued. 'We are also aware that imperialism has not changed

[20] Report on the Calcutta conference of November 4–5. *Afro-Asian Bulletin* 3 (September–October 1961), 14.

its character and is trying to regain its hold on our political, economic and cultural life.'[21] Second, that

> The Writers of the newly liberated countries of Asia and Africa, who are engaged in consolidating their freedom by rebuilding their economic, social and cultural life are also faced with similar problems as ours. . . . On the other hand, writers and intellectuals of these Afro-Asian countries, which are still under colonial rule – writers of Algeria, Angola, South Africa, Goa & other countries – are engaged in a life and death struggle along with their people[.][22]

What this meant in practical terms was that the Indian writers were identifying cultural development as a component of anti-colonialism, while recognizing the different phases of the same anti-colonial struggle unfolding in multiple locations, against both new and old modes of imperialism.

Anand, as general secretary of the Association, submitted a report on Tashkent, the wave of Afro-Asian awakening and the current global 'conflict of ideas'. He contrasted the colonial violence of the Western export of ideas with India's historically peaceful cultural influence on its neighbours – at least, as he wanted to see it – most recently in leading by example the way to decolonization. However, 'Recalling the fraternal cooperation extended by intellectuals abroad' during India's freedom struggle, 'Dr. Anand said that "India has, unfortunately, not repaid the debt."'[23] Solidarity was now owed to the rest of Afro-Asia. Zaheer disagreed that Indian intellectuals were neglecting Afro-Asian solidarity, though he admitted much more should be done. The peoples of Africa, engaged in a massive liberation effort, were looking to India, which had preceded them, for more support – so far inadequate. The delegates chosen in Calcutta for the upcoming Cairo conference 'must not go empty-handed. We must take the "finest flowers" from the works of Indian writers' to present to their counterparts. (And that would be adequate support?)

One way that India identified for itself a special link and a special lever to press in solidarity with African anti-colonialism (perhaps more powerful than the literary blossoms recommended by Zaheer) was through Goa, which as noted at Bandung and reported in the *Bulletin*, lay under the same regime as Angola, Mozambique and Guinea-Bissau. Zaheer, Anand, Aleem and other PWA veterans spoke prominently on Angola and Goa, yoked together as

[21] *Afro-Asian Bulletin* 3 (September–October 1961). Calcutta Conference Supplement: 'Writers, Unite and Uphold the Human Dignity!' ('A Declaration of the First National Conference of the Indian Writers' Association for Afro-Asian Solidarity'), 13.

[22] Ibid.

[23] *Afro-Asian Bulletin* 3 (September–October 1961), 17.

Portuguese colonies. Furthermore, Portugal was a NATO ally, and where it was – the subcontinent and the Indian Ocean – NATO bases could be. Thus Goan decolonization would be one tactical tumbler in the combination lock of the world anti-imperialist struggle.[24]

Goan independence activist Berta Menezes Braganza was a recurring contributor to the *Afro-Asian Bulletin*: an Indian military action there, she urged, could save the Goan people from the nightmare of 'fascist madness' under Antonio Salazar's control, and gladden the hearts of the anti-colonial forces throughout the world. She concluded, 'IT WILL . . . MEAN VALUABLE AND ACTIVE ASSISTANCE TO THE BRAVE ANGOLAN PEOPLE WHO ARE FIGHTING THE SAME ENEMY. IT WILL INDEED BE THE MOST EFFECTIVE SOLIDARITY WITH ANGOLA.'[25] Anand's concluding speech in Calcutta reinvoked 'the great potentiality' of Indian writers, were they 'to throw their full weight on the side of the still suffering millions in Africa and Asia'?[26]

The *Lotus* agenda

Following Tashkent, a nine-country AAWA Permanent Bureau was formed, including delegates from India (progressive poet Mr Zoheir), Japan, China, Indonesia, USSR, Ghana, Sudan and UAR, plus Faiz as an observer.[27] It was to be located in Colombo, under General Secretary Ratna Deshapriya Senanayake, head of the Ceylonese Writers' Association.[28]

Like its parent AAPSO, the AAWA consistently identified four main areas of global concern: American aggression in Southeast Asia, American-backed Israeli aggression in West Asia, the apartheid regime in South Africa and the remaining Portuguese colonies in southern Africa. Building upon

[24] Berta Menezes Braganza, 'The Goan Struggle Against Portuguese Colonialism', *Afro-Asian Bulletin* 3 (November–December 1961), 23.

[25] Ibid., 24 (her caps).

[26] *Afro-Asian Bulletin* 3 (September–October 1961), 19.

[27] As with the lack of a Pakistani delegation, the country's absence on the Bureau is also illustrative of its US bloc alignment under Ayub Khan. Furthermore, although the AAWA was not organized on an official state-to-state basis, many of its participants did play roles in their respective government as Carolien Stolte points out in '"The People's Bandung": Local Anti-imperialists on an Afro-Asian Stage' (*Journal of World History* 30, no. 1–2, June 2019), Faiz would not enjoy such official favour (nor did Afro-Asian internationalism) until Zulfikar Ali Bhutto's tenure in the 1970s.

[28] The founders of the Lanka Sama Samaja Party had emerged from the same cluster of leftist intellectuals in 1930s London that had produced the PWA and the Congress Socialist Party's left wing; all these entities were then very close. Though I cannot trace the precise trajectory of the Ceylon Writers' Association in relation to the splinterings of the left parties, the LSSP split into Stalinist and Trotskyist factions in the 1940s, re-merging in the 1950s. The Sri Lankan writers went with China after the 1962 Sino-Soviet/Sino-Indian split.

the Bandung principles (although far from non-aligned), AAPSO aimed 'to unite, consolidate and accelerate actions of solidarity with the struggle against imperialism, colonialism, neo-colonialism, racism, apartheid, Zionism, fascism and reaction; and to provide all-out moral, political and material support to the struggle for freedom, self-determination and national independence'.[29] It sought interdependence and economic parity, rallying the progressive and democratic forces of the developing countries against destabilization, disruption and cultural infiltration.

AAPSO's comprehensive analysis of neo-colonialism echoed framings that would have been familiar to readers of IPTA and PWA publications like *Unity* and *Indian Literature*. It could operate through economic, military or cultural/religious modes,[30] through tactics including manipulation of puppet governments, economic infiltration, integration into economic zones or security treaty blocs, fomenting internal subversion or intramural conflict, persecutions of dissident or minority groups, balkanization or partition, assassination of individuals, intimidation and blackmail, radio and print propaganda. The agents of these tactics could include embassies, missions, UN technical advisers, foreign military personnel advising local security and police forces, military bases sometimes cloaked as scientific research stations or training schools and operatives utilizing organizations like the Peace Corps, Moral Re-Armament, Africa Crossroads, trade unions, cultural, youth or philanthropic organizations as sites for pressure and espionage.

As part of the spectrum of hard and soft power through which the Cold War adversaries (or in AAPSO terms, the forces of imperialism and the forces of liberation) both operated, culture was crucial. This was where the task of writers came in – with the power to influence consciousness, hearts and minds. The AAWA's publications and educational initiatives would be a counter to those associated with the CIA-funded Congress of Cultural Freedom, which covertly supported a slate of journals including England's *Encounter* and India's *Quest*. These provided a platform for writers ranging from liberal democrats to leftist critics of Stalinism, whose work was opportunistically promoted to undermine the appeal of the Soviet bloc. *Lotus* was their opposite: the primary organ through

[29] AAPSO Constitution, *Permanent Secretariat of the Afro-Asian People's Solidarity Organization* (Cairo, UAR: [1960?]), 4.

[30] *Afro-Asian People's Solidarity Movement*, Permanent Secretariat of the Afro-Asian People's Solidarity Organization (Cairo, UAR: [1961]), 19–29; *Afro-Asian Bulletin* 3 (May–June 1961), 39–43. The discrepancy should of course be noted between AAPSO's reponse to the Anglo-French-Israeli invasion of Suez (in response to which Sahir Ludhianvi wrote his masterpiece 'Parchaiyan' as an epic against global militarism) and their non-response to the Soviet invasion of Hungary, both in 1956.

which the AAWA would (on their side, openly and unabashedly an instrument of the cultural Cold War) implement the indispensable cultural aspects of AAPSO's political agenda. *Lotus* was also the vehicle by which the ideas and images could be circulated, channeled and activated – which was the very substance of the AAWs' ultimate purpose, as it was of the PWs: to intervene in the way people think, feel, understand and thereby act.

The first few numbers were billed simply as *Afro-Asian Writings*.[31] The editorial board renamed it *Lotus* in 1969,[32] noting the flower's significance to multiple Afro-Asian cultures, including the iconography of Buddhism, Hinduism and Islam: 'Lotus is first of all a flower that possesses the specificity of its association with water . . . "And from water, we make everything alive."' (A footnote identifies this as a Koranic citation. Can this Lotus ever be reappropriated from Hindutva in South Asian mental associations?) Further, as 'A flower linked to water, Lotus, consequently, represents life' and youth, or enlightenment.[33]

Youssef el-Sebai was editor-in-chief (and general secretary of the Permanent Bureau); his fellow Egyptian Mursi Saad el-Din was deputy editor-in-chief and assistant general secretary. Zaheer and Anand were on the founding editorial committee; Faiz would eventually succeed El-Sebai as editor-in-chief.[34] It was published triennially in three languages: Arabic (printed in Cairo), English and French (printed in East Germany).

But much happened between the establishment of the AAWA and the launch of *Lotus*. The Cold War in the global south wasn't just between the United States and the USSR, proffering decolonizing countries' two rival models of economic development and freedom. It was also, to use Jeremy Friedman's phrasing, between the USSR and China, proffering two rival models of revolution. One prioritized anti-imperialism and decolonization, the other a more gradualist building of socialism from its territorial bastion; in other words, whether to make anti-capitalism subsidiary to anti-colonialism or vice versa.[35] The Sino-Soviet split after 1962 was also a Sino-Indian split, with China hoping to edge

[31] Countries represented in *Lotus*'s tables of contents include Algeria, Burma, Cape Verde, Congo, Egypt*, Gambia, Guinea, Indonesia, Iraq, Ivory Coast, Japan, Jordan, Laos, Lebanon, Malawi, Mongolia, Morocco, Nigeria, Palestine, Sao Tome, South Africa, Sudan, Syria,* Thailand, Tunisia, Turkey, UAR*, USSR (various Central Asian republics), Vietnam.

[32] *Lotus* 2:6 (#7) (October 1970), 5.

[33] *Lotus* #57 (1986), 6.

[34] The original editorial board included Anand, Faiz, Mouloud Mammeri (Algeria), Hiroshi Noma (Japan), Soheil Idris (Lebanon), Sononym Udval (Mongolia), La Guma, Sofronov. Mario Andrade (Portuguese Colonies), Abdulla Hamid el-Amin (Sudan) and Doudou Gueye (Senegal) were added subsequently. It was printed by a solidarity committee in East Germany.

[35] Jeremy Friedman, *Shadow Cold War: the Sino-Soviet Competition for the Third World* (University of North Carolina Press, 2015).

out the USSR as leader of the anti-capitalist world and India as leader of the anti-colonialist world, and within India, an intra-left and intergenerational one. The AAWA and PWA stuck close to Moscow, while a breakaway parallel Afro-Asian Writers Bureau was established in Beijing. Inside India, two writers' conferences in Delhi (the PWA in 1967 and the AAWA in 1970, for which the former seemed more or less to be a preview) came under attack both from the left and from the right as the PWA/AAWA were demonized by Cold Warriors and denounced by Maoists alike for its Moscow loyalism. This split had deeply impacted the international context by the time the journal began to circulate in 1968. So did the rifts opened up by the Six Day War in the Middle East, which would draw the *Lotus* administration ever closer to the Palestinian resistance movement, seen as a vanguard in the international anti-imperialist struggle. *Lotus* operations relocated from Cairo to Beirut in 1979, where it was hosted by the PLO after Anwar Sadat's signing of the Camp David accords. This was seen as a betrayal and a capitulation, and caused a rift between Egypt and the USSR.

Each issue of *Lotus* reiterated its mission of linking cultural awareness to political decolonization (as El-Sebai had linked cultural action to armed independence struggle, at the recent AAWA conference in Delhi), and restated its purpose: 'propagation of a wider knowledge of Afro-Asian literature; emancipation of Afro-Asian culture from colonialist and neo-colonialist chains; promotion of Afro-Asian literature and presentation of its new and genuine elements.' Each issue was stamped with the AAWA emblem, centred on a map outlining the two continents, resting upon a book, crowned with a burning torch and crossed horizontally by two clasped hands, one light and one dark, all encircled by 'Afro-Asian Writers' in its three official languages: The AAPSO emblem featured the same hands, torch and map, sans book and text.

They believed in culture as resistance; culture of resistance; the reclamation of culture as a component of decolonization, especially important in the Third World context. 'Art for life's sake, not art for art's sake' remained the lodestone it had been to the PWA: artistic and intellectual production were never neutral, but always contextually embedded and conscientiously committed. The ideal situation for an artist or writer was to be in the closest possible touch with 'the People' as a source of vitality and authenticity, serving as a transparent conduit for their aspirations and desires while simultaneously serving as teachers, guides or engineers of the New Man/New Woman who would in turn act upon progressive aspirations and desires.

There was an emerging international canon of Afro-Asian culture-heroes who exemplified this ideal: Pablo Neruda, Nâzım Hikmet, Alex La Guma,

Mahmoud Darwish, Ghassan Kanafany, Ngugi wa Thiong'o, Chinua Achebe, Wole Soyinka, Amilcar Cabral, Patrice Lumumba, Paul Robeson, Nazrul Islam, Kim Chi-ha, To Huy. Alongside these names, South Asian fiction and poetry in *Lotus* was represented almost exclusively by Progressive Writers: Faiz, Anand, Zaheer, Razia Zaheer, Ali Sardar Jafri, Sahir Ludhianvi, Amrita Pritam, Khwaja Ahmad Abbas and Mukhopadhyay made regular appearances.[36]

Different countries' Writers Unions would host one another (or sometimes even one another's friends, family or protegés) and help with travel arrangements: most often the Soviet Writers' Union, and the centrally located Arab ones. Crucially, Afro-Asian discursive and conceptual space (and the real physical space of meetings) made it possible for Indian, Pakistani and soon Bangladeshi writers to be reunited as Afro-Asian writers, sharing in a solidarity beyond national borders. It did not undo the partition of states, but it at least partially re-wove their epistemic communities, bypassing state barriers through an idea of connection that transcended (while still containing) national affiliation.

Language barriers had still to be dealt with, however. Translation in general was always a challenge. Submissions in each country first had to be rendered into one of the three languages for consideration, then into the other two for publication if accepted by the central editorial committee. Few readers would encounter most of the pieces in *Lotus* in the original, and many renditions were undeniably clunky. But content overrode form for the purposes of Afro-Asian Writing: the message to be conveyed was ultimately considered more important than the fine nuances of language. (Here is another example of the scaling up of the earlier PWA mission: Attar Singh's essay on the problems of translation in Afro-Asian literature compared it to the same issue within the subcontinent, referencing the variety of languages within India and the common languages shared between India and Pakistan.)[37]

Yet even if imperfectly, *Lotus* was a tool for counteracting the silo effect of the colonial period, replacing bilateral colony-metropole spokes with a web of direct south–south horizontal relations. In the process of becoming visible to one another through art, they would reveal themselves to themselves, as they wanted to be.

[36] There were also contributions from non-Progressive Writers like the more literarily than politically prominent R. K. Narayan, or the Progressively estranged Manto (who for some reason appears listed as a Bangladeshi); as well as a new generation of emerging writers like Tarun Sanyal, Pritish Nandy and Samar Sengupta, some of whose later politics were more divergent from the original programme.

[37] *Lotus* #21 (1974), 30–5.

The art of Lotus

Each *Lotus* cover featured sumptuous full-colour photographs or reproductions of some form of folk or classical art – paintings, textiles, masks, sculptures. The corresponding multi-page art features inside were curated and annotated by Abdel Aziz Sadek, who was also in charge of layout and design, glossing the plates with captions written rather in the manner of museum wall labels which served the instructive goal of learning about one another's cultures. There was no apparent hierarchical distinction between classical and artisanal work, in forms ranging from Islamic architecture to Buddhist statuary, Coptic and Pharoanic Egyptian art, Mughal miniatures (one month, the calligraphy of the *Babarnama* was featured), West African masks, Central Asian carpets or Japanese floral arrangement.

Starting in 1969, Lotus Prize winners were always generously featured in the journal, as exemplary Afro-Asian writers. The selection criteria illustrated the ideal for what Afro-Asian writers were supposed to do, and what Afro-Asian literature was supposed to be: the prize was awarded for literary merit in the portrayal of contemporary realities; taking a militant stance against all forms of discrimination, social injustice, inequality and imperialist 'infiltration and aggression', and 'express[ing] of the peoples; aspiration to a better life'.

Here is how *Lotus* implicitly finessed the relationship between ideology and art: for the true Afro-Asian writer, the Lotus Prize winner, there was no conflict between the two. Individualistic expression and aesthetic experimentation per se were irrelevant in this context. Rather, the point was how effectively individual artists conveyed the struggles and aspirations of their people, how closely they identified with the collective body, enabling them to serve as its conduit and amplifier. The best examples of this kind of work (i.e. work worthy of the Lotus Prize) emerged where that orientation coincided with an artist's own personal inclinations. In that case, what they wrote would follow naturally from who they were, where they were situated, what they cared about. So, to meet the criteria of both skill *and* passion, artists were essentially being judged as much on the qualities of their hearts and souls as for their mastery of craft.

Anand had been on the Lotus Prize jury for fiction since 1969; after 1971, Faiz was asked to judge poetry and La Guma fiction. The Soviet members were to judge criticism (on the basis of their congenitally advanced understanding of Marxist theory, of course, the single-most important qualification for criticism self-evidently consisting in the application of that theory to a piece of writing). Work was to be submitted in one of the three *Lotus* languages, along with a translation of key passages into the other two, a resumé and an analysis written by at least two major literary critics. The prize included £500, a diploma, a medal and high visibility through extensive propagation of the work in print and radio.

Many issues carried a special section devoted to the contemporary literature of a particular country, such as Palestine, Mozambique, the Philippines or Vietnam. The rest of the contents featured poetry, short fiction, essays and critical research studies, often on folklore, folkways, or tribal arts and music. Theatre was prominent, as it had been in the relationship between the PWA and IPTA. Sometimes there would be short plays or poetic dramas by the likes of Wole Soyinka, Leopold Sedar Senghor or the young Pakistani playwright Mirza Adib; sometimes an expository piece on contemporary people's theatre practices, or the radical theatre of Nigeria, Senegal, Syria or Lebanon.

Where the art spreads were musealogical and research articles anthropological, editorials and criticism were political. If one directive was to excavate and revitalize the arts and letters of each country, another was to continue grappling with artists' and writers' social responsibilities in the present moment, such as the role of revolutionary poets under occupation. There were articles on topics such as the meaning of freedom in the cultural Cold War, literary militance, dialectics of tradition and modernity, or motifs of resistance in Afro-Asian literature.

Stories and poems were windows onto life – or at least, in accordance with the principles of Progressive/Afro-Asian/Socialist-Realist aesthetics, they were supposed to be so. Representations were to be truthful and transparent; feelings expressed were expected to be appropriate to dedicated revolutionaries, lovers of the People. In this sense the windows sometimes gave onto landscapes that were as much aspirational as they were actual. Nevertheless it is the specificity of these aspirations, combined with the specificity of the actualities described, that defines the generic category of 'Afro-Asian' literature. What made a specimen of socialist realism Afro-Asian, according to AAWA critics, was that the social reality conveyed was a mid-twentieth-century African or Asian one, meaning that it was a context marked by the history of colonial occupation, economic dependency and underdevelopment, and the struggle against these; that the scenery and subjectivities evoked were particular to these places and moments, with locally rooted cultural textures embedded at a particular structural location within global modernity.

If perhaps clichéd, *Lotus*'s aesthetic motifs were also thoroughly compatible with the established repertory of Progressive imagery: the red of dawn, storms, blood, flags, horizons, roses; illumination of candles or lamps, signifying reason and enlightenment; long nights, of suffering if dark, of love if lit by moon and stars; mornings and awakenings; roads, destinations, journeys; sowing and reaping of emerald or golden harvests; all manner of stylized flowers, shrubs, trees, vines, horses and birds, of which a special category was peace doves; but also an iconography of guns – pistols or AK-47s – isolated in iconic silhouette, or toted by African-, Asian- or Arab-garbed guerrillas; hands: clasped together, raised in fists, clutching rifles or those other major weapons in their arsenal, pens and books: the books often appearing like towering architectural edifices and the pens upright like javelins, or bristling in a cluster like a quiver of arrows, with lethal-looking nibs sharp as chisels or spearheads, sometimes completely set free of the pens, flying in a flock of flechettes.

Lest this seem contradictory, for the *Lotus* discursive community there was no contradiction in juxtaposing militance and anti-militarism. They made a clear distinction between imperialist aggressors and Afro-Asian freedom fighters. Ideological pacifism was not the point, decolonization was. The establishment of a just global order of free, sovereign societies was the structural prerequisite for world peace.

Similar themes recur in the stories, the best of these which evoke a poignant empathy, a mix of pain and hope. The protagonists tend to be caught in the contradictions of development and dependency, reflecting the social and economic realities of the Third World. They are militant partisans, or farmers striving to provide for their families, or young people leaving the village to be educated, returning to face the paradoxical tensions between cultural pride and modern rejection of superstition, the mingled alienation and comfort of homecoming.

What signifies goodness in these stories: collective farming, the fertile land and its crops, especially fruit trees, and its cognate, the beautiful peasant woman sturdy of limb and fertile of womb. For even though authors could now define feminine beauty as strength, capable of carrying a weapon, a child or a water jug, bearing the burdens of a revolutionary household along with half the sky, they still had not managed to disconnect the ideal woman and her body from the heart of the beloved land and culture. In short they had not quite mastered feminism, though they were trying: 1975 was the UN's year of the woman, to which El-Sebai called attention in his editorials.

What signifies badness in these stories: imperialists, capitalists, neocolonialists and their collaborators (developers, land grabbers, mine owners, exploitative labour contractors); poverty and inequality; babies and children dead from sickness, malnutrition or violence; obliquely implied rape or sexual exploitation

– of wives, sisters, daughters and sometimes of men. Railroads and trains were ambiguous: radically disruptive, for better and worse.

Tradition and modernity

Lotus contributors, editors and readers from all the participating countries had set themselves to reclaiming their battered pasts, portraying their present realities and building from these materials their desired futures. The relationship of tradition and modernity was a recurring theme. To reconnect with folk forms was not a regression to lost 'purity', but the healing of a ruptured line; a restoration not of the past but of the possibility for unfettered unfoldment of life. Removing the colonial influence would revive the potential for autonomous, dynamic development into an alternate modernity to that presumed synonymous with the terms of Western colonialism, one defined as both progressive and authentic to Afro-Asian contexts.[38]

Anand and Faiz were each occupied with this task for their respective countries. From the 1950s onward, both played key roles in national cultural institutions while also travelling around world in connection with the WPC, AAWA and other bodies. Both worked in journalism, criticism, education, drama and film. Both valued internationalism as a national ideal – a way framing national character that was in fact common to many of the Afro-Asian decolonizing countries.[39] Both selected from among the subcontinental complex of contradictory, polyglot histories to try to define progressive Indian and Pakistani cultures in contrast to the ethnoreligious nationalist versions which were contending for space to monopolize 'authentic' national culture on both sides of the borders. While rejecting notions of politicized religion,

[38] Zeyad el Nabolsy shares this assessment of the Afro-Asian writers' understanding of the relationship between a dynamic living tradition, modernism and futurity, but suggests a different framing than 'alternative' modernity. Rather, he argues, the 'privileged epistemic standpoint' that Afro-Asian writers occupied with regard the operation of colonialism and global capitalism, plus the rationalist, Marxist framework of their critiques, made them even *more* quintessentially modern than the West; in other words, their aspirations would make them seekers not of alternatives to this modernity but greater fulfillment of it. Western imperialists, not colonized Asians and Africans, were the violaters of reason and of the values of democracy and equality, 'not modern enough'. To me, this indicates that it was never modernity per se the Progressive and Afro-Asian writers took issue with, but rather the presumed Western-ness and necessary coloniality of that modernity. 'Lotus and the Self-Representation of Afro-Asian Writers as the Vanguard of Modernity', *Interventions* (2020), 3.

[39] Nabolsy beautifully elaborates on this trait as characteristic of AAWA-member countries' sense of being Afro-Asian, constructing the desired traits of their own national identities through this ideal of solidarity. See 'Lotus and the Self-Representation of Afro-Asian Writers as the Vanguard of Modernity', 4–8.

the progressive imagination nevertheless sought historical precedent for the desired cultural character in egalitarian and emancipatory readings of Islamicate (for Pakistan), Buddhist and Vedantic (for India) philosophical and artistic traditions. Both envisioned their societies as diversely multinational, multi-ethnic and multi-linguistic confederations. Rebelling against the puritanical tendencies of left as well as right, both envisioned their cultures as sensual, rich in dance, music and physicality.

Ironically these two writers who represented two distinct countries in the AAWA bodies and *Lotus* mastheads shared neighbouring Punjabi roots, and drew upon many of the same multiregional materials in order to define themselves as separate cultures: Harappa/Mohenjo Daro, Iqbal, Tagore, Premchand, the bhakti and sufi saints, Chishti, Kabir, Tukaram, Khusrao, Hafiz, Jami, Guru Nanak. They shared much else besides: both were members (despite Anand's English oeuvre) of the same Hindustani progressive epistemic community whose rupturing Aijaz Ahmad laments in *In the Mirror of Urdu*.[40]

Note that although emphasizing that the country should be recognized as multi-ethnic and multi-lingual, Faiz's cultural construction of Pakistan is focused on the northwest of the subcontinent, not Bengal. Perhaps he felt that it was the task of Bengalis to elaborate that part of it. This comports with his and Sibte's idea of a cohesive Pakistani identity as rooted in history, territory and material culture, meaningful as a nation in secular terms; however, while this proposition was meant to counter the idea of the religious state, with religion as basis for national identity, it may also have had the effect of proving the logic of different nationalist identities for the western and eastern wings.

Internationalist humanist though he be, ultimately Faiz was a poet of Urdu, not Bengali. His faith that Urdu could serve as a universal language of the people was perhaps a blind spot regarding the Bangladeshi liberation movement. Some Bengalis were dissatisfied with Faiz's ambiguity regarding the Bangladesh war. The handful of poems through which he addressed it are sorrowful but muted and oblique, despairing and resigned. By personal accounts he was deeply grieved by the slaughter, and by the level of alienation he sensed between eastern and western Pakistanis, mourning the feeling that once fellow citizens had become strangers – a reopening of the scars of 1947.[41] But while he deplored the violence, it may be that he also in his heart did not support the call for independence and seemed to feel that reconciliation would have been preferable to separation.[42]

[40] See Aijaz Ahmad, *In the Mirror of Urdu*. Simla: Indian Institute of Advanced Study, 1993.

[41] See for example Hashmi, *Love and Revolution*, 225–6, 233.

[42] Mosarrap Khan, in 'Faiz Ahmed Faiz and the Bangladesh Liberation War (1971)' (*Cafe Dissensus*, 15 May 2015), speculates that after his previous prison experiences Faiz may have been wary of

Even so, without missing a beat, Bangladesh joined the list of countries appearing in the *Lotus* bylines. Qazi Nasrul Islam's poetry was prominently featured at this time, joined by other young Bangladeshi poets. India and the USSR had supported Bangladesh in 1971. I can only speculate with what pain or pleasure, discomfort or delight, the writers of all three countries encountered each other at AAWA meetings in the 1970s, but here nevertheless they could reunite.

For Pakistan, Faiz and Sibte Hasan, foremost intellectuals of the first-generation PWA, attempted to sketch the continuity of a blend of elite and folk, indigenous pre-Axial and Islamic ingredients, resulting in what was unique to the northwestern part of the subcontinent. Faiz suggested that the region's positioning in the peripheries between great empires had enabled a relatively high degree of flexibility and cross-fertilization of Central Asian, Iranian, Arabic and Indic elements over many centuries. Drawing on a literary canon of Iqbal, Abul Kalam Azad, Mohani, Ghalib and others, Sibte traced a proto-progressive legacy of humanism in Urdu and Persian mystic poetry with its messages of love, peace, ecumenism and anti-fundamentalism.[43]

For India, Anand's emphasis on Buddhism, in line with much Dalit scholarship,[44] organized the interpretation of cultural history as a dialectic between hierarchal and egalitarian elements, or in other words, between a Vedic-Aryan-Brahminical lineage and all its discontents: 'For a thousand years [the priestly elites] fought the Buddha. For the next thousand years they fought the egalitarianism of Islam. For the next thousand years they will fight Nehru.'[45] The same brahminism had led to gross patriarchal abuses, and twisted sexual morality. The revivalists were picking the wrong aspects of classical culture as the 'true' and 'pure' ones; you could just as *authentically* have chosen one that was egalitarian, rationalist and sex-positive, as one that was hierarchical, misogynistic and hypocritically ascetic. Anand remained embroiled in a running battle for a 'new myth' as India's master narrative, revealed as a subaltern, Dravidian, Dalit, working class, Buddhist, Sufi, composite.[46]

criticizing the west Pakistani government too overtly on Bangladesh. Or was it that he was too close to Bhutto?

43 Khalid Sohail, Omar Latif and Abbas Syed (eds), *Progressive Ideals and Ideas in Urdu Literature* (Whitby, ON: Green Zone Publishing, 2016) [loc 2083].

44 Anand's first novel *Untouchable* had made his name as a social realist and Anglophone Indian writer, although it would not be considered politically correct by later standards of representation. Perhaps aware of this, Anand much later co-edited with Eleanor Zelliott and prefaced *An Anthology of Dalit Literature* (Columbia, MO: South Asia Books, 1992).

45 Anand to Saros Cowasjee. *Author to Critic: The Letters of Mulk Raj Anand* (Calcutta: Writers Workshop, 1973), 22.

46 op.cit. 38, 44. As early as 1968–9 Anand was warning of the danger of Hindutva, noting the Shiv Sena as an menacing 'heatwave in Maharashtra', *Author to Critic*, 66.

Anand was working out his social/artistic criticism in essays and speeches, and in voluminous personal correspondence with several long-term interlocutors. But perhaps his main forum was *Marg*, a Bombay-based monthly review of art, architecture and design that he founded in 1946 and edited for many years along with Anil da Silva, the Sri Lankan feminist, writer, artist/art critic who had also been a founding leader of IPTA. *Marg* offered a graphic platform for visually displaying and annotating the best exemplars of a desired Indian culture, much as *Lotus* was doing for Afro-Asia, celebrating classical and artisanal work alike as riches of the people's treasure house. Anand travelled the country for material, visiting museums and modern architecture sites, craft villages and ancient cave sculptures.

Meanwhile, Faiz developed strikingly analogous ideas in his articles for *Viewpoint*, the magazine founded by Mazhar Ali Khan in 1975; in interviews and addresses to international bodies such as the AAWA or the WPC; and in a report written for a Standing Committee on Art and Culture the Ministry of Education had appointed him to chair in 1968 as head of the National Arts Council. Faiz's critical writings of the 1960s and 1970s focused on several intersecting issues: for his own country, the challenges of defining a cultural identity, with practical steps for promoting the arts as a component of national development, and for Third World countries more generally, the challenges of cultural decolonization and the role of literature in resistance and emancipation.

But first, he noted, the damage and socio-economic distortions of colonial intervention had to be repaired, ethnic and class inequities redressed, and alienation healed. Everything had to be critically assessed, to select what was beneficial and reject what was oppressive, establishing a useable past on which to build a desirable future. Some traditional elements 'basic to national identity' would be 'adjusted and adapted to the needs of a more advanced social structure, which help to strengthen and promote progressive social values and attitudes'. Other elements deemed 'irrelevant or repugnant to the more advanced system of social relationship, which hinder the progress of more rational enlightened and human values and attitudes', would be jettisoned. Meanwhile some Western elements conducive to technical, aesthetic and scientific advancement could be selectively assimilated, while others that 'deliberately aimed at promoting degeneracy, decadence, and social reaction', would be repudiated.[47]

In other words it was not the age or provenance of an element that made it good or bad, but rather its effects, weighed against a set of values. The choice was

[47] Faiz, 'Cultural Problems in Underdeveloped Countries', Sheema Majeed (ed.), *Culture and Identity: Selected English Writings of Faiz* (Oxford University Press, 2005), 35.

not categorically between past and future, nor between foreign and indigenous; it was about *which* foreign and *which* indigenous elements should be combined, which cross-border affinities and transnational alliances – those of imperialists with the country's landlords, capitalists and religious leaders, or those of anti-imperialists with the country's left intellectuals, workers and peasants – should be embraced in the present.

For Progressive writers recast as Afro-Asian writers, love of country was not a matter of exceptionalism, but of particularity – about being deeply rooted in a place, embedded in its history and landscape, with bodies and sense-memories shaped by its foods and lifeways, the specificities of its social relations and economic structures, institutions and practices, manifesting in its songs and sculptures, poems and paintings. But the struggle for a vision of global social justice transcended nationality, and no country was ahistorically and essentially on one side or the other of the epic fight for justice and liberation. That required continual iteration. In *Lotus*, the South Asian countries, like all the rest, iterated (illustrated, illuminated) themselves in accordance with progressive values, priorities and aesthetics. Each new country was fashioning as much as finding itself, in order to share the self it most wanted to be – emancipated, unalienated, egalitarian, creative, participating in an Afro-Asian ecumene. We see the delegates of this imagined community photographed in the special sections documenting AAWA conferences: a utopian rainbow of smiling or intent faces, crowned with heavy headphones, shaking hands or clutching papers, their countries named on sans serif placards at tiered seats and microphones. Freedom is an endless series of international meetings.

Conclusion

The AAWA built upon the same rhetoric, analysis, structures, aesthetics, aims and objectives that the PWA had been elaborating since the1930s, transposed intact and scaled up from (an always multinational) subcontinental into a transcontinental Third World space. The term 'progressive' continued to be used throughout, with a small p; in fact the duties of a true AAW and of a true PW sound much the same, and Afro-Asian(-ism) carried the Progressive tradition in its politics, poetics and mission, out to an expanding horizon. The fight moved; the fight remained. Furthermore the AAWA created a venue in which Indian, Pakistani and later Bangladeshi Progressive Writers could be reunited as fellows in Afro-Asian solidarity that transcended national borders.

They had developed an analysis that connected imperialism, colonialism and neo-colonialism, fascism and racism in all their forms, and a comprehensive strategy for opposing them through cultural means, replacing them with visionary alternatives. At both scales, Progressive and Afro-Asian writers tried to weave a sense of larger commonality based in shared ideals from a diversity of languages and ethnic identities (while still neglecting to fully account for the imbalance among them).

The PWA/AAWA project at the international level was (as it had always been in pre-partition India) to use culture as a weapon against capitalism and imperialism, and a tool for building horizontal solidarities, celebrating unity in diversity across linguistic barriers and ethnic differences, seeking commonalities while celebrating particularities. Moreover the late-stage PWA was virtually synonymous with the Indian and Pakistani branches of the AAWA, as seen for example in Lahore's Afro-Asian Book Club and film series, or the billing of *Lotus India* (edited by Bhisham Sahni, brother of IPTA star Balraj Sahni) in the 1970s as the organ of both the Indian branch of AAWA and the PWA, then undergoing something of a revival.

In a session at the 1967 Delhi PWA meeting on the organization's 'Achievements, Shortcomings and Future Programme', Zaheer affirmed that its two original objectives – freedom and socialist revolution – still remained, but located beyond their own national horizon. More than two-thirds of humanity continued marching onward: the one-third who were building socialism in the Second World and the one-third-plus who were liberating themselves from colonial chains in the Third World.[48]

As preparations began for the 1970 Delhi AAWA conference, El-Sebai noted that 'Our Indian friends must be given their due', for their contributions to the birth and growth of 'each initiative of the movement of Afro-Asian writers'. He editorialized afterward of 'The long road . . . from New Delhi to Tashkent by way of Cairo and Beirut, to return anew to Delhi' fourteen years on, reprising that 'famous encounter on the banks of the Jumna in . . . the magnificent and prestigious capital of India'.[49]

La Guma's comments on 'Literature and Life' (a title also shared by Akhtar Husain Raipuri's 1935 essay on Progressive literature) illustrated this continuity:

[48] Carlo Coppola, *Urdu Poetry, 1935-1970: The Progressive Episode* (diss. University of Chicago, 1975), 335.

[49] *Lotus* # 9–3, July 1971, 128. Again, note that while among the 'Indian friends' would also have been contemporary Pakistani writers, the Pakistani *state* was not a participant in the AAWA in the same way that the Indian *state* was, and could not have been hosting such a conference; the neighbouring South Asian governments leaned in opposite directions on the Cold War chessboard.

he quoted Gorky, a favourite of the PWs, on the interwar popular front, counterposing the defenders of human culture and freedom against the forces of destruction – in the 1930s, fascism. Only now it was the people of Vietnam, Namibia, Zimbabwe and South Africa, versus the US military and its proxies and puppets, who were cast in the roles previously played by the people of democratic Spain and France versus the armies of Hitler and Mussolini. The fight was still a fight for liberation, equality and their very material and spiritual existence, against the negation of their pasts and futures.[50]

Since both PWA and AAWA always ended their analytical and exhortatory declarations with a list of actionable resolutions, we too might ask ourselves:

- What were the cultural/aesthetic tasks to undertake, and how did artists and intellectuals of the PWA contribute to the relevant struggles in the 1930s–1940s?
- What were the cultural/aesthetic tasks to undertake, and what did artists and intellectuals of the PWA and AAWA contribute to the relevant struggles in the 1950s–1970s?
- What are the cultural/aesthetic tasks to undertake, and how might artists and intellectuals interested in the PWA and AAWA and their mission, but involved in forms and formations specific to our own moment (though perhaps not so different), contribute to the relevant struggles in the 2020s and beyond?

Lotus ceased publication after the break-up of the Soviet Union and the PLO withdrawal from Tunis (where the *Lotus* office had moved along with it, following the 1982 Israeli bombing of Beirut). But a new AAWA launched a new *Lotus* in 2016, for a renamed Writers' Union of Africa, Asia and Latin America (WUAALA).[51] In a moment when fascism and white supremacy are resurging globally, when reactionary interpretations of national culture stoking homicidal chauvinism continue to gain ground in South Asia, when the screws of crisis of the Middle East seem only to keep tightening despite one's thinking it can't possibly turn any further, a strong progressive Afro-Asian sensibility with access to a vigorous transnational vehicle for propagating its words and images seems like something it would be good to have in the world.

[50] *Lotus* 1:4, January 1970, 239.

[51] Nida Ghouse, 'Lotus Notes', *ARTMargins* 5, no. 3 (October 2016), 83; Hala Halim, 'Afro-Asian Third-Worldism into Global South: The Case of *Lotus* Journal', *Global South Studies: A Collective Publication with The Global South* (22 November 2017). https://globalsouthstudies.as.virginia.edu/key-moments/afro-asian-third-worldism-global-south-case-lotus-journal.

5

What got 'left' behind

The limits of leftist engagements with art and culture in postcolonial Sri Lanka

Harshana Rambukwella

Introduction

Writing in 1972, twenty years after its original publication, Ediriweera Sarachchandra – considered one of twentieth-century Sri Lanka's Sinhala-language artistic titans – attempted to defend his artistic philosophy in the preface to the second edition of his much-maligned book of literary criticism *kalpana lokaya* (*The World of the Imagination*):

> This book has been more objected to rather than being critiqued. The objections arose because of the phrase '*kalpana lokaya*' in its title. What is literature if it is not an imaginary product of mankind? It is true that literature has been imagined based on the physical world which is accessible to our senses. But it is a world that is only accessible to our minds and imaginations.
>
> I sometimes wonder if those who objected to '*kalpana lokaya*' did so due to their limited linguistic knowledge. I do not know if they understood it as 'THE IMAGINARY WORLD'. I used it in the sense of the 'THE WORLD OF THE IMAGINATION'. [*emphasis original*][1]

Sarachchandra was responding to the heavy materialist critique his book encountered in the two decades since its publication in 1958. The 1950s, when Sarachchandra emerged as a dominant artistic force in Sri Lanka, was a time of major artistic production and innovation in postcolonial Sri Lanka. It was also a time when the nascent Sri Lankan nation state was taking a decisive

[1] Ediriweera Sarachchandra, *Kalpana Lokaya* (*The World of the Imagination*) (Colombo: S. Godage and Sons, 2015 [1958]), i–ii.

turn towards the institutionalization of majoritarian Sinhala nationalism. In 1956, two years prior to the publication of Sarachchandra's *kalpana lokaya*, S. W. R. D. Bandaranaike, the fourth prime minister of independent Sri Lanka, came to power riding a wave of Sinhala and Buddhist nationalist sentiment. Bandaranaike was backed by a core village-based constituency – colloquially dubbed the *panca maha bala wēgaya* or 'the five great forces' – comprising Ayurveda doctors, school teachers, the Buddhist clergy, farmers and workers.[2] For many Sinhala nationalists the year 1956 rather than 1948 – the official year of independence – marked emancipation from a West-sympathizing comprador political class. Another seminal figure in twentieth-century Sinhala literary culture, Martin Wickramasinghe dubbed it the 'fall of the Brahmin/comprador' class – *bamunu kulaye biňda wætīma*.[3] There was much expectation that this was the dawn of an indigenous economic and cultural revival – though subsequent events dashed many of these hopes. The political economy of the moment in which Sarachchandra wrote *kalpana lokaya* was therefore one characterized by a strong decolonizing thrust and a turn to indigeneity. It was also a moment of cultural invention (Hobsbawm and Ranger 1983) when a new cultural and artistic script was being crafted for the newly independent nation. The Sinhala term for this trend in the 1950s was *deshiya*, meaning indigenous in a broad and inclusive sense. But jostling for influence was another discourse termed '*apekama*' (loosely translating as 'ourness'). *apekama* unlike *deshiya* was more about an exclusivist sense of Sinhala identity and pride premised not simply against a perceived 'West' but also premised against the culture and social practices of internal others such as Tamils, Muslims or Burghers or Eurasians.[4]

Kalpana Lokaya though emerging in this moment of cultural and political firmament was avowedly apolitical. As Sarachchandra's quote earlier alludes to, many of the critiques of the book came from a social realist perspective. Many leftist critics saw Sarachchandra's text as apolitical and a kind of liberal-humanist treatise on 'art for art's sake'. However, the leftist critique of Sarachchandra, while focusing on the manifest lack of 'politics' in his work, also missed a structural political factor. Sarachchandra's artistic production, though never overtly political, was nonetheless subtly informed by the nationalist politics of the moment – particularly the rise of Sinhala nationalism. The main critical thrust

2 Nalini Hennayake, *Culture, Politics and Development in Postcolonial Sri Lanka* (Oxford: Lexington Books, 2006), 84.

3 Martin Wickramasinghe, *Upan Da Sita* (*From the Day I Was Born*) (Colombo Tisara Publishers, 1961).

4 Harshana Rambukwella, *The Politics and Poetics of Authenticity: A Cultural Genealogy of Sinhala Nationalism* (London: UCL Press, 2018).

of this chapter is based on how leftist artistic criticism in Sri Lanka remained largely blind to the deep structural relationship between mainstream Sinhala artistic production and Sinhala nationalism up to the 1980s and how this in turn prevented leftist critique from recognizing the radical potential of Sinhala-language avant-garde artistic work that began to emerge in the 1960s and 1970s – work that was inspired by a sense of regional leftist solidarity that transcended ethno-nationalist frames and engaged with leftist imaginaries within the South Asian region. This was a trend that was particularly evident in the formal choices made by avant-garde artists.

However, this supranational orientation was not evident in leftist politics, which capitulated to rising Sinhala ethno-nationalism during roughly the same time period. At the same time, the leftist failures in relation to ethno-nationalism cannot be understood in isolation from the larger history of postcolonial Sri Lanka where Sinhala ethno-nationalism became an institutionalized norm – very little in Sinhala society evaded the allure of Sinhala ethno-nationalism and leftist artistic critique and political engagement were no exceptions. Framed by this overall critical orientation, this chapter explores leftist artistic production and critique in two phases of Sinhala-language artistic production in Sri Lanka's postcolonial history: the 1950s when artistic production was heavily shaped by the euphoria of independence, and the period from the 1960s leading up to the early 1980s when the promise of the nation state begins to crumble. It is in this period that one sees distinctive traces of how a South Asian imaginary of leftist progressivism intersects with the formal and thematic concerns of artists, as artists begin to experiment with form and its deep structural relationship with nation, nationalism and class – for instance, in the work of film-maker Dharmasena Pathiraja who was directly influenced by the work of Ritwik Ghatak and Mrinal Sen (see Dass's chapter in this volume).

I begin by looking briefly at the evolution of leftist politics in Sri Lanka, framing it against the rise of Sinhala cultural nationalism and how leftist cultural discourses in Sinhala society were unable to maintain a critical distance from the cultural articulation of majoritarian nationalism. Next, I explore the 1950s as a period during which a modern Sinhala aesthetic is formed. Framed by the cultural politics of the emergent nation state, it was a period when a discourse of 'authenticity', which associated the artistic and cultural life of the nation with an exclusivist Sinhala orientation, begins to emerge.[5] It was also a period of significant artistic innovation and ideas of authenticity were nestled

[5] Ibid.

within other discourses about formal and thematic artistic innovation, a spirit of decolonization and artistic commitments to socialist social transformation. It is in the next period from the 1960s that artistic expression begins to take a more recognizable leftist form. However, it is also in the 1960s that *apekama* or authenticity emerges as the more dominant alternative to *deshiya* or a more inclusive notion of indigeneity. From the 1960s onwards it is possible to see leftist art positioning itself as an anti-institutional critique of mainstream Sinhala cultural production. In contrast though the leftist critique of art lagged behind – often unable to contend with the artistic innovation of the avant-garde and unable to recognize how this work also questioned and probed the deep structural relationship between Sinhala art and culture and the postcolonial Sri Lankan nation state. What emerges is a situation where avant-garde art is shaped by a transnational South Asianist sense of left progressivism while left artistic criticism remains entrapped within a national imaginary.

A brief history of leftist politics in Sri Lanka

Sri Lanka has had an active left political movement since the 1920s. The beginnings of leftist political activity can be traced to the early labour movement which coalesced around trade union activity. A. E. Goonesinha, who formed the Ceylon Labour Union, is one of the main figures associated with early labour agitation.[6] Goonesinha was able to mobilize a substantial labour movement in the early 1920s, and in 1923 he provided leadership to a successful general strike against the British colonial administration. However, this early labour movement is viewed with some ambiguity by left-oriented scholars because they do not see it as a Marxist struggle in which class consciousness transcended 'ethno-racial' divisions. Instead, it is often seen as a bourgeois-led social democratic movement.[7] Scholars like Jayawardena (1974) also do not consider the movement to be anti-imperialist. One of the reasons for leftist reservations of the early labour movement was its behaviour when confronted with the threat of mass unemployment due to the global economic downturn in the late 1920s.[8] When Sinhala workers began to see Indian migrant labourers as a threat,

6 G. Anandalingam and Mary Abraham. 'Left-Wing Politics and Ethnic Conflict in Sri Lanka', *Comparative Studies of South Asia, Africa and the Middle East* 6, no. 2 (1986), 38–45.

7 Kumari Jayawardena, 'Origins of the Left Movement in Sri Lanka', *Social Scientist* 2, no. 6/7 (1974), 3–28.

8 Ambalavaner Sivanandan, *When Memory Dies* (London: Arcadia, 1997).

Goonesinha and the Labour Union paper *Veeraya* (*Hero*) played into these ethnic/racialist fears and exploited the emergent ethno-linguistic consciousness within the Sinhala community.[9]

The first leftist political parties to emerge in Ceylon – the 'Trotskyite' Lanka Sama Samaja Party (LSSP) (1935) and the 'Stalinist' Communist Party (CP) (1940), which was a breakaway faction of the LSSP – were self-consciously different to the labour movement. Both drew inspiration from an internationalist Marxist worldview and sought to mobilize people on a platform of class consciousness, rather than ethnic or religious solidarity.[10] This internationalist and non-communalist outlook had a lot to do with the background and education of the founders, most of whom were educated in England and were exposed to anti-imperialist, socialist and communist ideals of leftists like Harold Laski. N. M. Perera, Colvin R. de Silva, S. A. Wickramasinghe and Leslie Goonewardena, the main figures associated with the LSSP, received their education in England and were exposed to radical leftist thinking. The LSSP and CP were able to successfully challenge Goonesinha and win over substantial segments of the labour movement, including plantation sector workers of the *malaiyaka* community, which were of Indian Tamil origin. But soon after independence in 1948, the left movement deviated from its commitment to an internationalist proletariat principle. This change reflected larger changes in the political economy of the country. Since the introduction of universal franchise in 1931, under the Donoughmore Constitutional Reforms, many elite anglicized politicians sought ways of accruing mass appeal by adopting what they saw as discourses of indigeneity, such as language and religion.[11] These changes anticipate the nature and shape of the majoritarian nation state that began to consolidate itself in 1950s Sri Lanka. When the citizenship status of the *malaiyaka* community, a crucial political base for the left, became a thorny political issue in 1948 about belonging and unbelonging in the new nation state, the left response was lukewarm.[12] The left's failure to decisively intervene – in a context where elite Sinhala politicians like D. S. Senayanayke, the first prime minister of independent Sri Lanka, were stoking Sinhala majoritarian sentiments against *malaiyaka* Tamils – signalled the inability of left politics to resist the emerging

[9] Anandalingam and Abraham, 'Left-Wing Politics and Ethnic Conflict in Sri Lanka', 39.

[10] Ibid.; Ambalavaner Sivanandan, 'Ethnic Cleansing in Sri Lanka', *Race and Class* 51, no. 3 (2010), 59–65.

[11] James Manor. *The Expedient Utopian: Bandaranaike and Ceylon* (Cambridge: Cambridge University Press, 1989); Rambukwella, *The Politics and Poetics of Authenticity.*

[12] Anandalingam and Abraham, 'Left-Wing Politics and Ethnic Conflict in Sri Lanka', 40.

majoritarian trajectory of the post-independence Sri Lankan nation state.[13] In order to remain politically 'relevant', from the 1960s onwards the left began to form alliances with mainstream political parties which campaigned on explicit Sinhala nationalist electoral platforms. A key highlight in this trend was when Colvin R de Silva, one of the founders of the Sri Lankan left movement, became the main architect of a new republican constitution in 1972, which contained an explicit clause on the protection of Buddhism, the dominant religion of the Sinhala majority.[14]

In 1971 leftist politics in the country took another decisive turn. A radical 'new left' emerged in the form of the *Janatha Vimukthi Peramuna* (JVP) or People's Liberation Front, led by the charismatic Rohana Wijeweera, a rural Sinhala youth from southern Sri Lanka who had attended the Patrice Lumumba University in Soviet Russia. The JVP built a highly effective village-level network and used a system called the *panthi paha* (five classes) for ideological indoctrination[15] and positioned itself explicitly as a radical alternative to the 'old left'. In 1971 the JVP launched a failed military coup to capture state power and was bloodily suppressed in a brutal crackdown by the government in power, which included members of the 'old left' and was led by S. W. R. D. Bandaranaike's widow, Mrs Bandaranaike.[16] The JVP was not ethno-nationalist when it first emerged. However, after it regrouped in the 1980s it became explicitly Sinhala nationalist, particularly as the military conflict between the Sinhala majority state and militant sections of the Tamil minority intensified in the 1980s. The JVP attempted a second failed insurrection in the 1987–9 period and was again bloodily suppressed. As we shall see further, the emergence of the JVP in 1970s had a significant impact on the artistic practice and vision of a number of important Sinhala creative artists.

The cultural and aesthetic implications of this leftist trajectory of moving from an internationalist orientation to a majoritarian nationalist one are not clear cut. Artistic production in the 1950s occurred within a broad notion of indigeneity or *deshiya* arising from decolonization but nestled within this was also a more exclusivist notion of 'ourness' or *apekama*. Writers, dramatists and

[13] Amita Shastri, 'Estate Tamils, the Ceylon citizenship Act of 1948 and Sri Lankan Politics', *Contemporary South Asia* 8, no. 1 (1999), 65–86.

[14] A. Sivanandan, 'Ethnic Cleansing in Sri Lanka', *Race and Class* 51, no. 3 (2010), 59–65; Anandalingam and Abraham, 'Left-Wing Politics and Ethnic Conflict in Sri Lanka'.

[15] Nirmal Dewasiri, 'Mainstreaming Radical Politics in Sri Lanka: The Case of the JVP Post-1977', *PCD Journal: Journal of Power, Conflict and Democracy in South and South East Asia* 2, no. 1(2010), 69–94.

[16] Nira Wickramasinghe, *Sri Lanka In the Modern Age: A History of Contested Identities* (Honolulu, Hawaii: University of Hawai'i Press, 2006), 237.

film-makers operated in this complex and fluid arena of cultural politics. Much of the artistic work produced in this period looked at the emergent nation state with hope. There was a general expectation for a more egalitarian future within the new nation state. In some ways this paralleled how African writers, such as Ngugi wa Thiongo and Chinua Achebe, wrote with anticipation about the future of newly independent African states. While little of the artistic work produced by Sinhala artists of the 1950s can be characterized as 'leftist', many artists did profess ideals of social justice. In the next section I will explore the 1950s as a site where a cultural script for the newly independent nation state was fashioned – literally an invention of tradition (Hobsbawm and Ranger 1983) and how this tradition begins to take an essentially Sinhala character.

Sinhala cultural production in the 1950s: Social justice, authenticity and nationalism

I trace cultural production in the 1950s period through three seminal figures in Sinhala literary culture: Martin Wickramasinghe (1890–1976) – considered Sri Lanka's first truly 'modern' prose writer; Ediriweera Sarachchandra (1914–96) – considered the founding figure of modern Sinhala drama and a professor of Sinhala literature and language; and Gunadasa Amarasekara (1929–) – a seminal novelist, essayist and poet who was influenced by Wickramasinghe and Sarachchandra. The ideological interactions between Wickramasinghe, Sarchchandra and Amarasekara, who was a kind of protégé to the two older figures, provide insight into how Sinhala nationalist discourse overdetermined artistic production in this period. It also gives insight into how commitments to leftist social justice were framed by the larger discourse of the post-independence Sri Lankan nation state. In essence what you see in this period is a trajectory where Sinhala artists with socialist and leftist sympathies embark on a trajectory where their left progressivism is overdetermined by a commitment to a sense of ethnic and religious nationalist authenticity.

Martin Wickramasinghe – nationalist authenticity and social justice

Martin Wickramasinghe is important to the story of leftist aesthetics because of the seminal role he played in establishing realism as a literary genre in the country. Wickramasinghe's fictional practice was significantly informed by social realism. He was well versed in Russian literary traditions in addition to his familiarity with western European forms of fictional representation. The novel *Gamperaliya* (1981[1941]), translated as *Uprooted*, is seen as a landmark in establishing the realistic novel as a genre in Sri Lanka. Wickramasinghe's interest in issues of social justice is visible in *Gamperaliya*. The story is based on the disintegration of a feudal village-bound socio-economic system with the rise of merchant capitalism within the colonial economy. The fortunes of the *waluwa* or the manor house of the village decline, while Piyal, a youth from a low caste background who once served as an English tutor for the *waluwa* children, returns to the village having reinvented himself as a wealthy entrepreneur. Piyal had earlier wooed Nanda, the elder daughter of the *waluwa*, but was spurned due to his caste. Nanda in the meantime is forced to enter a loveless marriage with a high-caste man who loses his money due to the global economic downturn in the 1930s and eventually dies in the arid southeastern part of Sri Lanka trying to revive his fortunes by engaging in business. Piyal re-enters Nanda's life and marries her and even pays for the funeral of her dead husband. The novel is underwritten by ideological tensions about modernity and tradition that characterize Wickramasinghe's entire oeuvre. These are also tensions that influence writers like Gunadasa Amarasekara and leave a lasting imprint on post-independence Sinhala artistic production.

At one level the novel is about the idea of the village itself. There is clearly a critique of the feudal social and economic structures of the village. Change, as represented by Piyal, is seen as necessary and inevitable. But there is also romanticization of the village as a repository of authentic Sinhala values – a kind of country and city binary[17] in which Piyal, whose subjectivity is the product of colonial modernity, is seen as a diminished human being. This in turn is tied to Wickramasinghe's career-long fascination with the village as a site of Sinhala authenticity.[18] In a series of semi-autobiographical and quasi-anthropological books such as *Kalu Nika Seveema* or *In Search of the Kalu Nika* (1989 [1961]), *Sinhala Lakuna* or the *Sinhala Sign* (1995 [1947]) and *Upan Da Sita* or *From the Day I Was Born* (1961) Wickramasinghe both documents and recreates the village of his childhood from the vantage of someone who has been displaced from it. In most of these texts the village becomes a site of authenticity, simplicity and an index for a traditional Sinhala value system visualized in the symbolic triad of the *weva* (irrigation tank), *dagoba* (Buddhist stupa) and *yaya* (the paddy field). Wickramasinghe, more than any other twentieth-century Sinhala

17 Raymond Williams, *Country and the City* (Oxford: Oxford University Press, 1973).

18 Rambukwella, *The Politics and Poetics of Authenticity*, 125–50.

writer, contributed to the mainstreaming of this village-based sense of Sinhala authenticity as an aesthetic and cultural structure of feeling.[19] This village-based notion of authenticity, in addition to its romanticism, was also connected in a more insidious manner to the deep structures of the nation state.

From the 1940s onwards the idea of the village as a site of Sinhala authenticity was increasingly exploited by elite politics. Sinhala politicians outdid each other in presenting themselves as custodians of Sinhala authenticity denoted by the symbolic trinity of the *wewa, dagopba* and *yaya*.[20] They styled themselves as patrons of Buddhism and Paddy cultivation and projected themselves as inheritors of the mission of ancient Sinhala kings.[21] However, this did not result in artists like Wickramasinghe either ironizing or critiquing the political exploitation of this discourse of authenticity. Framed by the cultural politics of decolonization, there was tacit alignment between the institutionalized political articulation of authenticity and its cultural and aesthetic production. It is only much later in the 1980s that mainstream Sinhala artists begin to critique the political exploitation of authenticity as post-independence Sri Lanka faced grave political and economic threats.[22] The tacit compact between the institutionalized political discourse of authenticity and its cultural and aesthetic articulation blunts the progressivism of Sinhala artistic production. It stifles the emergence of progressivist leftist art that is critical of the nation state. It is only in the late 1960s and 1970s that artistic production explicitly critical of the nation state begins to emerge, with the economic and political promise of the postcolonial nation state beginning to fail.

The village-urban dynamic of Wickramasinghe's work and the search for social justice continues in two sequels to *Gamperaliya* – *Kaliyugaya* or *Age of Kali* (2001 [1957]) and *Yuganthaya* or *End of an Era* (1965 [1949]). The three books form a tri part saga in which Sinhala society, particularly its emergent middle- and upper-middle classes, are depicted as becoming increasingly unmoored from the organicism of village life. One figure who spans all three novels, Tissa, the son of the manor house in *Gamperaliya*, embodies a kind of 'ideal' postcolonial subjectivity. Tissa remains anchored to a set of core village-based values even though he migrates to the city and becomes part of the emergent middle class.

[19] Jonathan Spencer, 'Writing Within: Anthropology, Nationalism and Culture in Sri Lanka', *Current Anthropology* 31, no. 3(1990), 283–300; Stanley J. Tambiah, *Buddhism Betrayed? Religion, Politics and Violence in Sri Lanka* (Chicago: The University of Chicago Press, 1992).

[20] Rambukwella, *The Politics and Poetics of Authenticity*, 86–90.

[21] H. L. Seneviratne, *The Work of Kings: The New Buddhism in Sri Lanka* (Chicago: University of Chicago Press, 1999).

[22] Rambukwella, *The Politics and Poetics of Authenticity*.

Tissa's subjectivity represents an ontological dilemma of a decolonizing subject torn between tradition and modernity – between authenticity and inauthenticity. In contrast to this are other characters who in their desire for social mobility lose touch with authenticity and the values of village life – especially as they become anglicized in their attempts to climb the urban social ladder.

An abiding characteristic of Wickramasinghe's work is that the fidelity to a village-based sense of authenticity qualifies and overdetermines his sympathies towards leftist politics and social justice. As mentioned earlier, when S. W. R. D. Bandaranaike swept to power on a populist Sinhala and Buddhist political wave, Wickramasinghe publicly admired and endorsed the victory penning an essay titled *bamunu kulaye bindaweteema* or 'the fall of the *bamunu* (elite) comprador class'. However, Wickramasinghe's admiration for the victory was not about the rise of a proletariat class in the leftist sense but because it was a victory for an indigenous village-based lobby (Ayurveda doctors, school teachers, the Buddhist clergy, farmers and workers) marginalized by colonial power structures.

This ethno-religiously tempered socialism is also visible in *Yuganthaya* or *End of an Era*, the final book of the *Gampaeraliya* triology where Wickramasinghe's most explicit representation of leftist politics is found. In *Yuganthaya* (1965 [1949]) the daughter of Piyal and Nanda – the two main protagonists of *Gamperaliya* – is married to an anglicized Sinhala businessman named Simon Kabalana. Kabalana is depicted as a hard-nosed capitalist whose British-educated son Malin returns to Sri Lanka as a radical leftist. Malin has many ideological disagreements with his father about the exploitation of workers and ultimately leads a labour revolt against his father's business empire. Wickramasinghe crafts Malin's character ambiguously. The London-educated leftie is admired for his idealistic social commitment but is a rootless figure compared to his close friend Aravinda who is a British-qualified medical doctor but culturally far more rooted due to his village upbringing. Malin, arguably, also stands as a metaphor for the limitations of the old left in Sri Lanka – who were similar to Malin in their cultural outlook due to their anglophone upbringing.

Wickramasinghe later returns to a leftist theme in one of his last books *Bava Taranaya* (1973), *Transcending Existence*. The book was written within the context of the emerging JVP movement as a radical alternative to the old left. The book is an unconventional retelling of the life of Prince Siddartha before he attained Buddhahood. It departs from traditional representations of Siddartha and gives him a socialist character.[23] Siddartha is imagined similar to Malin in

[23] Chamila Somiratne, 'Re-envisioning a Discipline: Martin Wickramasinghe's Contribution to Comparative Literature' (MA Thesis, University of Massachusetts, Amherst, 2016), 66–70.

Yuganthaya – a young rebel from a noble and wealthy background who identifies himself with the 'common people'. However, by using the character and the story of the Buddha, Wickramasinghe in essence is couching a socialist theme, within an indigenist aesthetic and cultural register. Ironically though, Wickramasinghe was heavily criticized for the perceived profane representation of the Buddha's character.[24] As we shall see further, Gunadasa Amarasekara attempts a much more explicit 'indigenization' of leftist politics through a syncretic Buddhist–Marxist reading. What is common to both writers though is that their leftist or socialist sympathies are framed by an overarching Sinhala-centric worldview.

Ediriweera Sarachchandra: The longing for national form

Ediriweera Sarachchandra, though younger than Wickramasinghe, is considered Wickramasinghe's counterpart in theatre. While Wickramasinghe is seen as the figure invested in preserving and propagating a Sinhala and Buddhist ethos and identity, Sarachchandra is often seen as his cosmopolitan foil.[25] Such a division, however, is unhelpful. Both Sarachchandra and Wickramasinghe need to be seen as two expressions of a hegemonic Sinhala cultural discourse closely associated with the identity of the postcolonial Sri Lankan nation state. Neither Wickramasinghe nor Sarachchandra was a Sinhala nationalist in the sense the term is understood today. However, it is clear that for both figures the cultural identity of the newly independent nation was anchored primarily in a Sinhala and Buddhist ethos.

One reason why Sarachchandra is seen as the more cosmopolitan of the two figures is because his artistic practice was less overtly 'socially engaged'. He rarely professed a political ideology and was not invested in the kind of village-based authenticity or *apekama* that is identified with Wickramasinghe. Sarachchandra styled himself as a liberal-humanist interested in artistic form and content rather than the social relevance of art. Almost his entire dramatic oeuvre from the 1950s to 1960s period had a classicist and abstract quality. However, later in his career Sarachchandra did produce more 'socially engaged' theatre and also wrote fiction which had direct relevance to his contemporary social context. However, it is in his early theatrical practice and the way it was received, particularly by leftist critics, that the deep structural imprint of Sinhala nationalism and how it held

[24] R. Jayatunge, '*Bava Taranaya* – Reviewed after 37 Years', *News Article*, 2011. http://www.lankaweb.com/news/items/2011/01/04/bhava-tharanaya-reviewed-after-37-years/.

[25] Anupama Mohan, *Utopia and the Village in South Asian Literatures* (Basingstoke: Palgrave McMillan, 2012).

a fascination for leftist artistic criticism is apparent. In order to understand why Sarachchandra's theatre can be seen as a site of a bourgeois nationalist aesthetic production, I briefly sketch below the critical reception of two of his most iconic plays, *Maname* (1956) and *Sinhabahu* (1961), which have seen thousands of productions and remain popular.

Maname dramatizes the well-known *Chulla Dhanuddhara* Jathaka – from the Buddhist Jathaka story tradition (a cycle of 550 stories which chronicle the past lives of the Buddha before he attains Buddhahood) – where the virtuous Prince Maname is betrayed by his newly-wed wife. In the original story a band of wild men confront the prince and princess and assures the prince safe passage if the princess is left behind. The prince decides to fight for the honour of his wife. When he defeats the chief of the wild men in single combat and asks the princess for the sword to slay the chief, she is overcome by the masculine attraction of the wild man and gives the sword to the chief instead of her husband. In the end the wild men collect her jewellery and abandon her in the forest. The Jathaka story is a parable on lust and morality where the woman is censured for her passion.

Sarachchandra's retelling complicates this moral structure. Both the prince and princess are shown to be sensuous and excited by the freedom from the bonds of civility represented by the forest. In the climax of the play, when the prince asks for the sword, the princess argues that the wild man's life should be spared because he honourably agreed to single combat, when he could have easily overpowered the prince using his men. Temporarily fazed by this argument the prince relaxes his hold on the chief who then escapes and grabs the sword and kills the prince.[26] This slight change in plot throws up a number of questions about civility–uncivility, the place of passion in human life and the agency of a woman bound by tradition. The princess therefore becomes a complex figure and a passionate woman testing the boundaries imposed on her subjectivity by tradition. However, even in Sarachchandra's rendition the woman is ultimately blamed because the chief of the wild men abandons her after accusing her of being fickle. Haththotuwegama argues that the dramatic potential offered by the complex and 'modern' woman represented by the princess is lost in this didactic ending.[27] The play's content, therefore, reproduces a traditional moral structure

[26] A. J. Gunawardena, 'Asia's Modern Theatres: Encounters with Tradition', in *The World Encyclopedia of Contemporary Theatre: Asia/Pacific*, eds. Don Rubin, Chua Soo Pong and Ravi Chaturvedi (London: Routledge, 2000), 21.

[27] Gamini Haththotuwegama, '*Maname Natya saha Madyama Panthika Sanskruthiya* (The *Maname* Drama and Middle Class Culture)', in *Streets Ahead with Haththotuwegama*, ed. Kanchuka Dharmasiri (Piliyandala, Sri Lanka: Ravaya Publishers, 2012), 214.

which Sinhala audiences would have found familiar. The formal innovation of Sarachchandra's theatre, one can argue, is not matched by its thematic content.

Haththotuwegama also argues that a similar dynamic is visible in *Sinhabahu,* which is based on the founding anthromorphic myth of the Sinhala race, which holds that the Sinhalese descended from a union between a mythical lion and a human princess.[28] In *Sinhabahu* as well there is squandered dramatic potential in the character of Suppa Devi, the princess – a complex woman inhabiting many contradictory subjectivities – who runs away with the lion. Haththotuwegama (2012b) contends that this underdevelopment is due to the influence of bourgeois Sinhala culture. It is also significant to note that the two sources of Sarachchandra's most iconic plays are built on two main points of reference in postcolonial Sinhala nationalism: Buddhism and Sinhala ethnic identity. The enduring popularity of the two plays, therefore, may have much to do with how they speak to this cultural imaginary.

While Sarachchandra's theatre is not explicitly 'socially engaged' unlike the fiction of Wickramasinghe – which deals with social and cultural change in decolonizing Sri Lanka – Sarachchandra's theatre is also a product of this historical moment and invested in the emergent Sinhala nationalist nation state. This duality is apparent in how leftist critics admired Sarachchandra's theatre but criticized his views on aesthetics. One such significant leftist intervention was by Sucharitha Gamlath, a professor of Sinhala language and literature with a PhD in philosophy from University College, London. Gamlath was closely associated with the Trotskyist left in Sri Lanka and, in particular, the Revolutionary Communist League (RCL), which was founded in 1968 by the Keethi Balasooriya, a student member of the LSSP or Lanka Equal Society Party.[29]

Gamlath's strongest and most sustained critique of Sarachchandra appears in the 1986 publication *Kalpanalokavadaya, Sahithyakala ha Maaksvaadaya* (*Idealism, the Arts and Marxism*), co-authored with Keerthi Balasooriya (Balasuriya and Gamlath 1999 [1986]). This text is positioned as an extended Marxist refutation of Sarachchandra's 1959 *Kalpana Lokaya* (*The World of the Imagination*). Sarachchandra's text, as outlined earlier, is essentially a liberal-humanist treatise on the autonomy of art and the freedom of artistic choice – politics or social commitments are extraneous or at best marginal to the business of the artist. It is also a text that upholds the possibility of universal aesthetic

[28] Ibid., 215

[29] Dewasiri, 'Mainstreaming Radical Politics in Sri Lanka', 79.

criteria and the power of the individual imagination. Predictably Gamlath finds this position problematic and marshals a wide body of Marxist literary criticism to refute Sarachchandra. He sees Sarachchandra's ideas on art and culture as esoteric, idealistic and lacking in social commitment. He also sees Sarachchandra's encouragement of modernist and existentialist literary and artistic production in Sinhala as deeply problematic. Gamlath also contrasts Sarachchandra with Martin Wickramasinghe and argues the latter was more socially conscious. However, Gamlath argues that Wickramasinghe's understanding of Sinhala and Buddhist culture as a bulwark of authenticity against modernity fails to take into account how capitalism has radically remoulded Sri Lanka – implicitly suggesting that a combination of local authenticity with socialist ideology is necessary to understand contemporary Sri Lankan society. As we will see in the next section, Gmalath's views closely resonate with Amarasekara's explicitly nationalist approach to art and culture.

In contrast to this general critique of Sarachchandra's aesthetic views, Gamlath is at pains to establish that Sarachchandra's theatre, especially *Maname* and *Sinhabahu*, are sophisticated high points of postcolonial Sinhala theatre. Gamlath argues that Sarachchandra, the dramatist, was instinctively sensitive to the social world of the Sinhala people. In contrast, in his literary criticism Sarachchandra was a modernist idealist out of touch with society.[30] The irony of this dichotomizing of Sarachchandra is that Sarachchandra himself commented that he 'took drama from the village but never took it back'.[31] As scholars like Haththotuwegama have argued, Sarachchandra's theatrical experiments, innovative and significant as they were, served to make drama a thoroughly bourgeois form.[32] They allowed monolingual English-speaking and bilingual English- and Sinhala-speaking urban audiences to imagine a space of convergence between their urban lives and the larger cultural life of the country through their appreciation of Sarachchandra's theatre. It can be added to Haththotuwegama's critique that through Sarachchandra's theatre middle-class, urban Sinhala audiences found a cultural expression for the political project of *jathiya godanageema*, or 'nation building'[33] – a project infused with notions of

30 Sucharitha Gamlath and Keerthi Balasuriya, *Kalpanalokavadaya, Sahithyakala ha Maaksvaadaya* (*Idealism, the Arts and Marxism*) (Colombo: Godage, 1986 [1999]).

31 Gamini Haththotuwegama, 'Unresolved Contradictions, Paradoxical Discourses and Alternative Strategies in the Post-colonial Sinhala Theatre', in *Streets Ahead with Haththotuwegama*, ed. Kanchuka Dharmasiri (Piliyandala, Sri Lanka: Ravaya Publishers, 2012a), 210.

32 Haththotuwegama, '*Maname Natya saha Madyama Panthika*', 190.

33 Jayadeva Uyangoda, *Jathiya, Jathikawadaya Saha Jathika Rajya* (Nation, Nationalism and Nation-State) (Colombo: Social Scientists Association, 1994).

Sinhala authenticity or *apekama* which displaced the more inclusive discourse of *deshiya* or indigeneity.[34]

Gunadasa Amarasekara: Fusing Sinhala nationalism and leftist social transformation

Amarasekara began his literary career as a member of the so-called Peradeniya School – a 1950s artistic movement associated with the University of Peradeniya. It identified Sarachchandra as its artistic guru. A hallmark of the Peradeniya School was innovation – particularly in experimenting with different genres and artistic trends, especially those popular in Europe and the Anglophone world at the time. Amarasekara's own work from this period is marked by experimentation with literary modernism. Some of his early novels such as *Karumakkarayo* (*The Damned* 1955) and *Yali Upannemi* (*I am Reborn* 1960) were highly contentious due to their sexually explicit themes and critical probing of rural and urban Sinhala culture. Sarachchandra actively encouraged these works and praised Amarasekara – not necessarily for the social content of his writing but for the formal innovation and willingness to experiment.[35] However, Amarasekara experienced a 'nationalist turn' in the early 1960s – partly as the result of a public critique of his work by Martin Wickramasinghe, which accused Amarasekara of misrepresenting Sinhala culture – specifically its rural Buddhist ethos.[36] Amarasekara has also stated that he found the liberal humanism of the Peradeniya School stifling and culturally irrelevant.[37] Following this nationalist turn, Amarasekara's work begins to turn increasingly nativist, and he begins to see himself as a kind of literary didact whose primary mission is to artistically define and disseminate Sinhala and Buddhist authenticity within a socialist programme for social transformation.

Amarasekara first began systematically expressing these ideas in *Abudassa Yugayak* (A topsy-turvey time) (1976) and later elaborated them in *Anagarika Dharmapala Maaksvaadeeda?* (Is Anagarika Dharmapala Marxist?) (1980). Both texts attempt to construct a grand narrative of post-independence Sinhala nationalism. The basic contours of Amarsekara's argument are that a

34 Kanchuka Dharmasiri, 'From Narratives of National Origin to Bloodied Streets: Contemporary Sinhala and Tamil Theatre in Sri Lanka', in *Mapping South Asia through Contemporary Theatre: Studies in International Performance*, ed. A. Sengupta (London: Palgrave Macmillan, 2014).

35 Wimal Dissanayake, *Enabling Traditions: Four Sinhala Cultural Intellectuals* (Boralesgamuwa, Sri Lanka: Visidunu Publishers, 2005).

36 Ibid., 113–36.

37 Malinda Seneviratne, 'Gunadasa Amrasekara – The Dentist-philosopher Rooted in Sinhala Soil', *Infolanka*, 2000. http://www.infolanka.com/org/srilanka/people/57.htm.

form of Sinhala authenticity has survived the colonial encounter. Anagarika Dharmapala, an early-twentieth-century Buddhist missionary and social reformer, instinctively recognized this authenticity and tried to revive it for a modern social reform project but did not have the political backing or political understanding to do so. Later in 1956, S. W. R. D. Bandaranaike also instinctually tapped into this discourse of authenticity, though he came from an anglophone background. However, in both instances this discourse was thwarted by comprador interests. It is in this context that Amarasekara proposes a new social contract where Marxism can be synthesized with Buddhism to indigenize Marxism and make it 'authentic'. Amarasekara's views here are shaped by the same village-based discourse of Sinhala authenticity that Wickraramasinghe identified with. Amarasekara then links this social vision to a didactic artistic mission for the artist – a political role that the nationalist artist has to perform.[38] In the course of making this argument Amarasekara also engages in a critique of Sarachchandra that replicates Gamlath's – admiring Sarachchandra's theatre while critiquing his overall artistic vision.

Both *Abudassa Yugyak* (1976) and *Anagarika Dharmapala Maksvaadeeda* (1980) were written in a context in which leftist politics took a radical turn. While the post-Bandaranaike era saw the political institutionalization of Sinhala nationalism, economically the promise of decolonization hardly materialized and there was frustration, particularly among rural educated youth.[39] Parallel to the economic stagnation of the country was an emergent schism within the left movement where the 'old left' and the established political elite were seen as a comprador class by vernacular-educated rural youth who were entering the political process in the decades after 1956 – sometimes referred to as the 'children of '56'.[40] It is in this context that the radical 'new left' emerged in the form of the JVP, or People's Liberation Front, led by the charismatic Rohana Wijeweera, a rural Sinhala youth from southern Sri Lanka who had attended the Patrice Lumumba University in Soviet Russia. The JVP built a highly effective village-level network and used a system called the *panthi paha* (five classes) for ideological indoctrination,[41] and positioned itself explicitly as a radical alternative to the 'old left'. In 1971 the JVP launched a failed military coup to

[38] Amarasekara, Gunadasa. *Abudassa Yugayak* (A Topsy-turvy Time) (Boralesgamuwa, Sri Lanka: Visidunu Publishers, 1976); Gunadasa Amarasekara, *Anagarika Dharmapala Māksvādida?* (*Is Anagarika Dharmapala Marxist?*) (Kaluthara, Sri Lanka: Sampath Publishing House, 1980).

[39] K. M. de Silva, *A History of Sri Lanka* (Chennai, India: Oxford University Press, 1981), 504–5.

[40] Nalin de Silva, 'Bandaranaike's and '56', *The Island*, 2005 October 12. http://www.island.lk/2005/10/12/midweek3.html; Wickramasinghe, *Sri Lanka In the Modern Age*, 230–7.

[41] Dewasiri 'Mainstreaming Radical Politics in Sri Lanka, 69–94.

capture state power and was bloodily suppressed in a brutal crackdown by a coalition government led by Bandaranaike's widow in which the old left played a significant role.[42] It is in this context that Amarasekara makes his intervention to argue that a Sri Lankan leftist project needs a nativist element in order to succeed. In doing so, Amarasekara is also making an implicit appeal to the JVP to become more indigenist. This is a seemingly progressive argument, but the indigenist element Amarasekara proposes is exclusively Sinhala and Buddhist – a majoritarian political move at a time when Tamil youth unrest against elite political failures was also manifesting in the North of the country.

In concluding this section it should also be noted that there is anecdotal evidence that suggests ethno-nationalist overdetermination prevented potentially progressive inter-ethnic leftist artistic alliances. In 1947 Martin Wickramasinghe was the vice president of the inaugural committee of the Ceylon Writers Association (CWA), styled after the Indian Progressive Writers Association. However, by the mid-1950s he no longer played any active role in it.[43] Similarly Ediriweera Sarachchandra was also associated with the establishment of the CWA but is no longer active by the 1950s (Third Eye 2002). While this cannot be attributed to any explicit 'nationalist' orientation on the part of Wickramasinghe or Sarachchandra, what it does point to is the kind of identity politics that shaped this period of Sri Lankan history. The CWA did, however, achieve a more progressive role in Tamil society where it facilitated the emergence of literary voices from traditionally marginalized castes within the Tamil community and also challenged existing classical literary traditions in favour of more socially engaged forms.[44]

The early avant-garde left

By the 1960s discourses oppositional to mainstream Sinhala cultural and aesthetic discourse began to emerge. Collectively these efforts can be described as an avant-garde movement. Many of these avant-garde initiatives emphasized the social relevance of art, but with distinct differences to the artistic practice that preceded them. Within the bourgeois national aesthetic represented by

42 Wickramasinghe, *Sri Lanka In the Modern Age*, 237.

43 Selvy Thiruchandran, 'Progressive Writers and the Progressives: Some Thoughts', *Pravada* 3, no. 6, 26–9 (Colombo: Social Scientists Association, 1994).

44 Thiruchandran 1994; Karthigesu Sivathamby, '50 Years of Sri Lankan Tamil Literature', *Frontline* 16(9), May 1999.

figures like Sarachchandra, Wickramasinghe and Amarasekara social relevance was defined in terms of either a classicist orientation which looked to history, religion and myth for inspiration, or as in Wickremesinghe and the later Amarasekara, a pastoral, village-based notion of authenticity. For the avant-garde artists of the late 1960s and 1970s, social relevance was located in trying to come to terms with the major social, political and cultural shifts occurring in contemporary Sri Lankan society – particularly the problems of frustrated rural youth in the city. Both in form and content their responses were distinct to what preceded them and a left-leaning progressive stance characterized the work of most of these artists. Some of them were also critically self-conscious about how the forms and genres they used were politically and ideologically invested in bourgeois nationalism and drew inspiration from radical international and regional artistic movements. Leftist scholars such as Gamlath engaged with the avant-garde. However, given the hegemony of mainstream nationalist Sinhala cultural discourse, the avant-garde was often misread and misunderstood.

An early example of progressive artistic expression is the work of dramatist Sugathapala de Silva who formed the theatre group *apey kattiya* (our people) in the 1960s. de Silva's theatre was a direct reaction to what he saw as the classical elitism and social irrelevance of the work of Sarachchandra. The titles of some of his early plays, such as '*Boarding Karayo*' (Boarding-house Guys) staged in 1962 or *Thattu Geval* (Tenements) staged in 1963 indicate an earthy, urban realism. These plays implicitly question the postcolonial cultural euphoria and stylistic elitism in the works of Sarachchandra. de Silva and the members of *appey kattiya* considered themselves outsiders to the social and cultural milieu represented by Sarachchandra and the bourgeois postcolonial Sinhala cultural tradition of the 1950s.[45] For instance, *Boarding Karayo* dramatizes the lives of four lower-middle-class workers boarded in a 'chummery' – a term denoting a building that provides lodging for unmarried men. These four individuals represent rural youth who have migrated to the city in search of a better life. The play dramatizes their humdrum existence along with those of the landlady and her young daughter and the female cook and young odd-job boy who work for the 'chummery'.[46] The play speaks to the frustrations of rural lower-middle-class youth and the economic and social stagnation of post-independence Sri Lanka. It is also likely that Sugathapala de Silva was influenced by anti-establishment

[45] Ariyawansa Ranaweera, 'Diminishing legacy of Dr Sarachchandra and the Arrival of the "Outsiders"', *The Island* (10 June 2016). http://www.island.lk/index.php?page_cat=article-details&page=article-details&code_title=59933.

[46] *Dinamina*.

theatre like John Osborne's *Look Back in Anger* (1956) – which were available to young playwrights like de Silva within a vibrant Colombo-based cultural milieu. As Sarath Amunugama notes, embassies on either side of the Cold-War ideological divide regularly screened films and plays as part of their 'soft' cultural diplomacy efforts.[47]

Gamini Haththotuwegama's 'Wayside and Open Theatre' group was another significant alternative theatrical presence that emerged in this period. Though not aligned with a specific leftist political ideology, Haththotuwegama's theatrical practice throughout his career remained oppositional – refusing the proscenium theatre and other institutional performance spaces for street corners, bus stands and pavements.[48] The group also experimented with many forms, including absurdism, physical theatre and surrealism. The performers themselves were drawn largely from working-class backgrounds. One iconic moment in the group's history was when it 'gate crashed' an FAO (Food and Agriculture Organization of the United Nations) banquet meeting in Colombo to stage a satire on world politics and the exploitation of the Third World by the First World.[49] The group also consistently satirized and critiqued contemporary Sri Lankan society. One of their most popular productions was *Wesak Dekma* which speaks to the commodification of religion within the emerging neo-liberal economy following reforms in the late 1970s. In the play a father and son duo become reduced to the level of mendicants, unable to afford any of the goods or services on offer during *Wesak* (the Buddhist religious day and festivities celebrating the birth, enlightenment and death of the Buddha), leading them to conclude that they cannot 'afford' religion. Haththotuwegama's philosophy was of a truly 'open' theatre in which class, education or even geography were not barriers to artistic production and appreciation. In spirit and method it resembled Augusto Boal's theatre of the oppressed. However, his work also received limited recognition from the cultural establishment and remained very much on the margins of mainstream Sinhala cultural discourse. It was only in 2012, after his untimely death, that a volume covering his work was published by one of his former students (cited as Dharmasiri 2012 in this chapter).

One of the most significant presences in this avant-gardist movement was the film-maker Dhramasena Pathiraja who gained prominence in the 1970s

47 Sarath Amunugama, 'Tony Ranasinghe: From Angry Young Man to Star-crossed Lover', *The Island* (27 June 2015). http://island.lk/index.php?page_cat=article-details&page=article-details&code_title=127269.

48 Kanchuka Dharmasiri, 'Introduction', in *Streets Ahead with Haththootuwegama*, ed. Kanchuka Dharmasiri (Maharagama, Sri Lanka: Ravaya Publishers, 2012), 17.

49 Ibid., 18–19.

and has been described as a 'rebel with a cause'[50] and 'the left-bank (*Rive Gauche*) film maker'.[51] Pathiraja's films – much like Sugathapala de Silva's and Hathtotuwegama's plays – can be seen in part as a response to the bourgeois nationalist aesthetic of the 1950s and a response to a rapidly changing social and political reality. Collectively they were also deeply influenced by the rise of the JVP and its bloody suppression and what this represented in terms of the failure of the post-independence Sri Lankan nation state. However, unlike nationalist artists like Amarasekara, avant-garde artists like Pathiraja saw this as a collective national tragedy which victimized both Sinhala and Tamil youth. Pathiraja is also unique because he directed '*Ponmani*' (1976), Sri Lanka's one and only Tamil film by a Sinhala director based on his experiences while working as a lecturer at the Department of Sinhala at Jaffna University in the North of the country. Jaffna University at the time was also a hotbed of leftist artistic activity[52] and *Ponmani* can be seen as a product of this environment. The film has been hailed as a sensitive and critical interrogation of caste and class in middle-class Jaffna life.[53]

In film-making, the equivalent of Sarachchandra and Wickramasinghe was Lester James Peries, an internationally renowned and stylistically accomplished film-maker whose most celebrated cinematic work *Gamperaliya* was based on the iconic novel by Wickramasinghe – an indication of how dominant the bourgeois aesthetic was across different genres and modes of expression. Peries's cinema was characterized by a bourgeois realist aesthetic and an intense fascination with the village and themes of rural disintegration. Pathiraja has indicated that his cinema is an attempt to break free of this mould and explore new forms and thematic concerns in search of an alternative mode of cinematic expression.[54] Pathiraja has also compared his cinematic journey to that of Ritwik Ghatak in India and draws comparisons between his situation vis-à-vis Peries to that of Ghatak and Satyajit

50 Brandon Wee, 'In conversation with Sri Lankan Director Dharmasena Pathiraja', *Kinema: A Journal for Visual and Audiovisual Media* (2003). http://www.kinema.uwaterloo.ca/article.php?id=78&feature.

51 Manjula Wediwardena, '*Yuddhaya Pilibanda Gemburu Sinamawak Bihiwanu Aththe Uthuren*' (A Substantive Cinema about the War Can Only Emerge from the North) – Interview with Dharmasena Pathiraja (2016). http://www.jdslanka.org/s/index.php/2014-12-20-03-09-05/2014-12-20-03-12-04/560-2016-04-19-08-49-02.

52 Mahendran Thiruvagaran, 'Clash at Jaffna University: Conversation on Culture and History – Part II', *Colombo Telegraph*, 2016. https://www.colombotelegraph.com/index.php/clash-at-jaffna-university-conversations-on-culture-history-part-ii/.

53 Edwin Ariyadasa, Dr. Dharmasena Pathiraja: Revolutionary Film Maker', (2018). http://www.dailynews.lk/2018/01/29/local/141288/dr-dharmasena-pathiraja-revolutionary-film-director?page=71.

54 Dharmasena Pathiraja, 'It is Like An Incomplete Sentence: Pathiraja Speaks to Sumathy Sivamohan', in *An Incomplete Sentence: The Cinema of Dharmasena Pathiraja* (Boralesgamuwa, Sri Lanka: Network for the Promotion of Asian Cinema (NETPAC), 2009a), 5.

Rai.[55] Lester James Peries's cinema is often seen as the founding of a modern Sri Lankan (read Sinhala) cinema and therefore a norm against which alternative expressions like Pathiraja's became judged. The normative influence of Peries's cinema also meant that funding and production opportunities for avant-garde artists such as Pathiraja were limited. Peries's international acclaim can also be attributed to some extent to the themes he pursued and a kind of Orientalist fascination they may have held for Western critics.[56]

Pathiraja was briefly a member of a Trotskyite Party and, as he recounts in several interviews, was influenced by the major sociopolitical shifts in Sri Lankan society in the 1970s – the catalytic event being the JVP uprising of 1971.[57] Pathiraja was also what one might call a 'theoretically informed' film-maker who as a university academic studied film and critical theory and was particularly influenced by the radical cinema of Goddard, Rocha, Ghatak and Sen.[58] Many of his films probe issues such as youth culture, working-class urban life, the influence of capital on traditional structures of life and a Sri Lankan modernity shaped by market forces and neo-liberal capital. A significant feature of Pathiraja's cinema is a degree of self-reflexivity about his medium and thematic concerns – a feature he attributes to the influence of Ghatak on his cinema and the unease he had with the cinematic idiom of established figures like Rai and its relationship to normative and hegemonic notions of nation.[59]

However, within Sri Lankan leftist critical discourse Pathiraja's cinema had a mixed reception. This is evident in the divergent critical responses Pathiraja received for two of his most significant cinematic achievements, *Bambaru Awith* (*The Wasps are Here* 1978) and *Soldadu Unnahe* (*The Old Soldier* 1981). *The Wasps are Here* is a story about the clash of anonymous urban capital, personified by a charismatic young urban entrepreneur, with the established village order represented by an equally charismatic older fisherman in a remote fishing village in the north-west tip of Sri Lanka. Many leftist critics received the film with much approbation – primarily due to what they saw as its social realism. But as one leftist critic outside mainstream Sinhala cultural discourse observed, the

[55] Manjula Wediawardena, '*Yuddhaya Pilibanda Gemburu Sinamawak Bihiwanu Aththe Uthuren*' (A Substantive Cinema about the War Can Only Emerge from the North) – Interview with Dharmasena Pathiraja, 2016. http://www.jdslanka.org/s/index.php/2014-12-20-03-09-05/2014-12-20-03-12-04/560-2016-04-19-08-49-02.

[56] Pathiraja, 'It is Like An Incomplete Sentence'.

[57] Ibid.; Wediwardena, '*Yuddhaya Pilibanda Gemburu Sinamawak Bihiwanu Aththe Uthuren*'.

[58] Robert Crusz, An incomplete sentence. Booklet published on Dharmasena Pathiraja at the sixteenth Singapore International Film Festival, 2003.

[59] Dharmasena Pathiraja 'Where there is No Partition: Ghatak and I', in *An Incomplete Sentence: The Cinema of Dharmasena Pathiraja* (Boralesgamuwa, Sri Lanka: Network for the Promotion of Asian Cinema [NETPAC], 2009), 116.

film was much more than a political statement about capitalist exploitation. It was also a self-reflexive critique of the limits of bourgeois radicalism.[60] This critique is enacted by the figure of an educated Marxist urban youth who enters the fishing village as a friend of the young entrepreneur and pontificates about social justice from an idealistic theoretical stance, but is a helpless bystander in the conflict between the two forms of capitalism. In this film, Pathiraja seems to be turning the cinematic gaze inwards and questioning, at least partly, his own subjectivity as an urban bourgeois film-maker entering an unknown socio-cultural ethos, and holding naïve beliefs about the potential of radical politics – similar to the reflexivity in a film like *Akaler Sandhane* (*In Search of Famine* 1980) by Mrinal Sen (see Chapter 7 by Dass in this volume). However, for leftist critics like Sucharitha Gamlath the value of the film lay in what they saw as its faithful reproduction of social and material reality.

Pathiraja's other film, *The Old Soldier*, was a much more formally innovative work, which abandons the conventions of narrative cinema in favour of an episodic structure without a clear linear plot or storyline. The film centres on figures drawn from the peripheries of an urban underclass: a destitute soldier and a veteran of the Second World War, a prostitute, an alcoholic pimp and a pick-pocket. They interact over a three-day period leading up to and following Sri Lankan Independence Day. The film is about the meaning and meaninglessness of nation, nationalism and nation state and the violence of the state towards its subjects. The soldier who suffers from a form of PTSD is unnerved by the Independence Day military parade, and is treated as a madman for being afraid of this peacetime expression of national and military pride. However, in the final sequence of the film, when the police drag him away for being a public nuisance, a symbolic connection is drawn between statist violence and its consequences for the subjects of the state – even for those who fought and defended it. The film has been noted for its austere economy of style, and for how it deconstructs the nation from within.[61] However, for many mainstream leftist critics, including Gamlath, the film was a failure because of its lack of social realism (Gamlath 2008).

The early 1980s, when *The Old Soldier* was first screened, was also a watershed period in the post-independence history of Sri Lanka. In 1983, the ethnic riots against the Tamil community erupted, and from the 1980s onwards Sri Lankan society was subjected to aggressive neo-liberal reforms under an 'open

[60] Reggie Siriwardena, 'Pathiraja Politics and Cinema', in *An Incomplete Sentence: The Cinema of Dharmasena Pathiraja* (Boralesgamuwa, Sri Lanka: Network for the Promotion of Asian Cinema [NETPAC], 2009 [1978]), 54.

[61] Ibid.

economic' policy, which in turn had wide-ranging impacts on the social life of urban and rural Sri Lanka. In cultural terms it also marked the beginning of the end for the state-centred bourgeois nationalist aesthetic inaugurated by figures like Sarachchandra and Wickramasinghe.[62] By the late 1980s it is also possible to see a heightened sense of anxiety and despondency in figures like Amarasekara, as they attempt to salvage the discourse of authenticity they carefully nurtured.[63] There was an exponential increase in popular culture and popular artistic production in theatre, literature, music and cinema. This growth in popular culture was facilitated by various electronic forms of reproduction and dissemination, such as audio and video cassettes and terrestrial TV and FM radio channels. But the political left, along with mainstream Sinhala cultural discourse, did little to recognize or theorize the importance of popular cultural expression. Instead, critics used the dismissive term 'cassette culture' to describe this popular culture.[64] A challenge for progressive artists of the period was how to tap the mass potential of popular culture for progressive political work, which artistes like Pathiraja acknowledged.[65] However, even in the 1980s, the waning grip of mainstream Sinhala culture kept progressive cultural work and alternative artistic discourses on the sidelines.

What is left? Concluding thoughts on the forms of the left in Sri Lankan cultural discourse

While the political left in Sri Lanka emerged as a progressive force through the early labour movement and nascent anti-imperial struggles in the early twentieth century, by the 1950s and 1960s significant sections of the left movement were compromised by majoritarian Sinhala nationalism. The 1950s also saw a consolidation of Sinhala nationalism as a statist discourse. Both the political and cultural imagination of the nation state increasingly became identified with Sinhala majoritarian identity – pithily captured in the Sinhala word for nation, *jathiya*, which conflates the Sinhala ethnic identity with that of the nation state.[66] Leftist cultural discourse, as this chapter has argued, largely subscribed to the default Sinhala-centric bourgeois nationalist aesthetic. Operating on a

62 Rambukwella, *The Politics and Poetics of Authenticity*, 102–36.
63 Ibid.
64 Rambukwella, *The Politics and Poetics of Authenticity*, 128 .
65 Pathiraja, 'It is Like An Incomplete Sentence'.
66 Uyangoda, *Jathiya, Jathikawadaya Saha Jathika Rajya*.

limited model of 'social relevance' and 'social realism', leftist cultural discourse was unable to offer a more inclusive alternative to mainstream Sinhala cultural production. At the same time progressive avant-garde cultural production was marginalized due the 'national longing for form'. This was in contrast to other parts of South Asia, such as India and Bangladesh, where the political left and leftist cultural discourse had a more sustained and nuanced engagement with avant-garde and popular forms of art.

Sri Lanka's story of leftist engagements with art and culture does not end with the 1980s avant-garde movement. Though under-theorized and largely unrecognized by the cultural establishment, avant-gardist cultural efforts continued in Sri Lanka through the 1980s and beyond. Within contemporary history of progressive cultural production, perhaps the most sustained alternative and radical cultural critique emerged in the work of the X-Group (*X-Kandaayama*), led by Deepthi Kumara Gunaratne and Nirmal Dewasiri in the mid-1990s, which also maintained links with the JVP.[67] The X-Group was instrumental in introducing post-structuralist and post-modernist aesthetics to Sinhala art and cultural criticism, and was also sensitive to the need to engage substantively with popular culture. The work of the X-Group has coincided with a new generation of film-makers, dramatists, musicians and writers who have been experimenting with form and content in numerous ways. Some of these artists have also formed collectives which seek to systematically contest mainstream culture and, while not rejecting popular culture, have sought to resist its increasing and intense marketization.

It is difficult, however, to characterize all these efforts as 'leftist'. One commonality they share is consistently raising issues that question and probe normative ideas that have dominated Sinhala cultural discourse since the 1950s. The work of these artists and cultural critics has raised questions about ethnicity, gender, sexuality and a host of other 'taboo' subjects. These efforts, however, also raise fundamental questions about what is meant by contemporary leftist political practice and aesthetics. Is anything that is oppositional to the cultural and political mainstream leftist? Or does there have to be some recognizable form of commitment to leftist political ideology and theory? As traditional leftist politics have declined the world over and even the JVP in Sri Lanka has become increasingly mainstream,[68] the form and shape of leftist aesthetics remain an open question – and one that this chapter can only pose as a provocation for further reflection.

[67] Dewasiri, 'Mainstreaming Radical Politics in Sri Lanka', 80.
[68] Ibid.

6

The conscience whipper

Alamgir Kabir's film criticism and the political velocity of the cinema in 1960s East Pakistan

Lotte Hoek

In September 1971, while civil war raged in Pakistan, a letter arrived from Park Street in Calcutta, addressed to the acting president of Mujibnagar, the exiled government of Bangladesh. The letter contained a pointed indictment of filmmaker Zahir Raihan and his short documentary *Stop Genocide* (1971). The letter's author, the film producer and director Fazlul Huq, writes: 'I, personally, protest against this film and I request you to immediate action to stop this film before it is shown to the public through the Indian government.'[1] Having seen the film in a private show in Calcutta, Huq objects vehemently to the film's content. He writes:

> The film start[s] with a photo of V.I. Lenin and with his wordings shows nothing but little of refugees [*sic*] and a little part of our liberation Army Training Camp. But the serious setback is, in my opinion, that there is not a single shot or word about our beloved leader Sheikh Mujibur Rahman or Awami League or, the six points.[2]

This state of affairs is worrisome to Huq because 'I believe if this film is shown in India or abroad, the viewers shall have the belief that our liberation is being guided by something else and not the points we believe in.'[3]

Whether Fazlul Huq received any response is not clear from the *Bangladesher Swadhinota Juddho Dolilpotro* (Bangladesh Liberation War Documents),

[1] Hasan Hafisur Rahman (ed.), *Bangladesher Swadhinota Juddho Dolilpotro* [Documents of the Bangladesh Independence War]. Vol. 3 – Mujibnagar (Dhaka: People's Republic of Bangladesh, Information Ministry, 2009 [1982–5]), 125.

[2] Ibid., 125–6.

[3] Ibid., 126.

in which his letter is collected. What is clear is that Zahir Raihan's film was screened in India and elsewhere abroad to generate awareness about the crisis. 'During Liberation War a compelling necessity was felt to publicise the cause of Bangladesh to the outside world through film medium' and Zahir Raihan 'was assigned to produce a number of documentaries'.[4] These documentary films included *Liberation Fighters* (1971, dir. Alamgir Kabir), *Innocent Millions* (1971, dir. Babul Chowdhury), *A State is Born* (1971, dir. Zahir Raihan) and *Stop Genocide*. They were co-produced by the Bangladesh Shilpi-Kushali Shahayak Samity and the Bangladesh Liberation Council of the Intelligentsia.[5] The latter was formed of 'teachers, writers, painters, artists and journalists of Bangladesh who have been forced to take temporary refuge in India'[6] and Zahir Raihan was its general secretary.[7] The Mujibnagar government in Calcutta, however, appears to have been ambivalent about the films.[8] The exiled government's External Publicity Division, in suggesting a set of articles to be carried by the Bangladesh UN delegation in September 1971, included 'Mr. Zahir Raihan's documentary films after proper editing'.[9] What 'proper editing' consisted in is not laid out but a certain ambivalence around the films of Zahir Raihan is palpable.[10]

In Fazlul Huq's letter this ambivalence over Raihan's films is expressed as discontent over the visual predominance of Lenin over Mujib, of the lines of refugees over the Six Points. And in many ways, this sentiment has come to prevail over the interpretation of these documentary films. Zahir Raihan and his films have been understood primarily within a nationalist framework, with Raihan described as the 'veteran Bengali-nationalist film- maker'.[11] But *Stop Genocide*, as well as other films in his oeuvre, suggests a more complex political orientation. It can not only be found in the quote and image of Lenin at the start of *Stop Genocide*, and the sound of the *International*, but also in the experimental, formalist, structure of the film. Fahmida Akhter describes *Stop Genocide* as 'an

4 Alamgir Kabir, *Film in Bangladesh* (Dhaka: Bangla Academy, 1979), 48.

5 Ibid.

6 Rahman, *Bangladesher Shwadhinota*, 475.

7 Ibid.; Abul Khaer Mohammad Atikuzzaman and Priyam Pritim Paul, *Cholochitro O Jatiyo Mukti – Alamgir Kabir, Rochona Shomogro, 1* (Cinema and National Liberation – Collected Works of Alamgir Kabir), Vol. 1 (Dhaka: Agami Prokashani, 2018), 24.

8 And Kabir's writing suggests there was distance between the Bangladesh Liberation Council of the Intelligentsia and the Awami League, see Atikuzzaman and Paul, *Cinema and National Liberation*, 24.

9 Rahman, *Bangladesher Shwadhinota*, 784.

10 See also Naeem Mohaiemen, 'Simulation at Wars' End: A "Documentary" in the Field of Evidence Quest', *BioScope: South Asian Screen Studies* 7, no. 1 (2016), 6.

11 Zakir Hossain Raju, *Bangladesh Cinema and National Identity. In Search of the Modern?* (London: Routledge, 2015), 84.

ethical cinematic appeal . . . that creates a dialectical cinematic language'.[12] The montage of the opening sequence echoes the rhythm of a telegram, with hard 'stops' on the soundtrack echoed by freeze frames stilling the images of the refugees that Raihan uses to underscore the devastation and despair. Raihan's style was in conversation with the cinema of Santiago Álvarez, in particular, and Third Cinema, more generally.[13] Alamgir Kabir, who delivered the narration in *Stop Genocide* and was centrally involved in the making of these documentaries during the war, understood the film's central achievement to be that 'the film convincingly established the genocidal crimes and successfully identified Bangladesh Liberation War, not as an isolated phenomenon, but as an integral part of the relentless struggle for better life being waged all around the world by working men and women'.[14] To Kabir, the film was both documentary evidence of the atrocities as well as a visionary document that placed these events within the longer sweep of anti-imperial and revolutionary struggles. The content of the imagery, the nature of the voiceover and the highly stylized montage can all be considered under the category of the 'forms of the left', a formal aesthetic that is wedded to the quest for the freedom and liberation of the working people of East Pakistan centred on the promises of socialism. *Stop Genocide* uses aesthetic tropes within cultural repertoires in Bengal that were already understood to participate in political formations on the left, as well as being in conversation with international cinematic movements and experiments. *Stop Genocide* uses forms of the left, combining local and transnational themes and aesthetics associated with particular historical formations, ideals and networks. And the film was immediately and disagreeably recognized as such by Fazlul Huq. And in this form, it was understood by both Raihan *and* by Huq to be highly politically efficacious, either for better or worse.

In this chapter, I explore forms of the left in the context of the cinema in East Pakistan in the 1960s. I argue that in the run-up to the genocide and war in 1971 that led to the independence of Bangladesh, cinema emerges as one of the art forms through which progressive and left political commitments could be expressed and shared by a group of artists and writers who worked across media. In the context of the American left, Michael Denning has described the

[12] Fahmida Akhter, Zahir Raihan's '*Stop Genocide* (1971): A Dialectical Cinematic Message to the World', in *South Asian Filmscapes: Transregional Encounters*, eds. Elora Halim Chowdhury and Esha Niyogi De (Seattle: University of Washington Press, 2020), 234.

[13] Fernando Solanas and Octavio Getino, 'Toward a Third Cinema', *Cinéaste* 4, no. 3 (1970–71), 1; Vijay Prasad, 'Naeem Mohaiemen's Tragic History of the 1970s Left', *Afterall: A Journal of Art, Context and Enquiry* 47 (Spring, Summer 2019), 64.

[14] Kabir, *Film in Bangladesh*, 49.

'politics of form' as the aesthetic ideologies that accompanied the networks of artists and cultural institutions on the American left, expressed in the 'repertoire of forms and styles, genres and conventions; and the critical controversies and debates that surrounded them [which] established ways of seeing and judging, canons of value'.[15] In this chapter, I will focus on the latter part of this 'politics of form' – through an exploration of Alamgir Kabir's efforts at public education around cinema. I ask how Kabir understood the formal aspects of the cinema as politically efficacious in the 1960s in the context of the continuing political tensions and conflicts in the latter days of East Pakistan. I focus on two sites and modes of film education offered by Alamgir Kabir: in his critical writing on the cinema, particularly in newspaper columns; and through his work in the film society movement and his film institute in the late 1960s in East Pakistan. I will argue that through both he encouraged a reading and viewing public to be familiar with and participate in the debates and controversies around repertoires of cinematic form, style, genre and convention to transform established ways of seeing and judging; with the explicit understanding that this would generate political and social transformation on the part of the individual viewer as well as the collective. That is, formal literacy was considered a political position. To contextualize Alamgir Kabir's views on the progressive nature of the moving image and cinema, I will situate his work within the left aesthetic field in East Pakistan that fed the consolidation of the film industry in East Pakistan from the late 1950s, before turning to Kabir's short form criticism published in the newspapers and his efforts at instilling formal understanding of the cinema through educational initiatives. My engagement with Kabir's work shows the ways in which the formal language of cinema has been understood and practiced as a politically progressive force allied to the left within East Pakistan and was inherited by film-makers and critics in independent Bangladesh (Figure 6.1).

Artists, cinema and the left in East Pakistan

The background against which an exploration of East Pakistani cinema comes into focus as a site for progressive or left-wing aesthetics, is the place of culture in the complex history of the political left and Communist Parties in eastern

[15] Denning, Michael, *The Cultural Front: The Laboring of American Culture in the Twentieth Century* (London: Verso, 1997), xix–xx.

Figure 6.1 Flowers and candles before portraits of Alamgir Kabir during his annual memorial lecture in Dhaka, January 2014. Photograph by author.

Bengal. At Partition, East Bengal[16] inherited an active communist movement with significant centres of communist activism in Barisal, Mymensingh and Rajshahi.[17] Between 1947 and the early 1950s, East Bengal saw the continuation of significant peasant and labour conflicts, revolts and uprisings, in which sharecroppers and workers resisted the exploitative conditions under which they laboured.[18] Communist Party membership, however, dwindled fast in the early years of Pakistan. Observers suggest that the 12,000 party members in East Bengal in 1947[19] dropped down to 'a few hundred'[20] in the 1950s. The decline is, first, attributed to the mass population movements between East and West Bengal which relocated a significant part of the membership. More significant

[16] After the 1947 Partition of British India, the eastern part of Pakistan was called East Bengal. From 1955 it was known as East Pakistan. In 1971 it became independent Bangladesh.

[17] Marcus Franda, 'Communism and Regional Politics in East Pakistan', *Asian Survey* 10, no. 7 (1970), 589.

[18] Layli Uddin, '"Enemy Agents at Work": A Microhistory of the 1954 Adamjee and Karnaphuli Riots in East Pakistan', *Modern Asian Studies* (2020), DOI: https://doi.org/10.1017/S0026749X19000416; Willem van Schendel, *A History of Bangladesh* (Cambridge: Cambridge University Press, 2009), 89–92.

[19] Moni Singh, *Establishing the Communist Party of Pakistan*, trans. Meghna Guhathakurty, in Meghna Guhathakurta and Willem van Schendel, *The Bangladesh Reader: History, Culture, Politics* (Durham, NC: Duke University Press, 2013), 170; Badruddin Umar, *The Emergence of Bangladesh: Class Struggles in East Pakistan (1947-1958)* (Karachi: Oxford University Press, 2004), 47.

[20] Talukder Maniruzzaman, *The Bangladesh Revolution and Its Aftermath* (Dhaka: UPL, 2003 [1980]), 35; Umar, *The Emergence of Bangladesh*, 189.

were, second, the repressive conditions of the new Pakistan government,[21] which refused to release communists imprisoned by the British before 1947.[22] The party was not banned until 1954, yet many party workers were imprisoned and their activities violently disturbed.[23] Even in prison, the hunger strikes for better conditions in jail led by communist activists were violently and lethally repressed.[24] Third, at the Second Congress of the Communist Party of India in February 1948, when the Communist Party of Pakistan was established (with the East Bengal Party continuing to be guided by the [Indian] West Bengal Party), the direction charted by B. T. Ranadive to 'organize toiling masses to struggle for anti-imperialist and agrarian revolution so as to establish a people's democratic state led by the working class'[25] produced its own contradictions and resulted in the alienation of some party members in both parts of Pakistan[26] and in India, not least among artists and cultural workers, given Ranadive's 'apathetic attitude . . . to cultural action'.[27]

In light of the radical direction of the Communist Parties in India and Pakistan, and the repressive conditions in East Bengal, the remaining party workers operated largely underground even before 1954,[28] while left political work was undertaken via other fronts, such as the peasant and workers' organizations, the Youth League, the language movement, the East Pakistan Students Union and the Awami League.[29] By the 1960s, the Communist Party in East Pakistan had splintered into many rival factions, none of which were able to mobilize sufficient support and many were engaged deeply in doctrinal conflicts, while left-oriented front organizations operated across different social and cultural arenas.[30] This political splintering and use of other fronts allowed the diffusion of left political and cultural imaginaries. Talukder Maniruzzaman suggests that

> by 1969-70, the leftist movement in East Pakistan had moved a long way ahead of its poor start in 1947-8. Through the use of techniques . . . [such as] cultural subversion, infiltration of popular political organisations, manipulation

21 Kamran Asdar Ali, *Communism in Pakistan: Politics and Class Activism 1947-1972* (London: IB Taurus, 2015); Saadia Toor, *The State of Islam: Culture and Cold War Politics in Pakistan* (London: Hurst, 2011), Umar, *The Emergence of Bangladesh*, 48–9.

22 Umar, *The Emergence of Bangladesh*, 153.

23 Ibid., 47; Maniruzzaman, *The Bangladesh Revolution*, 35.

24 Umar, *The Emergence of Bangladesh*, 152–60.

25 Ali, *Communism in Pakistan*, 42.

26 Umar, *The Emergence of Bangladesh*, 189; Ali, *Communism in Pakistan*, 49–85.

27 Sunderason, *Partisan Aesthetics*, 127.

28 Umar, *The Emergence of Bangladesh*, 47.

29 Maniruzzaman, *The Bangladesh Revolution*, 37.

30 See Naeem Mohaiemen, '"Kothai Aj Shei Shiraj Sikder (Where Today Is that Shiraj Sikder)?" Terrorists or Guerrillas in the Mist', *Sarai Reader 06: Turbulence* (2006), 296–311. http://archive.sarai.net/files/original/aa81240315ea2e06d9a102b63fffe21.pdf.

> of sensitive issues of language, autonomy and economic distress, and anti-imperialist agitation – the leftists in Bengal achieved a major change in the political *atmosphere*, making it favourable for secular and radical politics.[31]

Cultural organizations were a significant part in the making of this atmosphere and culture was among the most significant arenas of ideological contestation in East Pakistan between 1947 and 1971.[32]

Cultural organizations had been and would be 'fronts' in the struggle towards social transformation and revolution in East Bengal. In pre-Partition eastern Bengal, the boundaries between cultural and political action were porous, as Somnath Hore's drawings from the Tebagha movement and Zainul Abedin's famine sketches illustrate. IPTA had been very active in eastern Bengal, especially around Chittagong, where songs were used 'to popularize anti-fascist and Marxist ideals among masses'.[33] IPTA songs remained in circulation in the decades after Partition.[34] After 1947, cultural organizations and movements in East Bengal, including the theatre movement, *Pragati Lekhak O Shilpi Sangha* (the Progressive Writers and Artists' Association), *Udichi Shilpi Goshthi* ('North Star' Artists' Group) and the *Mohilla Parishad* (Women's Council), had varying relations of proximity to left political organizations. Artists and writers such as Satyen Sen, Sufia Kamal, Zahir Raihan, Zainul Abedin and Munier Chowdhury had been associated with such left-oriented cultural front organizations, and the calls for radical transformation resounded in their work. Nazneen Ahmed, in her study of the place of poetry and song in political activism in East Pakistan, writes that '[f]rom 1947 to 1971, culture was the galvanizing object of the resistance movement, in terms of linguistic nationalism, and its vehicle for collective mobilization'.[35] Her account of poet Sufia Kamal's place within this field stresses the ambivalences of the gendered tropes by which her poetry calls for action on behalf of 'a reforming, secular nationalism'.[36] Yet Ahmed notes in passing how Kamal 'combined political activism within the resistance movement, socialist affiliations and social work for women's rights, throughout her long career as East Bengal's foremost female poet'.[37] Elsewhere, Ahmed has highlighted the

31 Maniruzzaman, *The Bangladesh Revolution*, 46 (emphasis mine).

32 Ali Raza, 'Dispatches from Havana: The Cold War, Afro-Asian Solidarities, and Culture Wars in Pakistan', *Journal of World History* 30, no. 1–2 (2019), 223–46.

33 Taj ul-Islam Hashmi, *Pakistan as Peasant Utopia: The Communalisation of Class Politics in East Bengal, 1920-1947* (Dhaka: University Press Limited, 1992), 223.

34 Ibid., 223–5.

35 Nazneen Ahmed, 'The Poetics of Nationalism: Cultural Resistance and Poetry in East Pakistan/ Bangladesh, 1952–71', *Journal of Postcolonial Writing* 50, no. 3 (2014a), 256.

36 Ibid., 264.

37 Ibid., 263.

connections Kamal maintained with the Progressive Writer's Movement.[38] On the cusp of the Liberation War, Kamal becomes the president of the 'Mahila Parishad, an off-shoot of the Communist Party'.[39] Culture was the site where underground workers and fellow-travellers met and works of art and criticism were among the means by which social criticism and utopian visions could be expressed.

Syed Jamil Ahmed describes a potent moment of prison theatre in Dhaka on 21 February 1953 that brings the political repression of leftist political activists together with artistic practice and cultural form. On that day, prisoners at Dhaka Central Jail covertly performed the play *Kabar* (The Grave) to commemorate the language martyrs who had been killed while demonstrating to have Bengali recognized as a state language of Pakistan.[40] The play was written by Munier Chowdhury, a playwright and English literature scholar who was also an active member of the Communist Party. In June 1948, a few months after the Second Congress of the CPI in Calcutta had led to the establishment of the CPP, Chowdhury had presided over the public meeting at the then Coronation Park in Dhaka where the Communist Party presented its programme. His 'presidential speech was cut short, since serious disturbances were apprehended, and the meeting was dissolved',[41] leading to a spate of violence against the activists. Chowdhury was jailed for his participation in protests against the police violence with which the language movement met in 1952.[42] He wrote *Kabar* while in prison. The play stages a spectral aftermath of the repressions of the language movement. It narrates the rising from the grave of a number of people shot by the police as they are buried under the cover of night by a political leader and a police officer. The ghostly corpses attempt to hold the leader to account but eventually fade as dawn arrives. Ahmed analyses the play as part of the staging of the Bengali nation and suggests that 'the performance of Munier Chowdhury's *Kabar* (The Grave) on 21 February 1953 can be indeed identified as the defining moment in the narration of the nation (Bangladesh now) in its theatrical context'.[43] His analysis of this significant occasion highlights, however,

[38] Ahmed, Nazneen, 'The Crafting of National Culture in East Pakistan', Conference paper presented at 'Once Upon a Time in East Pakistan', University of Edinburgh, May 1 (2014b).

[39] Ananya Jahanara Kabir, Utopias Eroded and Recalled: Intellectual Legacies of East Pakistan *South Asia: Journal of South Asian Studies* 41, no. 4 (2018), 906.

[40] Syed Jamil Ahmed, 'Designs of Living in the Contemporary Theatre of Bangladesh. In *Mapping South Asia through Contemporary Theatre: Essays on the Theatres of India, Pakistan, Bangladesh, Nepal and Sri Lanka*, ed. Ashish Sengupta (London: Palgrave Macmillan, 2014), 136.

[41] Umar, *The Emergence of Bangladesh*, 48.

[42] Afsan Chowdhury, 'Subsumed by History and Nation', *Himal Southasian* (January 2011), http://old.himalmag.com/himal-feed/53/3532-subsumed-by-history-and-nation.html.

[43] Ahmed, *Designs of Living*, 136.

that '[i]n attempting to crystallize the notion of the Bengali "nation" around the foci of language and culture . . . [Kabar] is heavily laden with Islamic worldview'.[44] This allows Ahmed to suggest the inevitable alignment or shadowing of Bengali nationalism by religion and he thus contributes to an account of the ambivalences of nationalist aspiration as read through cultural form and activism. However, in what appears as an aside to Ahmed's account of the prison performance, he notes: 'the performers played for a group of spectators held together by their common identity as political activists and members of the Communist Party'.[45] While not otherwise elaborated and given Chowdhury's very central role in the East Bengal Communist Party, there is another possible reading of the staging of the play, as a form of the left in which cultural and political activism converge alongside the repressions of the Communist Party in the context of civil resistance that is retrospectively read as nationalist and possibly religious.

The history of Bangladeshi cinema pre-Bangladesh is similarly told as a national cinema in waiting.[46] The films of the 1960s, the consolidation of the film industry in Dhaka and the development of new cultures of the cinema in the 1960s have rarely been a significant focus of analysis and are mostly read as part of the cultural forms accompanying a nationalist awakening. The landscape of the cinema in East Pakistan, however, was diverse and saw major transitions across all aspects of cinematic culture between 1947 and 1971. One significant strand of this was the involvement in film culture of artists and writers who were allied and related to progressive and left-aligned cultural organizations and venues. Among this large network of artists, many were more or less explicitly linked to left-wing political activism and the Communist Party. It is within this network of collaborators, friends and fellow activists, and of the aesthetic principles and institutions they inhabited, that we should place the consolidation of film-making and film education in 1950s eastern Bengal as well as the eventual arrival of Alamgir Kabir as a critic and educator in the mid-1960s.

In his biography of the artist S. M. Sultan, the author Abdul Hasnat Hye describes Sultan's engagement with the composer, singer, actor and director Khan Ataur Rahman and the actor, composer, journalist, writer, radio producer and film-maker Fateh Lohani. They lived together in London in the early 1950s, where Fateh Lohani was pursuing a course in cinematography and Khan Ata ran

[44] Syed Jamil Ahmed, 'Performing the Bengali Nation: Munier Chowdhury's Kabar and Syed Huq's Payer Awaj Pawa Jaye' *Depart* no.14/15 (2013). http://departmag.com/index.php/en/detail/266/Performing-the-Bengali-nation-and-Munier-Chowdhuryands-Kabar-and-Syed-Huqands-Payer-Awaj-Pawa-Jaye.

[45] Ahmed, *Designs of Living*, 136.

[46] Raju, *Bangladesh Cinema*.

a puppet theatre.[47] Both had spent significant amounts of time in West Pakistan, where they moved in progressive artistic circles.[48] Sultan met them in London around 1952,[49] and Hye describes them as follows:

> Both had a restless nature and a daredevil attitude to most things. Occasionally they went underground. The police looked for them. I learnt later that they, too, were communists. You see, during those days if you were an artist or a writer you had to be a communist almost automatically. No other ideology spoke so clearly and so earnestly on behalf of the common people as communism did.[50]

Before 1947, Fateh Lohani had been an actor in Calcutta, working with Bimal Roy and Utpal Dutt, and acting in the pre-independence film *Dukkhe Jader Jiban Gara* (1946, Those Who Live in Constant Misery, dir. Obaidul Haque).[51] He was the first to direct feature films at the newly instituted East Pakistan Film Development Corporation, releasing *Akash ar Mati* [The Sky and the Earth] in 1959 and *Asiya* in 1960. He was prolific in radio and cinema in East Pakistan. Khan Ata acted in *Jago Hua Savera* (1959, The Day Shall Dawn, dir. AJ Kardar) and all of Zahir Raihan's significant Bengali films – *Kokhono Asheni* [Never Came] in 1961, *Kancher Deyal* [Glass Wall] in 1963 and *Jibon Theke Neye* [Taken From Life] in 1970. Khan Ata also extensively composed music and songs for Bengali and Urdu films, including for Zahir Raihan. He directed numerous films, including most prominently *Nawab Sirujdaulla* (1967) and *Saat Bhai Chompa* [Seven Brothers and Chompa] (1968). The former, narrating the fall of Nawab Sirajdaulla in the wake of the Polashi battle, has been widely read as a not-so-veiled indictment of West Pakistani dominance.[52]

Other artists engaged with cinema in the East Pakistan period were more directly involved in the party's activities. Murtaja Baseer, remembered foremostly as a painter, also was an art director and wrote screenplays in the 1960s for the films *Karwan* (1964, dir. S.M. Parvez, *Urdu*) and *Nodi O Nari* (1965, dir. Sadek Khan, *Bengali*). In his autobiography, Basheer writes that 'as a student, I became associated with politics. Progressive politics. Communist Party. I used to draw pictures for the booklets or posters of that party. I drew the pictures of Marx,

47 Abdul Hasnat Hye, *Sultan*, trans. Kabir Chowdhury (Dhaka: Adorn Publications, 2008), 256.
48 Ibid.
49 Lotte Hoek and Sanjukta Sunderason, 'Journeying through Modernism: Travels and Transits of East Pakistani Artists in Post-Imperial London', *British Art Studies* 13, https://doi.org/10.17658/issn.2058-5462/issue-13/hoek-sunderason.
50 Hye, *Sultan*, 240.
51 Anupam Hayat, Fateh Lohani, *Banglapedia* (2012), https://en.wikipedia.org/wiki/Fateh_Lohani.
52 Gazdar, Mushtaq, *Pakistan Cinema 1947–1997* (Oxford: Oxford University Press, 1997), 105.

Engels, Lenin, Stalin, and other intellectuals.'[53] He recounts how he was arrested while putting up posters he had drawn that showed the Hajong liberated area and the hammer and sickle sign. These liberated areas were regions in East Bengal where peasant revolts and sharecropper resistance had been staged since the 1930s, often alongside peasant-focused Communist Parties and activists,[54] including Moni Singh,[55] and where significant land reform had taken place. Basheer had been called by members of the Communist Party to participate in liberation-day celebrations of such an area in Mymensingh. He was again arrested during the language movement in 1952 and spent a number of months in prison.[56] While he severed ties with the party, he remained politically engaged: 'my political expression happened through my drawing; through the art I made.'[57]

Most prominently among the film-makers aligned to the left in Dhaka after 1947 was Zahir Raihan. Well established as a writer before turning to film, Zahir Raihan's left-wing political commitments were clearly articulated in his work and in his interviews. As I have described elsewhere, Zahir Raihan's commitment to the cause of the proletariat lasted right through the 1960s and into 1971.[58] It was evident in his films, including in social melodrama's such as *Kokhono Asheni*. Zahir Raihan's film *Jibon Theke Neya* was released in 1970 and is generally credited with capturing and galvanizing both the discontent and the rising spirit of action in East Pakistan, on the brink of a brutal civil war that would eventually lead to the liberation of East Pakistan as Bangladesh.[59] Yet the film can easily be reread not just as a nationalist call for independence but as a much broader call to raise up, and awaken, the peasants and workers and lead them into the struggle ahead. *Jibon Theke Neya* tells the story of a household held in the iron grip of a matriarch that none of the family members dare to oppose while outside a political struggle for freedom unfolds, eventually inspiring a revolution within the house. It is a thinly veiled indictment of the injustices of Ayub Khan's military regime that had ended in 1969 and memorably included a rendition of Rabindranath Tagore's song

[53] Murtaja Baseer, *Amar Jibon O Onnano* (My Life and More) (Dhaka: Bengal Publications, 2014), 34 (my translation).

[54] Van Schendel, *A History of Bangladesh*, 89–92.

[55] Meghna Guhathakurta and Willem van Schendel, *The Bangladesh Reader: History, Culture, Politics* (Durham, NC: Duke University Press, 2013), 170.

[56] Baseer, *Amar Jibon*, 34 (my translation).

[57] Ibid., 35 (my translation).

[58] Hoek, Lotte, 'Cross-wing Filmmaking: East Pakistani Urdu Films and Their Traces in the Bangladesh Film Archive', *BioScope: South Asian Screen Studies* 5, no. 2 (2015), 99–118.

[59] Fahmida Akhter, '*Jibon Theke Neya* (Glimpses of Life, 1970): The First Political Film in Pre-Liberation Bangladesh', *Journal of the Asiatic Society of Bangladesh* (Hum.) 59, no. 2, (2014), 291–303; Naadir Junaid, *Bengali Political Cinema: Protest and Social Transformation* (PhD Thesis, The University of New South Wales, 2013).

Amar Shonar Bangla (My Golden Bengal) that was to become the national anthem of Bangladesh. Khan Ataur Rahman composed and sang for the film and acted the role of the effete artistic husband of the matriarch who embodies the dictatorial rule of Ayub Khan. Against her repression of his music and singing, Khan Ata's character repeatedly sings one of his own compositions decrying the complicity of those who stand by at moments of collective stirring: 'How will I break this cage? While everywhere the song of freedom sounds, I, like a thief, am busy praising the master.'[60] The song works to illustrate the immediate repressions of the household that is ostensibly the focus of the film but requires little imagination to link directly to the political movements unfolding in East Pakistan at the time. What this song of freedom might sound like, however, is articulated both poetically and visually in another of the songs in the film; this one sang by one of the brothers in the household who is deeply involved with the political movements outside the house. This song is sung as an illustration of the strike he attends, the chorus repeatedly calling to 'awaken all the poor of the world today' (*duniyar joto gorib ke aj jagiye dao*). The sequence is visually striking, consisting of a series of medium-long and close low-angle shots of raised fists, raised ploughs and the faces of the strikers only.[61] Cut rapidly and with no other contextualizing imagery, the visual markers of revolutionary and conscious raising cinema in the song sequence support the lyrics that are sung by the group who, with their ploughs and weathered faces, stand in for the agitating peasants. The film was photographed by one of Zahir Raihan's regular cinematographers, Afzal Chowdhury.[62] When I discussed the shooting of this particular song sequence in an interview with him in 2014, Chowdhury was adamant that what he executed was what Raihan had envisaged. This was important to him. He said that 'the images make visible the theme of the song' (*Chobi diye dekhano hochche gaantar theme*). This visual instantiation of the call to awaken the repressed was something that Chowdhury insisted had been Raihan's vision for the song, and something that he, as a cinematographer, had merely materialized. Here both the imagery and the montage underscore the left political coalition and uprising that was a central part of the movements within East Pakistan and that fed into the Liberation War.

Exploring *Jibon Theke Neya* for its forms of the left allows a re-reading of the film that has been fixed as a Bengali-nationalist allegory. It provides the

[60] My translation.

[61] The cover of this book references this shot from *Nibon Theke Neya*; the film can be found on YouTube.

[62] See Lotte Hoek, 'Mirrors of Movement: *Aina*, Afzal Chowdhury's Cinematography and the Interlinked Histories of the Cinema in Pakistan and Bangladesh', *Screen* 57, no. 4 (2017), 488–95.

possibility of analysing the imagery in the film anew and is an indication of the pluriform nature of the popular resistance movement that was the liberation struggle. The film, not just its narrative but all its aesthetic forms, suggests that the national popular of the 1960s was deeply informed by leftist and anti-imperial motifs, rhetoric and themes that also bespeak the wider international artistic networks and points of contact that imbued the struggle. These aesthetic forms also provide further insight into the international inspirations and cinematic exchange within the films made in the late 1960s in East Pakistan. These films can be positioned alongside global cinematic forms and debates, including with regard to movements within Latin American cinema, including the work of Santiago Álvarez,[63] part of the Third Cinema movement,[64] as well as the unexplored wider engagement with Afro-Asian film-making. The aesthetic traces in the films of Raihan and others give us access to the broader alliances and commitments across political and artistic communities that imbued the 'atmosphere' in 1960s East Pakistan and to which Alamgir Kabir would return as an impassioned film critic.

Alamgir Kabir: The conscience whipper

Alamgir Kabir returned to Dhaka in 1966, after spending seven years in London. He had travelled to Britain in 1959, aged twenty, to study physics and maths, but he was quickly disillusioned with his engineering work. He became involved with journalism and cinema, writing articles and criticism for various papers.[65] The turning point came when he saw *The Seventh Seal* (1957, dir. Ingmar Bergman) and became convinced of the power and possibility of the cinema.[66] He took courses at the British Film Institute and the University of London between 1961 and 1964, writing essays on all aspects of the cinema.[67] He moved in left-wing and revolutionary cultural and political circles, swept up in the liberation front for Palestine and wrote for the *Daily Worker*. He was centrally involved in forming the underground East Bengal Liberation Front in 1963 and published

63 Prasad, 'Naeem Mohaiemen's Tragic History', 64.
64 Junaid, *Bengali Political Cinema*.
65 Anupam Hayat, *Alamgir Kabirer Cholocchitro: Potbhumi, Bishoy o Boishishto* (Alamgir Kabir's Cinema: Background, Subject and Features), (Dhaka: Bangaza Prokashon, 2016), 15.
66 Atikuzzaman and Paul, *Cinema and National Liberation*, 216.
67 Hayat, *Alamgir Kabirer Cholocchitro*, 15–16; Atikuzzaman and Paul, *Cinema and National Liberation*, 244.

two magazines that were critical of the Pakistan regime.[68] This ensured his surveillance by the Pakistan government, which closely tracked the activities of politically engaged intellectuals, teachers, writers and journalists during this period of military rule in the country.[69] Kabir's political and cinematic interests dovetail in his understanding of the cinema as a medium of transformative possibilities (*shombhabonamoy*). As Kabir reflected in 1988 on this formative moment: 'At this time, I'm not sure why, I felt that film is part of national politics [*cholocchitro jatiyo rajnitir ekti ongo*].'[70]

The year of his return to Dhaka, Kabir attended the Mannheim film festival and the London Film Festival. He wrote reviews and critiques of the films screened for the Dhaka newspaper *The Pakistan Observer*[71] and the *Holiday* magazine.[72] When Kabir returned to Dhaka in 1966, he started to write film, television and radio reviews and criticism for *The Pakistan Observer* and the weekly *Chitrali* magazine.[73] His political activities and critical writing saw him arrested and jailed in 1966 not long after his return.[74] He was jailed twice in the period between 1966 and 1971. Nonetheless, during this time he became the senior editor of the weekly *Holiday* and, after meeting Zahir Raihan, edited *The Express*, which he described as a 'lively politico-cultural tabloid'.[75]

Today, Kabir is best known for his work with the Bangladesh Film Institute and Archive, the feature films he made in the 1970s and his continued engagement with the film society movement, particularly the Short Film Forum in the 1980s, until his tragic death in 1989. Kabir's serial institution building should be seen as not only an indicator of his energy and commitments but also the scale of his ambitions for the cinema. It was not until 1970 that Kabir would turn to film-making (working on an unfinished documentary about Maulana Bhashani),[76] subsequently collaborating with Zahir Raihan during the war on the documentaries discussed earlier and eventually making his feature and documentary films in independent Bangladesh.[77] I argue that his commitment

68 Atikuzzaman and Paul, *Cinema and National Liberation*, 271.

69 Ibid., 216.

70 Ibid., 271. Crucially, Kabir's writing in the 1960s is not particularly engaged with the question of the 'national,' this emerges in his writing subsequent to the national liberation in 1971.

71 Hayat, *Alamgir Kabirer Cholocchitro*, 18.

72 Alamgir Kabir, Mannheim Film Week, *Holiday* 2 January (1966c), 5, 7.

73 Ibid.; Anupam Hayat, *Alamgir Kabirer Cholocchitro*, 18.

74 Ayub Hossain, Alamgir Kabir. *Banglapedia* (2012), http://en.banglapedia.org/index.php?title=Kabir,_Alamgir.

75 Alamgir Kabir, *Film in Bangladesh* (Dhaka: Bangla Academy, 1979), 147.

76 Hayat, *Alamgir Kabirer Cholocchitro*, 39.

77 His films from the 1970s are understood to have progressive political aspirations too, see Naadir Junaid, 'Cinema that Raises a Critical Consciousness: The Films of Alamgir Kabir', in *South Asian*

to film criticism and film education that predates his career as a film-maker should be understood as a central part of his cinematic legacy and constitutes a powerful and lasting articulation of the forms of the left in Bangladeshi cinema. By looking at the two arenas where Alamgir Kabir mobilized film education in the 1960s, namely in film criticism and in film education, it becomes clear how he approached the cinema as a means of instilling political awareness, inspiring critical vision and galvanizing action.

Kabir's writing for *The Pakistan Observer* provided a source of critically engaged and consistent film journalism appearing in English in East Pakistan. Surveying Kabir's journalistic output from the mid-1960s, alongside his book *The Cinema in Pakistan* (1969), produces a clear statement on Kabir's perspective on the cinema as a socially progressive force and the film critic as the vehicle through which it might be amplified. As he writes in the opening pages of his 1969 book *The Cinema in Pakistan*: 'The cinema is probably the only art form whose political utility can be comparable to that of any political party, may be even more.'[78] He notes it was Lenin who 'realised this as early as in 1919'.[79] For Kabir, it was self-evident that 'the aim of every art is to contribute directly or indirectly to social development and also to act as a *catalyst* in the process of social evolution'.[80] The film critic, for whom 'socio-political consciousness is an indispensable quality',[81] had a key role to play in catalysing such social change:

> A concerted press campaign in favour of good films that try to tell sensible stories without forsaking the needs of the society while avoiding sermons and films that make honest efforts to exploit the resources of the cinema as vehicles of art as well as means of propagation of ideas: could act as an important *conscience-whipper* of audiences throughout the country.[82]

The job of the critic was to be 'an easily accessible link between people and art forms',[83] unlocking the potential of the art cinema for its audiences. Kabir's many writings and educational initiatives should be understood to build such accessible links between people and art forms. It responds to the central challenge before the radical cultural movement in South Asia: to connect the

Filmscapes: Transregional Encounters eds. Elora Halim Chowdhury and Esha Niyogi De (Seattle: University of Washington Press, 2020), 266–82.

78 Alamgir Kabir, *The Cinema in Pakistan* (Dhaka: Sandhani Publications, 1969a), 5–6.

79 Ibid., 6.

80 Ibid., 125, emphasis mine.

81 Kabir, *The Cinema in Pakistan*, 125.

82 Kabir, *The Cinema in Pakistan*, 184, emphasis mine.

83 Kabir, *The Cinema in Pakistan*, 120.

people to their texts and forms and thus foster an 'emancipatory pedagogy'.[84] To read Kabir's reviews and critical writing in the newspapers, then, is to witness the ways in which he builds such pedagogical links between the public and the cinema, which is understood as a potent political and progressive force; it is to witness the conscience whipper in action.

Kabir's film criticism is focused on connecting the formal aspects of individual films to their political potential. In the year of his return to Dhaka, Alamgir Kabir reviews Khan Ataur Rahman's film *Raja Sanyasi* (1966). Kabir writes that 'two elements of his direction impressed me. These are: a precise sense of proportion which is rare in this country and a potent sense of social consciousness. Obviously, he doesn't belong to the school of "art for art's sake.". . . he didn't miss any opportunity of injecting as many social comments as he found possible.'[85] This is high praise for Khan Ata's second feature film.[86] The significance that Alamgir Kabir attaches to cinema as an art that is not produced just for its own sake, and that is imbued with social conscience, can also be seen in his review of international cinematic trends, including the nouvelle vague and the Indian neorealists. His evaluation of directors associated with the New Wave hinges on the question of whether the abstractions in their work 'can make art really indispensable to the toiling millions.'[87] This means Kabir expresses great appreciation for Chris Marker and Jean Rouch but is less optimistic about others who 'ignoring the needs of the time and people, these pretentious philistines engaged themselves in examining their "esoteric neuroses" magnifying it a thousand times under the microscope of caprice and frivolity'.[88] It is only certain types of abstraction that are valued by Kabir for their capacity to present an 'indispensable' form of social comment.

In his evaluation of Pakistani films, Kabir's appreciation is reserved for films that combine social consciousness and commitment with a sense of realism. Repeated throughout his many reviews from 1966 onwards, he rejects or appreciates films for their capacity to instil a sense of realism and a realistic depiction of characters and their social world. In the *Holiday* newspaper Kabir explicates a formal grading system for the films he reviews. The grading system

[84] Priyamvada Gopal, *Literary Radicalism in India: Gender, Nation and the Transition to Independence* (London and New York: Routledge, 2005), 143.

[85] Alamgir Kabir, 'Raja Sanyasi', *Holiday* (10 October 1966a), 5.

[86] This amity between Alamgir Kabir and Khan Ataur Rahman will not last. Their positions during and after the Liberation War diverge significantly and is aired vociferously in the papers in independent Bangladesh.

[87] Alamgir Kabir, 'New Wave Cinema & Its Contribution to Art', *The Pakistan Observer* (24 May 1966c), 14.

[88] Ibid.

he applies to films newly released in Pakistan is based on a 5-star system. He explains how films are graded by noting that 'Any Pakistani film with a good authentic story and other elements of artistic standard comparable to that of "Jago Hua Savera" (1959) directed by A.J. Kardar is awarded five stars or more.'[89] The singling out of the little-seen and financially unsuccessful *Jago Hua Savera* bespeaks the standards that Kabir has in mind. Its excellent cinematography and strong commitment to realism, combined with the social urgency of its narrative,[90] (see Dadi's chapter in this volume) make *Jago Hua Savera* Kabir's benchmark for Pakistani films in the late 1960s. Kabir uses this standard to compare other Pakistani films. In his evaluation of *Aakhri Station* (1966), he deplores the lack of realism in the plot but notes that as Urdu scriptwriter Hajira Masroor 'is not an East Pakistani, it will be unjust to expect from her an authentic characterisation and background'.[91] Shabnam receives praise in her role of the 'mad girl conceived and realised with compassion, realism and without exaggeration'.[92] The value Kabir places on realism and such lack of 'exaggeration' also means that he is singularly dismissive of the many folk films that are released from the mid-1960s onwards in Pakistan.[93]

Kabir's unwavering appreciation of *Jago Hua Savera*'s aesthetic qualities illustrates Kabir's deep faith in the formal aspects of the cinema as the location of a film's political potentiality. In Kabir's 1979 edition of his book, now titled *Film in Bangladesh*, he dismisses *Jago Hua Savera* for inauthenticity due to its failure to capture 'an authentic Bengaliness'[94] and its 'language problem'.[95] A. J. Kardar's star had significantly faded between the two editions of Kabir's book (1969 and 1979) due to Kardar's role in the 1971 war. During the military attack on the East Pakistani population and the ensuing genocide, film-making had come to a standstill in Dhaka. Kabir notes that 'Cinemas were ordered to stay open. But the general atmosphere of terror that prevailed everywhere discouraged the captive population.'[96] Amidst this terror and civil war 'one long colour, propaganda documentary titled *Betrayal* was made by Ajay Kardar (of *Day Shall Dawn* [*Jago Hua Savera*]) for the occupation regime with active collaboration from at least one leading Bengali film director. It attempted to justify the military crackdown

89 Alamgir Kabir, Current Release *Holiday* (31 August 1969b), 5.
90 See Iftikhar Dadi, this volume.
91 Alamgir Kabir, Aakhri Station *Holiday* (13 March 1966d), 5.
92 Ibid.
93 Kabir, *The Cinema in Pakistan*, 46–7.
94 Kabir, *Film in Bangladesh*, 40.
95 Ibid.
96 Ibid., 48.

and the genocide.'[97] After 1971, *Jago Hua Savera* was no longer upheld as a benchmark as it had been in the *Holiday* reviews. Nonetheless, Kabir remained persuaded by its formal qualities, in particular the 'opening sequence that portrays the homecoming of the fishermen just before sunrise'.[98] Kabir suggests here that Kardar may have plagiarized this sequence from Visconti's *La Terra Trema* but concedes that either way it 'added a lyrical quality'.[99] The formal aspects of the film outlive the political betrayals of its director and Kabir's lasting appreciation powerfully illustrates Kabir's perspective on the nature of cinema as an art form. For Kabir, the critic's key tools for catalysing the political efficacy of cinema were raising public awareness and understanding of the ways in which film could be read and interpreted as well as initiating readers into the formal languages of cinema.

Debashree Mukherjee has described the emergence of film journalism in Bombay in the 1930s. She shows how in newspapers and magazines 'the film critic self-consciously promoted cinema as art, industry, and social document, thereby creating a space for the movies in everyday public consideration'.[100] Such everyday consideration was both a tool for the consolidation of the industry and a site for political intervention. Mukherjee narrates evocatively how the critic and film-maker K. A. Abbas made use of the public forum of the newspaper and the genre of film criticism in the 1930s and 1940s to connect the anti-imperial struggle to the narratives of the films screening in the Bombay cinema halls. 'Abbas saw himself as a political activist who had chosen cinema as his favoured object of inquiry.'[101] Not unlike Kabir's imagination of his role as a film critic for *The Pakistan Observer* in the 1960s, the film critics that Mukherjee discusses 'self-consciously took on the task of mediating between the film and the audience, preparing the viewer, as it were, on ways of seeing'.[102] This understanding of film criticism as a preparation in a way of seeing describes accurately how Alamgir Kabir approached newspaper film criticism in the late 1960s.

The understanding of the political role cinema could play in a society shackled by an exploitative and illegitimate government resonates strongly between K. A. Abbas's position in the late 1930s and Alamgir Kabir's in the late 1960s. Mukherjee cites K. A. Abbas's staunch defence of his 'prejudiced'

[97] Ibid.
[98] Ibid., 40.
[99] Ibid.
[100] Debashree Mukherjee, 'Creating Cinema's Reading Publics: The Emergence of Film Journalism in Bombay', in *No Limits: Media Studies from India*, eds. Ravi Sundaram and Sujata Patel (New Delhi: Oxford University Press, 2013), 168.
[101] Ibid., 173.
[102] Ibid., 169–70.

position with regard to certain films in 1940: 'I am not interested in motion pictures as motion pictures, but as an art medium for the reflection, and where possible, the enrichment of life, and a means for the reconstruction of society on healthier, more just, and rational lines.'[103] Nearly thirty years later, Kabir writes in a very similar vein of the political potential of cinema, and is similarly allied to left political movements and parties. For example, Kabir does not hesitate to critique Satyajit Ray, who he greatly admires, because 'Ray is never found to portray the 'evil' or 'violence' that are the real by-products of any society' while 'his social commitments are also too feeble, if not reactionary'.[104] This resonance between Abbas's and Kabir's position may be understood as the long legacy of the cultural fronts of the Communist Party in pre-independence South Asia, the 'hugely influential radical cultural movement that spanned several regions and languages across [pre-independence] India'[105] that included IPTA and the PWA. Through this movement, 'a new criticism was encouraged that gauged artists and writers according to their allegiance to anti-imperialism and their support for socialist ideals'[106] and 'borrowed heavily from the reports and speeches of the first Soviet Writers' Congress held in 1934'.[107] After 1948, the party's ever-narrowing ideological line with regard to the arts directly impacted the nature of criticism. Kamran Asdar Ali recounts how in the realm of literature the definition of 'progressive' writers was increasingly narrowed in the All Pakistan Progressive Writers' Association (APPWA).[108] Among those labelled 'reactionary' are those artists who believe in 'art for art's sake'.[109] Criticism, then, was itself a political category in the early years of Pakistan, its roots firmly in the pre-independence era. Kabir's writing in the 1960s shows the longevity of these ideological positions.

The links between the PWA/APPWA and Alamgir Kabir's nascent film criticism in the mid-1960s in East Pakistan are easily retrieved. As shown earlier, there were plentiful cultural activists on the left who had participated in the cultural and political life of the pre-1947 era. But also after Partition, connections to the APPWA in East Bengal were closer than might be imagined now. For example, the newspapers and magazines for which Alamgir Kabir wrote in the late 1960s also reprinted newspaper articles from fellow progressive

[103] K. A. Abbas in Mukherjee, 'Creating Cinema's Reading Publics', 173.
[104] Alamgir Kabir, Satyajit Ray. *Holiday* (17 June 1966b), 7.
[105] Gopal, *Literary Radicalism*, 1.
[106] Ali, *Communism in Pakistan*, 92.
[107] Ibid., 238n8.
[108] Ibid., 94.
[109] Ibid.

critics in West Pakistan. In December 1966, the *Holiday* reprinted an article by the Urdu poet Ahmed Nadim Qasmi titled 'Real Essence of Socialist Art'.[110] Ali describes Qasmi as 'a dedicated worker on the cultural front' and 'fellow-traveller'.[111] Qasmi's article in the *Holiday* was originally published in *Daily Jang*. In the article, Qasmi describes the performance of a cultural troupe from China that toured the major cities of both wings of Pakistan and concludes that the aesthetic value of the performances was strengthened by the unity of ideological purpose and the infusion of Mao's thought in the performance. He concludes that detractors are unfortunately afflicted by their belief in 'art for art's sake'.[112] The article appears alongside a long article on the life, work and ideas of Walt Disney, written by Alamgir Kabir.[113]

If Kabir's newspaper criticisms from the mid-1960s echo K. A. Abbas's writing in the 1940s, or the struggles in the APPWA in the 1950s, this is in part due to the historical ties that bind these writers and their political lineages. The ideas that they draw upon are part of national and international conversations that resonate globally after the revolution in Russia, whether in cinema or in literature. What is significant to note here, though, is that these particular ideas and concerns with the purpose of art, the place of the artists and the necessity of the commitment to an art and aesthetic dedicated to the people and their life-worlds emerge at particular historical junctions. Rather than untimely, belated or derivative, the resurgence of these particular modes of aesthetic criticism become *acute* and activated in particular historical moments, such as in the revving up of the anti-imperial struggle in the 1930s in colonial India and in the gathering revolutionary storm that sweeps East Pakistan in the late 1960s. Such 'conjunctures'[114] are particularly conducive to the reiteration of historical forms and ideas in new and acute ways. It is in this context that a particular historical inheritance of left and progressive modes of attentiveness to aesthetic form comes to the fore. Particular historical configurations make these forms appear recursively, and I understand Alamgir Kabir's film criticism in Dhaka between 1966 and 1971 as wedded to the political foment of the period.

The realism and social commitment that Kabir finds so important in the films he reviews are directly linked to how he understands cinema's functioning as a medium. For Kabir, cinema is a provocation that demands a response from its

[110] Ahmed Nadim Qasmi, 'Real Essence of Socialist Art', *The Holiday* (25 December 1966), 3.
[111] Ali, *Communism in Pakistan*, 88–9.
[112] Qasmi, *Real Essence*, 3
[113] Alamgir Kabir, 'Walt Disney: Tribute to a Charmer', *The Holiday* (25 December 1966), 5, 7.
[114] Gopal, *Literary Radicalism*, 18–22.

viewers. And this is what produces its political potency. He writes that 'A film provokes its audience much more directly than any other art form. . . . Hardly anyone is left un-committed.'[115] A realist film containing social commentary would provoke its audiences in socially progressive ways, 'whipping up' their conscience. Where does this capacity for generating commitment originate? Kabir does not consider cinema a joining together of existing art forms but, like many before him, sees 'proper' cinema as an autonomous form. When not weighed down by pre-existing forms, untethered from tradition, this independent form displayed what he termed 'radical breakaway tendencies'.[116] Kabir's example here, unsurprisingly, is Eisenstein, who he sees as animating the visual through 'invent[ing] newer cinematic methods for realising ideas in terms of photography'.[117] Kabir writes that 'there is . . . one particular characteristic that is unique to the cinema. . . . In a film everything is happening "now", in the present.'[118] This is why Kabir suggests that no-one remains 'uncommitted' in the face of cinema.[119] The power of this present-ness is famously phrased by Christian Metz as the capacity of cinema 'to inject the reality of motion into the unreality of the image . . . render[s] the world of imagination more real than it had ever been'.[120] For Kabir, this is what makes the cinema particularly suited to his political aspirations and ideals. The movement of the image, its montaged nature, actualizes both its autonomy from other art forms as well as its 'break-away tendencies', 'its dynamic qualities have room for great possibilities'.[121] For Kabir the movement of the image produces alongside it a political velocity: its present-ness is the invitation to empathic participation and has the force to move us, render the viewer committed, engage their conscience.

The provocation of film is lasting. Kabir writes that in the cinema 'images . . . fleetingly make their entrances and exits on the visual faculties of keen filmgoers. These possess their own movements, colours and rhythms waiting to be polished, classified, defined and termed in words.'[122] While it is the movement of the visual that is unique to the cinema and 'invites a most spontaneous response',[123] it also 'waits' to be grasped in language ('termed in words'). The

[115] Kabir, *The Cinema in Pakistan*, 120.
[116] Ibid., 4.
[117] Ibid.
[118] Ibid., 3.
[119] Ibid., 120.
[120] Metz in Tom Gunning, 'Moving Away from the Index: Cinema and the Impression of Reality', *Differences* 18, no. 1 (2007), 45.
[121] Kabir, *The Cinema in Pakistan*, 4.
[122] Ibid., 120.
[123] Ibid.

'keen filmgoer' would translate the film's galvanizing movement into words and texts, settling them into consciousness and inspiring action. I understand Kabir's dedication to film criticism as aiding this process of translation. Film education became central to Kabir's aim to realize cinema's political potential embedded in its formal qualities and animated by its physical movement. It was the trained viewer who would be best able to harness these qualities and Kabir was committed to produce such viewers not only through his prolific film criticism but also through his manifold initiatives towards film education, where it has had a lasting impact. Like criticism, film education was a means of producing accessible links between people and art forms that were premised on inviting people to pay close attention to the formal aspects of the cinema. To combat 'philistinism' in cinema 'it is essential to create a correct filmic awareness which is only possible through educational institutions and a virile cine-club movement'[124] (1969: 100). Kabir played a critical role in both the film society movement and the many initiatives to establish film education in East Pakistan and Bangladesh.

The first film society in Pakistan was set up in 1963 in the mould of the film societies in India and Britain.[125] By 1969 there were two clubs in Dhaka, one in Chittagong and one in Karachi.[126] Not only did the film societies screen a variety of international films for their paying membership, they were also linked to a history of radical and progressive political constituencies and put into practice their understanding of the cinema as socially transformative.[127] The pedagogic aims of the societies were deeply linked to the emancipatory and progressive politics that marked the development of the film societies. By 1968, Alamgir Kabir was the general secretary of the Pakistani Film Society.[128] In 1969, Kabir founded a parallel organization, the Dhaka Cine Club[129] and was on the board of directors of the Dacca Film Institute set up at the same time.[130] Kabir 'aspire[d] to develop it on the lines of the British Film Institute of London'.[131]

[124] Ibid., 100.

[125] Muhammad Khushru, *Bangladesher Cholocchitro Shongshod Andolon* (The Film Society Movement in Bangladesh) (Dhaka: Porua, 2004), 27; Rochona Majumdar, 'Debating Radical Cinema: A History of the Film Society Movement in India', *Modern Asian Studies* 46, no. 3 (2012), 731–67; Richard Lowell Macdonald, *The Appreciation of Film: The Postwar Film Society Movement and Film Culture in Britain* (Exeter: University of Exeter Press, 2016).

[126] Kabir, *The Cinema in Pakistan*, 101.

[127] Macdonald, *The Appreciation of Film*, 16; Majumdar, *Debating Radical Cinema*.

[128] 'Film Correspondent, Dacca Film Society Activities', *The Pakistan Times Magazine* (11 August 1968), vi.

[129] Raju, *Bangladesh Cinema*, 179.

[130] Anupam Hayat, *Bangladesher chalachitro itihash* (The History of Bangladeshi Cinema) (Dhaka: Bangladesh Film Development Corporation, 1987).

[131] Kabir, *The Cinema in Pakistan*, 100.

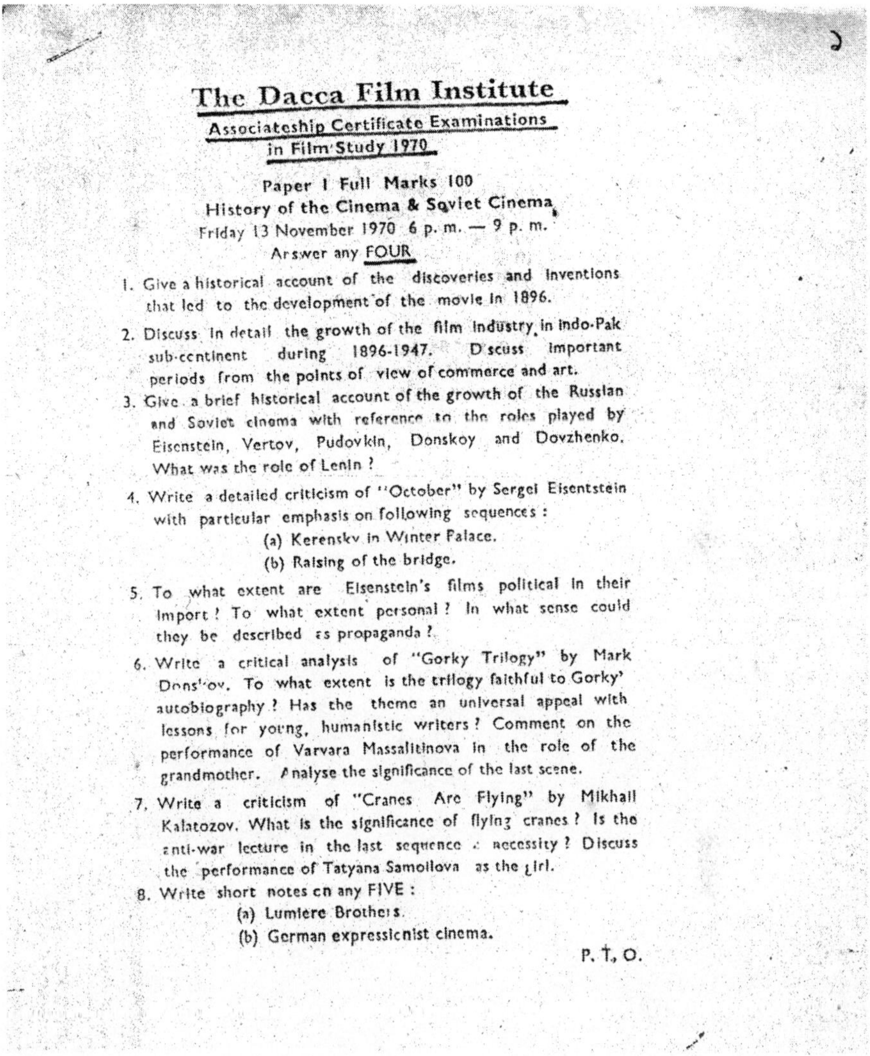

The Dacca Film Institute

Associateship Certificate Examinations in Film Study 1970

Paper I Full Marks 100
History of the Cinema & Soviet Cinema
Friday 13 November 1970 6 p. m. — 9 p. m.
Answer any FOUR

1. Give a historical account of the discoveries and inventions that led to the development of the movie in 1896.
2. Discuss in detail the growth of the film industry in Indo-Pak sub-continent during 1896-1947. Discuss important periods from the points of view of commerce and art.
3. Give a brief historical account of the growth of the Russian and Soviet cinema with reference to the roles played by Eisenstein, Vertov, Pudovkin, Donskoy and Dovzhenko. What was the role of Lenin ?
4. Write a detailed criticism of "October" by Sergei Eisentstein with particular emphasis on following sequences :
   (a) Kerensky in Winter Palace.
   (b) Raising of the bridge.
5. To what extent are Eisenstein's films political in their import ? To what extent personal ? In what sense could they be described as propaganda ?
6. Write a critical analysis of "Gorky Trilogy" by Mark Donskov. To what extent is the trilogy faithful to Gorky' autobiography ? Has the theme an universal appeal with lessons for young, humanistic writers ? Comment on the performance of Varvara Massalitinova in the role of the grandmother. Analyse the significance of the last scene.
7. Write a criticism of "Cranes Are Flying" by Mikhail Kalatozov. What is the significance of flying cranes ? Is the anti-war lecture in the last sequence a necessity ? Discuss the performance of Tatyana Samoilova as the girl.
8. Write short notes on any FIVE :
   (a) Lumiere Brothers.
   (b) German expressionist cinema.

P. T. O.

Figure 6.2 Exam in Film Study Paper 1 from Alamgir Kabir's Dacca Film Institute, 1970. © Catherine Masud, courtesy of Catherine Masud.

Kabir taught a rigorous curriculum at the Dacca Film Institute. 'It is essential to create a correct filmic awareness which is only possible through education institutions . . . [and] Lecture courses . . . to create not film-makers but serious students of the cinema with correct awareness.'[132] Figures 6.2 and 6.3 provide an example of the demanding examination that a 'serious student'

[132] Ibid., 101.

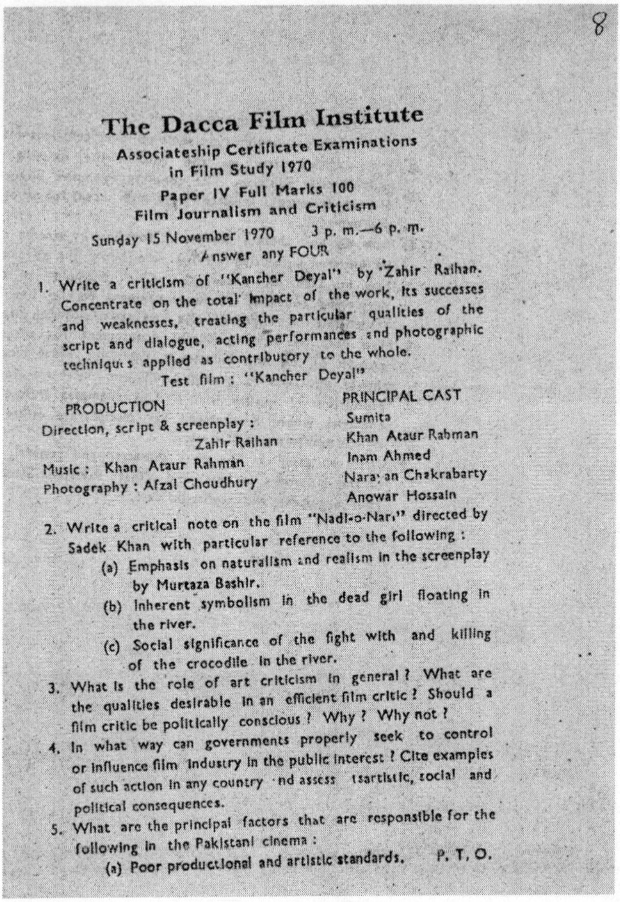

The Dacca Film Institute

Associateship Certificate Examinations
in Film Study 1970
Paper IV Full Marks 100
Film Journalism and Criticism

Sunday 15 November 1970 3 p. m.—6 p. m.

Answer any FOUR

1. Write a criticism of "Kancher Deyal" by Zahir Raihan. Concentrate on the total impact of the work, its successes and weaknesses, treating the particular qualities of the script and dialogue, acting performances and photographic techniques applied as contributory to the whole.

Test film : "Kancher Deyal"

PRODUCTION	PRINCIPAL CAST
Direction, script & screenplay : Zahir Raihan	Sumita
	Khan Ataur Rahman
Music : Khan Ataur Rahman	Inam Ahmed
Photography : Afzal Choudhury	Narayan Chakrabarty
	Anowar Hossain

2. Write a critical note on the film "Nadi-o-Nari" directed by Sadek Khan with particular reference to the following :
   (a) Emphasis on naturalism and realism in the screenplay by Murtaza Bashir.
   (b) Inherent symbolism in the dead girl floating in the river.
   (c) Social significance of the fight with and killing of the crocodile in the river.
3. What is the role of art criticism in general ? What are the qualities desirable in an efficient film critic ? Should a film critic be politically conscious ? Why ? Why not ?
4. In what way can governments properly seek to control or influence film industry in the public interest ? Cite examples of such action in any country and assess its artistic, social and political consequences.
5. What are the principal factors that are responsible for the following in the Pakistani cinema :
   (a) Poor productional and artistic standards. P. T. O.

Figure 6.3 Exam in Film Study Paper 4 from Alamgir Kabir's Dacca Film Institute, 1970. © Catherine Masud, courtesy of Catherine Masud.

at the Dacca Film Institute might face. If, in 1970, you wanted to become an associate of the Dacca Film Institute, you were required to sit four exams, each taking three hours. The four papers covered cinema history, international cinema, the theory of cinema and the art of the documentary, as well as film criticism. Over three weekend days in November 1970, you were asked to write on topics as diverse as the growth of Soviet cinema, produce a critical appreciation of *Meghey Dhaka Tara*, produce short notes on blimp, boom and dupe or the Kuleshov Experiments and evaluate 'to what extent are Eisenstein's films political in their import?'[133] The fourth paper, on criticism, included

[133] Paper I, History of the Cinema and Soviet Cinema, Associateship Certificate Examination in Film Study, The Dacca Film Institute, 1970, Private Collection of Catherine Masud.

questions such as 'Should a film critic be politically conscious?' and 'In what way can governments properly seek to control or influence film industry in the public interest?'[134] You were also required to be deeply familiar with the emerging cinema in East Pakistan, and Paper IV asks students to write pieces of criticism on *Kancher Deyal* (1963, Glass Wall, dir. Zahir Raihan) or *Nodi o Nari* (1965, River and Women, dir. Sadek Khan).[135] These exam papers provide clear insight into the types of knowledge and practice Kabir expected of his students: close textual study, detailed technical knowledge, a good grasp of the political nature of film, extensive historical awareness with regard to cinema in Pakistan, a grasp of film theory and an intimate familiarity with the classic film texts of a recognizably international film canon.

Kabir's efforts in the 1960s were to ground film education in independent Bangladesh in crucial ways. During the war, Kabir worked with Zahir Raihan and others to imagine 'the transformation of the film industry of the about-to-be-independent country on revolutionary lines'.[136] The socialist vision of a state-run film industry, in which directors would be on government payrolls and distribution and exhibition nationalized, required 'Zahir Raihan's presence and leadership'.[137] But devastatingly, he was killed immediately after the end of the war. And, as Kabir describes it in 1979, 'the people who ran the first government of free Bangladesh had no serious intention of introducing meaningful socialistic measures in any sphere of the newly independent country'.[138] Instead, the aspirations for the radical transformation of cinema in independent Bangladesh remained located among film society activists and film educational initiatives, many of which were spearheaded by Kabir.

Kabir, alongside others such as Mohammad Khusru, remained a driving force of the movement around cinematic art that emerged after the Liberation War in independent Bangladesh. They pushed for the state's support in developing film culture, leading to the establishment of the Bangladesh Film Institute and Archive. Kabir would continue to lead film appreciation courses at various institutes from 1979 into the 1980s and heading the efforts of the Short Film Forum, decisively shaping a new generation of film-makers, film critics and film enthusiasts (Figures 6.4 and 6.5). Those curricula have become the basis of the many film appreciation courses taught across the country today. Through these

[134] Paper IV, Film Journalism and Criticism, Associateship Certificate Examination in Film Study, The Dacca Film Institute, 1970, Private Collection of Catherine Masud.
[135] Ibid.
[136] Kabir, *Film in Bangladesh*, 50.
[137] Ibid.
[138] Ibid., 51.

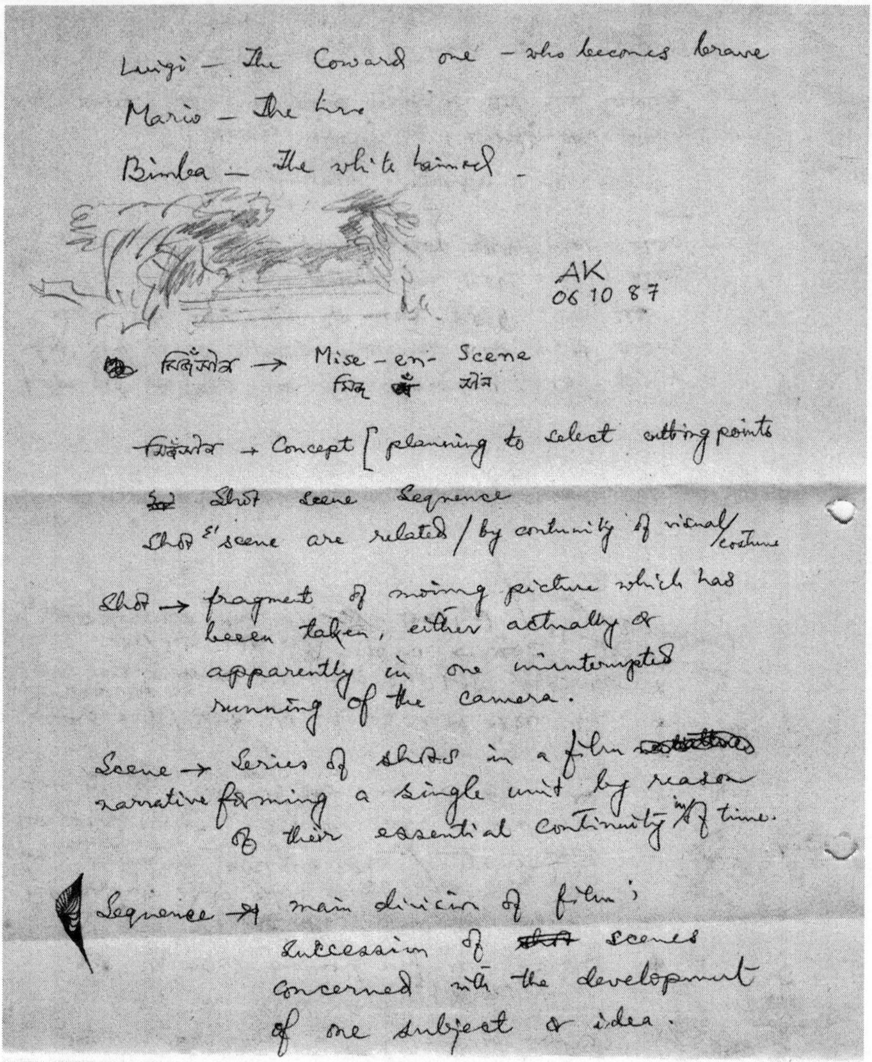
Luigi – The Coward one – who becomes brave
Mario – The hero
Bimba – The white haired –
AK
06 10 87
মিজঁসেন → Mise-en-Scene
মিজ্ অঁ সেন
→ Concept [planning to select cutting points
Shot Scene Sequence
Shot & scene are related / by continuity of visual/costume
Shot → fragment of moving picture which has been taken, either actually or apparently in one uninterrupted running of the camera.
Scene → Series of shots in a film narrative forming a single unit by reason of their essential continuity in/of time.
Sequence → main division of film; Succession of scenes concerned with the development of one subject or idea.

Figure 6.4 Handwritten notes taken during a class taught by Alamgir Kabir at NIMCO, 1987. © Catherine Masud, courtesy of Catherine Masud.

classes, film appreciation, as the practice of evaluating film texts through close reading and formal analysis, has remained the mainstay of film education in Bangladesh and continues to feed into film and media criticism today. It is here that the forms of the left, and the histories of politically progressive and left-wing cultural politics, have sedimented and remain available for contemporary articulation in the film and media culture of Bangladesh.

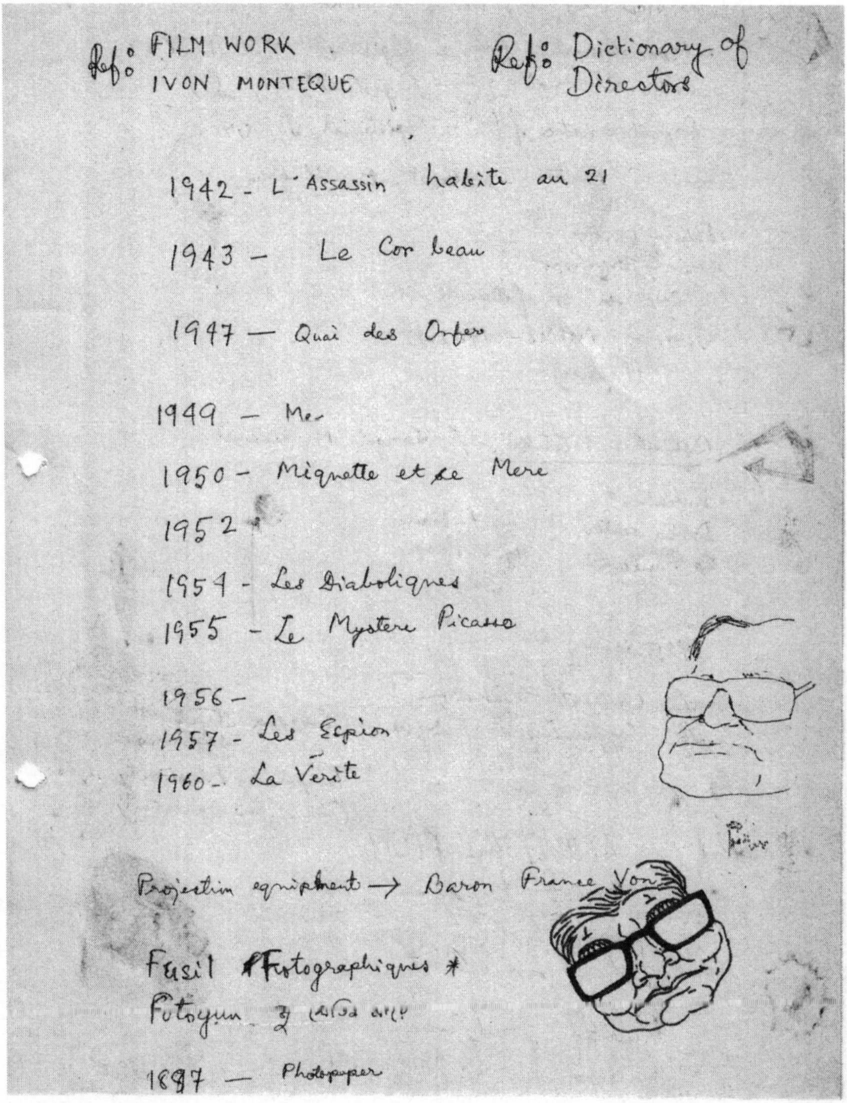

Refo: FILM WORK
IVON MONTEQUE

Refo: Dictionary of Directors

1942 - L'Assassin habite au 21

1943 - Le Corbeau

1947 - Quai des Orfevr

1949 - Me

1950 - Miquette et se Mere

1952 -

1954 - Les Diaboliques

1955 - Le Mystere Picasso

1956 -

1957 - Les Espion

1960 - La Verite

Projection equipment → Baron France Von

Fusil Fotographiques *

Fotogun

1897 - Photopaper

Figure 6.5 Portraits of Alamgir Kabir sketched in the margins of handwritten notes from a class taught by Alamgir Kabir at NIMCO, 1987. © Catherine Masud, courtesy of Catherine Masud.

Conclusion

Alamgir Kabir has been primarily celebrated and remembered as a film director and film society activist. In this chapter, I have argued that an important part of his continuing influence can be found in his film criticism and film education.

This is not only because of his important contributions to institutionalizing film education but also because training in the formal language of the cinema was, perhaps counterintuitively, a key aspect of his political aspirations. His ideological commitments in the 1960s were not only expressed through his political activism that landed him in jail. As he understood the formal characteristics of cinema to contain within them the capacity to move viewers politically, his commitments were also expressed in his endeavours to educate others about the formal qualities of cinema and raising awareness about film history and theory. He achieved these through publishing his critical evaluations in widely read newspapers and building numerous institutions that allowed people such access and insight. I suggest that for Kabir, formal film language was a part of the wider domain of forms of the left, aesthetic practices and ideas that actualized a left political orientation.

Placing a particular formalist aesthetic at the heart of the left political agenda of one of the key political artistic protagonists of the 1960s also expands how we might understand the place of the fine arts within this decade as it fed into the liberation struggle. It was within an environment of loose political affiliations to the left, state repression of the Communist Party and many strong ties among artists that East Pakistani cinema developed in the course of the 1950s and 1960s. This is the time when ideas of popular and art cinema were not yet fully articulated and cinema in eastern Bengal was a site of experimentation drawing on the cultural and artistic ferment that has so frequently been cited in studies of the language movement. The contributions of urban artists and intellectuals to the struggle have largely been read as both bourgeois and nationalist in nature. Tracing the forms of the left in the works and writings of these actors can suggest that there is a left progressive orientation within these works. Despite the ways in which we think of the cinema in the 1960s in East Pakistan as particularly concerned with family melodrama and folk features (in Urdu and Bengali), and as a steady build-up to the nationalist triumph of *Nawab Sirajdaulla*, *Jibon Theke Neya* and the urgent *Stop Genocide*, there is a social and aesthetic history of left political commitments of many of its key actors that can be recuperated through a close engagement with their texts. These can be discerned today in a continuing commitment to realism on the part of those who describe themselves as part of the avant-garde or art cinema; an emphasis on the rural in the cinema; and the faith in the possibility of cinema to be politically efficacious, as expressed by many associated with the film society movement. Following up these traces provides a starting point to ask what has happened to that progressive cultural politics, in the cinema and elsewhere, after the independence of Bangladesh, and to recuperate its energies alongside the political movements that shape the contemporary moment.

7

Look back in angst

Akaler Sandhaney, the Indian New Wave and the afterlife of the IPTA movement

Manishita Dass

Introduction

At the beginning of Mrinal Sen's meta-cinematic film *Akaler Sandhaney* (*In Search of Famine*, 1980, Bengali), an idealistic leftist director (Dhritiman Chatterjee) from the city of Calcutta sets out with his film unit for the village of Hatui, on a mission to shoot an 'authentic' film about the ravages of the Bengal famine of 1943–4.[1] By 1980, the year in which *Akaler Sandhaney* was set and released, the 'practice of trooping off to the villages with camera and crew'[2] in pursuit of authenticity and social realism had become fairly common within the 'Indian New Wave',[3] a heterogeneous and transregional cinematic constellation shaped by a groundswell of leftist critique and dissent on the one hand, and a state-sponsored attempt to promote a 'cinema of social significance and artistic sincerity'[4] on the other. The directors associated with this label were united not by their adherence to a common aesthetic or political agenda but by a disdain for entertainment-oriented cinema, and by a common vision of film-making as a serious artistic enterprise and an instrument of sociopolitical critique. Many of them also shared a preoccupation with the problems of the rural (and to a

1 An estimated 1.5–3 million people died in this famine, which was a man-made disaster. For a comprehensive account of this famine, see Paul Greenough, *Prosperity and Misery in Modern Bengal: The Famine of 1943-44* (Oxford: Oxford University Press, 1982) and Janam Mukherjee, *Hungry Bengal: War, Famine, and the end of Empire* (New York: Oxford University Press, 2015).

2 Sumita S. Chakravarty, *National Identity in Indian Popular Cinema, 1947-1987* (Austin: University of Texas Press, 1993), 236.

3 The terms 'New Indian Cinema' and 'Parallel Cinema' were and are also used to refer to these films.

4 Raghunath Raina, Foreword, *The New Generation: 1960-1980* (Delhi: Directorate of Film Festivals, 1981), 5.

lesser extent, the urban) poor, who had been historically denied access to the full rights of social citizenship, and a desire to capture the grim realities of their lives. This often led film-makers to villages, to make films that focused on poverty, exploitation, superstition, the conflict between tradition and modernity, and the unholy nexus between feudal power, patriarchal ideology, political corruption and violence. Take, for instance, *Samskara* (*Funeral Rites*, 1970, Kannada, Pattabhi Rama Reddy), which focuses on the turmoil caused in a rural Brahmin community by the death of a renegade; *Ghatashraddha* (*The Ritual*, 1977, Kannada, Girish Kasaravalli), which revolves around the ritual excommunication of a young Brahmin widow; Shyam Benegal's *Ankur* (*The Seedling*, 1974, Hindi), *Nishant* (*Dawn*, 1975, Hindi) and *Manthan* (*The Churning*, 1976, Hindi), all of which explore the workings of an oppressive feudal system in villages; *Thampu* (*The Circus Tent*, 1978, Malayalam, G. Aravindan), which traces the impact of a visiting circus on a village; *Aakrosh* (*Cry of the Wounded*, 1980, Hindi, Govind Nihalani), which investigates why a young tribal man accused of killing his wife refuses to speak; and Mrinal Sen's *Oka Orie Katha* (*The Marginal Ones*, 1977, Telegu), a fable-like drama of destitution set in Telengana.

These films gained critical acclaim both in India and abroad, media attention and a measure of government patronage and subsequently broke out of the 'art-house' circuit to gain a second lease of life through India's burgeoning television culture. However, the Indian New Wave did not quite succeed in reaching the masses, whose lives were central to its modernist enterprise of creating an alternative cinematic sphere. *Akaler Sandhaney*, made when the New Wave had already started to lose its initial momentum and self-confidence (as well as the government support that had fostered and buoyed it), foregrounds the differences of cultural capital and the politics of class distinctions that shaped the New Wave films and circumscribed their appeal to a mass audience. It also interrogates the uneasy relationship between the film-makers (mostly male middle-class intellectuals) and the 'people' they wanted to represent, as well as their aesthetic of realism and their valorization of the rural as the privileged site of authenticity and 'the real'. The film is, of course, an ironic exercise in self-reflexivity as Mrinal Sen (1923–2019) had been associated with the New Wave project of 'forging a progressive national consciousness'[5] ever since its inception. *Bhuvan Shome* (1969), Sen's quirky, ironic film about a curmudgeonly and anglicized bureaucrat's transformative journey to a village, is widely credited, along with Mani Kaul's experimental *Uski Roti* (*His Bread*, 1970), with having launched the Indian New

[5] Chakravarty, *National Identity*, 239.

Wave, and the bristling anger and formal experimentation of his 1970s films set the trend for a certain kind of political cinema within it. However, as I show in this chapter, the wryly meta-cinematic commentary in *Akaler Sandhaney* goes beyond the immediate context of the Indian New Wave and needs to be read in the inter-text of another pivotal moment in the longer history of the left-liberal Indian elite's aesthetic and political engagement with the rural: the left cultural movement spearheaded in the 1940s by the Indian People's Theatre Association (IPTA), the cultural wing of the undivided Communist Party of India (CPI).

This earlier moment – subsequently described as 'the only instance of a cultural avant-garde in contemporary Indian history'[6] – is invoked in the credit sequence through the soundtrack. As the camera tracks along a highway bordered by paddy-fields, following a number of vehicles carrying the film crew and their equipment, we hear the crew members cheerfully singing a classic IPTA song from the late 1940s, *Hei Samalo Dhaan Ho* ('Let's protect our crop'), written by Salil Chowdhury in the agitational context of the Tebhaga peasant movement in Bengal:

> Protect your crop, ho!
> Sharpen your sickle, ho!
> Stake your life and honor for it
> We shan't part ever again
> With the rice we planted with our blood,
> The rice that's our life, ho![7]

This song (which would be familiar to many Bengali viewers as well as to those members of a larger Indian audience with some knowledge of the left cultural movement of the 1940s) goes on to refer to the Bengal famine of 1943, a man-made disaster that was the product of administrative neglect and wartime profiteering, and killed an estimated 1.5–3 million people, mostly villagers, within a year. The horrors of the Bengal famine, which the film-within-the-film revisits, radicalized a generation of middle-class Indians, especially Bengalis, who came of age in the 1930s to 1940s, and brought many of them into the orbit of the IPTA, which played a central role in mobilizing popular outrage about the famine through street theatre performances and the visual arts and in organizing relief efforts.[8] While Mrinal Sen himself was more of a spectator than

[6] Ashish Rajadhyaksha and Paul Willemen (eds), *Encyclopedia of Indian Cinema* (New Delhi: Oxford University Press, 1999), 109.

[7] My translation from the Bengali original.

[8] See Sanjukta Sunderason, *Partisan Aesthetics: Modern Art & India's Long Decolonization* (Stanford, CA: Stanford University Press, 2020), especially the introduction and Ch. 2, for an extended

an active member of the IPTA (and a fellow-traveller rather than a card-carrying member of the CPI), its grassroots cultural activism in the context of the Bengal famine left an indelible mark on him and on his subsequent quest for a cinema of political commitment, as he acknowledged in several of his interviews and writings.[9] *Akaler Sandhaney*'s wryly self-reflexive commentary on the Indian New Wave, I argue, also attests to, and reflects on, the living legacy of the IPTA movement in postcolonial India: the continuing relevance of the questions this movement raised about the relationship between aesthetic form and progressive politics, as well as the long shadow of its constitutive contradictions and unfulfilled promises. Before trying to unravel some of the tangled issues *Akaler Sandhaney* raises about subalternity – or the predicament of disenfranchised communities and individuals excluded from, or at the margins of, hegemonic histories, discourses and socio-economic formations – and the politics of representation in postcolonial India, let me provide a context for my reading through a brief, and necessarily limited, overview of the New Wave and its place within the historical and political force-field of left-wing aesthetics in South Asia.

Situating the Indian New Wave

The term 'Indian New Wave' was first used by Indian film-makers and critics in the late 1960s and the early 1970s to refer to an upsurge of film-making outside the mainstream. It was then adopted by government agencies such as the Directorate of Film Festivals and the National Film Development Corporation (NFDC), which played a leading role in promoting these films as cultural exhibits in India and abroad. In part the result of government initiatives from the late 1960s onwards to foster an alternative film culture through institutions such as NFDC, the Film Finance Corporation (FFC) and the Film and Television Institute of India (FTII),[10] the Indian New Wave was never a cohesive movement with a governing manifesto. The films associated with this label were diverse in

discussion of the centrality of the Bengal famine for a generation of artists and the history of Bengali modernism.

9 See the essays and interviews in Mrinal Sen, *Montage: Life. Politics. Cinema* (Calcutta: Seagull Books, 2002).

10 The FFC and later the NFDC adopted a lending policy that encouraged low-budget, narrative and experimental film-making while the FTII, set up in 1961, provided formal training – a training that was not geared towards fitting into the commercial film industry, although there were some successful crossovers – to many of the directors, editors and actors later associated with the Indian New Wave.

terms of language, politics, stylistic range and thematic concerns, and ranged from realist depictions of everyday life to modernist experiments with film form.

However, the New Wave film-makers shared a distrust of commercial cinema's values, themes and styles,[11] as well as a vision of cinema as art and sociopolitical critique, a vision coloured by the internationalist impulses of the Indian film society movement and what the editors of this volume describe as 'the popular left-wing upsurge of the late-1960s and early 1970s' across South Asia. Their approach to cinema owed much to the pioneering work of Satyajit Ray, Ritwik Ghatak and Mrinal Sen (all from Bengal), as well as to the influence of regional Indian literatures and theatre, and international art cinemas, notably Italian neorealism, the French *nouvelle vague* and the New Latin American cinema of the 1950s to 1970s.[12] It was articulated in the increasingly volatile political context of the 1960s to 1970s in India, marked by the unravelling of the Nehruvian consensus and the hegemony of the Indian National Congress (which had been in power at the Centre and in several of the states ever since independence), the institutionalization of corruption, the brutal state repression of militant student and peasant movements, Indira Gandhi's authoritarian rule, escalating economic crises, blatant political opportunism, widespread social disaffection and a growing crisis of political legitimacy. All these contributed to a loss of faith in, and a general questioning of, the narratives and projects of Indian nationalism. This interrogative impulse shaped the emerging discourse, across India, about a new cinema of social commitment or a cinema committed to capturing 'the lives of ordinary people and the experiential voices of the marginalized'[13] (as well as a more academic discourse – that of Subaltern Studies – with remarkably similar concerns about subalternity and representation).[14]

At the heart of the cinema of social commitment associated with the 'Indian New Wave' label was a 'realist project' that 'addressed squarely the injustices of society, the realities of oppression, the social and cinematic repressions of

[11] The degree of distrust, however, varied from person to person. I do not mean to suggest that the New Wave directors were univocal in their condemnation of Bollywood. Obviously, someone like Benegal or Nihalani or Ketan Mehta (all of whom experimented with the conventions and narrative structures of commercial cinema) was less averse to Bollywood than directors such as Mani Kaul or Kumar Shahani who insisted on a more radical break with what they considered to be the 'bazaar realism' of Bombay cinema.

[12] For a historical overview of the Indian New Wave and a summary of the main critical debates around it, see Ira Bhaskar, 'The Indian New Wave', in *Routledge Handbook of Indian Cinemas*, ed. K. Moti Gokulsing, Wimal Dissanayake and Rohit K. Dasgupta (Abingdon: Routledge, 2013), 19–33. For a discussion of the antecedents and the shaping influences of the Indian New Wave, see Chidananda Dasgupta, 'The New Cinema: A Wave or A Future?' *Indian Cinema Super Bazaar*, ed. Aruna Vasudev and Philippe Lenglet (New Delhi: Vikas, 1983), 39–49.

[13] Bhaskar, 'The Indian New Wave', 27.

[14] Surprisingly enough, little has been written about the overlap between these two projects.

traumatic history, and critiqued the tradition that empowered the upper castes and legitimized the violence perpetrated in their name against caste, community and gender identities and roles'.[15] Not surprisingly, rural India, where a large segment of the Indian population lived in poverty and in thrall to oppressive social conventions and semi-feudal hierarchies, emerged in this cinema as a privileged locus of 'the real' or a crucial site for exploring and understanding the struggles and failures of postcolonial India. Girish Karnad, an actor, director and playwright closely associated with the Indian New Wave, articulated this imagination of the rural in no uncertain terms: 'If you want to know the real India, you cannot get it from an Indian who lives in the city. It is the village Indian who is the real Indian.'[16] Karnad's comment attests to the continuing influence of a colonial cartography of national space that dates back to the mid-nineteenth century[17] – the mapping of the urban–rural divide in terms of a contrast between the privileged and hybridized world of the urban elite and the social and economic realities of the villages. Whether idealized as a pastoral paradise (e.g. in poetry and paintings) or the site of an alternative modernity (as in Gandhian visions), or identified as the target of transformative projects of modernization (e.g. Nehruvian projects of development) or social justice (e.g. in the literature of social reform and revolutionary movements), rural India emerged in colonial literary, artistic and political discourses as the authentic or the central space of the nation. In postcolonial India, a gulf of class privilege and hegemonic cultural capital is still seen as separating the lived experience of the metropolitan artist or intellectual (such as Karnad or Sen or many other New Wave film-makers) from the 'real' India of the villages, or from rural India's cultural norms, socio-economic structures and disenfranchised communities.

As Chidananda Dasgupta points out in 'The New Cinema: A Wave or a Future?', the Indian New Wave's project of realism can be read as an attempt, on the part of the liberal urban intelligentsia, to bridge this gulf and to expiate a deep sense of guilt 'over its persistent legacy of privilege'.[18] The project thus ran the risk of falling prey to what Paul Willemen calls the fantasy of 'ventriloquist identification': 'the fantasy . . . of the middle-class intellectual or entrepreneur who is so traumatized by his or her privileged education that he or she feels compelled to abdicate from intellectual responsibilities and to pretend to be a

[15] Bhaskar, 'The Indian New Wave', 28.

[16] Girish Karnad, 'Interview', in, *Indian Cinema Super Bazaar*, ed. Aruna Vasudev and Philippe Lenglet (Delhi: Vikas, 1983), , 222.

[17] See S. K. Das, *A History of Indian Literature: 1911-1956* (Delhi: Sahitya Akademi, 1995), 406–9, for an overview of the country-city dichotomy in Indian literatures.

[18] Dasgupta, 'The New Cinema', 41.

mere hollow vessel through which the voice of the oppressed, the voice of other people, resonates.'[19] However, it would be facile to dismiss the films of the Indian New Wave merely as an expression of middle-class guilt or a collective left-liberal indulgence in ventriloquist identification. Such readings not only distort the complex terms, and long history, of the left-liberal Indian elite's engagement with the disenfranchised – which can lead, as is evident from *Akaler Sandhaney*, to both wryly self-reflexive critiques and lingering fantasies of breaking out of their class position – but also fail to account for the Indian New Wave's distinctive place in this history.

A preoccupation with the subaltern, especially the rural subaltern, is not exclusive to the Indian New Wave but had been one of the driving forces of progressive literary, artistic and political discourse in twentieth-century South Asia (as the trajectories traced in other chapters in this volume – for example, of the writers associated with the Progressive Writers' Association or the PWA, the work of Chittaprosad, the making of *Jago Hua Savera* and the Kagmari Festival of 1957 – make clear). *Akaler Sandhaney* alludes, time and again, to a watershed moment in this history, one that has emerged as a central point of reference for several chapters in this volume: the IPTA movement of the 1940s, which consolidated itself in the context of the Bengal famine of 1943 and the CPI-led peasant and workers' movements in Bengal, Kerala and Andhra Pradesh (Telengana), and brought the suffering subaltern – more specifically, the suffering peasant – centre-stage both as subject and spectator. The movement was sparked off by a cataclysmic eruption of the village into urban consciousness, in the form of the starving millions who poured into the cities and towns during the famine of 1943, and the peasant uprisings. It was sustained – up to a point – by close interactions between the IPTA activists (not all of whom were card-carrying members of the CPI) and the rural and urban working-class audiences for whom they often staged agitprop performances, using theatre, songs, dance, skits, puppetry and posters, and drawing on regionally specific traditions of dramatic performance: 'By performing for the rural and non-literate public instead of a limited elite audience, the IPTA made political theatre available to those who previously had little or no access to it.'[20]

The initial, pre-independence phase of the IPTA movement is still widely remembered as a heady moment of cultural ferment, radical idealism and political fervour. As Sen put it much later, it was a time of unimaginable horrors

[19] Paul Willemen, 'The National', *Looks and Frictions* (London: BFI, 1994), 213.

[20] Nandi Bhatia, *Acts of Authority/Acts of Resistance: Theater and Politics in Colonial and Postcolonial India* (Ann Arbor: University of Michigan Press, 2004), 93.

yet 'something called hope was just around the corner':[21] the hope of using art and performance as modalities of grasping and portraying contemporary realities, as political weapons and consciousness-raising tools in the 'struggle for freedom, cultural progress, and economic justice',[22] and as means of bridging the gap between middle-class radicals and 'the people'. Participants in, and historians of, the IPTA movement repeatedly – and, at times, nostalgically (as Sunderason mentions in her essay in this book) – recall this short-lived phase of the IPTA in Bengal and elsewhere as being successful in 'reaching the grassroots' and 'in bringing about an identification' between the activist performers and the audience.[23] Even when looking back at this period with a more critical eye, Hemanga Biswas, a prominent musician, composer and IPTA stalwart, acknowledged that, despite its many 'weaknesses, contradictions, and conflicts,' the IPTA was nonetheless briefly able to provide a platform that enabled Indian artists and intellectuals to come close to 'the toiling masses' by identifying with the latter's 'causes'.[24] Biswas argued that the IPTA thus temporarily succeeded in truly becoming a 'mass medium' in the 1940s, through an amalgamation of the political and the cultural fronts: IPTA songs, for instance, became powerful weapons of mass mobilization, and were amplified and popularized through the 'waves of the political movement'.[25] Salil Chowdhury, the renowned composer who was Biswas's comrade in the 1940s IPTA movement before their political and artistic paths diverged, also remembered the cultural movement as an unprecedentedly broad-based and organic formation. He described it as being shaped by the involvement of not just middle-class intellectuals and students but also peasants and workers, formal experimentation driven by the urgency of political communication, and the creation of 'art for the people and by the

[21] Reinhard Hauff and Anjum Katyal, *Ten Days in Calcutta: A Portrait of Mrinal Sen by Reinhard Hauff* (Calcutta: Seagull Books, 1987), 73.

[22] *Indian People's Theatre Association Bulletin* (July 1945).

[23] Anuradha Roy, *Cultural Communism in Bengal, 1936-1952* (Delhi: Primus Books, 2014), 250. A representative example of memoirs of the IPTA movement: Arun Mitra, 'Lekhak-Shilpi Sangha o *Nabanna*: Smriti' [The Writers & Artists' Association and *Nabanna*: Memories], *Bharatey Sanghatito Pragati Sanskriti Andolaner Ponchash Barsho-Poorti Smarak Sankalan* [*Commemoration Volume for the Indian Progressive Movement's 50th Anniversary*] (Calcutta: L. Aikatan, 1986), 140–3; Chinmohan Sehanobish, *No. 46: Ekti Sanskritik Andolan Prasange* [*No. 46: About a Cultural Movement*] (Calcutta: Seriban, 2008, originally published 1986); Reba Raychaudhuri, *Jibaner Tane, Shilper Tane* [*Drawn to Life, Drawn to Art*] (Calcutta: Thema, 1999); Sajal Raychaudhuri, *Gananatya Katha* [*On the People's Theatre Movement*] (Calcutta: Mitra and Ghosh, 1990), among other memoirs.

[24] Hemanga Biswas, 'Gana Natyo Andolaney Amar Gaan' ('My Songs in the People's Theatre Movement') in *Uttal Shaat-Sottor: Rajneeti, Samaj o Sanskriti* [*The Turbulent 1960s-1970s: Politics, Society, and Culture*], ed. Arjun Goswami (Kolkata: Chayanika, 2006), 94. My translation.

[25] Ibid., 91.

people', especially songs and poster drama that 'could directly communicate with the people' and speak eloquently to their experiences.[26]

In interviews and essays, Sen repeatedly spoke about his admiration of the artistic innovativeness and political reach of 1940s IPTA performances (plays, ballets, street theatre), and of their formative impact on him and many of his contemporaries. 'I cannot deny', he wrote in an essay published towards the end of his long film-making career, 'it was the play *Nabanna* [Bijon Bhattacharya's a groundbreaking play about the famine, first staged by the IPTA in 1944 and widely regarded as one of the IPTA movement's most important contributions to Indian political theatre] that tempted me to take that first step in the direction of cinema.'[27] His interest in film-making emerged in the late 1940s, growing stronger through animated discussions with like-minded friends (including IPTA activists such as Ritwik Ghatak, Salil Chowdhury and Tapas Sen, who would go on to achieve national and international recognition as a film-maker, a music composer and a lighting designer, respectively), and was inextricable from a collective preoccupation with politics and social justice: 'That is the time when we learned and realized how to live with our notions of cinema inexorably entangled with our notions of revolution.'[28]

While Sen's first cinematic project (envisioned as a collective one) – shooting and then exhibiting a clandestine agitprop film, titled *Jamir Lorai* (*The Struggle for Land*), in the Kakdwip region of Bengal, where a peasant uprising was in full swing in the late 1940s to early 1950s[29] – did not materialize, and the films he made in the late 1950s and the 1960s were not overtly political (despite being marked by an interest in situating the lives of individuals in a socio-economic perspective), the aesthetics and politics of the 1940s IPTA movement cast a long shadow across his film-making career. This is especially evident in his long-standing 'agenda of examining history, social change, and even individual relationships from a Left radical position';[30] his urge to document histories of poverty, deprivation, exploitation and class struggle; the 'pamphleteering' style, intense topicality and political bluntness of his 1970s films – such as *Interview* (1970), *Calcutta '71* (1972), *Padatik* (*Urban Guerilla*, 1973) and *Chorus* (1974);

26 Salil Chowdhury, 'Nijer Katha' ['My Story', interview by Kalpana Biswas, originally published in *Kalpurush*: Summer/Monsoon1980], in Goswami, ed. *Uttal Shaat-Sottor*, 100–2.

27 Sen, 'A Terrible Dearth of Dreams and Dreamers', *Montage*, 115.

28 Sen, 'Paradise Café', *Montage*, 106.

29 Mrinal Sen, 'Bhoot-Bartaman-Bhabishyat (1940-1970)' ['Past, Present, and Future' (1940-1970)], in Debashish Sengupta, ed., *Pragatir Chetana, Pragatir Pathikera* [*Progressive Consciousness, Progressive Travellers*] (Kolkata: Ekushey Sangsad, 2008), 64–70.

30 Sen, 'Over the Years', *Montage*, 78.

and in their tendency 'to point a finger at the enemy of the people'.[31] In retrospect, Sen traced this accusatory impulse back to the 'hangover' or the 'legacy left by the IPTA of the 40s', with its agitprop orientation, clear-cut moral distinctions and political battle-lines and unwavering focus on mobilizing 'friends' in order to fight easily recognizable 'enemies'[32] – tendencies that became increasingly anachronistic and unproductive after independence, when, as the editors of this volume point out, 'the logic of resistance in the postcolony morphed from an anti-colonial one to one where the enemy was not everywhere clear'[33] and could no longer be grasped in black-and-white terms.

Ek Din Pratidin (*And Quietly Rolls the Dawn*, 1979), which clinically examines how a middle-class Bengali family's anxieties, hypocrisies and patriarchal double standards are exposed when its eldest daughter and sole breadwinner fails to return home from work one night, marks the beginning of Sen's conscious attempt to move away from the anachronistic aspects of his IPTA legacy and the strident politics of his 1970s films, and towards an examination of middle-class life, an interest in the intersection of the personal and the political, and a hunt for the 'enemy within':

> I thought, now is the time to go into myself, to pull myself up by the hair, to point my accusing finger at myself. It is not masochism, it is not self-flagellation, it is not self-pity. What I used to do before was to locate my enemy outside me. Now I am trying to find my enemy within myself.[34]

This inward turn – praised as necessary political introspection by some of his Indian viewers, excoriated as a disappointing retreat from politics by others – was partly prompted by the formation, in 1977, of a Left Front government in the state of West Bengal, where Sen lived. As many of his friends and former allies now became part of the political power elite, Sen, like many others, was troubled by the growth of 'an irritating sense of self-complacency'[35] and rigidity among the left leadership, as well as by the rift between the establishment left and other leftist groups. Reading an open letter by Elio Vittorini, an Italian leftist intellectual, around the same time, he found his motto in Vittorini's reminder to the Italian Communist Party that 'the point is not to pocket the truth but to chase the truth'.[36] He would later describe the more contemplative, self-reflexive

[31] Sen, 'Interview: 1986', *Montage*, 240.
[32] Ibid.
[33] Hoek and Sunderason, 'Introduction: Forms of the Left in Postcolonial South Asia', 17.
[34] Shampa Banerjee, *Profiles: Five Filmmakers from India* (Festival of India, USA, 1985–6), 60.
[35] Sen, 'Interview: 1982', *Montage*, 181.
[36] Sen, 'An Uncertain Journey', *Montage*, 103.

films he made in the 1980s as being part of his pursuit of an elusive truth and 'the enemy within' – the limitations and contradictions of the urban middle classes, rather than an external foe or structure of oppression.

Akaler Sandhaney: In search of 'the enemy within'

Akaler Sandhaney is the most obviously personal of the series of reflections on the 'enemy within' that followed *Ek Din Pratidin*. It takes a satirical look at the illusions of the urban middle-class radical – who has, as Samik Bandyopadhyay rightly points out in his introduction to the English version of the script, not only initiated and led movements for political action and social reform in modern India but has also let them down in most cases[37] – by exploring the implications and outcome of the New Wave's quest for reality. In his foreword to the first published version (in Bengali) of the working script of *Akaler Sandhaney*, Sen describes the film as a re-assessment not only of his own work as 'a reality seeker'[38] and his class position but also of the New Wave's desire for realism – or, to borrow Hoek and Sunderason's characterization of left-committed artists' approach to realism, 'for a form that would capture the reality of a social context, make it legible and galvanising to its audiences, and imbue the aesthetic object with an urgency for social change':[39]

> It [the film] ultimately poses the question: Have we really succeeded in proving our tall claims to realism, to an objective presentation of the environment through our art? Or how far have we succeeded? In other words, how honest have we been in our artistic work, and where and when have we begun deceiving ourselves and hiding behind so-called aesthetics? . . . For I at least have reached a point where I can assert boldly: there is a gap between the physicality of reality and the artist's redemption of it, of which he may or may not be aware. The artist too often covers up the void with his technique and all those efforts we characterize as artistry. . . . In *Akaler Sandhaney*, we make a confession of our incapacities.[40]

As Sen makes it clear in an interview published in 1985, he became increasingly concerned not only with juxtaposing the New Wave's claims to realism with its

[37] Samik Bandyopadhyay, 'Introduction', in *In Search of Famine (Akaler Sandhaney): A Film by Mrinal Sen* (Calcutta: Seagull Books, 1983), vi.

[38] 'An Interview with Mrinal Sen', by Sumita S. Chakravarty, *Cine-Tracts* (Summer/Fall 1981), 29.

[39] Hoek and Sunderason, 'Introduction', 29–30.

[40] Quoted and translated by Samik Bandyopadhyay in his introduction to *In Search of Famine*, vii.

'incapacities' but also with exploring the contradictions and the power equations implicit in some of its representational practices, especially the ones shaped by a preoccupation with the rural poor:

> I go to the countryside, to a very poor village . . . and then I try to understand them and their problems. I have my subject, my equipment and the actors with me. I go on to make a film on them, their problems and their crisis – and on the contradictions they suffer from – on their struggles and their ability to get over these struggles or succumbing to situations. Well, at that time, I emphatically pray that I can develop a sort of respect for the circumstances in which they live. Now, if you question my integrity, I'll have a big fight with you. I do have respect for the circumstances in which my characters live and if I don't grow this feeling, I don't have any right to make a film on them. So I stay with them for a month or two. I shoot the entire film with my actors but I live with them – in the village, in a slum, on a pavement. And then I come back. . . . I come back to my furnished apartment and when I meet you, I give interviews. And the first thing you feel is that Mrinal Sen is a sensitive filmmaker. This is what I am realizing and what I've been trying to talk about.[41]

In *Akaler Sandhaney*, Sen uses the story of the making – and unmaking – of a film to interrogate his own class position and aesthetic agenda and to examine the political implications of the New Wave's realist project and the cinematic practice of directors who 'invade the villages with their cameras'.[42] An unnamed film-maker (played by the actor who had appeared in Sen's *Padatik* as a young middle-class Maoist activist) sets out, along with his crew, to recreate the reality of the Bengal famine of 1943 'on location', only to discover that famine is an ever-present reality in rural Bengal and to eventually return to the city without accomplishing his mission of shooting the 'authentic' famine film. The film-within-the-film remains unfinished due to its director's inability to resolve the tensions between a tragic past and a potentially tragic present, between urban and rural culture, between cinematic illusion and the reality it claims to portray. These fault lines become apparent in the film – to the audience, if not always to the members of the film unit themselves – through the interactions of the film crew and the villagers. The crew's reactions to the villagers vary from blatant insensitivity and unthinking intrusions to well-intentioned but ineffectual attempts to bridge a communication gap that is hardly commensurate with the actual physical distance between the village and the city of Calcutta.

41 Utpal Chatterjee, 'Mrinal Sen: "Film-making Is Like Climbing a Steep Hill!"' *Cinema-India International* 2, no. 1 (January–March 1985), 57–8.

42 Sen, 'Interview: 1981', *Montage*, 163.

The distance between the two worlds – the hierarchical distinctions of class and cultural capital that separate the two – is expressed through the movements, speech patterns and conversations of the characters. The members of the film crew navigate their unfamiliar surroundings confidently, their politeness towards the villagers often tinged with superciliousness and an ethnographic curiosity. They speak in accents of privilege, effortlessly switching from Bengali to English and vice versa in mid-sentence when talking among themselves, their banter laced with an urbane wit that reveals their bi-cultural, bi-lingual fluency and easy familiarity with high-culture icons ranging from Rabindranath Tagore and Jibanananda Das (major figures in the canon of modern Bengali literature) to Shakespeare, T. S. Eliot and Arthur Koestler. They tend to address the poorer villagers as 'tumi' (a vocative case in Bengali that is politer and less presumptuous than 'tui' but much less respectful than 'apni', which is used as a mark of deference or courtesy to elders and to strangers or distant acquaintances perceived as social equals or superiors), though the latter address them as 'apni'. The villagers are deferential, unsure and compliant, at least initially, as well as somewhat awed by the sophistication of the visitors and puzzled by their project. Although Calcutta is just a few hours' drive away from the rural settlement of Hatui, the world of the villagers, dominated by the ever-present threat of starvation and institutionalized orthodoxy, seems to be intellectually and emotionally inaccessible to, or at best, only dimly perceived by, the urban elite, and eludes the latter's attempts to represent it.

As the film unit arrives in Hatui an old villager remarks, 'The city folk have come to take pictures of the famine! The famine is present in every pore of our bodies.' His caustic comment (apparently inspired by a remark Sen overheard a villager make about his own crew when he was shooting *Akaler Sandhaney* on location[43]) satirizes the film's title (which also happens to be the title of the film-within-the-film) and sets up an ironic contrast between the film unit's pursuit of authenticity and the shortcomings of their well-intentioned critiques of rural power structures, a contrast which deepens as the film progresses. The members of the unit unintentionally disrupt the lives of the villagers in more ways than one. On an economic level, the bulk purchases made by the production manager to provide the unit with sumptuous meals push up prices in the local market, leading an old villager to accuse the 'city folks' of unthinkingly sparking off a new famine in the course of their search for the old one – a charge which points to the exploitative aspects of an artistic practice ostensibly committed to exposing

[43] Mrinal Sen, *Tritiyo Bhuban* (*The Third World*) (Kolkata: Ananda, 2011), 150.

exploitation. Eventually, the director's attempts to find a local replacement for the role of a prostitute, and his inability to understand the stigma that would be attached to any village woman who plays that role, generates so much hostility that some members of the unit contemplate calling in the police to protect themselves from the very people the film was supposed to be speaking for. At this point, the elderly headmaster of the village school, who himself had come to the village from the city and had 'broken himself' over the years, as he puts it, in a vain attempt to integrate himself into the rural world, asks the director to abandon his pursuit of authenticity and go back the city, to the safety of the make-believe world of film studios. Although the schoolmaster admits that part of the problem lies in the villagers' 'ignorance, superstition, greed, and selfishness', he does not absolve the director and his crew of all blame and accuses them of having partially provoked the crisis by imposing themselves, in the unthinking arrogance of their class privileges, on the rural community.[44]

The crew's lack of insight and self-awareness is most glaringly illustrated by their apparent obliviousness to the shadow of starvation that continues to loom over the lives of a large number of the villagers, and their tendency to overlook what Sen describes as the 'uneasy, uncomfortable, irresistible, and inevitable connection between the past and the present'.[45] They hardly seem to notice the parallel between the fictional story of Sabitri set in 1943 and being enacted by Smita Patil in the film-within-the-film (Patil, who was dubbed 'the queen of parallel cinema' by critics, plays herself in the framing film) and the life of Durga (Sreela Majumder), the village woman who does odd jobs for the unit. Watching Patil enact a sequence where she is humiliated by her screen husband who suspects her of selling her body for a handful of rice to feed her starving family, Durga instinctively cries out in pain. She identifies with Patil's screen persona, seeing in Sabitri's story a reflection as well as the inevitable outcome of her own struggle to support her disabled husband and ailing child. Her inarticulate anguish, however, remains unheeded for the most part. Even though the director and Patil gradually become aware of this poignant convergence between fiction and reality (which simultaneously illustrates the potential as well as the limitations of this cinema), they are ultimately unable to help Durga. The director's progressive politics and commitment to an aesthetic of social

44 For an insightful discussion of Sen's exploration of the power dynamic involved in the representation of rural worlds by privileged urban artists in *Akaler Sandhaney* and *Khandahar*, see Bhaskar Sarkar, 'The Inward Look: The Politics and Practice of Cinematic Representation', in *The Enemy Within: The Films of Mrinal Sen*, ed. Sumita S. Chakravarty (London: Flics Books, 2000), 98–130.

45 Mrinal Sen, 'Interview: 1980', *Montage*, 154.

realism do not help him to face contemporary reality when the past collides with the present. *Akaler Sandhaney* ends with several shots of Durga's expressionless face dissolving into each other and finally fading away, while an off-screen voice informs us that Durga's son died a few days after the crew went back to the city, that her husband subsequently abandoned her and that now she is all alone.

The fading away of Durga's image seems to visualize, as it were, the disappearance of 'the historically muted subject of the subaltern' – the spectral presence hovering at the edges of history – that Gayatri Spivak theorizes in her influential essay, 'Can the Subaltern Speak?'[46] Durga's image disappears, not into 'pristine nothingness', but into the 'violent aporia between subject and object status' that, according to Spivak, constitutes the space of the subaltern.[47] Spivak's discussion of subalternity is based on a reading of the body of work produced by the Subaltern Studies collective, a loosely knit group of scholars committed to exposing and undermining the elitism inherent in dominant approaches to South Asian society and culture (colonial, nationalist and traditional Marxist historiography) by highlighting the hidden histories of subordinated groups and subaltern resistance. While she acknowledges the importance of such a task, she also cautions against the perils of a politics of recovery: an uncritical celebration of subaltern agency and a presumption to speak for a consciousness that cannot be completely retrieved from the space of subalternity. As she argues in a *Socialist Review* interview, it is a space that, by definition, lies outside the arena within which postcolonial Indian intellectuals such as the members of the Subaltern Studies collective and she herself (and the director in *Akaler Sandhaney* and Sen) are located as citizen-subjects:

> There is a space in post-imperialist arenas which is displaced from empire-nation exchanges. Where one sees the 'emancipated bourgeoisie,' 'organized labor,' 'organized left movements,' 'urban radicalism,' the disenfranchised 'women's arena'. . . all of this is constituted within that empire-nation exchange, reversing it in many different kinds of ways. But in post-imperialist societies there is a vast arena which is not necessarily accessible to that kind of exchange. It is that space that one calls subaltern.[48]

As Spivak points out with characteristic irony later on in the interview, 'the subaltern is the name of the place which is so displaced from what made me

[46] Gayatri Chakravorty Spivak, 'Can the Subaltern Speak?' in *Marxism and the Interpretation of Culture*, ed. C. Nelson and L. Grossberg (Urbana: University of Illinois Press, 1988), 295.

[47] Ibid., 306.

[48] 'Gayatri Spivak on the Politics of the Subaltern', Interview by Howard Winant. In *Socialist Review* 20 (1990), 90–1.

and the organized resister that to have it speak is like Godot arriving in a bus.'[49] In other words, the subaltern would not be subaltern if s/he could speak – that is, speak in a way that would be audible or have some authority within the structures of inequality that constitute the subaltern. The inability to be heard within the discourses of hegemonic power, even if one makes a valiant effort to speak, is, in fact, a hallmark of subalternity. Thus attempts by the metropolitan intellectual to 'speak for' or 'give voice to' the subaltern (as in the film-within-the-film and many earlier New Wave films or in earlier moments of Indian cultural history) without acknowledging his own complicity in the structures of power and knowledge that render the subaltern silent are not only doomed to failure but are at risk of being caught up in a patronizing, and ultimately ineffectual and self-defeating, politics of representation. *Akaler Sandhaney* seems to endorse this view of the unrepresentability of the subaltern, making an implicit case for a more self-reflexive, socially responsive and historically responsible cinematic practice: one that would work towards making the conditions of subalternity visible without presuming to speak on the subaltern's behalf or give voice to the oppressed, and be aware of its 'incapacities,' its own entanglements in the exploitative structures that it purports to criticize, and its affective investment in the histories of loss that it is compelled to trace.

Akaler Sandhaney can, in fact, be read as Sen's cinematic attempt to cast a clinical eye on his own – and more broadly, the cultural left's – relationship to the famine of 1943 and, by extension, to the other cataclysmic events (communal riots, political turbulence, the violence of war, the horrors and the tragedy of the partition) that convulsed South Asia in the 1940s.[50] As mentioned earlier, Sen's experience of living through the famine that decimated rural Bengal and 'littered' Calcutta's pavements with 'visions from hell' significantly contributed to his artistic formation and political education.[51] (114) *Baishey Sravan* (*The Wedding Day*, 1960), his third film and, according to him, the first film that he made on his own terms, traces the corrosive and dehumanizing impact of the famine on the once-loving relationship between a middle-aged Bengali villager and his young wife. He revisits the ravages of the famine in the second episode of *Calcutta '71* (1972), through the eyes of an expatriate Bengali visiting Calcutta in 1943, and the spectre of hunger lurks in the background of many of

[49] Ibid., 91.

[50] Several years later, he reflected on this in an essay titled, 'Itihaser Ashroye' ('In the Refuge of History'), translated by Sunandini Bannerjee as 'A Terrible Dearth of Dreams and Dreamers', in Sen, *Montage* 112–16.

[51] Sen, 'A Terrible Dearth of Dreams and Dreamers', *Montage*, 114.

his other films. In *Akaler Sandhaney*, however, he focuses not so much on the devastation caused by the famine as on the class privilege undergirding (and perhaps undermining) the unnamed director's – and by extension, his own and the cultural left's – preoccupation with the famine as a historical tragedy that had to be documented and memorialized.

From the beginning, the film sets up a series of sustained contrasts: between the famine as experienced on a visceral level by the anonymous millions decimated by it, and the famine as imagined or inserted into history and cultural memory, 'through the works of novelists and poets, on the canvases and in the colours of the artists, the voices of our singers and in the play *Nabanna* by the Gana Natya Sangha [IPTA]';[52] between the pastness of the famine for the director and his unit and its continuing presence in the lives of Durga and many other villagers; and between those who get to record the history of suffering and those whose suffering remains hidden from history. These contrasts come into sharply satirical focus when we see the members of the film unit while away a rainy day of enforced rest by looking at photographs of famine victims (some from 1943, some from much later periods in Bengal's history) and trying to guess the years when they were taken. The game does not only expose the distance between the film crew and the grim realities of hunger and malnutrition but also illustrates some of the processes – of othering, objectification and reification – through which the persistence of these realities come to be normalized or evaded.

The ambivalence of auto-critique

The incisiveness of Sen's auto-critique, however, is blunted, to an extent, by his reluctance to question the concept of the 'authentic' itself even as he satirizes the New Wave's misguided search for authenticity. Durga remains, even at the end, an enigmatic emblem of the national authentic, the 'real India' which remains beyond the orbit of urban modernity and the reach of the metropolitan left-liberal imagination. As in other New Wave narratives of rural suffering and marginalization, Durga's status as the 'authentic' Indian is secured through what feminist critic Lauren Berlant describes – in a different national context – as 'the trumping power of suffering'. In her analysis of the role of pain in the construction of American citizenship, Berlant has argued that ever since the abolitionist and suffrage movements, the value of individual citizens in the United States has been

[52] Ibid., 115.

most compellingly established and secured not through the juridical notion of an abstract personhood protected equally under the law (which often fails to offer equal protection to all citizens) but through 'a capacity for suffering and trauma' which confers moral power and the right to recognition as a person.[53] I find Berlant's account of 'sentimental politics' in the United States useful for thinking about the representation of subalternity in *Akaler Sandhaney*, as well as in the Indian New Wave, and more generally, about the affective power of suffering in forms of the left:

> It would not be exaggerating to say that sentimentality has long been the more popular rhetorical means by which pain is advanced, in the United States, as the true core of personhood and political collectivity. It operates when relatively privileged national subjects are exposed to the suffering of their intimate Others, so that to be virtuous requires feeling the pain of flawed or denied citizenship as their own pain.[54]

Even as *Akaler Sandhaney* satirizes the New Wave's obsession with the rural 'reality' and its tendency to present an ethnographic spectacle of the suffering of disenfranchised others, it does not quite escape the 'sentimental politics' that it critiques, the depiction of Durga being a case in point.

Akaler Sandhaney's self-reflexive critique of the Indian New Wave is also tempered by an undercurrent of sympathy for its project and an implicit, if partial, valorization of the city over the country. The depiction of the conflict between the village elders and thc film crew does not cast the former in a very favourable light. As the schoolmaster points out, the anger of the affluent village elders, while apparently sparked off by what they perceive to be a lack of respect for 'their women,' is not entirely righteous; it is fuelled, to a large extent, by their discomfort with the content of the film being made and its political thrust. They feel especially threatened by the film's critique of the speculative and exploitative practices of traders and moneylenders which contributed to the famine of 1943, as many of them (or their families) had attained their wealth and positions of social eminence precisely through such transactions and continue to engage in similar activities in the present. Their indignation thus comes across as sanctimonious and hypocritical, as well as profoundly patriarchal, and their rhetoric about protecting 'the honour of the village' is clearly motivated by a desire to maintain their power.

53 Lauren Berlant, 'The Subject of True Feeling: Pain, Privacy, and Politics', in *Cultural Studies and Political Theory*, ed. Jodi Dean (Ithaca: Cornell University Press, 2000), 42–62.

54 Berlant, 'The Subject of True Feeling', 45.

The schoolmaster's confrontation with the village elders, in the course of which he systematically outlines the sources of their ill-begotten wealth and identifies the cause of their anger, is a particularly important episode in this respect. As the only person in the film who can claim to belong to both the urban and the rural worlds, the schoolmaster serves within the film as the voice of wisdom and the symbol of the much-respected idealism of an earlier generation (coded in part through his precise manner of speaking, demeanour and dress). The film obviously intends his reading of the situation to guide our responses to the characters. Even though he ascribes part of the blame to the film crew's insufficient awareness of their class privilege, his denunciation of the village elders is much harsher. What comes across in his final words to the crew is not so much a sense of anger or a dismissal of their cinematic and political project, as a profound sense of disappointment at their inability to execute it and to bridge the gap between the village and the city. Their project itself, one can argue, is validated through his disappointment in its failure, as well as by his earlier approving responses to the shooting of a scene from the film (when he tells the actor playing an exploitative landlord that there are still people like his character in the village) and his apparent affection for the idealism of the director and of Smita Patil, who plays Sabitri in the film-within-the-film. Patil, one of the most famous icons of the Indian New Wave, not only plays herself in the film but also, by virtue of her already iconic status, can be said to represent the Indian New Wave itself. As such, the unfailingly positive responses of the valorized rural characters (not just the schoolmaster but also Durga and Haren, the artistically inclined weaver who used to act in *jatras* and appoints himself as the director's local guide and advocate) towards Patil also serve to partly validate the ideals underlying the New Wave's pursuit of realism, a project that the film as a whole purports to critique.

Sen's decision to cast the veteran actor Radhamohan Bhattacharya as the village schoolmaster who plays the voice of wisdom in the film is also significant in this context. Bhattacharya was best known to Bengali audiences for his role in Bimal Roy's 1944 film, *Udayer Pathey* (*Towards the Light*, Bengali), a film with a reputation 'as a popularized version of IPTA theatre':[55] that of the idealistic and incorruptible Anup, a young writer and trade-union activist who leaves the city at the end of the film to devote himself to the cause of the people, or the nation. In the famous last shot of *Udayer Pathey*, we see Anup walk away towards the rising sun and the presumably glorious dawn of a genuine national

[55] Rajadhyaksha and Willemen, *Encyclopedia of Indian Cinema*, 303.

independence. Thirty-six years later, the casting of the elderly Bhattacharya in the role of the principled yet disillusioned village teacher in *Akaler Sandhaney* simultaneously pays homage to the spirit of the earlier role and film, and the political fervour of the 1940s, and highlights the gap between the dream of a free and just society and the disheartening reality of the postcolonial predicament, inviting us to reflect on what went wrong.

Similarly, the contrast between the radical sentiments expressed in the song we hear in the opening sequence, supposedly sung in the voice of peasants rising up in revolt, and the bourgeois/haute-bourgeois deportment of the members of the film crew singing it operates both as homage and ironic commentary. *Akaler Sandhaney* relies on intertextual resonances and re-contextualization to invoke both the IPTA movement's utopian promise and its gradual loss of radical momentum: a once-revolutionary IPTA song is shown to have become part of a stock musical repertoire of middle-class dissent and light-hearted entertainment, and the IPTA's idealized agent of historical change – the insurgent peasant – is reduced to a figure of pathos in the film-within-the-film and, much more disconcertingly, in the framing film as well. The latter, however, succeeds in bringing images from the past into view in a new constellation in the present (by blurring the boundaries between the past and the present), and in raising compelling questions about what Sen described as 'the redemption of physical reality' (e.g. by foregrounding the artifice of cinematic realism). This is in stark contrast with the film-within-the film's uncritical embrace of verisimilitude and historical accuracy,[56] which renders it incapable of registering or confronting the unsettling presence of the past, the limits of realism and its own politics of representation. *Akaler Sandhaney* can thus be read as an extended meditation on forms of the left – the aesthetic and political compulsions and dilemmas – shared by the IPTA movement and the Indian New Wave, and more generally, on leftist Indian intellectuals' and artists' aporetic relationship with the rural subaltern and their recurrent attempts to make the subaltern speak – or to speak to the subaltern – through their work.

Fantasies of subaltern spectatorship

I want to end with a brief note on *Akaler Sandhaney*'s oblique references to the problem of speaking *to* the subaltern, a problem that has not only plagued

[56] The film's critique of an aesthetic of verisimilitude and historical re-enactment contains a not-so-veiled dig at Satyajit Ray's film about the famine of 1943, *Ashani Sanket* (*Distant Thunder*, 1973) but this is not Sen's primary target.

parallel cinema ever since its inception but has also exerted a shaping influence on the forms of the left in South Asia. In their foundational 1968 'Manifesto of the New Cinema Movement', Sen and Arun Kaul lamented that the lack of an 'enlightened audience' for 'off-beat' films posed a major challenge to their project of creating a 'new cinema' of artistic significance, social relevance and progressive politics:

> If the number of discriminating spectators appears, at first sight, to be heartbreakingly small, the reason is that the established film industry, motivated by the grossest economic considerations, has been for decades dishing out crudest vehicles of their notions of mass entertainment and thus conditioning the tastes of the majority of film goers.[57]

While the Indian New Wave eventually became a kind of alternative national cinema for an elite (mostly middle-class) minority, it could not reach the majority of those whom it professed to represent, the rural poor and the urban working classes. In a 1981 interview, Sen admitted that the 'New Cinema' failed to reach rural audiences: 'there is a strange duality at work in the rural areas, one that seeks political change but rejects political entertainment.'[58] He was very aware that, despite the urge 'to communicate to the large masses', his chosen forms and subjects appealed only to a 'minority audience of discriminating spectators, spread throughout the world':[59] 'When I make these films, I make films about certain people, but not necessarily for them. I make the films for people who understand my films.'[60] Sen's and, more generally, the Indian New Wave's access to a mass audience was limited not only by the much-lamented lack of effective outlets for mass distribution and exhibition but also by the elitist orientation of their aesthetic strategies and values, for example, Sen's experiments in non-narrative form, non-linear story-telling and blending fiction with documentary. What some of the practitioners and theorists of the Indian New Wave decried as the 'bazaar realism' of commercial cinema was able to captivate a much wider audience, and, often, to address the subliminal frustrations, daily humiliations and sense of precarity created in non-elite sectors by the contradictions of modernity and the postcolonial state's flawed projects of modernization. New Wave films, in contrast, remain largely confined within a relatively elite and

[57] Arun Kaul and Mrinal Sen, 'Manifesto of the New Cinema Movement (1968)', in *Film Manifestos and Global Cinema Cultures*, ed. Scott MacKenzie (Berkeley: University of California Press), 166.
[58] Sen, 'Interview: 1981', *Montage*, 161.
[59] Sen, Interview: 1980', *Montage*, 153.
[60] Sen, Interview: 1983', *Montage*, 212.

minority taste-culture, speaking primarily to the anxieties, aspirations and aesthetic preferences of the left-liberal middle classes.

In light of these circumstances, Durga's spontaneous reaction to the film that is being shot within the film and her instinctive identification with Smita Patil's on-screen character seem to reflect a fantasy of subaltern spectatorship that lies at the heart of the Indian New Wave. In Sen's case, this fantasy (as well as his melancholy awareness of its unattainability) was no doubt reinforced by his memories of his formative encounter with the IPTA during its most vibrant and successful phase of mass outreach in the 1940s. Durga represents the New Wave director's and the IPTA activist's dream audience: an audience of the oppressed who will come to recognize themselves in the fictional characters on the screen or on stage, and come to an understanding of their lives through the mediation of the film or the performance, thereby completing the film or the performance and vindicating its politically charged aesthetic of realism and its claims to authenticity. Ironically enough, the-film-within-the-film that has this effect on Durga is not at all the kind of film that Sen would want to make or endorse. As Suranjan Ganguly points out, it differs from the self-reflexive framing film, with its insistence on foregrounding its artifice – and most of Sen's other films, with their rejection of seamless realism and narrative continuity – 'not only in its reliance on a simple and crude realism, but in its melodramatic excesses, the way it openly caters to the emotions and manipulates its audience into identifying with the characters'.[61] However, these narrative and performative strategies, though consistently debunked through the framing film as ideologically suspect and emotionally manipulative, are precisely the ones that trigger Durga's epiphanic identification.

What, then, are we to make of the moment when Durga cries out in pain, disrupting the shooting of the film-within-the-film? It is a magical moment of wish-fulfillment for Sen and perhaps for some of the progressive bourgeois spectators of the film, in spite of its pathos, as it represents a much-desired point of contact between the world of the rural subaltern and the world of the metropolitan intellectual, between the country and the city, between the subject and the object of representation. But this idealized moment of recognition and perfect communication is a fleeting one, and its efficacy in Durga's life is far from clear. It fades away, along with Durga's image and the director's plan of making an 'authentic' film about the famine, into a troubling darkness at the

[61] Suranjan Ganguly, 'A Cinema on Red Alert: Mrinal Sen's Interview and In Search of Famine', *The Journal of Commonwealth Literature* 35, no. 1 (March 2000), 3.

end of *Akaler Sandhaney*. However, the ironic overtones of the moment remain (that it is brought about by a melodramatic mode of social realism that Sen finds ideologically suspect, cannot be registered by the film-in-making that sparks it, and lacks political efficacy), reminding the (bourgeois) spectator of the double bind of the progressive aesthetic project: the quest for effective 'forms of the left' that can 'give concrete shape to, and insight into, the experiences of the people'[62] and its apparently inevitable failure, the near-impossibility of retrieving the experience of subalternity or of speaking to the subaltern, and the inescapable political responsibility or compulsion (incurred by the very fact of privilege) of engaging in such efforts.

The pathos of the ending and of the earlier moment of wish-fulfillment thus stem not only from Durga's predicament and what she represents but also from Sen's melancholic reflections on the incapacities of his chosen form to achieve his desired political and aesthetic ideals, his perception of the unbridgeable gap between those who represent and those who are represented, and the temporal loop of the traumatic history that shaped his political sensibility and his approach to film-making. The affective force of the film for the audience of the Indian New Wave lies precisely in Sen's own political and aesthetic investments and failures, and in the melancholia that suffuses the film. Rather than reading this melancholia as a symptom of leftist self-indulgence or political retreat[63] or, in Freudian terms,[64] as an unproductive form of grief that refuses to relinquish what has been lost (the utopian horizons and convictions of the progressive movement), I see it as an attempt to look back in order to move forward, and as the modality of 'an ongoing and open relationship with the past – bringing its ghosts and specters, its flaring and fleeting images, into the present'[65] in order to emphasize the urgency of re-animating a political project – of social justice and transformative change – that remains unfinished.[66]

[62] Hoek and Sunderason, 'Introduction', 13.

[63] For an example of this reading, see Basab Dasgupta, 'Mrinal Sen: Kromagoto Anweshan' [Ceaseless Search], in *Nirbachito F [Selected F]* ed. Biren Das Sharma and Ujwal Bandopadhyay (Kolkata: Britter Baire, 2013), 55–8.

[64] Sigmund Freud, 'Mourning and Melancholia', in *The Standard Edition of the Complete Psychological Works of Sigmund Freud*, vol. 14, 1914–16, trans. James Strachey (1917; repr., London: Hogarth Press, 1957), 243–58.

[65] David L. Eng and David Kazanjian, 'Introduction: Mourning Remains', in *Loss: The Politics of Mourning*, ed. David L. Eng and David Kazanjian (Berkeley: University of California Press, 2003), 3–4. My approach to melancholia is indebted to Eng and Kazanjian's reconceptualization of melancholia as a generative openness to the past, rather than as a form of unhealthy grief (as Freud sees it).

[66] A Leverhulme Research Fellowship facilitated part of the research for this chapter.

Afterword

Kamran Asdar Ali

There is a desire in me to write. But when I sit down to write my thoughts become chaotic. Even after trying, I cannot separate Hindustan from Pakistan and Pakistan from Hindustan. Continuously this question arises in my mind. Will Pakistan's literature be different? If yes, then how? All that was written in undivided Hindustan who will claim that literature, will it now also be divided? Are the basic problems of our people on both sides not the same?[1]

The Urdu short-story writer Sa'adat Hasan Manto (1912–55), in the preceding quote, expresses how the division of British India (1947) created deep ambivalences regarding the continuity of what till then was a shared heritage for many North Indian intellectuals (of all religious persuasions). Intellectuals, who in many cases had known each other through their writings in Urdu/Hindi and who were developing a shared South Asian literary idiom, all of a sudden found themselves on different sides of a political, social and cultural border that was becoming more difficult to cross.

The editors (Lotte Hoek and Sanjukta Sunderason) in the Introductory chapter of this important volume similarly trace how the broader South Asian left borrowed idioms, ideas, themes and content while experimenting with form during the process of decolonization (and in the postcolonial period) in the earlier decades of the twentieth century. As if heeding Manto's anxieties, the editors consciously brought together a group of scholars who through their research remain involved in conversations and exchanges across borders of nation states that were formed through histories of anti-colonial struggles either in the 1940s or in 1971. For example, Iftikhar Dadi in Chapter 3 discusses the making of the film *Jago Hua Savera* (1959) by the first-time director A. J. Kardar. The acclaimed Pakistani progressive poet Faiz Ahmad Faiz (1911–84)

1 Sa'adat Hasan Manto, *Zehmat Meher Darakhshan*. The lines were cited in, Shemeem Hanfi, '*Adab Me Insan Dosti ka Tassawar*' (The Concept of Humanism in Literature), *Dunyazad* 21 (2008) (Karachi), 24.

wrote the dialogue and lyrics for the film which was a loose adaptation of the realist novella, *Padma Nadir Majhi* (*Boatman on the River Padma*) by the Indian writer Manik Bandopadhay (1908–56). Set in rural East Pakistan in the first decade after the country's independence and using a neorealist cinematic form, the film tells the story of poor fishermen and their struggle to survive. Kardar, while based in Pakistan, chose a team of experienced professionals from India; the assistant director, music director and the lead actress (Tripti Mitra) who herself was also involved with the Indian People's Theatre Association (IPTA), a leftist cultural association founded in the early 1940s and linked to the Progressive Writers Association (PWA) and the Communist Party of India (CPI). Dadi argues that the director in making these choices sought to broaden the scope of progressive cultural production beyond the narrow limits of the nation state. Further, Zahir Raihan was an assistant director on this team and Khan Ataur Rahman was one of the leading actors. Both were well trained and travelled Bengali artists/intellectuals who, as Lotte Hoek in Chapter 6 reminds us, collaborated professionally during the 1960s. During this period, Zahir Raihan also matured as a nationalist and left-wing film-maker in East Pakistan and introduced broader socialistic and class-based themes into his cinematic projects. Similarly, Maia Ramnath's contribution to the volume (Chapter 4) about the literary journal, *Lotus* details how intellectuals of the cultural left from India and Pakistan jointly participated in the journal's editorial process along with writers from other parts of the global South. In what follows, the chapters guide me in exploring the thematic insights of connectivity and conversations provided by the volume in order to further pursue questions related to difference, exclusion and violence while evaluating the cultural left's contribution to the creative processes and aesthetic forms in South Asia.

* * *

Manto's lamenting, the insightful framing of the introductory argument, and the various connections and associations between progressive artists, intellectuals and performers in South Asia highlighted in this text, reminds me of Aamir Mufti's important essay[2] on Faiz Ahmad Faiz' – who keeps appearing in several chapters in this volume – borrowing from a range of North Indian linguistic registers to compose his poetry. Despite his heavy reliance on high Persianate Urdu idiom, Mufti partly places Faiz, who was a Marxist and internationalist,

[2] See Aamir Mufti, 'Towards a Lyric History of India', *Boundary 2*, 31, no. 2 (2004), 245–74.

as using the Sufi idiom of South Asian Islam as a tool to critique religious orthodoxy. He shows how Faiz is immersed in the language of mystical Indian Islamic tradition that can be expressed in high Urdu diction and yet can also espouse a cultural lingua franca of North Indian poetic conventions. For Faiz, Mufti emphasizes, this appropriation of the Sufi expression is not merely a nostalgic embracing of syncretistic religious life, a merging of different traditions populating the social arena, but rather it is to emphasize the dialectic between the religious and the secular (worldly).[3] For example, Faiz's use of the idiom of *hijr* (leave, dislocation) in his poetry clearly relies on the Sufi invocation of the term as one of pain and joy of separation, the distancing from the beloved. Yet it is also a moment of love's consummation, of death and of self-extinction. However, Mufti argues, that for Faiz the issue of dislocation, intertwined as it is with the history of partition of British India, is one of prolonged separation and is connected to the desire to attain social justice despite the suffering and oppression related to the 'partitioned' nature of the larger collective self (people on both sides of the divide)

Mufti further traces the complex spatial geography of the shared linguistic idiom of North India (Urdu and Hindavi) present in Faiz's prose and poetry to argue that despite the barriers and divisions, there is a desire of an imagined union with the 'beloved' left behind on the 'other side', never completely forgotten. For Faiz, the predicament of the division is a continuous attempt to overcome the boundaries of the new nation state(s) by creating a dialogue with the other, which uncannily is also the self. In opening up this space Faiz in his poetry refuses to reify the self or the other while simultaneously creating utopian possibilities to end antagonisms and differences by foregrounding the shared linguistic idiom of the 'other'. For example, in a reading of Faiz's poem *Sipahi Ka Marsia* (Soldier's Elegy), Mufti shows how the poet abandons 'high' Urdu (Persianate) vocabulary and borrows from the Hindavi idiom, a register of language use that is not recognized in the official history of modern Urdu (or accepted as part of Pakistan's new emphasis on a more Persianized form of Urdu).

Utho ab mati se utho
Jago mere lal,
Ab jago mere lal
Tumri sej sajavan karan
Dekho ai rain andhyaran . . .

[3] Ibid., 260.

[Stand, get up from the dust
Wake up, my son
You wake up now, my son
Look, to make your bed
Dark night has arrived . . .][4]

First, to convey a particular emotion, Faiz uses the form of the modern *nazm*, rather than rely on *ghazal* (the more traditional, romantic and bounded form of lyric poetry in Urdu), the choice of form hence becomes important here to convey a more direct message.[5] By bringing the grieving voice of the parent to the fore through the vocabulary of cultural and idiomatic history, of images and rituals, the poem pushes us to encounter submerged sounds and meaning that are still retrievable and can be shared. Precisely at the moment of loss of the child in war (written immediately after the India-Pakistan war of 1965) the modern Urdu idiom, for Faiz, remains inadequate to express grief and hence he turns to Hindavi to explore the chequered history of nation state, communal difference and language preference. Mufti argues that this choice perhaps also makes clear that the elegy cannot be for the fallen Pakistani soldier alone.

Similarly, in a late poem by Faiz, *Tum Hi Kaho Kiya Karna Hai* (You Tell, What Needs to Be Done), the poet uses similar Hindavi idiomatic phrases to lament how despite the passing of years the promised 'dawn' of social justice had yet to arrive.

He starts the poem;

Jab dukh ki Nadiya Mai Hum Nai
Jeewan Ki Nao Daali Thi
Tha Kitna Kas Bal BahoN Mai
Lahu Mai Kitni Lali Thi
YuN lagta tha Kai Do Haath lagai
Aur Nao Puram Paar Lagi
Aisa Na Hua, Har Dharay Mai
Kuch an Dheki ManjhdharaiN theeN . . .

4 Faiz Ahmad Faiz, *Nuskhaha-e-Wafa* (Lahore: *Maktaba-e-Karavan*), 356–7. Translation by Aamir Mufti, see Mufti, 'Towards a Lyric History of India'.

5 *Ghazal* and *Nazm* are the two dominant lyric forms in Urdu poetry. Ghazal, borrowed from Persian, is a centuries older form of poetic expression; it has a bounded structure, meaning centered around a couplet, and rhyming elements at the end of each line. There is no overarching theme, but the basic message of the *ghazal* is romantic. *Nazm* has a more open structure and has thematic coherence as opposed to the ghazal. Mufti argues that Faiz's lyrics poetry has to be read in terms of the social significance of identity in the aftermath of the partition (the expression and dialectics of self and other) of British India. see Mufti, 'Towards a Lyric History of India'.

[When we put our life's boat in the river of sorrows
There was strength in our arms and our blood was warm
It seemed that in a couple of strokes the boat would cross the river
It did not happen, as in each wave there were unseen currents . . .] [6]

The poem, also a *nazm*, is not dated but is written most probably in the early 1980s. Faiz intertwines 'high' Urdu and Hindavi in this poem to reflect on the history of the postcolonial state and how even after years of sincere struggles, on either side of the border (India and Pakistan), the utopic moment of social justice was still illusory. To reiterate Aamir Mufti's argument, Faiz, in his use of both idiomatic registers, does not place himself in a particular geography or nation state (Pakistan), but his lament is for the entire region that equally suffered the vagaries and promise of the new dawn of freedom from colonial rule (1947). His choice in using the shared vernacular form undermines the dominant high idiom in Urdu – the use of *nadiya* (Hindavi/or Hindustani) for river, instead of *darya* (Urdu), *jeewan* (Hindavi) instead of *zindagi* (Urdu), *nao* (Hindavi and Bangla) instead of *kashti* (Urdu), but *lahu* (Urdu) for blood – and points to a borrowing from different, yet overlapping, linguistic traditions to show continuity and connectivity, while suggesting that the 'self' and the 'other' even in their separation have faltered in achieving common emancipatory goals. Where in the Soldier's Elegy, the grieving was not for the Pakistani self alone – here the struggle was supposed to be collective and not bifurcated. The division of British India had created a fracture that many North Indian progressives like Faiz in their own creative work were seeking to heal by making linguistic overtures.

In contrast, perhaps writers like Manto were seeking to make sense of the catastrophe that befell South Asia in 1947 in a different register. Published in 1948, *Siah Hashiye* (*Black Margins*)[7] is Manto's book of very short stories that depict the absurdness and the arbitrary nature of Partition's violence. A story from this collection, called 'Sorry', as in the English word, depicts the act of stabbing. The knife continues beyond the abdomen and cuts open the trousers. The killer laments and just says, 'uh oh, I committed a mistake',[8] leading the reader to believe that as the trousers fall down the 'identity' of the victim is revealed in some capacity.[9] In the post-partition climate when everyone was

6 Ibid., 603–5. Translation by the author.
7 Sa'adat Hasan Manto, *Siah Hashiye* in *Manto Numah* (Lahore: *Sang-e-Meel* Press, 1991).
8 The word is pronounced 'mishtake' in English.
9 The issue here is what becomes visible when the trousers fall down, a circumcised or uncircumcised man, which would make him either a Muslim or a Hindu, respectively. We of course assume that the

trying to understand or perhaps forget the carnage of the past year, such pieces of fiction had an uneasy aura about them.

Manto, in a less prescriptive mode than the more recognized progressive writers, in such stories opens an arena for us to appreciate the emergent debate on post-Partition identity. The Pakistani state emphasized national unity on the basis of a single national language (Urdu) and a unified religious identity (Islam) which remained in conflict with the cultural and linguistic diversity of the people who had become part of this new land. In an earlier published essay, I read some of Manto's short stories written after the carnage of 1947 during the early years of Pakistan's existence as representing his already developing ambivalence and uncertainty about the consolidation of a unitary identity in the Pakistani state.[10] For example, if we take the above-mentioned short story, 'Sorry', it may not only deal with the similarity and distance between self and the other, Hindu or Muslim, but may also allude to how in the new country, people—much like Manto's own uncertainty—were still unsure about who they were or had become. What lay under the trousers after the violent act of ripping them open could be read in terms of religious or for that matter sexual/gender identity. But the 'exposure' or the 'unveiling' of what lies underneath may also be understood as the ambiguous nature of identity itself in a post-catastrophic moment, the early years of Pakistan's history. The act of stabbing had created a lesion which could not be correctly identified or healed. These early fissures festered to trouble subsequent Pakistani history, whether in the form of the struggle for independence in East Pakistan/Bangladesh, or in the insurgencies for regional autonomy in Baluchistan.[11]

Such wounds, within the body politic, remain very much part of the history of postcolonial South Asia. We observe similar historical trajectories in Harshana Rambukwella's chapter in this volume as it shows how in Sri Lanka even the most progressive and left-oriented writers retained a Sinhala-centric worldview and could not democratically address the persistent Tamil question in the country's political and social life (or foresee the extreme violence that the country suffered for several decades). Similarly, Lotte Hoek in Chapter 6 depicts how for intellectuals in East Pakistan left-wing commitments were intertwined

killer and the victim are both males; it was more likely that a female victim would be raped and then killed or left to die.

[10] Kamran Asdar Ali, 'Progressives and "Perverts": Partition Stories and Pakistan's Future', *Social Text* 29, no. 3 (2011), 1–29.

[11] There have been major uprisings in Baluchistan for national self-determination of the region. These started in 1948 when the province was forcefully incorporated into Pakistan, and continued to 1973 when a full-scale war was fought in the region with the Pakistan Army on one side and armed rebels on the other. Even currently a low intensity war continues in many parts of Baluchistan.

with nationalist sentiments in the struggle for Bangladesh. She shares how as early as 1953, after the language struggle, the young playwright, Munier Chowdhury, a member of the Communist Party, staged the play *Kabar* (*The Grave*) while imprisoned with other activists and cadres of the party. The play itself had religious, nationalistic and leftist connotations.[12]

Further, in his above-mentioned paper on *Jago Hua Savera*, Dadi argues how despite Faiz's sensitivity to the issue of class and ethnic difference, he prefers a folk Bhojpuri diction (from the Hindi-speaking belt of North India, but not from Bengal) for his poems that are sung musically in *bhatliali*, a popular folk form used by boatmen in East Bengal (which was also popular in the left's cultural representation in the 1940s). Faiz's experimentation in terms of lyrical style and musicality does show a social concern and nudges toward folk forms, yet he uses a non-Bangla linguistic register in rendering his dialogue for the film. Perhaps sensitive to the idea of communicating with a potentially Bengali audience in East Bengal, Dadi maintains, Faiz created a mixture of simplified Urdu with some Bangla words. Ironically the rendition was not understandable by audiences of either linguistic communities. Hence, as one appreciates the earlier use of Hindavi diction by Faiz to find a resolution to the violent division of South Asian geography, in this particular case Urdu remains the dominant diction to address the question of difference within the Pakistani nation state (there are echoes of the process of Sinhala dominance in Sri Lanka here).

I have argued elsewhere[13] that although the Communist Party of Pakistan (CPP) in the early years of Pakistan recognized the rights of the Bangla language, the progressive movement continued to also think of Urdu as a national language that could eventually serve the purpose of a language of communication. Unlike the Pakistani state that pushed for Urdu's exclusive right to be the only national language (including Jinnah, the founder of Pakistan), the progressives were against the imposition of one language over the cultural and linguistic diversity of the land. However, in putting forward the argument for Urdu as the language of communication the communists thought that rather than impose Urdu on the population, conditions had to be created whereby different linguistic groups would by consensus agree to accept it as a common language of interaction among the various provinces. This was indeed a more democratic resolution

[12] Lotte Hoek draws on material from, Syed Jamil Ahmed, 'Raising the Dead in a Prison by the Light of Lanterns: A Study of a Fragment of Political Theatre', in *Gender, Politics and Performance in South Asia*, ed. Sheema Kirmani et al. (Karachi: Oxford University Press 2015), 35–54.

[13] Kamran Asdar Ali, *Communism in Pakistan* (London: I B Tauris, 2015).

of the language question, and a partial acknowledgement of cultural diversity within the populace that was taking shape in Pakistan in the late 1940s.[14]

This said, many progressives were (including Faiz) also steeped in the cultural traditions of the North Indian Urdu–Hindi belt.[15] They were sympathetic to the idea that eventually people would gravitate towards accepting Urdu not only as the major national language of communication but also of national unity.[16] Their arguments were almost exclusively for Urdu to attain its eventual pivotal place in national culture, and not for any other major language.[17] Hence, despite the issue of connectivity, it is clear that ethnic, sectarian and religious differences continued to remain a major fissure in the history of modernizing South Asian nation states like Pakistan.

* * *

The Introduction of the volume also discusses the history of the formation of the All India Progressive Writers Association (AIPWA) in 1935, leading to the later formation of IPTA and other forums of the cultural left in British India which had strong links with the CPI. In the anti-colonial atmosphere of the 1940s, a number of young writers, artists, musicians and aspiring film-makers were influenced by it. Under CPI's guidance there was also a serious attempt by the leaders of the movement to excavate folk themes and poetic genres. As we witnessed with Faiz's experiment with style and form for *Jago Hua Savera*, poets were encouraged to compose their work in the vernacular and local dialects of

[14] The Communist Party of Pakistan (CPP) indeed showed its solidarity with the Bangla question and the linguistic rights of the various peoples of Pakistan, yet under the influence of the CPI's hard line in the late 1940s it remained hostile, at least in this early phase of its existence, towards the emergent nationalist leadership of various linguistic groups, whether Pashtun, Baluch, Sindhi or Bengali. See Ferozuddin Mansur, *Pakistan Mai Quami ZabanoN ka Masla* (The Problem of National Languages in Pakistan). (Lahore: Sujeet Kitab Ghar (reprinted from first edition in 1952). For a somewhat detailed discussion of the Bengali question, see Yunus Samad, *A Nation in Turmoil: Nationalism and Ethnicity in Pakistan, 1937–1958* (New Delhi: Sage, 1995). Also see Saadia Toor, 'A National Culture for Pakistan: The Political Economy of a Debate', *Inter-Asia Cultural Studies* 6, no. 3(2005), 319–40.

[15] This is not to say that the intellectual elite in Pakistani Punjab, where the medium of instruction had been in Urdu since the late nineteenth century, did not itself have an investment in making Urdu the national language.

[16] In Pakistan, progressives constantly argued for the supremacy of Urdu in relation to English which had gained currency in government circles, in the process sidelining Urdu as the national language. Hajra Masroor,'Tul'u', *Nuqush* 9 (1949), 3.

[17] There is not enough space to discuss in detail the ambiguities of CPPs position on the language question; perhaps the leadership was not clear itself. Here we are reminded of how the Soviet Union, after a vigorous nationalities-policy in the immediate aftermath of 1917 period, had by the 1940s started the process of Russification where Russian had become the Soviet lingua franca. For an excellent discussion on the USSR's nationality policy, see Yuri Slezkine, 'The USSR as a Communal Apartment, or How the Socialist State Promoted Ethnic Particularism', *Slavic Review* 53, no. 2 (1994), 414–52.

different regions of British India (Andhra, UP, Bihar). This was then rendered into folk music and sung/read at gatherings of workers and peasants. There was an emphasis on art serving the people and putting their struggle against oppression and for freedom at the centre of all creative work. New forms were experimented with as poets started writing in free or blank verse (without meter and rhyme) and worked within the tradition of folk forms (ballads) by introducing new ideas and themes, and IPTA members wrote and performed progressive plays for a range of audiences. Further, a new criticism was encouraged that gauged artists and writers according to their allegiance to anti-imperialism and their support for socialist ideals (at times this was narrowly defined as support for the Soviet Union).

Sajjad Zaheer (1905–73) an accomplished short-story writer and literary critic, who later became the secretary general of the Communist Party of Pakistan (CPP), along with a group of Indian students such as Mulk Raj Anand and Ahmed Ali initially formed the Progressive Writers' Association (PWA) while studying in England during the 1930s. Carlo Coppola (1974),[18] who has written a history of the PWA, argues that young Zaheer and others were influenced by Marxist writings while studying at Oxford and the person who encouraged them to establish a formal organization was the leftist writer Ralph Fox (Fox later died in the Spanish Civil War). However, what is missing in Coppola's account (and also from *Roshnai*[19] the biographical account of the PWA that Sajjad Zaheer wrote later) is any discussion of how the manifesto borrowed heavily from the reports and speeches of the first Soviet Writers Congress in 1934, especially if we see the speeches by Andrei Zhdanov and Maxim Gorky.[20] There is much thematic similarity between Zhdanov's position and that of the emerging manifesto of the young Indian students in Britain.

In my own work, I have followed the progression of the PWA after the creation of Pakistan, where the All Pakistan Progressive Writers Association (APPWA) was similarly closely affiliated with the newly formed CPP. The newly appointed secretary general, Zaheer himself, as a founding member and past president,

[18] Carlo Coppola, 'The All India Progressive Writers' Association: The European Phase', in *Marxist Influences and South Asian Literature*, vol. 1, ed. Carlo Coppola (East Lansing: Michigan State University, 1974), 1–34.

[19] Sajjad Zaheer, *Roshnai* (lit. Ink) (Lahore: Maktab-e-Urdu, 1956). Also see, The Light (Karachi: Oxford University Press, 2006).

[20] Zhdanov, Andrei (1896–1948), senior member of the Soviet Communist Party in 1934, was the secretary of the Communist Party. See , A. A. Zhdanov 'Soviet Literature – The Richest in Ideas, the Most Advanced Literature', in *Problems of Soviet Literature: Reports and Speeches at the First Soviet Writers' Congress*, ed. A. Zhadanov, Maxim Gorky, N. Bukharin, K. Radek and A. Stetsky (Moscow: Cooperative Publishing Society of Foreign Workers in the USSR, 1935), 15–35.

was keen on pushing the role of intelligentsia in society. In his communiqués he asserted the need for writers to have a thorough mastery of Marxist ideology and insisted on study circles so that intellectuals and creative people, especially those linked to the CPP, could study the works of Marx, Lenin and Stalin, as well as literature coming from the Soviet Union and progressive literature from Europe and Britain. Writers were also encouraged to write essays, articles and literary criticism for popular consumption to counter bourgeois and 'reactionary' ideologies that were being propagated by, according to him, state and class enemies.[21] Within this context, by the late 1940s the CPP, in control of APPWA and influenced by the CPI's changed radical line, under its new secretary general, B. T. Ranadive, had started to purge from its ranks those that did not completely toe the new party line. This became more evident after the introduction of the new manifesto which targeted 'non-progressive' writers during the first APPWA conference held in Lahore in November 1949.

Following the prevalent Ranadive line, the 'non-progressive' intellectuals were severely criticized during this conference for their perceived political failings, alliance with the state machinery, sexual perversions and lack of social consciousness.[22] The manifesto lumped Islamists, nationalists and liberals (art for art's sake) into the same basket and painted them as reactionaries. The published manifesto then turned toward those writers who, according to its analysis, used bourgeois psychology and Freudian parameters to understand society. These authors were rendered as obscene, perverse, pornographic and decadent for their depiction of life through the lens of sexuality. They distorted people's experience, the manifesto asserted, and disrespected love as a pure form of desire.[23] Hence the manifesto portrayed these writers as anti-humanists who could only make fun of the people's creative faculty and were insensitive to the struggle for human existence. The protagonists of their works were killers, thieves, prostitutes and those elements of society that did not contribute to society's productive process; they wrote pessimistic stories about darkness and of death (this was a clear reference to Manto as a writer).

Progressive stalwarts like Ali Sardar Jafri (1913–2000)[24] and even Sajjad Zaheer argued that these freethinkers and liberal artists possessed a sick mentality that made them avoid people's problems. To be sure in Pakistan's early years there

[21] See, Ali, *Communism*.

[22] See Hafeeez Malik, 'The Marxist Literary Movement in Pakistan', *Journal of Asian Studies* 26 (1967), 649–64.

[23] Ibid. It will take a longer article to unpack the puritanical bent in progressive discourse of this era.

[24] Progressive Urdu poet.

was much anxiety present among progressive writers to distance themselves from those who were perceived by them as standard bearers of middle-class values and obscene literature. For example, Sardar Jafri attacked poets like N. M. Rashid (d.1975),[25] a major modernist poet of the era,[26] by arguing that he and others like him were perpetrators of the death wish, escapists and obsessed with sexual themes, and condemned Manto for elevating such topics to the level of religious belief.

Sanjukta Sunderason's contribution to the volume (Chapter 1) traces the history of another one such artist, Chittaprosad, who distanced himself from CPI and the progressive cultural movement during this period in India. Chittaprosad was associated with the Communist Party of India (CPI) from the early 1940s, being part of the 'Marxist Cultural Movement' of the era. He was a promoter of Social Realism in Indian art and created documentary drawings (famine sketches) along with performing grassroots relief work during the famine in Bengal in 1943–4. He also organized and composed popular ballets for IPTA in the 1940s and identified as a dedicated cultural worker for the future revolutionary change led by CPI. However, Sunderason reminds us that Chittaprosad moved away from such activities in 1948 when the party took a radical left turn under the new leadership of B. T Ranadive who enforced a more stringent ideological control over cultural expression. His story, as it unfolds, is one of a relationship between the creative imagination of the non-conforming individual artist who is committed to a notion of politically progressive art that may not always adhere to the doctrines of the more formal left formations.

What I have briefly recounted about the new manifesto is fairly common knowledge among some literary circles in South Asia. What is not so well known is that the language of the manifesto may have been influenced by, as did the first manifesto in 1935, the Congress of Soviet Writers, the renewed Soviet criticism of writers and intellectuals who were not following the state-sponsored ideological line. As discussed briefly in the Introduction by the editors of this volume, one example of this form of attack was by the same Andrei Zhdanov in 1946 on the journals *Zvezda* and *Leningrad* for publishing the works of Mikhail

[25] Ali Sardar Jafri, *Taraqi Pasand Adab* (Progressive Literature) (Aligarh, India: *Anjuman Tariqui-e-Urdu*, 1957), 198.

[26] N. M. Rashid (1910–75) was one of the most original Urdu poets of mid-twentieth-century South Asia. Although criticized by the progressives for his writing style and also for the themes he wrote upon, he was personal friends with many of them and also wrote the introduction to the progressive poet Faiz Ahmed Faiz's first book of poetry. He was under-appreciated as an intellect during his lifetime.

Zoshchenko (1895–1958) and Anna Akhmatova (1889–1966).[27] This became the basis for what was later to be called the Zhdanov Doctrine in cultural debates within global socialist circles. The journals were reprimanded for giving space to Zoshchenko's short stories. They were deemed commonplace, rubbish, devoid of ideas and apolitical literature that aimed at disorienting the youth and poisoning their minds. He is called a vulgar lampoonist for the satirical short stories he published during the war.

Similarly, the poet Akhamotova, who has now become the icon of modern Russian poetry, was condemned for ideologically empty poetry of pessimism reflective of a spirit of decline. She was accused of bourgeois aristocratic aestheticism, of 'art for art's sake', which does not follow in the footsteps of the people. She is portrayed as a poet of the elite that mixes fornication and prayer, a kind of religious eroticism (we see the echoes in this of how N. M. Rashid and Manto and others were condemned during the period of the new manifesto in Pakistan).

It would be obvious to even a lay reader that there are connections between the Soviet positions on culture and literature and the PWA during the late colonial and the early postcolonial period in South Asia. As was the case with the APPWA manifesto of 1949, the ideas put forward in Zhdanov's argument were acceptable in order to counteract the bourgeois individualistic moral code and literary forms. Within this context, we can surely understand why artists like Chittaprosad, while committed to a politics of social progressivism, sought to distance themselves from the more doctrinaire ideological positions.

* * *

Layli Uddin in Chapter 2 of this volume describes the politically important, yet celebratory Kagmari Festival (1957) organized by the peasant and nationalist leader Maulana Bhashani. The *mela* or *sammelon* in East Pakistan along with its structured pedagogical message incorporated a range of folk and religious idioms and performances to constitute the unique experience for its participants. Bhashani's stature as a foremost leader of the peasantry and the downtrodden in East Bengal (or in Pakistan) is widely known. What Layli Uddin also suggests in her contribution is that his populist politics had its roots within the aesthetic tradition (and experimentation) in prose, poetry, theatre, art and other genres of performative expression that constituted the creative landscape of Bengal during

[27] See Zhdanov's speech on 14 August 1946 on the journals *Zvedzda* and *Leningrad* (Zhdanov's speech was published in *Pravda*, 21 September 1946).

the late colonial and early postcolonial moment. For this last section I focus on Bengal, as several chapters in this volume have, to trace the use of the folk idiom in order to bring it into a dialogue with prevalent progressive and socialist ideals. In following this trajectory, for example, we are reminded of the Bengali artist Zainul Abedin (1914–76), who was close to the Progressive movement (also drew iconic representations of the Bengal famine) in the 1960s and painted Santhal (indigenous) women of East Bengal. As an artist and teacher, he was at the forefront of Bangladesh's war of liberation from West Pakistan and his work continued to frame the cultural life of the new country until his passing away.[28]

Abedin's influence hence helps me in sharing some concluding thoughts on form, art, aesthetics and political futures in a more contemporary postcolonial moment. For example, if we take the late Bangladeshi director Tareque Masud's *Clay Bird* (*Matir Moina*, 2002), the film is set in the period immediately before the war of liberation in Bangladesh, and through a sensitive lens he captures the life of rural East Bengal showing its rich heritage of tolerance of various religious practices. The film introduces several Baul performers who sing of religious co-existence and gender equity from within Islam's cultural traditions (perhaps similar to Faiz's reliance on the Sufi idiom to convey social causes). These songs remind us of Lalon Faqir (died 1890) the Bengali mystic, teacher and songwriter who sang about a life where all religions and beliefs are in harmony. This trajectory connects us to the larger role minstrels, *mirasis* and *devdasis* have played in the development of art and aesthetics in South Asia. These seemingly denigrated and at times gendered subaltern voices have overwhelmingly contributed to the ongoing history of music, dance and singing in the region. In the examples I have shared with you, these folk traditions are rethought and reconnected to modernist forms of creative expression; whether used in the *sammelon* organized by Bhashani to expand political mobilization in the new nation state, or the depictions of the Santhal in Zainul Abedin's modernist paintings, or using Baul songs as political critique by Tareque Masud in his film, or for that matter, Faiz's choice of Bhojpuri lyrics to represent the voices of exploited fishermen in *Jago Hua Savera*.

Masud's *Matir Moina* does help us remember the violence during Bangladesh's liberation war, but it should also be studied in light of the history of the cultural and political struggle conducted through the cinematic form by Zahir Raihan and

[28] Another such iconic figure in the history of theatre in South Asia is Habib Tanvir (1923–2009), who again through his immersion into folk forms made an important contribution to popular theatre in India. Habib Tanvir was famous for working with indigenous groups from Central India and he helped create and original a new language in theatre performance.

Alamgir Kabir in East Bengal of the 1960s and 1970s (see Lotte Hoek's chapter in this volume). Further, by incorporating papers that depict Chittaprosad's addressing of social and economic deprivation (his work was broader than Bengal of course) through various forms of artistic expression (Sunderason), and Mrinal Sen's self-reflective (and critical) cinematic engagement with the history of the Bengal famine (Manishita Dass), this volume compels us as readers to consider the postcolonial history of Bengal on both sides of the border.

To remind ourselves, while war raged in East Bengal, Kolkata (Calcutta then) in the early 1970s was a city under siege. This was due to the radical movement that is remembered in relation to Naxalbari, a small village in West Bengal that was the site of the 1967 peasant uprising supported by the Communist Party of India (Marxist). Soon the uprising spread across the state with major participation by indigenous groups such as the Santhals (who were painted by Zainul Abedin in East Bengal) and other scheduled castes. Driven by Maoist ideological fervour and Charu Majumdar's (1918–72) writings, the revolutionary movement was joined by a number of urban intellectuals and became popular among students in elite Kolkata colleges. Following Charu Majumdar's arrest and his death in custody (1972), the movement dissipated (to be resurrected later in various forms). By the time of his death the movement had already lost its force due to severe state suppression and also because of internal divisions within the CPI (ML) leadership. Yet this violent past continues to haunt the city as it lost some of its best and brightest to the cause of revolutionary violence (not to mention the hundreds of peasants and 'tribals' who were killed in the countryside).

To date the deaths of these young are mourned and remembered in Kolkata. Contemporary West Bengal literature and cinema itself have created avenues for rethinking and recalling the era. Foremost among them of course was Mrinal Sen's by now classic film, *Kolkata Ekattor* (*Calcutta '71*).[29] In 2009 another film on the period was released that detailed the student struggles, showing the devastating effects the violence had on individual lives and the larger society. Adapted from the novel *Kaalbela* (*Inauspicious Times*) by Samaresh Majumdar, the film (*Calcutta My Love*, in English) is directed by Goutam Ghosh, which traces the life of a young man who leaves his middle-class rural home to come to the city where he gets involved in radical politics. Through the male protagonist Animesh, the film shows the various forms in which communist politics, with its multiple internal contradictions, radicalizes the youth and forces them to

[29] Also see the Hindi film, *Hazaar Chaurasi ki Maa* (*The Mother of 1084*) based on a novel by the famous Bangla novelist, Mahasweta Devi.

shun bourgeois lives and head for the countryside to politicize the peasantry. Eventually internal differences, state infiltration of the movement and its severe suppression lead to the arrest (and killing) of thousands of cadres and supporters.

The film portrays how those arrested were tortured and kept in jail for years, not as political detainees but under various permutations of the criminal procedure code. The protagonist himself is captured in a shoot-out, tortured and loses the use of both his legs. He is left to rot in a bare cell with another student from the elite Presidency College; a torture victim who stares at a wall all day. This is the tragic aftermath that is only rectified when a new Left Front government comes into power led by CPI(M) in 1977 and the protagonist is released from jail to be reunited with his lover/partner and his, by then, school-going son.

The romantic partner, Madhabilata, comes from an upper-middle-class family and is a college mate of Animesh. She becomes the most hopeful character in terms of social transformation. She is among the many women of her class background who, during the political activism of the early 1970s, left their sheltered lives and joined the struggle; at times in solidarity with the ideological position of the party and at others, as did Madhabilata, in solidarity with those they loved. The ending shows her living in the urban fringes in a small shack, where she is raising her son and educating him. The de-classing of her existence comes at a social and economic price but offers her other kinds of liberation, that of being an independent woman leading her life by her own choice and not surrendering to middle-class notions of gendered respectability and sexual norms.

The film represents one among many aftermaths of the 'inauspicious times'. Another depiction is found in the award-winning Bangla novel, *Herbert* by Nabarun Bhattacharya, which details the continuous haunting of Kolkata by spirits. This tragicomic story has an eccentric and marginalized character, Herbert as its protagonist. Herbert is an orphan who grows up in a family home and is close to his cousin Binu, who like Animesh of *Kaalbela* also comes from a smaller town to Calcutta in the late 1960s only to be absorbed in left politics (a trope of travel and transformation is common in these depictions). Binu is shot and arrested by the police during the early 1970s. Soon after he dies while being tied by chains to his hospital bed. Later in the novel, Herbert who has a short and successful career as a psychic/clairvoyant who can call on spirits (the many that haunted the city), himself commits suicide. His body is taken to the public crematorium along with the mattress he slept on (one that was also used by Binu) and as the heat of the electric pyre reaches the mattress the entire crematorium is blown up by the dynamite that Binu and his friends had hidden in the mattress years ago. This incident in the book occurs in the early 1990s, but shows how the city keeps on experiencing various kinds of metaphorical, symbolic and real explosions related to the underlying structural causes of violence of the earlier era. The ghosts of the past (Binu), the marginalized, the poor, the traumatized and the tortured (like Animesh from *Kaalbela*), continue to co-exist and seek their space in this city, Kolkata.

My sharing of details from Tareque Masud and Gautum Ghosh's films and Nabarun Bhattacharya's novel is to suggest how past themes/histories and aesthetic forms are re-introduced into the contemporary moment. It also helps me to conclude my chapter from where I had started and raise, albeit in a different register, the issues related to connections, influences, borrowing and experimentation. In what follows I share a poem that addresses postcolonial traumas (distinct from the aura of the partition). Most of us are aware of brutal violence unleashed by the standing Pakistan Army on its own Bengali citizens in 1971. The horror of the nine months of killings, rapes and general mayhem is actually an unwritten and unremembered part of Pakistan's history. Despite the amnesia about the events surrounding the liberation of Bangladesh in contemporary Pakistan, poets and writers in Pakistan have sought to address the history of death and destruction in 1971. Sarwat Hussain (1949–6) was one such poet whose haunting rendition of the trauma of that era I share here:

Ek Insaan Ki Maut[30]

ruk kiyu gai tumharay hath Mujumdar.
ganna peesnay ki machine ka pahiya ruk gaya
zameen ruk gai

aadhay sayyaray peh humaisha kai liyai raat aa gai
laltain kon jlai ga?

hawaaiy guzarti haiN patoN ko girati hui

milad kai kitab kai warq ur rahai haiN
bahir algani par banyan sukh raha hai
tanki ki toti sai pani gir raha hai

yeh itnai saray kam kon karai ga Mujumdar!
ruk kiyu gai tumharay hath

[30] *Ek Insaan Ki Maut*, in Sarwat Hussain, 2015, *Kulliyat* (Sarwat Hussain), (Karachi: City Press, 2015), 49–51.

dekho ranga mati mai din nikal aya hai
baaNs kai darakhtoN mai koplaiN phut pari haiN
hathia aur bhola ko namoodar hotai huay nahin dekho gai kiya
tumharay baitay apni beewiyoN kai saath ghat sai kishti khol rahay haiN

un sai nahi milo gai kiya?
wahaN krishna chura kai sayai mai
tumhari biwi ki qabr
insaano aur badaloN ko guzartai dekhti hai

kiya fateha nahi parho gai?
agar bati nahi jalao gai Mujumdar!

tum meri zaban jantay ho
mai tumhari zaban nahi janta, laikin aaj tumharay sirhanay
ek geet kai bol duhrata hun

gao Mujumdar!
jaisay bachay gatay haiN
jaisay burhi ganga gati hai

shokolay uthia
aami monay monay boli
shara din aami janay
bhalo huay choli
aadesh Koray Jahan
mor guro janay
aami janay shii Kaaj
kori bhalo manay

(transliterated from Bangla)
ruk kiyu gai . . . boltay kiyu nahi Mujumdar!
tumhay kailay kai baghoN aur paani sai pyar tha na
hum tumhay kailay kai patoN sai kafnai gai
tumhari qabr pani mai banai gai
Mujumdar!

fauji boot dhan ki paneeri sai ziyada taqatwar hota hai
nahi
dhan ki paneeri fauji boot sai ziyada taqatwar hoti hai
is boot mai mera pao tha mujumdar!
loh yeh ganna cheelnai ki katar

kaat do is pao ko

alag aar do issay
mujhai apnai pao sai khof ata hai
mujhai murda admi ki hasi sai khof ata hai
mujhai rukay hui zamin sai khof ata hai
ruk kiyu gai tumharay hath Mujumdar!

A Human's Death[31]

Why have your hands stopped, Mujumdar!
The machine to press the sugarcane stopped
The earth stopped

Half the planet is forever steeped in darkness
Who will light the lantern?

The Wind passes by blowing the leaves
The *milad* book's leaves scatter
Outside the vests are drying on the clothesline
Water is dripping from the tank's tap

Who will do all this work, Mujumdar!
Why have your hands stopped?

Look! the day has risen on Ranga Mati[32]
Flowers are blossoming on the bamboo plants
Will you not witness the rising of *hatia* and *bhola* [33]
Your sons along with their wives are untying the boats at the *ghat*
Will you not meet them?

There in the shade of the *krishna chura* [34]
is your wife's grave

Watching humans and clouds pass by
Will you not recite the *fateha* [35]?
Not light the incense sticks Mujumdar!

You know my language
I do not know your language, but today lying next to you
I will recite a song

[31] Translation by the author.
[32] A hilly southeastern part of Bangladesh that borders India and Myanmar.
[33] Hatia and Bhola, two islands in East Bengal/Bangladesh that suffered immense death and destruction during the November 1970 cyclone.
[34] A flowering plant/shrub/tree that grows in South Asia.
[35] Prayers for the dead at the graveside.

Sing Majumdar!
The way children sing
The way old *ganga* sings

Translated from Bangla
Mornings I get up
To utter in my mind
The whole day
I should be good
Whatever my elders command
I must obey
With a mind full of content.

You loved banana fields and water
Banana leaves will be your shroud
And your grave will be in the water
Mujumdar!

The military boot is stronger than the rice stalk
NO
The rice stalk is stronger than the military boot
My feet were in those boots, Mujumdar!
Take the sickle that peels the sugarcane

Cut of these feet
Chop them

I am afraid of my feet
I am afraid of the dead man's laughter
I am afraid of the unmoving land
Why have your hands stopped, Mujumdar!

Sarwat Hussain's poem, perhaps written in the late 1970s (published in the mid-1980s), reminds us of the horrors of 1971. For Faiz, the generational trauma was the violence of partition, the fracturing of the collective self. His poems, by borrowing from the Hindavi idiom, attempted to suture the wounds of separation. For Hussain's generation the self was never one. there were multiple identities – differences – that were forcefully being kept together by the nation state. The excision when it came was brutal and horrific. By invoking the land and flora of East Bengal (*Hathia*, *Bhola*, *Krisna Chura*, Ranga Mati) and by using *Bangla* idioms, Hussain forces us to question the myth of Muslim nationalism, of a unitary identity (along with the dominance of Urdu). Yet, much like Manto in the story 'Sorry', Hussain shows that attempts or palliatives for healing cultural wounds remain unresolved and are a continuing process (it may not be very different in Sri Lanka after the violent history of the past few decades). However, in contrast to Faiz's use of Bhojpuri/Hindi idiom to write his lyrics for *Jago Hua Savera* (or his use of 'pidgin' Urdu for his dialogues), Hussain uses *Bangla* verses to further disrupt his own poetic authority in a gesture that depicts an expression of regret if not a sense of guilt on the part of an Urdu-speaking writer in relation to the events in East Pakistan/Bangladesh. His poem may hence be considered a gesture of apology or reckoning of past behaviour, may be a first nudge towards imagining a potential space – a possibility of sorts – to show how people of different ethnic backgrounds can share common destinies, the struggle by the collective self for social justice.

For Sarwat Hussain's generation the ending of the Soviet experiment (that motivated the earlier group of progressives), along with the failure of a redemptive project of left-wing liberation, the necessity to rethink past certainties before generating visions for a new future is perhaps crucial. However, with the destruction and desolation in the last few decades across South Asia, imagining a future is not always an easy task. Currently, with the resurgence of Sinhala nationalism in post-conflict Sri Lanka, the religious right-wing government in India, populist government in Pakistan that is narrowing the space for rights and freedoms and an increasingly authoritarian government in Bangladesh, the question faced by the various intellectuals remains: How does one even think or write about or seek to build a future under such circumstances?

Forms of the Left in Postcolonial South Asia, by assembling a series of chapters that show how a particular generation addressed such crucial questions, enables us (guides us) to start looking for new answers. Hence, poems, such as Hussain's, along with films such as produced by the late Tareque Masud or Gautam Ghosh, become necessary signposts when our postcolonial dreams have been shattered and the 'old language(s) of moral–political vision and hope are no longer in sync with the world they are meant to describe and normatively criticize' (this is not the world that the stalwarts of IPTA and PWA inherited).[36] Rather than creating grand narratives of change, resistance and working-class solidarity (sometimes based on the invocation of 'Rights'), this may perhaps be a moment of introspection and rethinking. Maybe the answer is not to again turn to an already available teleology that takes us there from here. What is needed is not be seduced by the immediacy of the present and

[36] David Scott, *Conscripts of Modernity* (Durham, NC: Duke University Press, 2004), 2.

perhaps take our time to ask new questions for the future.[37] Perhaps a new politics and aesthetics, building on the inheritance and contributions of an earlier generation, is yet to evolve, a creative energy that is restructured and redefined with a politics that seriously retains the category of difference while simultaneously emphasizing social equity.[38]

[37] Ibid.

[38] I borrow this argument from the historian, Joan Scott (1986). See J. W. Scott, 'Gender: A Useful Category of Historical Analysis', *The American Historical Review* 91, no. 5 (1986), 1053–75.

Bibliography

Abeysinghe, W. A. 'Amardeva, the Immortal'. *The Island* (4 November 2016). http://www.island.lk/index.php?page_cat=article-details&page=article-details&code_title=154954.

Adorno, Theodor, Walter Benjamin, Ernst Bloch, Bertolt Brecht and Georg Lukács. *Aesthetics and Politics, The Key Texts of the Classic Debate within German Marxism*, afterword by Fredric Jameson. London: NLB,1977. Reprinted, London: Verso, 1990.

Afro-Asian Peoples' Solidarity Movement. Cairo: Permanent Secretariat of the Afro-Asian People's Solidarity Movement, 1962.

Ahad, Oli. *Jatiyo Rajniti 1945 theke 1975*. 5th edn. Dhaka: S. M Raisuddin, 2012.

Ahmad, Aijaz. 'Jameson's Rhetoric of Otherness and the "National Allegory"'. *Social Text* 19 (fall 1987): 3–25.

Ahmad, Aijaz. *Lineages of the Present: Ideology and Politics in Contemporary South Asia*. London: Verso, 2002.

Ahmed, M. A. 'River Craft in Modern Bengal'. *Pakistan Quarterly* 4, no. 2 (Summer 1954): 37–9.

Ahmed, Nazneen. 'The Poetics of Nationalism: Cultural Resistance and Poetry in East Pakistan/Bangladesh, 1952–71'. *Journal of Postcolonial Writing* 50, no. 3 (2014a): 256–68.

Ahmed, Nazneen. 'The Crafting of National Culture in East Pakistan'. Conference paper presented at 'Once Upon a Time in East Pakistan', University of Edinburgh, May 1 (2014b).

Ahmed, Rafiuddin. *The Bengal Muslims, 1871–1906: A Quest for Identity*. Delhi: Oxford University Press, 1996.

Ahmed, Sara. 'The Politics of Good Feeling'. *Australian Critical Race and Whiteness Studies Association e-journal* 4, no. 1 (2008): 1–18.

Ahmed, Syed Jamil. 'Performing the Bengali Nation: Munier Chowdhury's Kabar and Syed Huq's Payer Awaj Pawa Jaye'. *Depart*, no. 14/15 (2013). http://departmag.com/index.php/en/detail/266/Performing-the-Bengali-nation- and-Munier-Chowdhury ands-Kabar-and-Syed-Huqands-Payer-Awaj-Pawa-Jaye.

Ahmed, Syed Jamil. 'Designs of Living in the Contemporary Theatre of Bangladesh'. In *Mapping South Asia Through Contemporary Theatre: Essays on the Theatres of India, Pakistan, Bangladesh, Nepal and Sri Lanka*, edited by Ashish Sengupta, 135–76. London: Palgrave Macmillan, 2014.

Ahmed, Syed Jamil. 'Raising the Dead in a Prison by the Light of Lanterns: A Study of a Fragment of Political Theatre'. In *Gender, Politics and Performance in South Asia*, edited by Sheema Kirmani et al. Karachi: Oxford University Press, 2015.

Ahmed, Talat. *Literature and Politics in the Age of Nationalism: The Progressive Episode in South Asia, 1932–56*. New Delhi: Routledge, 2009.

Ahmed, Wakil. *Bangla Loksangit: Bhawaiya*. Dhaka: Shilpakala Academy, 1995.

Ahmed, Wakil. *Bangla Loksangit: Bhatiali Gan*. Dhaka: Shilpakala Academy, 1997.

Ahmed, Wakil. *Bangla Loksangit Sari Gan*. Dhaka: Shilpakala Academy, 1998.

Akhter, Fahmida. 'Jibon Thekey Neya (*Glimpses Of Life*, 1970): The First Political Film in Pre-Liberation Bangladesh and a Cinematic Metaphor for Nationalist Concerns'. *Journal of the Asiatic Society of Bangladesh* 59, no. 2 (2014): 291–303.

Akhter, Fahmida. 'Zahir Raihan's *Stop Genocide* (1971): A Dialectical Cinematic Message to the World'. In *South Asian Filmscapes: Transregional Encounters*, edited by Elora Halim Chowdhury and Esha Niyogi De, 233–49. Seattle: University of Washington Press, 2020.

Ali, Kamran Asdar. 'Communists in a Muslim Land: Cultural Debates in Pakistan's Early Years'. *Modern Asian Studies*, 45, no. 3 (2011): 501–34.

Ali, Kamran Asdar. 'Progressives and "Perverts": Partition Stories and Pakistan's Future'. *Social Text* 29, no. 3 (2011): 1–29.

Ali, Kamran Asdar. *Communism in Pakistan: Politics and Class Activism 1947–1972*. London: IB Taurus, 2015.

Ali, Kamran Asdar. *Surkh Salam: Communist Politics and Class Activism in Pakistan 1947–1972*. Karachi: Oxford University Press, 2015.

Amarakirthi Liyanage, W. D. 'Radical Traditionalism: Post-realist Modes of Representation in Modern Sinhala Fiction and Post-coloniality'. *Phoenix- The Sri Lanka Journal of English in the Commonwealth* IX (2012): 83–98.

Amarasekara, Gunadasa. *Karumakkarayo (The Fateful Ones)*. Colombo: Dayawansha Publishers, 1955.

Amarasekara, Gunadasa. *Yali Upannemi (I was Reborn)*. Gampaha, Sri Lanka: Sarasavi, 1962.

Amarasekara, Gunadasa. *Abudassa Yugayak (A Topsy-turvy Time)*. Boralesgamuwa, Sri Lanka: Visidunu Publishers, 1976.

Amarasekara, Gunadasa. *Anagarika Dharmapala Māksvādida? (Is Anagarika Dharmapala Marxist?)*. Kaluthara, Sri Lanka: Sampath Publishing House, 1980.

Amin, Shahid. *Event, Metaphor, Memory: Chauri Chaura, 1922-1992*. Berkeley: University of California Press, 1995.

Amunugama, Sarath. 'Binda Vetunu Sanskruthika Balakanuwa [The Fallen Cultural Pillar]'. *Vichitra* (23 July 1987), 9.

Amunugama, Sarath. 'Tony Ranasinghe: From Angry Young Man to Star-crossed Lover'. *The Island* (27 June 2015). http://island.lk/index.php?page_cat=article-details&page=article-details&code_title=127269.

Anandalingam, G. and Mary Abraham. 'Left-Wing Politics and Ethnic Conflict in Sri Lanka'. *Comparative Studies of South Asia, Africa and the Middle East* 6, no. 2 (1986): 38–45.

Anderson, Benedict. *Imagined Communities: Reflections on the Origin and Spread of Nationalism*. London: Verso, 2006.

Anjaria, Ulka. *Realism in the Twentieth-Century Indian Novel : Colonial Difference and Literary Form*. New York: Cambridge University Press, 2012.

Appadurai, Arjun. *Modernity at Large: Cultural Dimensions of Globalization*. Minneapolis and London: University of Minnesota Press, 1996.

Appadurai, Arjun and Carol Breckenridge. 'Why Public Culture'. *Public Culture* 1, no. 1 (1988): 5–9.

Arasaratnam, S. 'The Ceylon Insurrection of April 1971: Some Causes and Consequences'. *Pacific Affairs* 45, no. 3 (Autumn 1972): 356–71

Ariyadasa, Edwin. 'Dr. Dharmasena Pathiraja: Revolutionary Film Maker'. 2018. http://www.dailynews.lk/2018/01/29/local/141288/dr-dharmasena-pathiraja-revolutionary-film-director?page=71.

Aslam, Feriyal Amal. 'Choreographing (in) Pakistan: Indu Mitha, Dancing Occluded Histories in the "Land of the Pure"'. PhD diss., University of California, Los Angeles, 2012.

'At Least 3 Killed and 4 Injured in Police Firing'. *Morning News* (5 September 1956).

Atikuzzaman, Abul Khaer Mohammad and Priyam Pritim Paul. *Cholochitro O Jatiyo Mukti – Alamgir Kabir, Rochona Shomogro, 1* [Cinema and National Liberation – Collected Works of Alamgir Kabir, Vol 1]. Dhaka: Agami Prokashani, 2018.

Babiracki, Patryk and Austin Jersild, eds. *Socialist Internationalism in the Cold War*. Cham, Switzerland: Palgrave Macmillan, 2016.

Back, Jean and Viktoria Schmidt-Linsenhoff, eds. *The Family of Man 1955–2001: Humanismus Und Postmoderne: Eine Revision von Edward Steichens Fotoausstellung = Humanism and Postmodernism: A Reappraisal of the Photo Exhibition by Edward Steichen*. Marburg: Jonas Verlag, 2004.

Badiou, Alain, Pierre Bourdieu, Judith Butler, Georges Didi-Huberman, Sadri Khiari, Jacques Rancière, Bruno Bosteels, Kevin Olson and Jody Gladding. *What Is a People? New Directions in Critical Theory*. New York: Columbia University Press, 2016.

Bakhtin, Mikhail. *Rabelais and His World*, translated by Hélène Iswolsky. Bloomington: Indiana University Press, 1984.

Balasooriya, Keerthi and Sucharitha Gamlath. Kalpanalokavadaya, Sahithyakala ha Maaksvaadaya *(Idealism, the Arts and Marxism)*. Colombo: S. Godage and Sons, 1986.

Bandopadhyay, Manik. *Padma River Boatman*. translated by Barbara Painter and Yann Lovelock. St. Lucia: University of Queensland Press, 1973.

Bandyopadhyay, Samik. 'Introduction'. In Mrinal Sen, *In Search of Famine (Akaler Sandhaneyy): A Film*. Calcutta: Seagull Books, 1983.

Bandhyapadhya, Samik. 'Introduction'. In Somnath Hore, *Tebagha: An Artist's Diary and Sketchbook*, translated by Somnath Zutshi, v–viii. Kolkata: Seagull Books, 2009.

Bandopadhyay, Sekhar. *Decolonization in South Asia: Meanings of Freedom in post-Independence West Bengal, 1947–52*. London and New York: Routledge, 2009.

Banerjee, Prathama. *Politics of Time: "Primitives" and History-Writing in a Colonial Society*. New York: Oxford University Press, 2006.

Banerjee, Prathama. *Elementary Aspects of the Political: Histories from the Global South*. Durham, NC: Duke University Press, 2020.

Banerjee, Sumanta. *India's Simmering Revolution: The Naxalite Uprising*. London: Zed Press, 1984.

Banerji, Subrata, 'Jottings'. *Illustrated Weekly of India* (30 June 1968).

Barthes, Roland. *Mythologies: The Complete Edition, in a New Translation*. translated by Richard Howard and Annette Lavers. 2nd edn. New York: Hill and Wang, 2013.

Baseer, Murtaja, *Amar Jibon O Onnano* [My Life and More]. Dhaka: Bengal Publications, 2014.

Basu, Pradip. *Towards Naxalbari (1953–1967): An Account of Inner-party Ideological Struggle*. Calcutta: Progressive Publishers, 2000.

Bayly, C. A. *Rulers, Townsmen and Bazaars: North Indian Society in the Age of British Expansion, 1770–1870*. Cambridge: Cambridge University Press, 1983.

Bazin, André. *Jean Renoir*. New York: Simon and Schuster, 1973.

Bazin, André. *What Is Cinema? Volume II*. translated by Hugh Gray. Berkeley: University of California Press, 1971.

BBC News. 'The India-Pakistan Masterpiece That Fell through the Cracks'. *sec. India* (5 June 2016). https://www.bbc.com/news/world-asia-india-36417007.

Benjamin, Walter. 'Left-wing Melancholy'. In *The Weimer Republic Sourcebook*, edited by A. Kaes, M. Jay and E. Dimendberg. Berkeley: University of California Press, 1994.

Berlant, Lauren 'The Subject of True Feeling: Pain, Privacy, and Politics'. In *Cultural Studies and Political Theory*, edited by Jodi Dean, 42–62. Ithaca: Cornell University Press, 2000.

Bhabha, Homi, ed. *Nation and Narration*. New York: Routledge, 1990.

Bharucha, Rustom. *Rehearsals of Revolution: The Political Theater of Bengal*. Honolulu: University of Hawaii Press, 1983.

Bharucha, Rustom. 'The Indian People's Theatre Association (IPTA)'. In Rustom Bharucha, *In the Name of the Secular: Contemporary Cultural Activism in India*. Delhi: Oxford University Press, 1998.

'Bhashanir khuje-dwityo porbo/Joinal Fakir'. *Maulana Bhashani Archive* 30/04/2021. https://www.facebook.com/111882550723553/videos/788333825454026.

Bhaskar, Ira. 'The Indian New Wave'. In *Routledge Handbook of Indian Cinemas*, edited by K. Moti Gokulsing, Wimal Dissanayake and Rohit K. Dasgupta, 19–33. Abingdon: Routledge, 2013.

Bhatia, Nandi. 'Staging Resistance: The Indian People's Theatre Association'. In *The Politics of Culture in the Shadow of Capital*, edited by Lisa Lowe and David Lloyd, 432–60. Durham: Duke University Press, 1997.

Bhatia, Nandi. *Acts of Authority/Acts of Resistance: Theatre and Politics in Colonial and Postcolonial India*. Ann Arbour: University of Michigan Press, 2004.

Bhattacharya, Malini. 'The Indian People's Theatre Association: A Preliminary Sketch of the Movement and the Organization, 1942–47'. In *Modern Indian Theatre: A Reader*, edited by Nandi Bhatia, 158–81. Delhi: Oxford University Press, 2009.

Bhattacharya, Sandipan, ed. *Chhobi-r Rajneeti, Rajneeti-r Chhobi*. Calcutta: Deepayan, 1990.

Biswas, Hemanga. 'Gana Natyo Andolaney Amar Gaan' [My Songs in the People's Theatre Movement]. In *Uttal Shaat-Sottor: Rajneeti, Samaj o Sanskriti [The Turbulent 1960s-1970s: Politics, Society, and Culture]* edited by Arjun Goswami, 67–98. Kolkata: Chayanika, 2006.

Biswas, Moinak. 'In the Mirror of an Alternative Globalism: The Neorealist Encounter in India'. In *Italian Neorealism and Global Cinema*, edited by Laura E. Ruberto and Kristi M. Wilson, 72–90. Detroit: Wayne State University Press, 2007.

Biswas, Moinak. 'The City and the Real: *Chinnamul* and the Left Cultural Movement of the 1940s'. In *City Flicks: Indian Cinema and the Urban Experience*, edited by Preben Kaarsholm. London, Calcutta, and New York: Seagull, 2007.

Boggs, Carl. 'Marxism, Prefigurative Communism, and the Problem of Workers' Control'. *Libcom.org* (13/09/2010). https://libcom.org/library/marxism-prefigurative-communism-problem-workers-control-carl-boggs.

Bose, Buddhadeb. *Amader Kabita Bhaban*. Calcutta, 1974.

Bose, Neilesh. *Recasting the Region: Language, Culture and Islam in Colonial Bengal*. New Delhi: Oxford University Press, 2014.

Bose, Sugata and Kris Manjapra, eds. *Cosmopolitan Thought Zones*. London: Palgrave Macmillan, 2010.

Bourdieu, Pierre. *The Field of Cultural Production, Essays on Art and Literature*, edited and introduced by Randall Johnson. New York: Columbia University Press, 1993.

Brennan T.. 'The National Longing for Form'. In *Salman Rushdie and the Third World*. London: Palgrave Macmillan, 1989.

Brinkema, Eugenie. *The Forms of the Affects*. Durham: Duke University Press, 2014.

Brueck, Laura R. *Writing Resistance: The Rhetorical Imagination of Hindi Dalit Literature*. New York: Columbia University Press, 2014.

Caute, David. *The Fellow-Travellers: A Postscript to the Enlightenment*. London: Weidenfeld and Nicolson, 1973.

Chakraborty, Dipesh. *Provincializing Europe, Postcolonial Thought and Historical Difference*. Princeton Studies in Culture/Power/History. Princeton and Oxford: Princeton University Press, 2000.

Chakraborty, Dipesh, Rochona Majumdar and Andrew Sartori, eds. *From the Colonial to the Postcolonial: India and Pakistan in Transition*. New Delhi: Oxford University Press, 2007.

Chakravartty, Gargi, ed. *People's Warrior: Words and Worlds of P. C. Joshi*. New Delhi: Tulika Books, 2014.

Chakravarty, Sumita S. 'An Interview with Mrinal Sen'. *Cine-Tracts* (Summer/Fall 1981): 27–32.

Chakravarty, Sumita S. *National Identity in Indian Popular Cinema, 1947–1987*. Austin: University of Texas Press, 1993.

Chatterjee, Partha. *The Nation and its Fragments*. Princeton: Princeton University Press, 1993.

Chatterjee, Partha. *The Present History of West Bengal, Essays in Political Criticism*. Delhi: Oxford University Press, 1997.

Chatterjee, Partha. *A Brief History of Subaltern Studies, In Empire and Nation: Selected Essays by Partha Chatterjee*, with Nivedita Menon. New York: Columbia University Press, 2010 [1998].

Chatterjee, Partha. 'The Nation in Heterogeneous Time'. *Indian Economic and Social History Review* 38, no. 4 (2001): 399–418.

Chatterjee, Saibal. 'A Treasure Regained: A Neo-Realist Gem Shows Pakistani Cinema in a New Light'. *DNA India* (11 June 2016). https://www.dnaindia.com/analysis/column-a-treasure-regained-2222123.

Chatterjee, Utpal. 'Mrinal Sen: 'Film-making Is Like Climbing a Steep Hill!'. *Cinema-India International* 2, no. 1 (January–March 1985): 57–8.

Chittaprosad. 'Chhobi-r Sankat'. *Arani*, Saradiya no., 1943.

Chittaprosad. *Hungry Bengal, A Tour through Midnapore District, by Chittaprosad, in November 1943*. Bombay: New Age Printing Press, 1944.

Chittaprosad. *Kshudartho Bangla (Hungry Bengal)*. Kolkata: Kathabarta, 2002.

'Chittaprosad-er Chithi o Chhara'. *Parichoy* (Saradiya, 1994).

Chowdhury, Afsan. 'Subsumed by History and Nation'. *Himal Southasian* (January 2011), http://old.himalmag.com/himal-feed/53/3532-subsumed-by-history-and- nation.html

Chowdhury, Salil. 'Nijer Katha' [My Story], interview by Kalpana Biswas, originally published in *Kalpurush*: Summer/Monsoon1980. In *Uttal Shaat-Sottor: Rajneeti, Samaj o Sanskriti [The Turbulent 1960s-1970s: Politics, Society, and Culture]*, edited by Arjun Goswami, 100–2. Kolkata: Chayanika, 2006.

Chowdhury, S. H. Harun. 'The Working of Parliamentary Government in Pakistan, 1947 - 1958: With Particular Reference to the Central Government and Major Political Trends'. PhD diss., Durham University, 1970.

Chowdhury, Zirwat. 'An Imperial Mughal Tent and Mobile Sovereignty in Eighteenth Century Jodhpur'. *Art History* 38, no. 4 (September 2015): 668–81.

Committee for Rational Development. *Sri Lanka, The Ethnic Conflict: Myths, realities and perspectives*. New Delhi: Navrang Publishers and Booksellers, 1984.

Cook, Alexander C., ed. *Mao's Little Red Book: A Global History*. Cambridge: Cambridge University Press, 2014.

Cooper, Sarah. 'Henfi Agel's Cinema of Contemplation: Renoir and Philosophy'. In *A Companion to Jean Renoir*, edited by Alastair Phillips and Ginette Vincendeau, 313–27. Chichester, West Sussex, UK: Wiley-Blackwell, 2013.

Coppola, Carlo. 'The All India Progressive Writers' Association: The European Phase'. In Carlo Coppola, ed. *Marxist Influences and South Asian Literature*, vol. 1, 1–34. East Lansing: Michigan State University, 1974.

Cowasjee, Saros. *Author to Critic: The Letters of Mulk Raj Anand*. Calcutta: Writers Workshop, 1973.

Crusz, Robert. An incomplete sentence. Booklet published on Dharmasena Pathiraja at the 16th Singapore International Film Festival. 2003.

Custers, Peter. 'Maulana Bhashani and the transition to secular politics in East Bengal'. *The Indian Economic and Social History Review* 47, no. 2 (2010): 231–59.

Dadi, Iftikhar. *Modernism and the Art of Muslim South Asia*. Chapel Hill: University of North Carolina Press, 2010.

Daily Sangbad. 'Awami League O Birat Sanskritik Sammelon' (1 February 1957).

Dalmia, Yashodhara. *The Making of Modern Indian Art: the Progressives*. New Delhi: Oxford University Press, 2001.

Damodaran, Sumangala. *The Radical Impulse: Music in the Tradition of the Indian People's Theatre Association*. New Delhi: Tulika Books, 2017.

Darnton, Robert, *The Great Cat Massacre: And Other Episodes in French Cultural History*. New York: Basic Books, 1984.

Das, Dhananjay, ed. *Bangla Sanskritite Marxbadi Chetana-r Dhara*, Anustup Special volume. Kolkata: Anustup, 1991.

Das, Dhananjay, ed. *Marxbadi Sahitya Bitarka*, vol. II. Kolkata: Notun Poribesh Prakasani, 1976.

Das, S. K. *A History of Indian Literature: 1911–1956*. Delhi: Sahitya Akademi, 1995.

Das, Susnata, ed. *Fascibad-birodhi Sangrame Abibhakta Bangla*. Kolkata: Prima Publications, 1989.

Dasgupta, Basab. 'Mrinal Sen: Kormagoto Anweshan' [Ceaseless Search]. In *Nirbachito F [Selected F]*, edited by Biren Das Sharma and Ujwal Bandopadhyay, 55–8. Kolkata: Britter Baire, 2013.

Dasgupta, Chidananda. 'The New Cinema: A Wave or A Future?' In *Indian Cinema Super Bazaar* edited by Aruna Vasudev and Philippe Lenglet, 39–49. New Delhi: Vikas, 1983.

Dass, Manishita. 'Cinetopia: Leftist Street Theatre and the Musical Production of the Metropolis in 1950s Bombay Cinema'. *positions: Asia Critique* 25, no. 1 (1 February 2017): 101–24.

Datta, Pradip Kumar. *Carving Blocs: Communal Ideology in Early Twentieth Century*. Oxford: Oxford University Press, 1999.

Datta, Sudhindranath. *The World of Twilight, Essays and Poems, and Other Essays*. Bombay, etc: Oxford University Press, 1970.

de Mel, Neloufer. *Women and the Nation's Narrative: Gender and Nationalism in Twentieth Century Sri Lanka*. New Delhi: Kali for Women, 2001.

Denning, Michael. *The Cultural Front: The Laboring of American Culture in the Twentieth Century*. London: Verso, 1997.

Desai, M. V. 'The Asian Writers' Conference December 1956: New Delhi'. *Books Abroad* 31, no. 3 (Summer 1957).

De Silva, K. M. 1981. *A History of Sri Lanka*. Chennai, India: Oxford University Press.

De Silva, Nalin. 'Bandaranaike's and '56'. *The Island*, 12 October 2005. http://www.island.lk/2005/10/12/midweek3.html.

Dewasiri, Nirmal. 'Mainstreaming Radical Politics in Sri Lanka: The Case of the JVP Post-1977'. *PCD Journal: Journal of Power, Conflict and Democracy in South and South East Asia* 2 , no. 1(2010): 69–94.

Dey, Bishnu. *In the Sun and the Rain: Essays on Aesthetics*. New Delhi: People's Publishing House, 1972.

Dey, Bishnu. *Bishnu Dey Prabandha Samgraha*, 1 and 2. edited by Dhrubakumar Mukhopadhyay, Calcutta: Dey's Publishing, 1997.

'Dhakai Michiler Upar Pulisher 27 Round Gulibarshan'. *Daily Azad*. 5 September 1956

Dharmasiri, Kanchuka. 'Introduction'. in *Streets ahead with Haththootuwegama*, edited by Kanchuka Dharmasiri. Maharagama, Sri Lanka: Ravaya Publishers, 2012.

Dharmasiri, Kanchuka. 'From Narratives of National Origin to Bloodied Streets: Contemporary Sinhala and Tamil Theatre in Sri Lanka'. In *Mapping South Asia through Contemporary Theatre: Studies in International Performance*, edited by A. Sengupta. London: Palgrave Macmillan, 2014.

Dikeç, Mustafa. *Space, Politics and Aesthetics*. Edinburgh: Edinburgh University Press, 2015.

Dissanayake, Wimal. *Enabling Traditions: Four Sinhala Cultural Intellectuals*. Boralesgamuwa, Sri Lanka: Visidunu Publishers, 2005.

Djagalov, Rossen. 'Tashkent 1968: A Cinematic Contact Zone'. *Slavic Review* 75, no. 2 (Summer 2016).

Djagalov, Rossen. 'The Afro-Asian Writers Association and Soviet Engagement with Africa'. *Monthly Review* (November 2017).

Djagalov, Rossen. 'Premature Postcolonialists: the Afro-Asian Writers Association and Soviet Engagement with Africa'. *Lefteast* (3 November 2017).

Documents of the Extraordinary Conference of the Afro-Asian Peoples' Solidarity Organization, Cairo, 1–3 July, 1967. Cairo, U.A.R.: Permanent Secretariat of the A.A.P.S.O, 1967.

Doss, Erika, ed. *Looking at LIFE* Magazine. Washington, DC: Smithsonian Institution Press, 2001.

Drachewych, Oleska and Ian Mckay, eds. *Left Transnationalism: The Communist International and the National, Colonial, and Racial Questions*. Montreal; Kingston; London; Chicago: McGill-Queen's University Press, 2019.

Duara, Prasenjit, ed. *Decolonization: Perspectives from Now and Then*. London: Routledge, 2004.

Dunham, Mary Frances, *Jarigan: Muslim Epic Songs of Bangladesh*. Dhaka: University Press, 1997.

Dutt, Utpal. *Towards a Revolutionary Theatre*. Calcutta: M. C. Sarkar, 1982.

Dutt, Utpal. *Utpal Dutt on Cinema*. Kolkata: Seagull Books, 2009.

Dutta Gupta, Shobhan Lal. *Comintern and the Colonial Question: the Decolonization Controversy*. Calcutta: Centre for Studies in Social Sciences, 1976.

Eastern Film. 'Introducing A. J. Kardar'. 5, no. 5 (June 1963): 44.

Ek Insaan Ki Maut, in Sarwat Hussain, 2015, *Kulliyat* (Sarwat Hussain). Karachi: City Press, 2015.

Elias, Khondoker Mohammed. *Bhashani Jakhan Europe-e*. 6th edn. Dhaka: Muktadhara, 1978.

Eng, David L. and David Kazanjian. 'Introduction: Mourning Remains'. In *Loss: The Politics of Mourning*, edited by David L. Eng and David Kazanjian, 1–25. Berkeley: University of California Press, 2003.

Enwezor, Okwui. 'Modernity and Postcolonial Ambivalence'. *South Atlantic Quarterly* 109, no. 3 (Summer 2010).

Enwezor, Okwui, Katy Siegel and Ulrich Wilmes. *Postwar: Art between the Pacific and the Atlantic, 1945–1965*. Munich: Haus der Kunst, 2017.

Eusufzai, Atiqur. 'Memoirs: As We Saw A Great Leader'. In *Moulana Bhashani: Leader of the Toiling Masses*, edited by Anisuzzaman Chowdhury, 269–322. New York: Maulana Bhashani Foundation, 2012.

Faiz, Faiz Ahmad. *Nuskhaha-e-Wafa*, 356–7. Lahore: Maktaba-e-Karavan, 2009.

Featherstone, David. *Solidarity: Hidden Histories and Geographies of Internationalism*. London: Zed Books, 2012.

Fernando, Laksiri. 'The State and Class Struggle in Sri Lanka: The General Strike of July 1980'. *Labour, Capital and Society / Travail, capital et société* 16, no. 2 (November 1983): 204–25.

Field, Garret. 'Veiling the Modular: Literary Language and Subjective Nationalism in Sinhala Radio Song of Sri Lanka, 1957–1964'. *The South Asianist* 4, no. 1 (2015): 1–24.

Film correspondent. Dacca Film Society Activities, *The Pakistan Times Magazine* (11 August 1968): vi.

Finkelstein, Sidney, 'Chittaprosad'. *Daily Worker* (16 November 1965).

Franda, Marcus. 'Communism and Regional Politics in East Pakistan'. *Asian Survey* 10, no. 7 (1970): 588–606.

Freitag, Sandria B., 'Consumption and Identity: Imagining "Everyday Life" Through Popular Visual Culture', *Tasveer Ghar: A Digital Archive of South Asian Popular Visual Culture*, 2010.

Friedman, Jeremy. *Shadow Cold War: The Sino-Soviet Competition for the Third World*. Chapel Hill: University of North Carolina Press, 2015.

Foucault, Michel, *This Is Not a Pipe*, translated by James Harkness. Berkeley, University of California Press, 1983.

Freud, Sigmund. 'Mourning and Melancholia'. In *The Standard Edition of the Complete Psychological Works of Sigmund Freud*, vol. 14, 1914–1916, translated by James Strachey (1917; repr., London: Hogarth Press, 1957), 243–58.

Fukuyama, Francis. 'The End of History?' *The National Interest* 16 (1989): 3–18.

Gamlath, Sucharitha. *Maname Natya Sevanaya (Appreciation of the Maname Drama 1996)*. Colombo: S. Godage and Sons, 1996.

Gamlath, Sucharitha. *Maaksvaadaya ha Saahithyakala (Marsim and the Arts)*. Colombo: Sarasavi, 2008.

Gamlath, Sucharitha and Keerthi Balasuriya. *Kalpanalokavadaya, Sahithyakala ha Maaksvaadaya (Idealism, the Arts and Marxism)*. Colombo: Godage, 1986 [1999].

Gandhi, Leela. *Affective Communities: Anticolonial Thought, Fin-de-Siècle Radicalism, and the Politics of Friendship*. Durham, NC: Duke University Press, 2006.

Gangopadhyay, Sunil. *East West: Purbo-Paschim*, vol. 1, translated by Enakshi Chatterjee. New Delhi: Sahitya Akademi, 2000.

Ganguly, Suranjan. 'A Cinema on Red Alert: Mrinal Sen's Interview and In Search of Famine'. *The Journal of Commonwealth Literature* 35, no. 1 (March 2000): 55–70.

Gankovsky, Y. V and L. R. Gordon-Polonskaya, *A History of Pakistan (1947–58)*. Lahore: People's Publishing House, 1962.

Garimela, Annapurna, ed. *Mulk Raj Anand: Shaping the Indian Modern*. Mumbai: Marg Publications, 2005.

'Gayatri Spivak on the Politics of the Subaltern'. Interview by Howard Winant. In *Socialist Review* 20 (1990): 81–97.

Gazdar, Mushtaq. *Pakistan Cinema, 1947–1997*. Karachi: Oxford University Press, 1997.

Ghatak, Ritwik. *On the Cultural Front*, A thesis submitted by Ritwik Ghatak to the Communist Party of India in 1954. Calcutta: Ritwik Memorial Trust, 2000.

Ghatak, Ritwik. 'On *Subarnarekha*', trans. Moinak Biswas, *Cinema Journal* 54, no. 3, (2015).

Ghosh, Ajoy. *Pakistan Portent*. New Delhi: Communist Party of India, 1958.

Ghosh, Chilka. *Chhabir Bishoy, Bishoyer Chhabi: Pratibad o Pratirodh*. Calcutta: N. I. Publishers, 2005.

Ghouse, Nida. 'Lotus Notes'. Mada Masr, 14 May, 15 June, 15 July, 20 August, 2014. http://www.madamasr.com/contributor-profile/nida-ghouse.

Ghouse, Nida. 'Lotus Notes'. *ARTMargins* 5, no. 3 (October 2016).

Giovacchini, Saverio and Robert Sklar, eds. *Global Neorealism: The Transnational History of a Film Style*. Jackson: University Press of Mississippi, 2011.

Glynn, Sarah. *Class, Ethnicity and Religion in the Bengali East End: A Political History*. Manchester: Manchester University Press, 2014.

Gopal, Priyamvada. *Literary Radicalism in India: Gender, Nation and the Transition to Independence*. London: Routledge, 2005.

Gould, William. *Hindu Nationalism and the Language of Politics in Late Colonial India*. Cambridge: Cambridge University Press, 2004.

Graeber, David and Marshall Sahlins, *On Kings*. Chicago: Hau Books, 2017.

Gramsci, Antonio. *Selections from Prison Notebooks*. Edited and translated by Quintin Hoare and Geoffrey Nowell-Smith. London: Lawrence and Wishart, 1971.

Gramsci, Antonio. *Prison Notebooks: Volume II*. Edited and Translated by Joseph A. Buttigieg. New York: Columbia University Press, 1996.

Greenough, Paul. *Prosperity and Misery in Modern Bengal: The Bengal Famine of 1943–44*. New York: Oxford University Press, 1977.

Groys, Boris. *The Total Art of Stalinism: Avant Garde, Aesthetic Dictatorship, and Beyond*. Translated by Charles Rougle. Princeton: Princeton University Press, 1992.

Guha, Ranajit. 'On Some Aspects of the Historiography of Colonial India'. In *Subaltern Studies I: Writing on South Asian History and Society*, edited by Ranajit Guha, 1–9. Delhi: Oxford University Press, 1982.

Guha, Ranajit. *Elementary Aspects of Peasant Insurgency in Colonial India*. Delhi: Oxford University Press, 1983.

Guhathakurta, Meghna and Willem van Schendel, eds. *The Bangladesh Studies Reader: History, Culture, Politics*. Durham: Duke University Press, 2013.

Guha-Thakurta, Tapati. 'The Making of a New "Indian" Art: Artists, Aesthetics, and Nationalism in Bengal, c. 1850–1920'. Cambridge: Cambridge University Press, 1992.

Gunasinghe, Newton. 'May Day after the July Holocaust'. In *Newton Gunasinghe: Selected Essays*, edited by Sassanka Perera. Colombo: Social Scientists Association, 1996 [1984].

Gunawardena, A. J. 'Asia's Modern Theatres: Encounters with Tradition'. In *The World Encyclopedia of Contemporary Theatre: Asia/Pacific*, edited by Don Rubin, Chua Soo Pong and Ravi Chaturvedi. London: Routledge, 2000.

Gunning, Tom. 'Moving Away from the Index: Cinema and the Impression of Reality'. *Differences* 18, no. 1 (2007): 29–52.

Gupta, Atreyee. 'The Promise of the Modern: State, Culture and Avant-Gardism in India (ca. 1930–1960)'. PhD diss., University of Minnesota, 2011.

Gupta, D. N. *Communism and Nationalism in Colonial India, 1939–1945*. New Delhi: Sage Publications, 2008.

Haaland, Torunn. *Italian Neorealist Cinema*. Edinburgh: Edinburgh University Press, 2012.

Habashi, Hasan. 'Historical Studies on the "Inba' al-Ghumr" of Ibn Hajar'. PhD diss., SOAS, UK, 1955.

Haldar, Gopal. 'Culture O Communist Dwaityo' (Culture and Communist Responsibility). In *Sanskritir Biswarup, Gopal Haldar*, edited by Dr. Bhattacharya, Debipada, Dr. Aruna Haldar and Dr. Amiya Dhar. Calcutta: Manisha, 1986.

Haldar, Gopal. *Gopal Haldar Rachanasamagra*, vol. 1. Calcutta: A Mukherjee and Co. Pvt. Ltd., 1991.

Halim, Hala. 'Lotus, the Afro-Asian Nexus, and Global South Comparatism'. *Comparative Studies of South Asia, Africa and the Middle East* 32, no. 3 (2012).

Halim, Hala. 'Afro-Asian Third-Worldism into Global South: The Case of *Lotus* Journal'. *Global South Studies: A Collective Publication with The Global South* (22 November 2017). https://globalsouthstudies.as.virginia.edu/key-moments/afro-asian-third-worldism-global-south-case-lotus-journal.

Hall, Stuart. 'Constituting an Archive'. *Third Text* 15, no. 54 (2001): 89–92.

Hall, Stuart. 'Black Diaspora Artists in Britain: Three "Moments" in Post-war History'. *History Workshop Journal* 61, no. 1 (2006).

Hall, Stuart and Doreen Massey. 'Interpreting the Crisis'. *Soundings: A Journal of Politics and Culture* 44 (Spring 2010): 57–71.

Hallaq, Wael B. and Donald P. Little, eds. *Islamic Studies Presented to Charles J. Adams*. Leiden: E.J Brill, 1991.

Hanfi, Shemeem. 'Adab Me Insan Dosti ka Tassawar' (The Concept of Humanism in Literature), *Dunyazad* 21 (2008) (Karachi): 24.

Hansen, Thomas Blom. 'Politics as Permanent Performance: The Production of Political Authority in the Locality'. In *The Politics of Cultural Mobilization in India*, edited by John Zavos, Andrew Wyatt and Vernon Marston Hewitt, 19–36. New Delhi: Oxford University Press, 2004.

Harney, Elizabeth. *In Senghor's Shadow*. Durham: Duke University Press, 2004.

Harney, Elizabeth. 'The Densities of Modernism'. *South Atlantic Quarterly* 109, no. 3 (Summer 2010).

Hartman, Saidiya. 'An Unnamed Girl, A Speculative History'. *New Yorker*, (9 February 2019). https://www.newyorker.com/culture/culture-desk/an-unnamed-girl-a-specu lative-history.

Hashmi, Madeeh Ali. *Faiz Ahmed Faiz: Love and Revolution*. New Delhi: Rupa Publications. 2016.

Hashmi, Taj ul-Islam. *Peasant Utopia: the communalisation of class politics in East Bengal, 1920–1947*. Dhaka: University Press Limited, 1994.

Haththotuwegama, Gamini. 'Unresolved Contradictions, Paradoxical Discourses and Alternative Strategies in the Post-colonial Sinhala Theatre'. In *Streets ahead with Haththotuwegama*, edited by Kanchuka Dharmasiri. Piliyandala, Sri Lanka: Ravaya Publishers, 2012a.

Haththotuwegama, Gamini. 'Maname Natya saha Madyama Panthika Sanskruthiya (the Maname drama and Middle Class Culture)'. In *Streets ahead with Haththotuwegama*, edited by Kanchuka Dharmasiri. Piliyandala, Sri Lanka: Ravaya Publishers, 2012b.

Hauff, Reinhard and Anjum Katyal. *Ten Days in Calcutta: A Portrait of Mrinal Sen by Reinhard Hauff*. Calcutta: Seagull Books, 1987.

Hayat, Anupam. *Bangladesher chalachitro itihash [The History of Bangladeshi cinema]*, Dhaka: Bangladesh Film Development Corporation, 1987.

Hayat, Anupam. 'Fateh Lohani'. *Banglapedia* (2012). https://en.wikipedia.org/wiki/Fateh _Lohani.

Hayat, Anupam. *Alamgir Kabirer Cholocchitro: Potbhumi, Bishoy o Boishishto [Alamgir Kabir's Cinema: Background, Subject and Features]*. Dhaka: Bangaza Prokashon, 2016.

Hennayake, Nalini. *Culture, Politics and Development in Postcolonial Sri Lanka*. Oxford: Lexington Books, 2006.

Hobsbawm, Eric and Terrence Ranger. *The Invention of Tradition*. Cambridge: Cambridge University Press, 1983.

Hoek, Lotte. 'Cross-Wing Filmmaking: East Pakistani Urdu Films and Their Traces in the Bangladesh Film Archive'. *BioScope: South Asian Screen Studies* 5, no. 2 (1 July 2014): 99–118.

Hoek, Lotte. 'Mirrors of Movement: *Aina*, Afzal Chowdhury's Cinematography and the Interlinked Histories of Cinema in Pakistan and Bangladesh'. *Screen* 57, no. 4 (Winter 2016): 488–95.

Hoek, Lotte and Sanjukta Sunderason. 'Journeying through Modernism: Travels and Transits of East Pakistani Artists in Post-Imperial London'. *British Art Studies* 13.

Hore, Somnath. 'Wounds', a booklet published to coincide with an exhibition of sculptures, and works on paper (1992).

Hore, Somnath. *Until the Rain: Fragments from an Artist's Life*. Kolkata: Seagull Books, 2008.

Hore, Somnath. *My Concept of Art*. Kolkata: Seagull, 2009.

Hore, Somnath. *The Tea-Garden Journal*. Calcutta: Seagull Books, 2009.

Hossain, Ayub. 'Alamgir Kabir'. *Banglapedia*. (2012). http://en.banglapedia.org/index.php?title=Kabir,_Alamgir.

Hung, Chai-tai. 'Two Images of Socialism: Woodcuts in Chinese Communist Politics'. *Comparative Studies in Society and History* 39 (1997).

Husain, Intezar. *Chiraghon Ka Dhuan: Yadon Ke Pachas Baras*. Lahore: Sang-e-Meel Publications, 2003.

Huyssen, Andreas. 'Geographies of Modernism in a Globalizing World'. *New German Critique* 100 (Winter 2007): 189–207.

Hye, Abdul Hasnat. *Sultan*, translated by Kabir Chowdhury, Dhaka: Adorn Publications, 2008.

Indian National Congress. *Report of the 51st Indian National Congress: Haripura (Dt. Surat. Gujarat) 1938*. Ahmedabad: Navajivan Press, 1938.

Iyer, Usha. *Dancing Girl: Choreographing Corporeal Histories in Hindi Cinema*. New York: Oxford University Press, 2020.

Jafri, Ali Sardar. *Taraqi Pasand Adab (Progressive Literature)*. Aligarh, India: Anjuman Tariqui-e-Urdu, 1957

Jago Hua Savera [Booklet]. np: np, nd.

Jaikumar, Priya. *Where Histories Reside: India as Filmed Space*. Durham: Duke University Press, 2019.

Jain, Kajri. *Gods in the Bazaar: The Economies of Indian Calendar Art*. Durham, NC: Duke University Press, 2007.

Jain, Kajri. *Gods in the Time of Democracy*. Durham: Duke University Press, 2021.

Jalil, Rakhshanda. *Liking Progress, Loving Change: A Literary History of the Progressive Writers' Movement in Urdu*. Delhi: Oxford University Press, 2014.

James, C. Vaughan. *Soviet Socialist Realism: Origins and Theory*. London: Macmillan, 1973.

Jameson, Fredric. *Marxism and Form: Twentieth Century Dialectical Theories of Literature*. Princeton: Princeton University Press), 1971.

Jameson, Frederic. 'Third World Literature in the Age of Multinational Capital'. *Social Text* 15 (fall 1986): 65–88.

Jamil, Sayyid Mazhar. *Zikr-e-Faiz*. Karachi: Department of Culture, Government of Sindh, 2013.

Jasimuddin. 'The Fisherman', translated by Winfred Holmes. *Pakistan Quarterly* 4, no. 2 (1954): 40.

Jasimuddin. 'The Folk Songs of East Bengal'. *Pakistan Quarterly* 6, no. 3 (1956): 45–50.

Jayatunge, R. 'Bava Taranaya – Reviewed after 37 Years'. *News Article*. (2011). http://www.lankaweb.com/news/items/2011/01/04/bhava-tharanaya-reviewed-after-37-years/.

Jayawardena, Kumari. 'Origins of the Left Movement in Sri Lanka'. *Social Scientist* 2, no. 6/7 (January–February 1974): 3–28.

Jeffrey, Craig and Jane Dyson. 'Geographies of the Future: Prefigurative Politics'. *Progress in Human Geography* 20, no.10 (2020): 1–18

Jeganathan, Pradeep and Qadri Ismail, eds. *Unmooring the Nation: The Politics of Identity and History in Modern Sri Lanka*. Colombo: The Social Scientists Association, 1995.

Jennings, Ivor. 'Politics in Ceylon Since 1952'. *Pacific Affairs* 27, no. 4 (December 1954): 345–52.

'Jibaner Sheshdin Parjonto Shakti Diya Shamasto Sarbaprokar Samarik Cuktir Biruddhita Kariba', *Daily Sangbad*, 7/2/1957.

Joshi, P. C. *The New Situation and our Tasks, Resolution of the Central Committee of the Communist Party of India*, passed at its meeting in December 1945, Bombay: New Age Printing Press for the Communist Party of India, 1945.

Jumabhoy, Zehra and Boon Hoi Tan. *The Progressive Revolution: Modern Art for a New India*. Asia Society Museum, New York, 14 September 2018 to 20 January 2019.

Junaid, Naadir. *Bengali Political Cinema: Protest and Social Transformation*. PhD Thesis, The University of New South Wales, 2013.

Junaid, Naadir. 'Cinema that Raises a Critical Consciousness: The Films of Alamgir Kabir'. In *South Asian Filmscapes: Transregional Encounters* edited by Elora Halim Chowdhury and Esha Niyogi De, 266–82. Seattle: University of Washington Press, 2020.

Kabir, Alamgir. 'Raja Sanyasi'. *Holiday* (10 October 1966a): 5, 7.

Kabir, Alamgir. 'Satyajit Ray'. *Holiday* (17 June 1966b): 5, 7.

Kabir, Alamgir. 'New Wave Cinema & Its Contribution to Art'. *The Pakistan Observer* (24 May 1966c): 12, 14.

Kabir, Alamgir. 'Aakhri Station'. *Holiday* (13 March 1966d): 5.

Kabir, Alamgir. 'Walt Disney: Tribute to a Charmer'. *The Holiday* (25 December 1966e): 5, 7.

Kabir, Alamgir. *The Cinema in Pakistan*. Dhaka: Sandhani Publications, 1969a.

Kabir, Alamgir. 'Current Release'. *Holiday* (31 August 1969b): 5.

Kabir, Alamgir. *Film in Bangladesh*. Dhaka: Bangla Academy, 1979.

Kabir, Ananya Jahanara. 'Utopias Eroded and Recalled: Intellectual Legacies of East Pakistan'. *South Asia: Journal of South Asian Studies* 41, no. 4 (2018): 892–910.

Kamal, Ahmed. *State Against the Nation: The Decline of the Muslim League in Pre-independence Bangladesh, 1947–54*. Dhaka: The University Press Limited, 2009.

Kang, Liu. 'Maoism: Revolutionary Globalism for the Third World Revisited'. *Comparative Literature Studies* 52, no. 1 (2015): 12–28.

Kantorowicz, Ernst H. *The King's Two Bodies: A Study in Medieval Political Theology*. Princeton: Princeton University Press, 1957.

Kapur, Geeta. 'Realism and Modernism: A Polemic for Present-Day Art'. *Social Scientist* 8 [Marxism and Aesthetics], no. 5/6 (December 1979–January 1980): 91–100.

Kapur, Geeta. *Place for People: An Exhibition of Paintings By: Jogen Chowdhury, Bhupen Khakhar, Nalini Malani, Sudhir Patwardhan, Gulam Mohammed Sheikh, Vivian Sundaram*, Jehangir Art Gallery, Bombay 9th November–15th November 1981; Rabindra Bhavan, New Delhi 21st November–3rd December 1981.

Kapur, Geeta. *When was Modernism: Essays on Contemporary Cultural Practice in India*. New Delhi: Tulika, 2000.

Kapur, Geeta. 'Partisan Modernity'. In *Mulk Raj Anand: Shaping the Indian Modern*, edited by Annapurna Garimella. Mumbai: Marg Publications, 2005.

Kapur, Geeta. 'Secular Artist, Citizen Artist'. In *Art and Social Change, A Reader*, edited by Will Bradley and Charles Esche. London: Tate Publishing in association with *Afterall*, 2007.

Karnad, Girish. 'Interview'. In *Indian Cinema Super Bazaar* edited by Aruna Vasudev and Philippe Lenglet. Delhi: Vikas, 1983.

Kaul, Arun and Mrinal Sen. 'Manifesto of the New Cinema Movement (1968)'. In *Film Manifestos and Global Cinema Cultures* edited by Scott MacKenzie, 165–8. Berkeley: University of California Press.

Kaur, Raminder. *Performative Politics and the Cultures of Hinduism: Public Uses of Western Religion in Western India*. Delhi: Permanent Black, 2003.

Kaviraj, Sudipta. 'Filth and the Public Sphere: Concepts and Practices about Space in Calcutta'. *Public Culture* 10, no. 1 (1997): 108–9.

Kaviraj, Sudipta. *The Imaginary Institution of India: Politics and Ideas*. New York: Columbia University Press, 2010.

Kaviraj, Sudipta. 'The Art of Despair: The Sense of the City'. In *The Invention of Private Life*. New Delhi: Permanent Black, 2014.

'Khadyar Janya Dabi Janaite Giya Dhakar Rajpathe ghate 8 Jan Nihat O 7 Jan Ahat'. *Daily Sangbad* (5 September 1956).

Khan, Naveeda. 'Flaws in the Flow: Roads and their Modernity in Pakistan'. *Social Text* 24, no. 4 (2006): 87–113.

Khan, Naveeda. 'The Acoustics of Muslim Striving: Loudspeaker Use in Ritual Practice in Pakistan'. *Comparative Studies in Society and History* 53, no. 3 (2011): 571–94.

Khanduri, Ritu Gairola. *Caricturing Culture: Cartoons and History in the Modern World*. Cambridge: Cambridge University Press, 2015.

Khullar, Sonal. *Worldly Affiliations: Artistic Practice, National Identity, and Modernism in India, 1930–1990*. Berkeley: University of California Press, 2015.

Khushru, Muhammad, *Bangladesher Cholocchitro Shongshod Andolon [The Film Society Movement in Bangladesh]*. Dhaka: Porua, 2004.

Kleff, Michael. 'Speaker of the (Carnegie) Hall: An Interview with Harold Leventhal'. https://www.woodyguthrie.org/harold.htm#kleff.

Koch, Ebba. *Mughal Architecture: An Outline of its History and Development, 1526–1858*. Munich: Prestel, 1991.

Kornbluh, Anna. *The Order of Forms: Realism, Formalism, and Social Space*. Chicago: The University of Chicago Press, 2019.

Koselleck, Reinhart. *Futures Past: On the Semantics of Historical Time*. Translated and Introduced by Keith Tribe. New York: Columbia University Press, 2004.

Lahiri, Madhumita. 'An Idiom for India: Hindustani and the Limits of the Language Concept'. *Interventions: International Journal of Postcolonial Studies* 18, no. 1 (2016): 60–85.

Lahusen, Thomas and Evgeny Dobrenko, eds. *Socialist Realism without Shores*. Durham: Duke University Press, 1997.

Lanba, Urmila. *Life and Films of Dilip Kumar, the Thespian*. New Delhi: Vision Books, 2002.

Lapidus, Ira. 'Knowledge, Virtue, and Action: The Classical Muslim Conception of Adab and the Nature of Religious Fulfillment in Islam'. In *Moral Conduct and Authority: The Place of Adab in South Asian Islam*, edited by Barbara Daly Metcalfe, 62–90. Los Angeles: University of California Press, 1984.

Larkin, Brian. 'The Politics and Poetics of Infrastructure'. *Annual Review of Anthropology* 42 (2013): 427–43.

Lassally, Walter. *Itinerant Cameraman*. London: J. Murray, 1987.

Lefebvre, Henri. *Critique of Everyday Life: Volume 1*, translated by John Moore. London: Verso, 1991.

Lefebvre, Henri. *Writing on Cities*, translated and edited by Eleonore Kofman and Elizabeth Lebas. Oxford: Blackwell Publishers, 1996.

Lewis, Su Lin and Carolien Stolte. 'Other Bandungs: Afro-Asian Internationalisms in the Early Cold War'. *Journal of World History*, Special Issue, 30, no. 1–2 (2019): 1–20.

Lukács, György. 'Realism in the Balance'. In *Aesthetics and Politics*, edited by Theodor W. Adorno, Walter Benjamin, Ernst Bloch, Bertold Brecht, György Lukács and Fredric Jameson. London: Verso, 2007 [1938], 38.

Lukács, Georgy. *Soul and Form*, edited by John T. Sanders and Katie Terezakis, introduction by Judith Butler, translated by Anna Bostock. New York: Columbia University Press, 2010 (First Published 1910).

Lunn, David. 'The Eloquent Language: Hindustani in 1940s Indian Cinema'. *BioScope: South Asian Screen Studies* 6, no. 1 (1 January 2015): 1–26.

Macdonald, Richard Lowell. *The Appreciation of Film: The Postwar Film Society Movement and Film Culture in Britain*. Exeter: University of Exeter Press, 2016.

Maclean, Kama. *Pilgrimage and Power: The Kumbh Mela in Allahabad, 1765–1954*. New York: Oxford University Press, 2008.

Maclean, Kama. *A Revolutionary History of Interwar India: Violence, Image, Voice and Text*. London: Hurst, 2015.

Majeed, Sheema, ed. *Culture and Identity: Selected English Writings of Faiz*. Oxford University Press, 2005.

Majumdar, Neepa. 'Importing Neorealism, Exporting Cinema: Indian Cinema and Film Festivals in the 1950s'. In *Global Neorealism: The Transnational History of a Film Style*, edited by Saverio Giovacchini and Robert Sklar, 178–93. Jackson: University Press of Mississippi, 2011.

Majumdar, Neepa. 'Importing Neorealism, Exporting Cinema: Indian Cinema and Film Festivals in the 1950s', In *Global Neorealism: The Transnational History of a Film Style*, edited by Saverio Giovacchini and Robert Sklar. Jackson: The University Press of Mississippi, 2012.

Majumdar, Rochona. 'Debating Radical Cinema: A History of the Film Society Movement in India'. *Modern Asian Studies* 46, no. 3 (2012): 731–67.

Majumdar, Rochona. 'Art Cinema: The Indian Career of a Global Category'. *Critical Inquiry* 42, no. 3 (1 March 2016): 580–610.

Maksud, Syed Abul. *Maulana Abdul Hamid Khan Bhashani*. Dhaka: Agami Prokashoni, 2014.

Maksud, Syed Abul. *Kagmari Sammelon: Maulana Bhashani Purbo Banglar Swadhikar Samrajyobadbirodhi Sangram*. Dhaka: Prothoma Prokashon, 2017.

Malik, Anushay. 'Alternative Politics and Dominant Narratives: Communists and the Pakistani State in the 1950s'. *South Asian History and Culture* 4, no. 4 (2013).

Malik, Hafeeez. 'The Marxist Literary Movement in Pakistan'. *Journal of Asian Studies* 26 (1967): 649–64.

Mallik, Sanjoy. 'Social Realism in the Visual Arts: "Man-Made" Famine and Political Ferment, Bengal 1943–46'. In *Art and Visual Culture in India, 1947–2007*, edited by Gayatri Sinha. Bombay: Marg Publications, 2009.

Mallik, Sanjoy. *Chittaprosad, Vol 1 and 2*. New Delhi: Delhi Art Gallery, 2011.

Mallik, Sanjoy, ed. *A Sketchbook of 30 Portraits by Chittaprosad*. New Delhi: Delhi Art Gallery, 2011.

Mallik, Sanjoy. *Yours Chitta: Translated Excerpts from Select Letters of Chittaprosad*. New Delhi: Delhi Art Gallery, 2011.

Maniruzzaman, Talukder. *The Bangladesh Revolution and its Aftermath*. Dhaka: University Press Ltd, 1980.

Manor, James. (1989). *The Expedient utopian: Bandaranaike and Ceylon*. Cambridge: Cambridge University Press.

Mansur, Ferozuddin. *Pakistan Mai Quami ZabanoN ka Masla (The Problem of National Languages in Pakistan)*. Lahore: Sujeet Kitab Ghar (reprinted from first edition in 1952).

Manto, Sa'adat Hasan. *Siah Hashiye* in *Manto Numah*. Lahore: Sang-e-Meel Press, 1991.

Marcuse, Herbert. *The Aesthetic Dimension: Toward a Critique of Marxist Aesthetics*. New York: Beacon Press, 1979. First published 1977.

Marcuse, Herbert. *Art and Liberation: Collected Papers of Herbert Marcuse*, vol. 4. New York: Routledge, 2007.

Margolies, David, ed. *Writing the Revolution: Cultural Criticism from Left Review*. London: Pluto Press, 1998.

Martins, Susana S. 'Failure as Art and Art History as Failure'. *Third Text Online*, no. 2 (August 2015).

Masroor, Hajra. 'Tul'u', *Nuqush* 9 (1949).

Mazumdar, Charu. 'Undertake the work of Building a Revolutionary Party'. *Liberation* (October 1968).

Mazzarella, William. *Shovelling Smoke: Advertising and Globalization in Contemporary India*. Delhi: Oxford University Press, 2004.

Menon, Dilip. 'Lost Visions? Imagining a Left Culture in the 1950s'. In *Land Labour and Rights – Ten Daniel Thorner Memorial Lectures*, edited by Alice Thorner. New Delhi: Tulika, 2001.

Metcalf, Barbara Daly, ed. *Moral Conduct and Authority: The Place of Adab in South Asian Islam*. Los Angeles: University of California Press, 1984.

Mirzoeff, Nicholas. 'On Visuality'. *Journal of Visual Culture* 5, no. 1 (2006): 53–79.

Misrahi-Barak, Judith, K. Satyanarayana and Nicole Thiara, eds. *Dalit Text: Aesthetics and Politics Re-imagined*. New Delhi: Routledge, 2020.

Mitchell, Timothy. 'The Stage of Modernity'. In *Questions of Modernity*, edited by Timothy Mitchell. Minneapolis: University of Minnesota Press, 2000.

Mitra, Arun. 'Lekhak-Shilpi Sangha o *Nabanna*: Smriti' [The Writers & Artists' Association and *Nabanna*: Memories]. *Bharatey Sanghatito Pragati Sanskriti Andolaner Ponchash Barsho-Poorti Smarak Sankalan [Commemoration Volume for the Indian Progressive Movement's 50th Anniversary*], 140–3. Calcutta: Aikatan, 1986.

Mitra, Asok. *Calcutta Diary*. London: Frank Cass, 1977. Reprint, Calcutta: Paranjoy Guha-Thakurta, 2014.

Mitter, Partha. *The Triumph of Modernism, India's Artists and the Avant-garde, 1922–47*. London: Reaktion Books, 2007.

Mitter, Partha. 'Interventions: Decentering Modernism: Art History and Avant-Garde Art from the Periphery'. *Art Bulletin* 90, no. 4 (December 2008): 531–48.

Moffat, Chris. *India's Revolutionary Heritage: Politics and the Promise of Bhagat Singh*. Cambridge: Cambridge University Press, 2019.

Mohaiemen, Naeem. '"Kothai Aj Shei Shiraj Sikder (Where Today Is that Shiraj Sikder)?" Terrorists or Guerrillas in the Mist'. *Sarai Reader 06: Turbulence* (2006): 296–311. http://archive.sarai.net/files/original/aa81240315ea2e06d9a102b63fffe21.pdf.

Mohaiemen, Naeem. 'Simulation at Wars' End: A 'Documentary' in the Field of Evidence Quest'. *BioScope: South Asian Screen Studies* 7, no. 1 (2016): 31–57.

Mohan, Anupama. *Utopia and the Village in South Asian Literatures*. Basingstoke: Palgrave McMillan, 2012.

Moin, A. Azfar. *The Millennial Sovereign: Sacred Kingship and Sainthood in Islam*. New York: Columbia University Press, 2012.

Moorhouse, Geoffrey. *Calcutta*. London: Weidenfeld and Nicolson, 1971.

Morcom, Anna. *Hindi Film Songs and the Cinema*. Aldershot: Ashgate, 2007.

Mouffe, Chantal. *On the Political*. New York: Routledge, 2005.

Movies & Music of India. 'Movies & Music of India – Timir Baran'. https://iyerbhaskar.wordpress.com/2012/03/29/movies-music-of-india-timir-baran/.

Mufti, Aamir. 'Towards a Lyric History of India'. *Boundary 2*, 31, no. 2 (2004): 245–74.

Mufti, Aamir. *Enlightenment in the Colony : The Jewish Question and the Crisis of Postcolonial Culture*. Princeton: Princeton University Press, 2007.

Mukherjee, Debashree. 'Creating Cinema's Reading Publics: The Emergence of Film Journalism in Bombay'. In *No Limits: Media Studies from India*, edited by Ravi Sundaram and Sujata Patel, 165–98. New Delhi: Oxford University Press, 2013.

Mukherjee, Hiren. *Tari Hote Tir*. Calcutta: Manisha Granthalaya, 1974.

Mukherjee, Janam. *Hungry Bengal: War, Famine and the End of Empire*. London: Hurst, 2015.

Nasir, Agha. *Ham jitay ji masruf rahe*. Lahore: Sang-e-Meel Publications, 2008.

Nersessian, Anahid. 'Two Gardens: An Experiment in Calamity Form'. *MLQ: Modern Language Quarterly* 74, no. 3 (2013).

Nersessian, Anahid. *The Calamity Form: on Poetry and Social Life*. Chicago: The University of Chicago Press, 2020.

Nowell-Smith, Geoffrey. 'The Second Life of Italian Neo-Realism'. *Journal of the Moving Image*, 2014, 46–58.

Obeysekere, Ranjini. 'Ediriweera Sarachchandra: A Renaissance Man'. *The Island* (28 June 2014). http://www.island.lk/index.php?page_cat=article-details&page=article-details&code_title=105881.

O'Hanlon, Rosalind. 'Recovery of the Subject: Subaltern Studies and Histories of Resistance in Colonial South Asia'. *Modern Asian Studies* 22, no. 1 (1988): 189–224.

Overstreet, Gene and Marshall Windmiller. *Communist Party of India, Miscellaneous Pamphlets*. Berkeley and Los Angeles: University of California Press, 1959.

Pakistan Film Magazine. 'Movies from East Pakistan, Dacca'. https://pakmag.net/film/db/EastPakistanFilms.php.

Pandey, Gyan. 'In Defense of the Fragment: Writing about Hindu-Muslim Riots in India Today'. *Representations*, no. 37, Special Issue: *Imperial Fantasies and Postcolonial Histories* (Winter 1992): 27–55.

Panikkar, K. N. 'Left Cultural Intervention, Perspectives and Practice'. *Economic and Political Weekly* 32, no. 15 (12–18 April 1997).

Parvez, Amjad. 'Rakhshi — The First Vamp/Dancer of Lollywood'. *Daily Times* (14 April 2020). https://dailytimes.com.pk/595320/rakhshi-the-first-vamp-dancer-of-lollywood/.

Pathiraja, Dharmasena. 'It Is Like an Incomplete Sentence: Pathiraja Speaks to Sumathy Sivamohan'. In *An Incomplete Sentence: The Cinema of Dharmasena Pathiraja*. Boralesgamuwa, Sri Lanka: Network for the Promotion of Asian Cinema (NETPAC), 2009a.

Pathiraja, Dharmasena. 'Where there Is No Partition: Ghatak and I'. In *An Incomplete Sentence: The Cinema of Dharmasena Pathiraja*. Boralesgamuwa, Sri Lanka: Network for the Promotion of Asian Cinema (NETPAC), 2009b.

Phạm, Quỳnh N. and Robbie Shilliam, eds. *Meanings of Bandung: Postcolonial Orders and Decolonial Visions*. London: Rowman & Littlefield, 2016.

Pinney, Christopher. 'Things happen: Or, from which moment does that object come?' In *Materiality*, edited by Daniel Miller, 256–72. Durham and London: Duke University Press, 2005.

Pinney, Christopher. *Photos of the Gods: The Printed Image and Political Struggle in India*. London: Reaktion, 2010.

Pinney, Christopher and Rachel Dwyer, *Pleasure and the Nation: The History, Politics, and Consumption of Public Culture in India*. Delhi: Oxford University Press, 2001.

Posmentier, Sonya. *Cultivation and Catastrophe: The Lyric Ecology of Modern Black Literature*, Baltimore: Johns Hopkins University Press, 2017.

Pradhan, Sudhi, ed. 'The All India People's Theatre Association: Annual Report –1946'. In *Marxist Cultural Movement in India: Chronicles and Documents*, 236–304. Calcutta: Santi Pradhan, 1979.

Pradhan, Sudhi, ed. *Marxist Cultural Movement in India: Chronicles and Documents*. Calcutta: Santi Pradhan, 1979.

Prasad, Vijay. *No Free Left: The Futures of Indian Communism*. New Delhi: LeftWord Books, 2015.

Prasad, Vijay. 'Naeem Mohaiemen's Tragic History of the 1970s Left. *Afterall: A Journal of Art, Context and Enquiry* 47 (Spring/Summer 2019): 56–65.

Pucci, Lara. 'History, Myth, and the Everyday: Luchino Visconti, Renato Guttuso, and the Fishing Communities of the Italian South'. *The Oxford Art Journal* 36 (2013): 417–35.

Qader, Mirza Tarekul. *Bangladesher Chalachitra Shipla [The Cinema of Bangladesh]*. Dhaka: Bangla Academy, 1993.

Qasmi, Ahmed Nadim, 'Real Essence of Socialist'. *Art, The Holiday* (25 December 1966): 3, 6.

Rahman, Hasan Hafisur, ed. *Bangladesher Swadhinota Juddho Dolilpotro [Documents of the Bangladesh Independence War]*, vol. 3 – Mujibnagar, Dhaka: People's Republic of Bangladesh, Information Ministry, 2009 [1982–85].

Rahman, Mahfuzur. 'Kagmari Sammelone Koyekjon Sangit Shilpi'. In *Kagmari Sammelon Smarakgrantha*, edited by Mohsin Shoshtropani, 75–80. Tangail: Kagmari Sammelon 50 Borsho-Purti Palon Jatiyo Kamiti, 2011.

Rahman, Saeed-ur, ed. *Maulana Bhashani: Bhashan o Bibroti*. Dhaka: Jagroti Prokashani, 2000.

Raina, Raghunath. 'Foreword'. *The New Generation: 1960–1980*. Delhi: Directorate of Film Festivals, 1981.

Raj, Ali. 'Pakistan's First Oscar Submission "Jago Hua Savera" Goes to Cannes'. *The Express Tribune*, 1 May 2016. http://tribune.com.pk/story/1095386/pakistans-first-oscar-submission-jago-hua-savera-goes-to-cannes/.

Rajadhyaksha, Ashish and Amrit Gangar, eds. *Ritwik Ghatak – Argument and Stories*. Bombay: Screen Unit/Research Centre for Cinema Studies, 1987.

Rajadhyaksha, Ashish and Paul Willemen, ed. *Encyclopedia of Indian Cinema*. New Delhi: Oxford University Press, 1999.

Rajput, A. B. 'River Life in East Pakistan'. *Pakistan Quarterly* (Summer 1964): 40–2.

Raju, Zakir Hossain. *Bangladesh Cinema and National Identity: In Search of the Modern?* London: Routledge, 2015.

Ramaswami, Shankar. 'Masculinity, Respect and the Tragic: Themes of Proletarian Humor in Contemporary Industrial Delhi'. *International Review of Social History* 51, supplement no. 14: Coolies, Capital and Colonialism: Studies in Indian Labour History (2006): 203–27.

Ramaswamy, Sumathi. *Beyond Appearances? Visual Practices and Ideologies in Modern Art*. New Delhi; Thousand Oaks, CA: Sage, 2003.

Rambukwella, Harshana. 'Reconciling What? History, realism and the problem of an inclusive Sri Lankan Identity'. ICES Research Paper No. 3. Colombo: International Centre for Ethnic Studies, 2012.

Rambukwella, Harshana. 'Locations of authenticity: S. W. R. D. Bandaranaike of Sri Lanka and the Search for Indigeneity'. *Journal of Asian Studies* 76, no. 2 (2017): 383–400.

Rambukwella, Harshana. *The Politics and Poetics of Authenticity: A Cultural Genealogy of Sinhala Nationalism*. London: University College London Press, 2018.

Ramnath, Nandini. 'Made in Pakistan with Some Help from India, Lost and Found Again: The Story of "Jago Hua Savera"'. *Scroll.in* https://scroll.in/reel/817995/made-in-pakistan-with-some-help-from-india-lost-and-found-again-the-story-of-jago-hua-savera.

Ranaweera, Ariyawansa. 'Diminishing Legacy of Dr Sarachchandra and the Arrival of the "Outsiders"'. *The Island* (10 June 2016). http://www.island.lk/index.php?page_cat=article-details&page=article-details&code_title=59933.

Rancière, Jacques. *Disagreement: Politics and Philosophy*, translated by Julie Rose. Minneapolis, London: University of Minnesota Press, 1999.

Rancière, Jacques. *Dissensus: Politics and Aesthetics*, edited and translated by Steven Corcoran. London: Continuum, 2010.

Rancière, Jacques. *Staging the People: The Proletarian and His Double*. London: Verso, 2011.

Rancière, Jacques. *Figures of History*, translated by Julie Rose. London: Polity Press, 2014.

Ray, Satyajit. *Our Films, Their Films*. 3rd edn. Bombay: Orient Longman, 1976.

Raychaudhuri, Reba. *Jibaner Tane, Shilper Tane* [*Drawn to Life, Drawn to Art*]. Calcutta: Thema, 1999.

Raychaudhuri, Sajal. *Gananatya Katha* [*On the People's Theatre Movement*]. Calcutta: Mitra and Ghosh, 1990.

Raza, Ali. 'Dispatches from Havana: The Cold War, Afro-Asian Solidarities, and Culture Wars in Pakistan'. *Journal of World History* 30, no. 1–2 (2019): 223–46.

Raza, Ali. *Revolutionary Pasts: Communist Internationalism in Colonial India*. Cambridge: Cambridge University Press, 2020.

Reza, Shah Ahmed. *Bhashani-r Kagmari Sammelon O Swayatsashoner Shongram*. Dhaka: Gonoprokashoni, 1993.

Richard, S. 'Azurie'. *Dances on the Footpath* (24 May 2013). https://roughinhere.wordpress.com/2013/05/24/azurie/.

Richards, John F. *The Mughal Empire*. Cambridge: Cambridge University Press, 1995.

'Road Building in E. Wing Stalled'. *Dawn* (1 February 1957).

Robbins, Christa and Kris Cohen, 'Beyond Formaldehyde, An Interview with Lauren Berlant'. *Open Set* (2015). http://www.open-set.com/cnrobbins/o-s-form-issue/an-interview-of-form-with-lauren-berlant/.

Rodgers, Daniel T. 'Cultures in Motion, An Introduction'. In *Cultures in Motion*, edited by Daniel T. Rodgers, Bhavani Raman and Helmut Reimitz. Princeton and Oxford: Princeton University Press, 2013.

Rogers, John. 'Post-Orientalism and the Interpretation of Premodern and Modern Political Identities: The case of Sri Lanka'. *Journal of Asian Studies* 58, no. 1 (1994.): 10–23.

Rooney, Ellen. 'Form and Contentment'. *MLQ: Modern Language Quarterly* 61, no. 1 (2000): 17–40.

Roy, Anuradha, compiled and ed. *Challish Dashaker Bangla-i Ganasangeet Andolan*. Calcutta: Anustup, 1992.

Roy, Anuradha. *Cultural Communism in Bengal, 1936–1952*. Delhi: Primus Books, 2014.

Roy, Srirupa. *Beyond Belief: India and the Politics of Postcolonial Nationalism*. Durham: Duke University Press, 2007.

Roy, Subodh, ed. *Communism in India, Unpublished Documents 1935-45*. Calcutta: Ganashakti Printers, 1976.

Roychodhury, Ranu. 'Documentary Photography, Decolonization, and the Making of 'Secular Icons': Reading Sunil Janah's Photographs from the 1940s through the 1950s'. *BioScope: South Asian Screen Studies* 8, no. 1 (2017): 46–80.

Ruberto, Laura E. and Kristi M. Wilson, eds. *Italian Neorealism and Global Cinema*. Detroit: Wayne State University Press, 2007.

Russell, Jane. *Our George: A Biography of George E. de Silva*. Colombo: Times of Ceylon, 1981.

Rydell, Robert W. *World of Fairs: The Century-of-Progress Expositions*. Chicago: University of Chicago Press, 1993.

Sa'aduddin, K. A. M. 'Kagmari Sammelan: Age O Pore'. In *Kagmari Sammelon Smarakgrantha*, edited by Mohsis Shoshtropani, 15–25. Tangail: Kagmari Sammelon 50 Borsho-Purti Palon Jatiyo Kamiti, 2011.

Sachse, F. A. *Bengal District Gazetteers: Mymensingh*. Calcutta: Bengal Secretariat Book Depot, 1971.

Samad, Yunus. *A Nation in Turmoil: Nationalism and Ethnicity in Pakistan, 1937–1958*. New Delhi: Sage, 1995.

Samaddar, Ranabir. *The Marginal Nation: Transborder Migration From Bangladesh to West Bengal*. Calcutta: Sage, 1999.

Sanjay, Seth. 'Indian Maoism: The Significance of Naxalbari'. In *Critical Perspectives on Mao Zedong's Thought*, edited by Arif Dirlik, Paul Healy and Nick Knight. New Jersey: Humanities Press, 1997.

Sanyal, Hiran Kumar. *Parichoy-er kuri Bochor o Ananyo Smritichitra*. Calcutta: Papyrus, 1975.

Sarachchandra, Ediriweera. *Kalpana Lokaya [The World of the Imagination]*. Colombo: S. Godage and Sons, 2015 [1958].

Sarkar, Bhaskar. 'The Inward Look: The Politics and Practice of Cinematic Representation'. In *The Enemy Within: The Films of Mrinal Sen* edited by Sumita S. Chakravarty, 98–130. London: Flics Books, 2000.

Sarkar, Bhaskar. *Mourning the Nation: Indian Cinema in the Wake of Partition*. Durham: Duke University Press, 2009.

Sarkar, Nikhil. *A Matter of Conscience: Artists bear Witness to the Great Bengal Famine of 1943*, translated by Satyabrata Dutta. Foreword by Amartya Sen. Calcutta: Punascha, 1998.

Sarkar, Shipra and Anamitra Das, eds. *Bangalir Samyabad Charcha* [Socialist Thinking in Bengal]. Calcutta: Ananda Publishers, 1998.

Saunders, Frances Stonor. *The Cultural Cold War: The CIA and the World of Arts and Letters*. New York: New Press, 1999.

Schendel, Willem van. *A History of Bangladesh*. Cambridge: Cambridge University Press, 2009.

Scott, David. *Conscripts of Modernity* Durham, NC.: Duke University Press, 2004.

Scott, J. W. 'Gender: A Useful Category of Historical Analysis'. *The American Historical Review* 91, no. 5 (1986): 1053–75.

Scott-Smith, Giles. *The Politics of Apolitical Culture: The Congress for Cultural Freedom, the CIA and Post-war American Hegemony*. Routledge, 2002.

Sehanbish, Chinmohon. *46 No. Ekti Sanskritik Andolon Prashange* [*No. 46: About a Cultural Movement.*] Calcutta: Research India Publications, 1986.

Selim, Lala Rukh. 'Art of Bangladesh: the Changing Role of Tradition, Search for Identity and Globalization'. *South Asia Multidisciplinary Academic Journal* 9 (2014): 1–21.

Sen, Mrinal. *Montage: Life. Politics. Cinema*. Calcutta: Seagull Books, 2002.

Sen, Mrinal. 'Bhoot-Bartaman-Bhabishyat (1940–1970)' [Past, Present, and Future (1940–1970)], In *Pragatir Chetana, Pragatir Pathikera [Progressive Consciousness, Progressive Travellers]* edited by Debashish Sengupta, 64–70. Kolkata: Ekushey Sangsad, 2008.

Sen, Samar. *Babubrittanto o Prasangik (The Annals of the Babu and Relevant Writings).* Calcutta: Dey's Publishing, 2004.

Seneviratne, H. L. *The Work of Kings: The new Buddhism in Sri Lanka.* Chicago: University of Chicago Press, 1999.

Seneviratne, Malinda. 'Gunadasa Amrasekara – The Dentist-philosopher Rooted in Sinhala Soil'. *Infolanka* (2000). http://www.infolanka.com/org/srilanka/people/57.htm.

Seth, Sanjay. 'Smashing Statues, Dancing Sivas'. *Humanities Research* XI, no. 1 (2004): 42–53.

Shahed, Syed Mohammad. *Romesh Shil Rochonabali.* Dhaka: Bangla Academy, 1993.

Shastri, Amita. 'Estate Tamils, the Ceylon Citizenship Act of 1948 and Sri Lankan Politics'. *Contemporary South Asia* 8, no. 1 (1999): 65–86, DOI: 10.1080/09584939908719856.

Shoshtropani, Mohsin, ed. *Kagmari Sammelon Smarakgrantha.* Tangail: Kagmari Sammelon 50 Borsho-Purti Palon Jatiyo Kamiti, 2011.

Shridharani, Krishnalal. 'Association and Isolation at Tashkent'. *Indian Literature* 2, no. 1 (October 1958–March 1959).

Siddique, Salma. 'Meena Shorey: The Droll Queen of Partition'. *BioScope: South Asian Screen Studies* 6, no. 1 (1 January 2015): 44–66.

Siddique, Salma. 'Archive Filmaria: Cinema, Curation, and Contagion'. *Comparative Studies of South Asia, Africa and the Middle East* 39, no. 1 (1 May 2019): 196–211.

Simone, Abdou Maliq. 'Muslim Hoedowns, Tenuous Language and the Uncertain Lives of an Urban Majority'. *International Journal of Urban and Regional Research* 43, no. 6 (2019): 1193–208.

Singh, Devika. 'Indian Art and the Bangladesh War'. *Third Text* 31, no. 2–3 (2017), 459–76.

Singh, Moni. 'Establishing the Communist Party of Pakistan', translated by Meghna Guhathakurty. In *The Bangladesh Reader: History, Culture, Politics* edited by Meghna Guhathakurta and Willem van Schendel, 170–4. Durham: Duke University Press, 2013.

Sinopoli, Carla M. 'Monumentality and Mobility in Mughal Capitals'. *Asian Perspectives* 33, no. 2 (1994): 293–308.

Siriwardena, Reggie. 'Pathiraja Politics and Cinema'. In *An Incomplete Sentence: The Cinema of Dharmasena Pathiraja.* Boralesgamuwa, Sri Lanka: Network for the Promotion of Asian Cinema (NETPAC), 2009 [1978].

Sivanandan, Ambalavaner. *When Memory Dies.* London: Arcadia, 1997.

Sivanandan, Ambalavaner. 'Ethnic cleansing in Sri Lanka'. *Race and Class* 51, no. 3 (2010): 59–65.

Sivathamby, Karthigesu. '50 Years of Sri Lankan Tamil Literature'. *Frontline* 16, no. 9 (May 1999).

Slezkine, Yuri. 'The USSR as a Communal Apartment, or How the Socialist State Promoted Ethnic Particularism'. *Slavic Review* 53, no. 2 (1994): 414–52.

Solanas, Fernando and Octavio Getino, 'Toward a Third Cinema'. *Cinéaste* 4, no. 3 (1970–71): 1–10.

Somiratne, Chamila. 'Re-envisioning a Discipline: Martin Wickramasinghe's Contribution to Comparative Literature'. MA Thesis, University of Massachusetts, Amherst, 2016.

Spencer, Jonathan. 'Writing Within: Anthropology, Nationalism and Culture in Sri Lanka'. *Current Anthropology* 31, no. 3 (1990a): 283–300.

Spencer, Jonathan, ed. *Sri Lanka: History and the Roots of Conflict*, 1–18. London: Routledge, 1990b.

Spencer, Jonathan. 'Postcolonialism and the Political Imagination'. *Journal of the Royal Anthropological Institute* 3, no. 1 (1997).

Spivak, Gayatri Chakravorty. 'Can the Subaltern Speak?' In *Marxism and the Interpretation of Culture*, edited by C. Nelson and L. Grossberg, 271–313. Urbana: University of Illinois Press, 1988.

Srinivas, S. V. 'Maoism to Mass Culture: Notes on Telangana's Cultural Turn'. *BioScope: South Asian Screen Studies* 6, no. 2 (2015).

Staniszewski, Mary Anne. *The Power of Display: A History of Exhibition Installations at the Museum of Modern Art*. Cambridge, MA: MIT Press, 1998.

Statements and Appeals. Cairo: Permanent Secretariat of the A.A.P.S.O, 1958–60.

Steimatsky, Noa. *Italian Locations: Reinhabiting the Past in Postwar Cinema*. Minneapolis: University of Minnesota Press, 2008.

Stille, Max. *Islamic Sermons and Public Piety in Bangladesh: The Poetics of Popular Preaching*. London: I.B. Tauris, 2020.

Stimson, Blake. *The Pivot of the World: Photography and Its Nation*. Cambridge, MA: MIT Press, 2006.

Stolte, Carolien. '"The People's Bandung": Local Anti-Imperialists on an Afro-Asian Stage'. *Journal of World History* 30, nos. 1–2 (2019): 125–56.

Stolte, Carolien and Su Lin Lewis, eds. 'Other Bandungs: Afro-Asian Internationalisms in the Early Cold War'. *Journal of World History* 30, nos 1–2 (June 2019).

Sunderason, Sanjukta. 'As Agitator and Organiser: Chittaprosad and the Art for the Communist Party of India'. *Object* no. 13 (2010): 75–95.

Sunderason, Sanjukta. 'Making Art 'Modern': Revisiting Artistic Modernism in India'. in *Modern Makeovers: A Handbook of Modernity in South Asia*, edited by Saurabh Dube. New Delhi: Oxford University Press, 2011.

Sunderason, Sanjukta. 'Shadow Lines: Zainul Abedin and the Afterlives of the Bengal Famine of 1943'. *Third Text* Special volume on Partitions, 31, nos 2–3 (November 2017): 239–59.

Sunderason, Sanjukta. 'Framing Margins: Mao and Visuality in Twentieth Century India'. In *Art, Global Maoism and the Chinese Cultural Revolution*, edited by Jacopo Galimberti, Noemi de Haro-García and Victoria H. F. Scott. Manchester: Manchester University Press, 2019.

Sunderason, Sanjukta. *Partisan Aesthetics: Modern Art and India's Long Decolonization*. Palo Alto: Stanford University Press, 2020.

Talukder, Maniruzzaman, *The Bangladesh Revolution and Its Aftermath*. Dhaka: UPL, 2003 [1980].

Tambiah, Stanley J. *Buddhism betrayed? Religion, politics and violence in Sri Lanka*. Chicago: The University of Chicago Press, 1992.

Tartakov, Gary Michael. *Dalit Art and Visual Imagery*. New Delhi: Oxford University Press, 2012.

Terracciano, Emilia. *Art and Emergency*. London: I. B. Tauris, 2017.

Thakur, Tanuk. 'Under Pressure, Mumbai Film Festival Drops Classic Pakistani Film'. *The Wire* (17 October 2016). https://thewire.in/diplomacy/classic-pakistani-film-jago-hua-savera-dropped-mumbai-film-festival.

Third Eye. 'K. Ganesh: A pioneer in Sri Lankan Tamil Literature'. *Third Eye* 8th issue. Chankalady, Sri Lanka: Department of Fine Arts, Eastern University, 2002.

Thiruchandran, Selvy. 'Progressive Writers and the Progressives: Some Thoughts'. *Pravada* 3, no. 6 (1994): 26–9. Colombo: Social Scientists Association.

Thiruvarangan, Mahendran. 'Clash at Jaffna University: Conversation on Culture and History – Part II'. *Colombo Telegraph* (2016). https://www.colombotelegraph.com/index.php/clash-at-jaffna-university-conversations-on-culture-history-part-ii/

Thomas, Paul. 'Gone Fishin'? Rossellini's "Stromboli," Visconti's "La Terra Trema"'. *Film Quarterly* 62, no. 2 (Winter 2009): 20–5.

Toor, Saadia. 'A National Culture for Pakistan: The Political Economy of a Debate'. *Inter-Asia Cultural Studies* 6, no. 3 (2005): 319–40.

Toor, Saadia. *The State of Islam: Culture and Cold War Politics in Pakistan*. London: Pluto Press, 2011.

Traverso, Enzo. *Left-Wing Melancholia: Marxism, History, and Memory*. New York: Columbia University Press, 2016.

Trnd, David. 'Nationalities, Pedagogies and Media'. *Cultural Studies* 7, no. 1 (1973): 89–106

Uddin, Layli. *In The Land of Eternal Eid: Maulana Bhashani and the Political Mobilisation of Peasants and Lower-Class Urban Workers in East Pakistan, c. 1930s-1971*. PhD diss., Royal Holloway, University of London, 2016.

Uddin, Layli. '"Enemy Agents' at Work": A Microhistory of the 1954 Adamjee and Karnaphuli Riots in East Pakistan'. *Modern Asian Studies* 55, no. 2 (2021): 629–64.

Umar, Badruddin. *The Emergence of Bangladesh: Class Struggles in East Pakistan (1947–1958)*. Karachi: Oxford University Press, 2004.

Uyangoda, Jayadeva. *Jathiya, Jathikawadaya Saha Jathika Rajya (Nation, Nationalism and Nation-State)*. Colombo: Social Scientists Association, 1994.

Van Schendel, Willem. *A History of Bangladesh*. Cambridge: Cambridge University Press, 2009.

Venugopal, Rajesh. 'Sectarian socialism: The politics of Sri Lanka's Janatha Vimukthi Peramuna (JVP)'. *Modern Asian Studies* 44, no. 3 (2010): 567–602.

Wediwardena, Manjula. 'Yuddhaya Pilibanda Gemburu Sinamawak Bihiwanu Aththe Uthuren' (A substantive cinema about the war can only emerge from the North) – Interview with Dharmasena Pathiraja. (2016). http://www.jdslanka.org/s/index.php/2014-12-20-03-09-05/2014-12-20-03-12-04/560-2016-04-19-08-49-02.

Wee, Brandon. 'In conversation with Sri Lankan director Dharmasena Pathiraja'. *Kinema: A Journal for Visual and Audiovisual Media*. (2003). http://www.kinema.uwaterloo.ca/article.php?id=78&feature.

Weidman, Amanda. 'Voices of Meenakumari: Sound, Meaning, and Self-Fashioning in Performances of an Item Number'. *South Asian Popular Culture* 10, no. 3 (2012): 307–18.

Wernicke, Günter, 'The Unity of Peace and Socialism? The World Peace Council on a Cold War Tightrope Between the Peace Struggle and Intrasystemic Communist Conflicts'. *Peace and Change* 26 (2001): 332–51.

Wickremasinghe, Martin. *Upan Da Sita (From the Day I Was Born)*. Colombo Tisara Publishers, 1961.

Wickremasinghe, Martin. *Yuganthaya (End of an Era)*. Maharagama: Samantha Publishers, 1965 [1949].

Wickremasinghe, Martin. *Bava Taraṇaya (Transcending Existence)*. Dehivala: Tisara, 1973.

Wickremasinghe, Martin. *Gamperaliya (Uprooted)*. Dehiwala, Sri Lanka: Thisara Publishers, 1981 [1941].

Wickremasinghe, Martin. *Kalu Nika Seveema (In Search of the Kalu Nika)*. Colombo: Tisara Publishers, 1981 [1961].

Wickremasinghe, Martin. *Martin Wickremasinghe Kruthi Ekathuwa (Martin Wickremasinghe Collected Works)*. Colombo: Tisara Publishers, 1989.

Wickremasinghe, Martin. *Sinhala Lakuna (The Sinhala Identity)*. Rajagiriya, Sri Lanka: Sarasa Publishers, 1995 [1947].

Wickremasinghe, Martin. *Kali Yugaya (Age of Kali)*. Rajagiriya, Sri Lanka: Sarasa Publishers, 2001 [1957].

Wickramasinghe, Nira. *Sri Lanka In the Modern Age: A History of Contested Identities*. Honolulu, Hawaii: University of Hawai'i Press, 2006.

Williams, Raymond. *Country and the City*. Oxford: Oxford University Press, 1973.

Wille, Simone. 'A Transnational Socialist Solidarity. Chittaprosad's Prague Connection'. *Stedelijk Studies 9*, Modernism in Migration. Relocating Artists, Objects, and Ideas, 1910–1970, Gregor Langfeld, Tessel M. Bauduin (eds.), Fall 2019.

Wille, Simone. 'Chittaprosad's Linocut Prints at the National Gallery in Prague: Understanding Indo-Czech Cultural Relations in the Postwar Era'. *Bulletin of the National Gallery in Prague*, 2020.

Williams, Raymond. 'Lecture on Realism'. *Screen* 18, no. 1 (Spring 1977). Reprinted in *Afterall: A Journal of Art, Context and Enquiry*, Issue 5 (2002): 106–115.

Williams, Raymond. *The Politics of Modernism, Against the New Conformists*. London: Verso, 2007.

Wilson, Rob and Christopher Leigh Connery, eds. *The WO R L D I N G Project: Doing Cultural Studies in the Era of Globalization*. Berkeley: North Atlantic Books, 2007.

Wilson, William A. 'Herder, Folklore and Romantic Nationalism'. *The Journal of Popular Culture* 6, no. 4 (1973): 819–35. DOI: 10.1111/j.0022-3840.1973.00819.

Younger, Prakash. 'The River: Beneath the Surface with Andre Bazin'. In *A Companion to Jean Renoir*, edited by Alastair Phillips and Ginette Vincendeau, 166–75. Chichester, West Sussex: Wiley-Blackwell, 2013.

Zachariah, Benjamin. *Nehru*. London: Routledge, 2004.

Zaheer, Hasan. *The Times and Trial of the Rawalpindi Conspiracy, 1951: The First Coup Attempt in Pakistan*. Karachi: Oxford University Press, 1998.

Zaheer, Sajjad. *Roshnai* (lit. Ink). Lahore: Maktab-e-Urdu, 1956.

Zaheer, Sajjad. 'Yaden'. In *Marxist Cultural Movement in India: Chronicles and Documents (1936–47)*, edited by Sudhi Pradhan. Delhi: National Book Agency, 1979.

Zaheer, Sajjad. *The Light*. Karachi: Oxford University Press, 2006.

Zavattini, Cesare. 'Some Ideas on the Cinema (Italy, 1953)'. In *Film Manifestos and Global Cinema Cultures: A Critical Anthology*, edited by Scott MacKenzie, 124–33. Berkeley: University of California Press, 2014.

Zhadanov, A., Maxim Gorky, N. Bukharin, K. Radek and A. Stetsky, eds. *Problems of Soviet Literature: Reports and Speeches at the First Soviet Writers' Congress*. Moscow: Cooperative Publishing Society of Foreign Workers in the USSR, 1935.

Zieleniec, Andrzeg. 'Lefebvre's Politics of Space: Planning the Urban as Oeuvre'. *Urban Planning* 3, no. 3 (2018): 5–15.

Zimmerman, Tanja, 'Yugoslav Partisan Poetry: Songs for the Leader', in *Partisans in Yugloslavia, Literature, Film and Visual Culture*, eds. Miranda Jakisa and Nikica Gilic. Verlag: Bielefeld, 2015.

Zitzewitz, Karin. *Aesthetics of Secularism*. London: Hurst, 2015.

Zulfiqar, Mohsin and Fabbeh Husein. *Elusive Dawn: Faiz Ahmed Faiz: A People's Poet, A Centenary Publication*. Bradford: Kala Sangam, 2011.

Index

Page numbers followed with 'n' refer to footnotes.